Catholic communities
in Protestant states

Manchester University Press

STUDIES IN EARLY MODERN EUROPEAN HISTORY

This series aims to publish
challenging and innovative research in all areas
of early modern continental history.
The editors are committed to encouraging work
that engages with current historiographical
debates, adopts an interdisciplinary
approach, or makes an original contribution
to our understanding of the period.

SERIES EDITORS

Joseph Bergin, William G. Naphy, Penny Roberts and Paolo Rossi

Already published in the series

Sodomy in early modern Europe
ed. Tom Betteridge

The *Malleus Maleficarum and the construction of witchcraft*
Hans Peter Broedel

Latin books and the Eastern Orthodox clerical elite in Kiev, 1632–1780
Liudmila V. Charipova

Fathers, pastors and kings:
visions of episcopacy in seventeenth-century France
Alison Forrestal

Princely power in the Dutch Republic:
Patronage and William Frederick of Nassau (1613–64)
Geert H. Janssen, trans. J. C. Grayson

Power and reputation at the court of Louis XIII: the career of Charles d'Albert,
duc de Luynes (1578–1621)
Sharon Kettering

Popular science and public opinion in eighteenth-century France
Michael R. Lynn

Religion and superstition in Reformation Europe
eds Helen Parish and William G. Naphy

Religious choice in the Dutch Republic: the reformation of
Arnoldus Buchelius (1565–1641)
Judith Pollmann

Witchcraft narratives in Germany: Rothenburg, 1561–1652
Alison Rowlands

Authority and society in Nantes during the French Wars of Religion, 1559–98
Elizabeth C. Tingle

The great favourite:
The Duke of Lerma and the court and government of Philip III of Spain, 1598–1621
Patrick Williams

Catholic communities in Protestant states

Britain and the Netherlands
c.1570–1720

edited by
BENJAMIN KAPLAN, BOB MOORE,
HENK VAN NIEROP AND
JUDITH POLLMANN

Manchester University Press

Copyright © Manchester University Press 2009

While copyright in the volume as a whole is vested in Manchester University Press, copyright in individual chapters belongs to their respective authors, and no chapter may be reproduced wholly or in part without the express permission in writing of both author and publisher.

Published by Manchester University Press
Altrincham Street, Manchester M1 7JA, UK
www.manchesteruniversitypress.co.uk

British Library Cataloguing-in-Publication Data is available

Library of Congress Cataloging-in-Publication Data is available

ISBN 978 0 7190 9993 9 *paperback*

First published by Manchester University Press in hardback 2009

This paperback edition first published 2016

The publisher has no responsibility for the persistence or accuracy of URLs for any external or third-party internet websites referred to in this book, and does not guarantee that any content on such websites is, or will remain, accurate or appropriate.

Printed by Lightning Source

Contents

List of illustrations *page* xi
List of contributors xii
Preface xiii

1 Shifting identities in hostile settings: towards a comparison of the Catholic communities in early modern Britain and the Northern Netherlands
   Willem Frijhoff 1

2 Cooperative confessionalisation: lay–clerical collaboration in Dutch Catholic communities during the Golden Age
   Charles H. Parker 18

3 'So they become contemptible': clergy and laity in a mission territory
   Michael Mullett 33

4 Integration vs segregation: religiously mixed marriage and the 'verzuiling' model of Dutch Society
   Benjamin Kaplan 48

5 'Getting on' and 'getting along' in parish and town: Catholics and their neighbours in England
   William Sheils 67

6 Burying the dead; reliving the past: ritual, resentment and sacred space in the Dutch Republic
   Judith Pollmann 84

7 Beads, books and bare ruined choirs: transmutations of Catholic ritual life in Protestant England
   Alexandra Walsham 103

8 The Southern Netherlands connection: networks of support and patronage
   Paul Arblaster 123

9 Priests, nuns, presses and prayers: the Southern Netherlands and the contours of English Catholicism
   Claire Walker 139

CONTENTS

10 Second-class yet self-confident: Catholics in the Dutch Generality Lands
    Charles de Mooi — 156

11 Between conflict and coexistence: the Catholic community in Ireland as a 'visible underground church' in the late sixteenth and early seventeenth centuries
    Ute Lotz-Heumann — 168

12 Orphans and students: recruiting boys and girls for the Holland Mission
    Joke Spaans — 183

13 Harbourers and housekeepers: Catholic women in England 1570–1720
    Marie B. Rowlands — 200

14 Paintings for clandestine Catholic churches in the Republic: typically Dutch?
    Xander van Eck — 216

15 Cultures of dissent: English Catholics and the visual arts
    Richard L. Williams — 230

16 Conclusion: Catholic communities in Protestant states, Britain and the Netherlands c.1580–1720
    Benjamin Kaplan and Judith Pollmann — 249

Index — 265

List of illustrations

4.1	Rembrandt, *The Syndics of the Clothmakers' Guild* (1662). Courtesy of the Rijksmuseum, Amsterdam.	*page* 49
6.1	Funeral near the ruin in Eikenduinen (1729). Engraving in Jacob de Riemer, *Beschryving van 's Graven-Hage* dl. 1 (1730). By permission of Haags Gemeentearchief, The Hague.	87
6.2	Gerrit Pietersz. de Jong, *Portrait of a family in front of the ruins of the chapel of Our Lady of Succour in Heiloo* (1630). By permission of Museum Catharijneconvent, Utrecht, inv. nr. BMH s473b.	88
6.3	Pieter Saenredam, Interior of the Cathedral of St Jan at Den Bosch (1646). By permission of National Gallery of Art, Washington.	92
7.1	B[ernard] G[arter], *A newe yeares gifte dedicated to the popes holiness and all the Catholikes addicted to the sea of Rome* (London, 1579), fold-out plate ('Certaine of the Popes Merchandize lately sent over into Englande'). By permission of the British Library, shelfmark 3932.dd. 15.	107
7.2	John Bucke, *Instructions on the Use of the beades* (Louvain, 1589), fold-out plate ('Lady Hungerforde's Meditations upon the Beades'). By permission of the British Library, shelfmark Huth 75.	108
7.3	Pilgrimage to the ruined chapel of Our Lady of Runxputte near Heiloo. Engraving by Frederik de Wit, first published Amsterdam c.1690. By permission of Museum Catharijneconvent, Utrecht.	114
10.1	Jan de Beijer, *The village church of Boxtel* (1740). Noordbrabants Museum.	157
10.2	Anonymous, *Departure of the Roman Catholic clergy and the royal garrison from 's-Hertogenbosch on 17 September 1629, after the capitulation in favour of Frederik Hendrik, Prince of Orange* (1629). Brabant Collection, Library of the University of Tilburg.	161
14.1	Anonymous, *Laudes Marianae* triptych. By permission of Museum Catharijneconvent, Utrecht (photo: Catharijneconvent).	218
14.2	Abraham Bloemaert, *The supper at Emmaus* (1622). Brussels, Musées Royaux des Beaux-Arts (photo: Utrecht University).	220
14.3	Pieter de Grebber, *St Bavo blessed by St Amand*. Haarlem, Roman Catholic Church of St Mary (photo: Utrecht University).	222
14.4	Interior of the former clandestine church 't Hert (now Museum Amstelkring), Amsterdam (photo: Museum Amstelkring).	223

ILLUSTRATIONS

14.5 N. Roosendael, *Christ after the Flagellation* (1677). By permission of Museum Catharijneconvent, Utrecht (photo: Catharijneconvent).   224

14.6 Jacob de Wit, oil study for *The Resurrection*. By permission of Museum Catharijneconvent, Utrecht (photo: Catharijneconvent).   226

15.1 Unknown sculptor, plaster relief of the Crucifixion (1577). Rushton Hall, Northamptonshire.   232

15.2 Rushton Triangular Lodge 1594–97. Rushton, Northamptonshire.   240

15.3 Lyveden New Bield (Northamptonshire), begun 1594 but left unfinished at the death of Sir Thomas Tresham in 1605.   242

15.4 Book title page of *The Betraying of Christ* (London: Adam Islip, 1598). By permission of the British Library.   243

List of contributors

Paul Arblaster is currently teaching at the Faculty of Philosophy and Letters at the Université Catholique de Louvain (Louvain-le-Neuve). He is the author of *A history of the Low Countries* (Palgrave, 2006) and *Antwerp and the world: Richard Verstegan and the international culture of Catholic reformation* (Leuven University Press, 2004) and has published articles on early-modern news, translation, exiles and accounts of martyrdom, focusing on interactions between the Low Countries and the British Isles.

Xander van Eck was Senior Lecturer in Art History at Utrecht University and is now Associate Professor of Art History at the Faculty of Fine Arts and Design at the Izmir University of Economics. He specialises in Dutch Renaissance and Baroque art. His dissertation *Kunst, Twist en Devotie* (Free University, Amsterdam 1994) is about the decoration of clandestine Catholic churches in the city of Gouda, 1572–1795. In 2002 he published a Corpus Vitrearum catalogue of the stained-glass windows by Dirck and Wouter Crabeth. His latest book is *Clandestine splendour: painting for the Catholic Church in the Dutch Republic* (Waanders, 2007) in their series Studies in Netherlandish Art and Cultural History.

Willem Frijhoff is Professor Emeritus of Early Modern History at the Vrije Universiteit, Amsterdam, and was chair of the Humanities and Social Sciences Division of the Royal Netherlands Academy of Sciences. Among his publications are *Embodied belief: ten essays on religious culture in Dutch history* (Hilversum 2002); *1650: Hard-Won Unity* (Assen/Basingstoke 2004) and *Fulfilling God's mission: the two worlds of Dominie Everardus Bogardus 1607–1647* (Leiden/Boston, 2007) which won the Hendricks Manuscript Award of the New Netherland Institute (Albany).

Benjamin Kaplan is Professor of Dutch History at University College London and also holds an appointment at the University of Amsterdam. He received his B.A. from Yale University in 1981 and his Ph.D. from Harvard University in 1989. Before moving to London, he taught at Brandeis University and the University of Iowa. His previous books include *Calvinists and Libertines: confession and community in Utrecht, 1578–1620* (Oxford University Press, 1995), which received the Philip Schaff Prize and the Roland Bainton Prize in History and Theology. His most recent book, *Divided by faith: religious conflict and the practice of toleration in Early Modern Europe*, was published by Harvard University Press in 2007.

CONTRIBUTORS

Ute Lotz-Heumann is Heiko A. Oberman Professor in the Division for Late Medieval and Reformation Studies at the University of Arizona. She is the author of *Die doppelte Konfessionalisierung in Irland: Konflikt und Koexistenz im 16. und in der ersten Hälfte des 17. Jahrhunderts* (2000) and co-editor of *Konversion und Konfession in der Frühen Neuzeit* (2007). She has published books and articles on the history of the Reformation and the confessional age in Ireland and Germany.

Charles C. M. de Mooij is Director of the Noordbrabants Museum in 's-Hertogenbosch and has published books and articles on the material culture and on the religious and political history of Brabant in the early modern period. In 1998 he received his Ph.D. from the Katholieke Universiteit Nijmegen for his thesis *Geloof kan bergen verzetten. Reformatie en katholieke herleving te Bergen op Zoom 1577–1795* (Hilversum: Verloren, 1998).

Bob Moore is Professor of Twentieth-Century European History at the University of Sheffield. He is the author of *Refugees from Nazi Germany in the Netherlands, 1933–1940* (1986); *Victims and survivors: the Nazi persecution of the Jews in the Netherlands, 1940–1945* (1997) as well as other works on the history of the Second World War. He has been the co-editor of the 'Britain and the Netherlands' volumes since 1999.

Michael Mullett is Professor of Cultural and Religious History at the University of Lancaster, where he has taught for forty years. His more recent books are *Catholics in Britain and Ireland 1558–1829* (Basingstoke, London and New York, 1998); *The Catholic Reformation* (London and New York, 1999); *Martin Luther* (London and New York, 2004) and *English Catholicism 1680–1830* (6 vols, London, 2006). Professor Mullett is currently working on *The historical dictionary of the Reformation and Counter-Reformation*.

Henk van Nierop is Professor of Early Modern History at the University of Amsterdam and Academic Director of the Amsterdam Centre for the Study of the Golden Age. Among his publications are *The nobility of Holland: from knights to regents, 1500–1650* (Cambridge, 1993) and *Het verraad van het Noorderkwartier. Oorlog, terreur en recht in de Nederlandse Opstand* (Amsterdam, 1999).

Charles H. Parker, an Associate Professor of History at Saint Louis University, works primarily on the religious and cultural history of the Dutch Republic. His primary publications include *The reformation of community: social welfare and Calvinist charity in Holland, 1572–1620* (Cambridge University Press, 1998) and *Faith on the margins: Catholics and Catholicism in the Dutch Golden Age* (Harvard University Press, 2008).

Judith Pollmann is Professor of the History and Culture of the Dutch Republic at Leiden University. She is the author of *Religious Choice in the Dutch Republic. The Reformation of Arnoldus Buchelius (1565–1641)* (Manchester University Press, 1999) and of numerous articles on the religious history of the early modern Netherlands. She is currently working on a book on Catholic identity and religious change in the Habsburg Netherlands, 1520–1635.

CONTRIBUTORS

Marie B. Rowlands is a research fellow Newman University College, Birmingham. Her research has been concerned with regions and communities in England in the seventeenth and early eighteenth centuries and her principal publications have been *Masters and men in the small metalware trades of the West Midlands 1660–1760* (Manchester, 1975); *The West Midlands from 1000 A.D.* (London, 1987); 'Recusant Women', in M Prior (ed.) *Women in English Society* (Methuen 1986) and *Catholics of parish and town* (1999) for the Catholic Record Society. She is currently developing further work on Catholic missions in their parish setting.

William Sheils is Professor of History at the University of York, where he teaches early modern religious and social history. He has published widely in the field and has been active as editor with Studies in Church History, the Church of England Record Society and the Oxford Dictionary of National Biography. He is President of the Ecclesiastical History Society for 2008–9.

Jo Spaans is Senior Lecturer in Church History in the Department of Theology, within the Faculty of Humanities at Utrecht University. She has held academic posts at the University of Amsterdam, Fryske Academy, Catholic Theological University of Amsterdam and the Free University of Amsterdam. In 1997–8 she was Visiting Professor in the History Department at the University of Michigan, Ann Arbor. Her doctoral dissertation was published as *Haarlem na de Reformatie. Stedelijke cultuur en kerkelijk leven 1577–1620* (1989) and she has subsequently written a study of early-modern poor relief in the Dutch province of Friesland: *Armenzorg in Friesland, 1500–1800. Publieke zorg en particuliere liefdadigheid in zes Friese steden. Leeuwarden, Bolsward, Franeker, Sneek, Dokkum en Harlingen* (1998). More recently, she edited a volume on the revival movement in the middle of the eighteenth century: *Een golf van beroering. De omstreden opwekking in de Republiek in het midden van de achttiende eeuw* (2001).

Claire Walker lectures in early modern European history at the University of Adelaide in Australia. She has written extensively about religious women, in particular, post-Reformation English nuns. Her publications include *Gender and politics in Early Modern Europe: English convents in France and the Low Countries* (Palgrave Macmillan, 2003) and an edition of *The admirable life of the Holy Virgin S. Catharine of Bologna* (Ashgate, 2006).

Alexandra Walsham is Professor of History at the University of Exeter. She is the author of *Church papists: Catholicism, conformity and confessional polemic in Early Modern England* (Woodbridge, 1993); *Providence in Early Modern England* (Oxford, 1999) and *Charitable hatred: tolerance and intolerance in England 1500–1700* (Manchester, 2006) and is currently completing a monograph entitled *The Reformation of the Landscape: Religion, Memory and Legend in Early Modern Britain and Ireland.*

Richard Williams teaches at Birkbeck College, University of London. Having previously studied theology, he then completed a doctorate at the Courtauld Institute which examined the impact of the Reformation on the visual culture of England. He has recently co-edited a book entitled, *Art reformed: reassessing the impact of the Reformation on the visual arts (2007) and is* currently working on another volume supported by a post-doctoral fellowship awarded by Yale University (the Paul Mellon Centre).

Preface

In August 2006 leading scholars from Britain, the Netherlands, Ireland, Belgium, Germany, the USA and Australia met in Amsterdam and Leiden to discuss the position, experiences and strategies of Catholics in the British Isles and the Dutch Republic, two Protestant countries that harboured, in the seventeenth century, important Catholic minorities. The conference was part of a triennial series of British–Dutch encounters that started in 1959. Since that year the conference proceedings have been published regularly in an informal series called *Britain and the Netherlands*, of which this volume is the sixteenth. Little would the organisers of the first meeting, the late professors Bromley and Kossmann, have recognised the present volume as a legitimate heir to their first conference at St Anthony's College, Oxford. Their meeting had little other purpose than to create contacts between scholars in two countries who knew little of each other's work, although the histories of their respective countries had been often intertwined. Volume 1 of *Britain and the Netherlands* covered a wide variety of topics ranging from the sixteenth to the twentieth centuries. The present volume explores a particular set of problems and the authors were asked to address, as much as possible, the similarities and differences between the two countries. Further, the authors of this volume do not represent two national communities of historians, but a global community of scholars with a truly international and comparative research agenda. The forty-ninth anniversary of the *Britain and the Netherlands* conferences thus reflects the significant changes that have taken place over the last half century in the historical profession as a whole.

The editors gratefully acknowledge the generous financial and logistical support from a number of institutions in two countries. They are, in the Netherlands, the Institute for Culture and History and the Amsterdam Centre for the Study of the Golden Age, both at the University of Amsterdam; the National Organisation for Scientific Research (NWO); the History Department and University Library at Leiden University; and, finally, a private foundation of Catholic signature, which has generously contributed towards the conference on condition that its name remains undivulged. In the UK, the conference was sponsored by the Department of History of University College London and the Association for Low Countries Studies in Great Britain and Ireland (ALCS).

On a more personal note, the editors would like to thank Dr Michiel van Groesen, without whose skilled and cheerful assistance the conference, and the ensuing volume, would have been less of a success. Finally, we would like to acknowledge the support of Tony Mason, Alison Welsby, Emma Brennan and their colleagues at Manchester University Press who helped us to bring the present volume to light.

> Ben Kaplan, London
> Bob Moore, Sheffield
> Henk van Nierop, Amsterdam
> Judith Pollmann, Leiden

1
Shifting identities in hostile settings: towards a comparison of the Catholic communities in early modern Britain and the Northern Netherlands[1]

WILLEM FRIJHOFF

Changing perspectives

Until the last quarter of the twentieth century religious history suffered from two major restrictions: it was monopolised by ecclesiastical views and narrowed by national historiography. In order to be able to grasp the quintessence of Catholicism, Catholic historians had to be Catholics; similarly, for a Calvinist, history written by a Catholic may still be considered as an encroachment on the God-given world order.[2] A clerical historian was a still better choice: he understood from within the institutional and intellectual situation of Catholicism and could direct his story the way his fellow-faithful expected. However, not all Dutch or British historians of Catholicism were clerics. For early modern Dutch Catholicism, Louis J. Rogier (1894–1974), a history professor and militant lay member of the national Catholic community, set the tone. The same was true for Protestantism. Ministers wrote about ministers, professors of theology drafted church histories, and continue to do so.

In the historical self-consciousness of all religious communities, even lay historians themselves systematically underrated lay agency. Women were excluded from the male-based institution of the Catholic Church – except those who followed an ecclesiastical rule and were somehow part of the institutional church – nuns, for instance, or noblewomen, or those clerical helpers known as *klopjes* in the Netherlands.[3] The Catholic community considered its fate a national problem and consequently looked inwards. Motives, reasons and context were described in national terms, and transnational relations were marginalised, with the exception of those with Rome and the Vatican. As was the case in Britain, the Dutch community considered ultramontanism a virtue. The resulting historical image was that of self-sufficient national churches, Catholic or Protestant, in unison with triumphant national states.

Religious minorities suffered from a third obstacle: a sense of victimisation. To assert their national belonging, they fostered a group identity that contrasted with the characteristics of the ruling opponents but was always closely confined within the categories of national pride and virtue. Minorities thus forged nationalistic narratives for themselves, reflections of the national church, painting in white what they perceived in others as black. Not all these narratives are fundamentally false. Religious culture in the public space, and to a certain extent even in private and domestic settings, is primarily a matter of transaction and negotiation between all the parties involved. Those who master the public space, public values, and public communication have achieved a major advantage that others have to take into account. One example, which I have studied myself, is that of 'popular religion'.[4] The leaders of the Catholic Reformation in the Netherlands tended to reject popular ritual as superstition. Confrontation with the similar views of the ruling Protestant churches, however, led them to claim some such popular forms –possession by spirits, pilgrimage to healing shrines, or the use of indulgences, be it in a more or less purified form – as identifiers of true Catholicism and to reappropriate them for the demarcation and consolidation of their own religious community.

Yet the real change that occurs since the last two decades of the twentieth century is not the transition from clerical towards professional historical scholarship, but a change in scope and methods. The prevailing empiricist methods and theological visions in church history make room for a more problem-oriented, cultural and anthropological approach, using social science-based methods. This transition commands a triple revision: re-evaluating the transnational dimensions, comparing national evolutions, and reconstructing the changing strategies for defining new religious group identities and group cultures.

It is rather surprising that, despite their proximity in many fields and their common interests throughout early modern and modern times, neither the Dutch nor the British Catholic community has ever felt the need for a close comparison of their respective histories and the way their own narratives, ideals, and agency shaped their identity as a religious minority. Both were gradually set apart in a predominantly Protestant state with an internally divided ruling church. Both enjoyed the support of social and intellectual elites, and continued for some time to play on the uncertainties of a substantial portion of the population. Both were considered politically dangerous, often suspected of treason and conspiracy, and therefore felt themselves victimised. Both were profoundly and durably upset by the loss of their public means of expression, primarily church buildings but also printing presses, schools, and universities. Both actively entertained expectations for the recovery of their former possessions, which gradually became invested with huge symbolic meaning. Both tried to develop educational alternatives at home and abroad. Both communities developed privileged relations with Catholic neighbours. Both received a missionary status from outside, contrasting with their strong indigenous convictions of continuity and feelings of authenticity. Finally, each, within the framework of its own state, was confronted with a massive yet socially and politically marginalised Catholic majority in a separate political territory – the Generality Lands for the Dutch Republic, and Ireland for the British crown.[5] Although Catholicism followed rather different paths in both territories, it remained strong and continued to motivate political resistance, and even some measure of re-catholicisation.[6]

A problem-oriented approach to religious history, rooted in new forms of social and cultural history, asking questions about the very concepts at stake in the narratives of the Catholic communities, should be able to compare these two communities at different levels: structural, political, social, and experiential. How did they create or discover and define themselves? How did they cope – from the top down but also from the bottom up, through clergy and laity, women and men, elites and the common people – with social and economic adversity, persecution, subordination, political distrust, and loss of state support? How did they manage to create new ways for the assertion of their (changing) values and their group identity, in interaction with an ever more self-confident nation and with the changing world around them? It goes without saying that such comparison should not accentuate the particularities of each Catholic community but, on the contrary, examine the similarities of their historical strategies and the resemblances of their answers to the hostile environments in which they evolved. Yet comparison needs not only method but also knowledge and documentation. We must scrutinise the local situations, contexts, and evolutions of both communities. Close awareness of time and space, and their interconnected change, is the major virtue of the historian.

Re-evaluating the transnational dimensions

In spite of the variety of its local appearances, the Roman Catholic Church was not a local, nor even a national organisation. It was what I would call a transnational institution, working with historically moulded national communities in an international setting but unable and perhaps also unwilling to ignore national boundaries and historical contingencies. The nationalisation of the church structure was precisely the issue of the Anglican experience but also, to a certain extent, that of the measures taken by the Habsburg sovereigns for the rationalisation of ecclesiastical organisation in the Netherlands and the internal surveillance of the national community by a national version of the Inquisition. Both monarchies desired keenly to remain in control, for reasons of church discipline, state cohesion, and religious culture. Both monarchies desired to enforce a national religion as a symbiosis between state and church for the benefit of the political community, gradually identified as 'national'.[7] In the Reformation era, both communities went through a process of delocalisation, loosening the links between popular religion, national community, and international church organisation. 'Local' increasingly meant 'regional', if not national, defined by higher authorities, themselves mostly disconnected from the local experience of everyday community life.

Paradoxically, Calvinism, in spite of its emphasis on local church organisation, appeared in the Netherlands from the start as a rather open confession with more border-crossing potential, just like the loose varieties of Lutheranism which initially prevailed outside Germany, including in the Netherlands. Both reform movements promised a future of civil freedom in answer to the compelling social and political force of ordered Catholicism. It is useful to keep this in mind, for Protestantism not only claimed to offer freedom of choice in religion and grace, it initially offered a real escape from the constraints of an increasingly oppressive church organisation supported by an increasingly powerful state. Even before the imposition of the Reformed Church monopoly in the public space, priests and monks deserted massively from Catholic Church structures in the Netherlands. This may be considered not only as a result of Protestant persecution but also as a vote of no confidence in the prevailing church organisation and a cry for fresh air and religious liberty, in whatever denominational context. The remaining secular priests upon whom the Catholic Church could rely – not more than seventy around the year 1600, according to the Dutch Apostolic Vicar Sasbout Vosmeer[8] – must have been saintly persons but, persisting as they did in such extreme conditions, several may have been conservative diehards or control freaks whom normal people preferred to avoid. We know that throughout the second half of the sixteenth century and far into the seventeenth century, lay desertion from religious practice and even from church membership was widespread in the Netherlands, especially in the coastal provinces of Holland and Friesland.[9] Yet, religion remaining a basic dimension of individual consciousness and community life, many must have been seekers, 'reli-shoppers' as we would call them today, changing churches several times during their lifetime, distancing themselves from ecclesiastical authorities, and picking bits and pieces from whichever religious guru passed by. The painter Rembrandt van Rijn may have been such a reli-shopper, but one with excellent biblical knowledge, profound religious needs, and a quite personal religious experience.[10] At a more basic level, the probate inventories of many Dutch citizens show marks of such religious syncretism: books from several denominational backgrounds converge in one person's library, signifying a personal appropriation of religion within the context of a broadly shared spirituality.[11]

By that time, the Catholic Church had redefined and reorganised itself.¹² The most evident transnational issue of early modern religion is obviously the by now inseparable pair, Reformation/Counter-Reformation. Both played over a wide range of regions and states and had a lasting influence on the shape that religious communities took in later centuries. During the whole period under review, the Counter-Reformation looms large in the Catholic countries bordering Britain and the Netherlands, such as France, the Southern Netherlands, or Westphalia, though this is barely visible in the narratives on these two countries themselves. The problem with the Counter-Reformation is probably its stereotyped image. In current historiography and in the classical imagery of many of our contemporaries, Counter-Reformation is roughly equivalent to Roman baroque sculpture, Bavarian Benedictine libraries, or Jesuit church façades. It is at any rate exuberant, emotive, and extreme. However, the Catholic Reformation – as we prefer to name it now – started in Northern Europe before the breakthrough of the baroque and went, in some respects, quite different ways. We should reserve the term Counter-Reformation for a specific aesthetic style and moral or spiritual message. This Counter-Reformation style – or stereotype – displays itself in some of the artistic achievements, clandestine or not, of the Catholic churches of Britain and the Northern Netherlands. But it should not prevent us from discovering two other realities: on the one hand all the resources of reform Catholicism in that era, including popular education, social discipline, new ethics and morals, and the revival of spirituality; on the other hand the specific local or regional, indeed broadly 'national' shape the Catholic Reformation took in the countries involved. A more open approach would consider the Catholic Reformation as a broad movement of regeneration, embracing the Counter-Reformation of course, but leaving space for 'national' varieties that at first sight may seem to be in contrast, even in contradiction, with the Counter-Reformation in the classical Roman or Mediterranean sense.¹³ It is only under this condition that we may compare the Catholic Reformations in Protestant nations.

One of the issues of the Catholic Reformation in our countries was the return to a national church organisation as a Catholic survival strategy. Catholics wanted to give a national character to internationally promoted values, movements, and institutions. International movements start, however, in particular places. Such a movement was Jansenism. Nourished by local needs, local grievances, and local thinking it evolved into a largely unlocalised doctrine. In the words of Lucien Ceyssens, it really was a Jesuit-born 'Anti-anti-Jansenism' without initial consistency.¹⁴ Analysed not as a theological but as a social and cultural issue, however, Jansenism may reveal the interaction between the local, the national and the transnational in Catholicism. Why did Jansenism take root so strongly in the Netherlands, both North and South, but – as far as I know – barely in Britain? Such a comparison may reopen a historical debate that by now totally revolves around itself. Jansenism has obviously been central to the community experience of large groups and is probably also intimately connected with the rise of international Pietism that found its specific ways in Britain.[15] Clearly, we must distinguish here between doctrine, church structure, and community life. One of the reasons for the differing impact of Jansenism in the two communities may be, as far as structure is concerned, the strong link between the local Catholic Church in Britain and Jansenism's enemies, the Jesuits. Besides, socially, Jansenism appears as an upper middle-class phenomenon, unable to attract the masses but also suspicious in the eyes of the higher nobility who continued to dominate the political and social scene of English Catholicism more than in the Dutch Republic.

Comparing national developments

At first sight, at the end of the sixteenth century Dutch and British Catholicism were in somewhat similar positions and suffered similar fates. The Protestant states were far from being Protestant nations, even if they proclaimed themselves as such. Catholicism was not only a forbidden and persecuted remnant, but it had to be conquered, precisely because of its symbolic value for social, political, or cultural groups, or for local, regional, or national power relations. Catholicism had lost its public privileges. Restricted to a private or domestic level, religious expression even was barely tolerated because of the permanent suspicion of connivance with internal or foreign enemies. Traditional narratives emphasise feelings of fear, subordination, and nostalgia, not to mention the clandestine character of religious practice. Yet there is certainly room for other approaches, stimulated by a comparison between the two communities. Both were mission territories, and as such the object of actively organised missionary work. Catholics did survive individually, in family settings, as social groups, as local communities, and even as a national church. Conversions became apologetic tools, hopes were cherished, and young people developed ideals for community service or a Catholic *reconquista*. Overall, the community held together, sometimes even grew. The decline of Catholicism was far from taken for granted. It is this positive, vivid aspect of the community's life experience, largely neglected until now, that may benefit from systematic comparisons between Britain, Ireland, and the Netherlands.

Other comparisons may be enlightening too. In many respects, Protestantism acted similarly to Catholicism, since the differences between the religious creeds and institutions were largely superseded by the common cultural background and social context within which the religious groups identified themselves in relation to each other. The confrontation of Protestant experience with Catholic life is therefore necessary for a better understanding of the communities. In a beautiful book on persecution and resistance in sixteenth-century England, Sarah Covington has recently compared the history of the Catholic and Protestant martyrs. She found a strikingly similar pattern of persecution and the assimilation of martyrdom in both communities.[16] In their public expression and political fate, martyrs are virtually interchangeable, but the appropriation of martyrdom by the community differs according to the local and national context. A twofold confrontation is therefore necessary: between the Protestant and Catholic experiences, and between the Catholic community's appropriations on either side of the North Sea.

Yet, if the stories of martyrdom were memorised in the Netherlands and in Britain, Catholic martyrs of the Reformation were not honoured with the same intensity everywhere. In the Holland Mission, there was barely any local cult of these martyrs, mostly known in local clusters, like 'the martyrs of Gorcum', but without a personal face – quite unlike Edmund Campion (1540–81) and his fellow martyrs in England. The canonisation procedures, including that for the murderer of William of Orange, Balthasar Gérard (executed in 1584), were all interrupted or delayed before conclusion. Martyrologies were scarce and remained very much the work of individual clerics, such as the theologian Willem van Est (Estius) or the Apostolic Vicar Vosmeer. It was not until the resumption of a national Catholic consciousness in the nineteenth century that the Catholic martyrs of the Reformation period received their consecration, and even then, almost nobody knew them by name. In recovering their self-consciousness Dutch Catholics didn't systematically oppose the surrounding Protestant context but used a consensus policy, asking for tacit accommodation and achieving an 'ecumenicity of everyday life'[17] that, in the daily intercourse of the national community, conveniently put between brackets everything that was not vital for denominational – or confessional – identity. Of course, when identity feelings really were involved, apologetics played its role. We know a number of textbooks, popular catechisms, and semi-learned treatises intended to provide the Catholic layperson with intellectual, spiritual, or political munitions for defence against the surrounding heretics.

It is precisely this point of confessional identity that is probably the most controversial and the least studied of all. It is the most difficult too, because it involves all the social and cultural groups of the confessional community, many of whom left barely any written, visual, or material trace in history, due to the illegitimate status of their community in the public order. Other complications come from the confessionalisation thesis of Reinhard and Schilling, which only very partially, if at all, applies to the two communities but has provoked an important international discussion that we cannot avoid.[18] Ever since the rise of recusant history (in Britain) and of pillarisation or *verzuiling* (in the Netherlands), confessional identity has in fact been supposed always to have existed. There *was* a Catholic community only waiting for the opportunity to assert itself – such is the implicit contention.

Yet what do we (and what did ordinary Catholics three or four centuries ago) understand by such notions? Peter Marshall has shown that the notion 'Catholic' was rather slow to gain consistency in sixteenth-century Britain, and that it should not yet be taken for the denominational concept that later historiography has designed and retro-projected onto the early Catholic Reformation era.[19] How far, then, did 'Catholics' continue to identify with the national community and the national church? Did they claim to embody its continuity, or to represent a newly conceptualised Catholic community?[20] Moreover, which Catholic Church did they have in mind? Was it the old medieval order, or a purified version accommodated by some form of Catholic Reformation, Revival or Restoration? How did they separate the true faithful from the heretics, both in the 'imagined community' and in real life? How did they fill the gap between these two extremes? Where, exactly, in that idyllic and seemingly coherent picture, was there room for dissimulators, traitors, seekers, critics, *liefhebbers* (simple sympathisers), the ungodly, or the undecided?

The notion of 'Catholic' is itself a historical construct. We have to use the straitjacket of historical prejudice in order to adjust loose historical evidence to our denominational discourse. Yet, through a close analysis of the sources we discover a variety of persons involved in community building, including laypeople, women, children, and the whole fringe of those who hesitated, the 'sociological Christians' (as they were called in the twentieth century) uniquely interested in useful sacraments, not in creed or confession. That mass of people obstructs our pre-established intellectual concepts and historical categories. Therefore, we must keep an open mind. Let us first look at the evidence before categorising, and remain sensitive towards local solutions for local problems in spite of the Catholic Church's compelling tendency to unify everything and remodel it according to the instructions of the central Roman agencies.

One more item is central to the understanding of the internal evolution of the two communities: that is the concept of loyalty. In spite of the basic similarity of the British and Netherlandic situations – that is, the legal inferiority and political non-existence of the Catholic underdog – the political framework of the two countries was very different. There were certainly common features in the attitude of the political authorities towards the Catholic minority. Every now and then suspicions of treachery surfaced concerning the pope, considered as Antichrist and rightly seen as a foreign sovereign with particular interests, different from those of the national Catholic community. Another common enemy, partly real, partly mythical, and largely metonymical for militant Catholicism as such, was the Jesuit order. Yet Jesuits apparently played very different roles in Britain and the Netherlands. Their role may have been pivotal in Britain, it was much less so in the Northern Netherlands, where they were more subject to competition with the secular clergy and other religious orders.

Even before the formal imposition of the Reformation, the Jesuit order had started to have a strong impact on those urban and social sectors of the Northern Netherlandic provinces that had been won over to the idea of a Catholic Reformation, some of them even prior to the Council of Trent. The emblematic figure here is, of course, Petrus Canisius (1521–97), canonised in the nineteenth century as *doctor ecclesiae*, the true Counter-Reformation hero of the Northern Netherlands beside the host of largely nondescript martyrs of the Beggars. Nevertheless, Canisius, the 'apostle of Germany', shows at the same time the ambiguity of the Dutch case. His working area was not the Netherlands but greater Germany, the natural hinterland of his home town of Nijmegen. The political unity of the Burgundian Northern Netherlands still had to go a long way before it was converted into a truly 'national' mental map for all its citizens. One aspect of our theme is precisely the strong role played by religion in the process of nation building in that area. I would contend that, through its survival strategy and ways of identity finding, the Catholic community has contributed as much to this nationalisation of the common political space as Protestantism, for which this role is traditionally reserved. However, the story of the Catholic Reformation in the Northern Provinces, before the breakthrough of Calvinism, and the way it is linked with what happened afterwards, is still waiting for a historian able to disentangle the archival, literary, and visual evidence from Protestant mythology and Catholic nostalgia.

In the political context of the Northern Netherlands, Catholics enjoyed individual toleration. As long as they did not ritually or publicly confess a non-Reformed creed, and no threat to public order was involved, there was room for a – sometimes rather surprising – Catholic presence in the public space, and especially for diverging visions of the Catholic Church and its impact on Dutch society. The vision of the secular clergy confined itself to national needs; it intended to promote a vision of institutional continuity between the pre-Reformation church and that of the post-Reformation order. It opposed the internationalism of the Jesuits and their allies. Altogether, Jesuits seem to have played a more 'national' role in Britain and to have been to a greater degree the guardians of Catholic consciousness. In the Netherlands, both visions managed to impose themselves in discussions within the Catholic community and to secure for themselves a proper and enduring space. Seen from above, the Holland Mission was, and remained, strongly divided between two diverging conceptions of Catholic ecclesiology, pastoral care, apologetics, and even moral theology. In fact, Dutch local communities may have largely resembled each other. Yet specific features of morals (either 'laxism' or 'rigorism' in penitential affairs), liturgical practice (the frequency of Holy Communion), popular piety, devotions, and spirituality continued to divide the two groups and gave way to regular, occasionally even fierce, competitions between the mission stations (substitutes for the parishes) in the larger towns.

The rising ideals of priestly spirituality had profoundly influenced the secular clergy, and especially the leaders of the Holland Mission. Almost all the secular Dutch church leaders of the seventeenth century were active members of the Oratory of Cardinal Pierre de Bérulle, which soon became the main institutional, theological, and spiritual antipodes to the Jesuit order. For Bérulle and his fellow priests, church organisation was primarily episcopal. Priests had first to obey their bishop and then other, eventually higher authorities; the spiritual care of their flock had to fit into the diocesan format, in response to diocesan, that is, regional, needs and norms. Consequently, a clash with the international strategy of the Jesuits, Franciscans, Capuchins, and other religious orders was inevitable, and the Dutch church was virtually predisposed for the episcopal and conciliarist views of later Jansenism that would result in the Utrecht Schism of 1723, and in the radicalisation of the Old Catholic leaders at the time of the Revolution.

Such tensions may have passed through the British Catholic communities too, but, in the long run, the cleavage between two radically opposed ecclesiological views seems to have affected the coherence of the Catholic community less. At any rate, the twelve Oratorians who came to London in the suite of Queen Henrietta Maria at the request of her confessor Bérulle, had to leave England pretty soon and, as far as I know, they left no visible trace in British history. Ecclesiastical loyalty was thus easier to achieve in the British Catholic community, where the guiding role of Rome was apparently much less disputed than in the Holland Mission, at least at lay level. Did this difference in conflicts of loyalty result in a greater homogeneity of the Catholic community in Britain than in the Netherlands? Loyalty certainly was one of the key elements of the community's identity and one that may have resulted in major shifts.

Seen from the political point of view, however, the context in which the two Catholic communities evolved was barely comparable. To put it plainly, British Catholics looked for a re-establishment of Catholic rule from within the state structure, Dutch Catholics from without. The British situation reflected a state that every now and then was more or less consensual towards Catholicism, either because of the sovereign's personal inclinations, or as a result of the power balance between the clans of the nobility, at court or in society at large. In Britain – I realise that Ireland is a case in its own right – political loyalty always leaned towards values, symbols, or people inside the national community, even if the sovereign involved was thrown out of the country for the time being. As the Jacobites were still Pretenders at the end of our period, Catholics had to rally to and obey their own, indigenous king. Loyalty may have been difficult to enforce, but the choice was always clear.

The citizens of the Northern Netherlands lacked such clarity. Dutch Catholics faced not so much a loyalty *conflict* as a loyalty *puzzle*. Whom exactly could they consider as their legal sovereign? The very subject of political loyalty had to be argued. They had no indigenous sovereign, no natural bearer of the monarchy and self-evident focus of the cult of his subjects. At least, the ruling sovereign – be it the one in Spain or his substitute in Brussels – did not really provoke feelings of national pride or enthusiastic adhesion. He was just the distant authority the Catholics needed to fulfil their expectations. Judging by the initiatives taken by nobles, merchants, or academics, Dutch Catholics probably felt as much at ease with the emperor as with the Spanish king or the Brussels sovereign, provided he was Catholic. The provincial States and the States General were purely formal bearers of sovereignty, without being the symbolic object of veneration. Therefore, civil religion in the public space was for Dutch Catholics a very questionable issue, and this fact probably had far-reaching consequences for their political behaviour and loyalty in later centuries. Of the king's two bodies, only one was left, but Catholics obviously sought compensation abroad. Anyway, Catholic political theology as taught in Louvain and Douai, Cologne and Rome, considered the political state as a natural monarchy. Even the Apostolic Vicar Philip Rovenius, in his learned treatise *Respublica Christiana* published in Antwerp in 1648 – the very year of the international acknowledgement of the Dutch commonwealth as a republican state – put a king at the head of his ideal and, quite naturally, monarchic state structure, barely less than a utopia, given the situation.[21] His successor Joan (Johannes) van Neercassel went so far as to offer the loyalty of the Dutch Catholics to the French invader, King Louis XIV, provided he guaranteed them the liberty of their cult beside that of the Reformed citizens that Neercassel considered irreversible.[22]

We must not underestimate this loyalty problem, because it was at the very heart of the construction of Catholic identity in the hostile, post-Reformation context. When reading Dutch lay sources, or texts that expressly address non-clerics, we are surprised to discover how long Catholics, especially laypeople of the lower social classes, hesitated to embrace a new state structure corroborated by international law. For generations, they not only hankered after a restoration of the old order but also thought that restoration feasible in the short term. Yet I will not suggest that relations between the religious communities were permanently strained by antagonistic emotions. People managed quite well to live together consensually. Somewhere in the background, however, a fundamental change was always hoped for, precisely because of the structural and humiliating subordination to a hostile state of those who confessed themselves to be members of the Catholic community.

Anti-Protestant emotions were therefore limited to the context of community events but, under propitious circumstances, they could then suddenly appear quite forceful and compelling. There was no Gunpowder plot in Dutch history, yet conspiracy suspicions arose every now and then during the first century after the foundation of the Dutch Republic. Even in that accommodating society, some Protestants panicked as late as the summer of 1734 about a political revolution and a general massacre by Catholics, and quite evidently some Catholics themselves hoped at the time to regain possession of the churches and to overthrow the political regime.[23] The question is, therefore, to analyse to what extent private religious feelings and religious group identity may have differed, and how they interacted with political and social evolutions in the national communities. It is obvious that, though within comparable contexts, the two communities did not follow the same path throughout the seventeenth century. How much room could an individual believer or his local community gain in the two contexts, British and Netherlandic? What can such comparisons teach us about the flexibility of early modern society and the place of the individual Catholic believer?

Survival strategies for religious group identity: a research agenda

To conclude, I will outline elements of the research agenda addressed by my fellow authors in this volume and highlight additional lines of enquiry that may be pursued in future. One of the key phrases of present-day social history is 'survival strategy'. Historians are aware that individuals, groups, or communities often have to live in hostile settings. This leads them to search for ways in which people in the past and in profoundly different economic, political, social, and cultural settings, sought to cope with poverty, adversity, social inferiority, political pressure, or religious persecution. This conceptual approach is most promising for the renewal of religious history, because it quits the too-simple paths of traditional, empiricist church history. Turning towards the living community itself, it requires the alliance of cultural history, cultural and social anthropology, social psychology, and related disciplines. In fact, it implies also a post-denominational and post-national attitude, since historians can no longer take for granted the definitions and limits set for the field of research by the more or less implicit convictions of prevailing confessional ideology and national interests.

Thus, the historiographic space formerly occupied by denominationally committed church historians needs a conceptual redefinition. The historical object itself must be reworded as 'the construction of minority group identities in changing settings', in order to make it a general research object, available to all, and not limited by the need for an intimate religious involvement of the historian. The main shift towards a new vision probably depends on exchanging the approach based on confessional supply for that of religious demand and on favouring from the start agency, daily life, and experience over institutions, ideas, and norms. Group survival can never be taken for granted in a hostile environment. People have constantly to deploy initiatives and consciously or unconsciously to develop adequate strategies to ensure the cohesion of the group as such, and thereby its survival. Such strategies have to respond closely to the actual context, in order to be effective. Any analysis should therefore take into account the interactions of the group with dominant or competing communities, and from as many perspectives as possible.

Survival strategies may involve a great variety of features. Let me enumerate some of them. We may distinguish between internal and external strategies. Internal strategies should foster the cohesion of the group; external strategies define its image and position within the global community or the nation. The very first and indeed basic condition of existence of any community is a place to gather, in order to realise and embody the community socially, physically, and visibly. Hence the importance, both symbolically and in practice, of the church property question, and the recurrent role it plays especially for Catholics throughout the whole minority period of the community. Even the smallest or remotest space will do, provided the community can recognise itself as both plural and united. Church attendance and community gathering require a minimum of organisation, an agenda, a ceremonial, or a liturgy: hence the importance of a community bond, a formal or unspoken but recognised set of rules, texts, songs, and rituals meant to reaffirm the identity of the group each time.

Second, internal cohesion may be reached by demographic means, for example by a marriage strategy — which confronts us with the degree of observance of the tacitly or formally established rules of the *connubium* and the efficacy of the sanctions applied by the community or its leaders in the case of a mixed marriage.[24]

Third, internal strategies may concern aspects of group survival through social agency.[25] How and by whom are the expenses linked to community work financed: church buildings, salaries of priests, ministers, admonishers and school teachers, poor relief, care of orphans and the elderly, and so on? How does protection and patronage work? Who depends socially and economically on whom within the community? Are family ties and kinship essential to inner cohesion? Do Catholic consumers buy in Catholic shops, Catholic artisans engage Catholic apprentices, and Catholic laypeople socialise in Catholic unions, clubs, or organisations of whatever kind they may be? Do the members of the group monopolise any one profession or translate a general profession into a community-linked occupation (such as money lending, banking, the wholesale or retail trade in specific commodities)? Given the exclusion of adherents of minority religions from public office, do people, in particular the minority elites, take refuge in specific intellectual occupations (for instance the law or medicine), or do they manage to escape the prohibitions, and with the connivance of whom? Do they invest their money in common enterprises?

A fourth range of internal strategies is about feelings of belonging and common destiny. How does the group define its inner structure, its limits, its *raison d'être*? Who is entitled to claim membership and under what conditions, both formal and informal? Who decides about membership, how is it obtained and through which rituals? Are outsiders welcome, and what kind of initiation rites (open or disguised) are they put through? How are members mobilised? By what practices, discourses, or other forms of persuasion? How are internal obligations communicated? Is there a coherent publication and communication strategy? How are the community's leaders recruited, educated, appointed, and controlled? Is there a common strategy for their intellectual formation? Are there specific moral requirements for the behaviour of the community's members, and how are sanctions applied in order to be effective inside the group?

Internal cohesion and external strategies

Internal cohesion is, of course, subject to a variety of strategy types, depending on the interaction with others: strategies of continuity, of change and renewal, or of a utopian and prophetic character, strategies of exclusion and inclusion, not only of persons, objects, and rituals, but also of myths, legends, stories, and narratives. The most important feature, however, is that, in order to survive, any minority has to develop a coherent narrative about its existence or survival as such, a historical 'canon' telling us from what founding events that community derives its historical legitimacy and uniting all the faithful in a single spirit and a single perspective. The narrative will be stronger when expressed in its own visual language, but also if it achieves the intellectual legitimisation of the group's existence, through a common philosophical or theological vision of its destiny. The Old-Catholic Schism in the Northern Netherlands (1723), strongly legitimised by a vision of past and present of the community different from that of the Roman Catholics, is a clear proof of the importance of such a common narrative and of the dangers incurred by the minority community if such a narrative is not shared by all those involved.

External strategies have to foster the image of the group as a whole, and to anchor its existence firmly and recognisably in the social and political environment. Theology and political philosophy play an important role in the legitimisation of the community as a minority with its own inalienable right to existence, and so does historiography. What is the social, political, and cultural image that the community wants to give of itself? Jan Andriessen demonstrated, many decades ago, how the Jesuit strategy strengthened the feelings of the Catholics in the Northern and Southern Netherlands that they fundamentally belonged together and one day had to recover their common destiny and, indeed, their common identity.[26] The Generality Lands figured in this constellation as a bridge, a sluice-gate of permeability, permitting at first the maintenance of the perspective of unity and, after the Peace of Westphalia, the realisation of a steady stream of books, prints, devotional objects, ideas, and transfers of ritual agency. Though an enemy of their state, the Southern Netherlands were for the Dutch Catholics in the North an ally upon whom they could rely.

However, the question has a wider sense. Whose support for survival is sought outside the community: that of foreign sovereigns, of befriended communities, of influential intellectuals? What arguments about the minorities' treatment elsewhere are brought forward to improve the community's position, and how far do problems across the borders affect the community's home situation? Are conversion stories capitalised on for the community's justification towards its opponents or rivals? How openly does a minority community want to express itself? Does it publicly claim continuity of functions, institutions, buildings, or at least of appearances? Does it take refuge in semi-clandestine behaviour, or make itself invisible to the outside world, and for what reason? Does it develop an aggressive self-assertion in its hostile environment, claiming its rights against the established political order? What is the relation between domestic settings, the private sphere, and public order? Where exactly does the domain that the community may claim as its own begin, and what degree of tolerance does it enjoy outside? Was it possible to create a simulation of normality for the minority church, could one survive individually as a heterodox believer, or was Nicodemism a realistic option? What were the formal and informal limits of denominational expression in the public space and – not quite the same thing – in the public order?

In a final analysis, however, it is not the strategy that must interest us but the minority group identity that it intends to protect, create, or promote. Therefore, all the aspects, elements and dimensions of survival strategy must be taken together in order to analyse as such the community they created. The key question here, of course, is about the nature and the strength of the community's self-consciousness. How strong exactly was the sense of community? Was it able to resist pressures from outside or centrifugal tendencies from within the group? Actually, Catholic minorities had the advantage over other persecuted or undesired religious minorities, like the Mennonites and the different groups of Dissenters, of having been the first practitioners of Christendom in their countries. Therefore, their self-consciousness played heavily with the historical argument, either in the form of priority claims or as an argument for continuity.

Having been the first to realise the Gospel's message in its ecclesiastical mantle, the Catholic Church thought of itself as the prime owner of Christendom and, in the mentality of that time, primacy was not only a fact but also a privilege with inalienable rights. No wonder that as late as 1632 Leiden University appointed a special Huguenot professor of European fame, the French philologist Claudius Salmasius, to combat Cardinal Baronius's works on the primacy of the Roman Church.

Once we have started to carry out this research agenda on a comparative scale, one final question remains and that is the evolution of the minority communities involved. As a historical construct, their identity was not stable. It proceeded from a changing and evolving balance between self-image, external context, objective conditions, and subjective achievements, impulsions, and responses, which had to be realised time and again. Minorities, too, had to organise their future in spite of the past. Some of them may have felt they were victims of a hostile history; others certainly took their destiny in their own hands. The very complexity of this multifaceted movement makes such an approach to religious history a challenge and a stimulating enterprise.

Notes
1 I am grateful to Mary Robitaille for tidying up my English.
2 Thus A.Th. van Deursen, 'Godslastering in Kuyperbiografie', in Nederlands Dagblad (22 May 2006) in response to the biography of Abraham Kuyper by Jeroen Koch.
3 Marit Monteiro, Geestelijke maagden: Leven tussen klooster en wereld in Noord-Nederland gedurende de zeventiende eeuw (Hilversum 1996).
4 Willem Frijhoff, 'Popular religion', in Stewart J. Brown and Timothy Tackett (eds), Cambridge history of Christianity, vol. VII (Cambridge 2006), pp. 185–207; Frijhoff, Embodied belief. Ten essays on religious culture in Dutch history (Hilversum 2002).
5 The condominium town of Maastricht, however, formally enjoyed a bi-confessional status.
6 Christine Kooi, 'Popish impudence. The perseverance of the Roman Catholic faithful in Calvinist Holland', Sixteenth Century Journal 26 (1995), 75–85. For the Generality Lands: Gerard Rooijakkers, Rituele repertoires: Volkscultuur in oostelijk Noord-Brabant 1559–1853 (Nijmegen 1994); Charles de Mooij, Geloof kan Bergen verzetten. Reformatie en katholieke herleving te Bergen op Zoom 1577–1795 (Hilversum 1998).
7 National, but not a 'local religion' as defined by William Christian, Jr, Local religion in sixteenth-century Spain (Princeton, NJ 1981), i.e. religious experience based on local needs and using traditional, localised customs, stories and rituals to remedy or redress them (in other words, 'popular religion').
8 L.J. Rogier, Geschiedenis van het katholicisme in Noord-Nederland in de 16e en de 17e eeuw (2nd edn, Amsterdam 1947), II, pp. 38–9. These 'seventy' have a semi-mythical status; note the similarity with the number of Christ's disciples, Luke 10: 1.
9 Holland: Joke Spaans, Haarlem na de Reformatie. Stedelijke cultuur en kerkelijk leven, 1577–1620 (The Hague 1989); Friesland: Wiebe Bergsma, Tussen Gideonsbende en publieke kerk. Een studie over het gereformeerd protestantisme in Friesland, 1580–1650 (Leeuwarden/Hilversum 1999).
10 S.A.C. Dudok van Heel, De jonge Rembrandt onder tijdgenoten. Godsdienst en schilderkunst in Leiden en Amsterdam (Nijmegen 2006).
11 Examples in Frijhoff, Embodied belief, pp. 54–5, and the special issue on reading culture of Tijdschrift voor Nederlandse kerkgeschiedenis 9:2 (June 2006).
12 Cf. John W. O'Malley, Trent and all that. Renaming Catholicism in the early modern era (Cambridge, MA 2000).

13 See also the well-known synthesis by Jean Delumeau, *Catholicism between Luther and Voltaire. A new view of the Counter-Reformation*, trans. Jeremy Moiser (London 1977).
14 Lucien Ceyssens, 'Les voies détournées dans l'histoire du jansénisme', in J. van Bavel and M. Schrama (eds), *Jansénius et le jansénisme dans les Pays-Bas* (Louvain 1982), pp. 11–26.
15 Cf. F.A. van Lieburg (ed.), *Confessionalism and Pietism. Religious reform in early modern Europe and North America* (Mayence 2006) [Veröffentlichungen des Instituts für Europäische Geschichte].
16 Sarah Covington, *The trail of martyrdom. Persecution and resistance in sixteenth-century England* (Notre Dame, IN 2003); see also Anne Dillon, *The construction of martyrdom in the English Catholic community 1535–1603* (Aldershot 2002).
17 For this notion, see Frijhoff, *Embodied belief*, pp. 39–65.
18 On the Netherlands: Olaf Mörke, "Konfessionalisierung" als politisch-soziales Strukturprinzip? Das Verhältnis von Religion und Staatsbildung in der Republik der Vereinigten Niederlande im 16. und 17. Jahrhundert', *Tijdschrift voor sociale geschiedenis* 16 (1990), 31–60; Heinz Schilling, 'Nationale Identität und Konfession in der europäischen Neuzeit' [1991], in Heinz Schilling, *Ausgewählte Abhandlungen zur europäischen Reformations- und Konfessionsgeschichte*, hrsg. v. Luise Schorn-Schütte and Olaf Mörke (Berlin 2002), 541–87 (with a few remarks on Britain). Also Wim Janse and Barbara Pitkin (eds), *The formation of clerical and confessional identities in early modern Europe* (Leiden 2006).
19 Peter Marshall, 'Is the Pope Catholic? Henry VIII and the semantics of schism', in Ethan Shagan (ed.), *Catholics and the 'Protestant nation'. Religious politics and identity in early modern England* (Manchester and New York, 2005), pp. 22–48.
20 I simply refer to the discontinuity thesis of John Bossy, *The English Catholic community 1570–1850* (London 1975) and the lively revisionist debate around the works of Christopher Haigh, Eamon Duffy and others (summarised by Ethan Shagan, 'Introduction. English Catholic history in context', in Shagan, *Catholics*, pp. 1–21), that has no equivalent for the Dutch Republic.
21 J. Visser, *Rovenius und seine Werke. Beitrag zur Geschichte der nordniederländischen katholischen Frömmigkeit in der ersten Hälfte des 17. Jahrhunderts* (Assen 1966), pp. 70–1.
22 M.G. Spiertz, *L'Église Catholique des Provinces-Unies et le Saint-Siège pendant la deuxième moitié du XVIIe siècle* (Louvain 1975).
23 Frijhoff, *Embodied belief*, pp. 181–213.
24 Benjamin J. Kaplan, "For they will turn away thy sons". The practice and perils of mixed marriage in the Dutch Golden Age', in Marc R. Forster and Benjamin J. Kaplan (eds), *Piety and family in early modern Europe. Essays in honour of Steven Ozment* (Aldershot 2005), pp. 115–33.
25 These aspects are at the core of the pillarisation thesis of Simon Groenveld, *Huisgenoten des geloofs: was de samenleving in de Republiek der Verenigde Nederlanden verzuild?* (Hilversum 1995).
26 J. Andriessen SJ, *De Jezuïeten en het samenhorigheidsgevoel der Nederlanden 1585–1648* (Antwerp 1957).

2

Cooperative confessionalisation: lay–clerical collaboration in Dutch Catholic communities during the Golden Age

CHARLES H. PARKER

The most fundamental circumstances common to Catholic communities in England and the Netherlands derived from the marginal conditions of their existence in the post-Reformation period. Marginalisation in the early modern period has also made its influence felt in the modern study of English and Dutch Catholic history. Launched by John Bossy (for England) and L.J. Rogier (for the Netherlands), the major lines of historical scholarship have stressed the significance of Protestant political ascendancy for Catholic identity.[1] The debate among English scholars has centred upon the degree of continuity or discontinuity in Catholic religious culture after the Reformation. The primary concern in the Netherlands has been to account for the slow-forming and uneven confessional allegiances across the Northern Provinces in the seventeenth century. Both Bossy and Rogier framed research agendas that led scholars in both lands to concentrate on conditions within each country that circumscribed Catholic communities and that necessarily distanced them from the international Roman Church.[2]

As a result of this attention to internal, national concerns, it has only been since the 1990s that historians have begun to situate Catholicism in the Netherlands within a broader European framework. As late as 1985, James Tracy observed that the Northern Netherlands lacked a Counter-Reformation.[3] Since then a number of studies have pointed to the international dimensions of Catholic life in the Golden Age Netherlands. Innovative work has examined such issues as the formation of the clergy, the pious energy of spiritual virgins, the art and architecture of hidden churches, the ongoing importance of pilgrimages, and the function of miracles.[4] Taken as a whole, this research indicates that although the Catholic Church in the Netherlands did not possess the backing of the state, the Roman faithful encountered many of the same religious trends as

Catholics elsewhere in Europe. From this more international perspective, the topic of lay–clerical interaction offers a useful way to contextualise Catholic communities in the Netherlands within the general reforming movements in European Catholicism.

Several studies in different areas of Europe since the 1990s have pointed out the limits of the 'top-down' imposition of religious discipline, central to the standard confessionalisation thesis.[5] Even in Iberia, home to the Spanish Inquisition, research has revealed the survival of popular religious customs and the limitations of priestly authority over lay behaviour.[6] Marc Forster's important study of south-west Germany concludes that 'religious change took place through a process of negotiation and exchange involving state officials, bishops, and their officials, local clergy, city and village leaders, and the common people'.[7] In other words, the Catholic Reformation was neither a simple matter of the clergy whipping the laity into shape nor a programme of elites imposing reform on common folk. Rather, religious reform was a complex movement requiring compromise as well as compulsion.

Despite greater awareness of negotiation and compromise, the assumption underlying much of the scholarship on discipline and reform posits two dichotomies —cleric versus lay and elite versus popular — with each faction possessing its own distinct objectives. Even Forster, whose work emphasises the extensive overlap between lay piety and clerical initiative, makes a distinction between a popular Catholicism and reform programmes promoted by elites. 'Despite the growing popularity of individual devotional practices, which were generally promoted by the clergy, popular Catholicism never succumbed to the other efforts by lay and clerical elites to regularise, systematise, and simplify religious practice.'[8]

The experience of Roman Catholic communities in the seventeenth-century Netherlands introduces a very different way of conceiving interaction among priests and laypeople. The particular political environment in the post-Reformation Netherlands made it necessary for priests and lay Catholics at all social levels to adopt an interdependent relationship. Political authorities carried out repressive policies against Catholic congregations, ranging from financial exactions to destruction of properties, to seizure, ransom, and banishment of priests. Consequently, laymen and women who chose to become or to remain Catholic generally possessed a steadfast commitment to their faith and to the priests who administered the sacraments to them.

As a result, Dutch Catholic communities in the seventeenth century exhibited what we might call a cooperative confessionalisation, fuelled by a lay leadership that supported Catholic reform. Collaboration did not always translate into harmony, however, since priests often locked horns with individual parishioners, larger segments of the community, and nearby congregations. By and large, though, conflicts involving lay folk and priests grew out of a mutual commitment to the institutions and offices of the Catholic Church. This essay will examine lay–clerical interaction in the Netherlands by highlighting the priorities of the Holland Mission (the Catholic pastoral organisation for the Netherlands) and the functions of local lay leaders.

The circumstances related to the Dutch Revolt against Spain and the ensuing religious settlement go a long way in explaining the cooperative relations in Catholic congregations. In particular, the massive reduction of an active priestly corps, the emergence of political repression, and the survival of a remnant of elite families loyal to Rome greatly influenced the nature of lay and clerical engagement in the seventeenth century.

Fearing violence from marauding soldiers, most priests, including all the bishops, fled lands held by Beggar forces, changed vocations, or went into hiding in the 1570s. Sasbout Vosmeer, the first apostolic vicar of the Holland Mission, counted only seventy priests in the Netherlands around 1600.[9] This estimate probably significantly undercounted active priests, though it is clear that men of the Roman collar were few and far between in the early Dutch Republic. The scarcity of priests motivated Sasbout Vosmeer, Philip Rovenius, Albert Eggius, and other leaders of the Holland Mission to create two seminaries, the *Collegium Alticollense* in Cologne (1602) and the *Collegium Pulcheriae Mariae Virginis* (1617) in Louvain. These seminaries trained a new generation of priests for the Netherlands in the Tridentine piety of the Catholic Reformation.[10] Since the Mission virtually had to start from the ground up in forming new priests, professionalisation of the clergy did not encounter the institutional obstacles to reform that plagued most bishoprics in Europe.[11] The apostolic vicars mandated seminary training and they controlled most aspects of it. Clergy numbers continued to be relatively low throughout the seventeenth century, ranging from 165 priests in 1614 to 241 in 1635 and 442 in 1645 (including religious).[12] The English mission offers an intriguing contrast, as approximately 400 priests served a much smaller Catholic population, leading Michael Mullett to conclude that England suffered from an 'over provision of underemployed priests'. In the Netherlands, the chronic scarcity of priests enhanced their value to Catholics who endured hardship in order to stay faithful.[13]

Various levels of repression emerged from the early phase of the Revolt. During the first ten years of the Republic, the States General and assorted provincial states issued a spate of edicts aimed at marginalising the Catholic faith in the Netherlands. By the early 1580s, Dutch laws had abolished all Catholic institutions, secularised all ecclesiastical properties, and proscribed all forms of 'papist' religious expression. Though hardly any functioning priests and benefices remained, Catholics did not have to join the public church, conform to a creed, or attend services as their co-religionists in England did. The States General guaranteed all Netherlanders freedom of conscience, meaning that they could hold their own private religious beliefs without fear of recrimination. This critical concession allowed for a more moderate coexistence among people of all religious persuasions than did the harsher regime in England. Nevertheless, Dutch Catholics frequently pointed out that the freedom of conscience principle did not extend to any liberty of worship.[14] The irksome paradox for those wishing to remain fully faithful to Rome was that they could identify themselves as Catholic, but could not worship as such.

While Catholics realised that they enjoyed far more liberal conditions than did religious minorities elsewhere, they still regarded themselves as victims of persecution. Many local authorities, especially in Holland and Utrecht, were willing to overlook private and discreet celebrations of the Mass, as well as other activities, for exorbitant bribes, which over time acquired a quasi-official status as 'recognition money'. However, connivance actually guaranteed little. Authorities regularly seized, roughed up, incarcerated, ransomed, and banished priests when Catholic expression impinged in some way on public space or consciousness. This structure of repression represented the management of religious pluralism by mingling connivance with aggression, potential violence, and extortion. For Catholic congregations, repression greatly reduced the number of priests, especially in provinces that took a harsher line, such as Zeeland, Gelderland, and Overijssel, and inculcated a strong sense of commitment among those who chose to remain Catholic.[15]

The political upheaval in the 1560s and 1570s forced regents and nobles to choose between the rebel forces or to stay loyal to Spain. While some Catholic families fled the Northern Provinces and others resisted the Beggars out of religious principle, most took a more pragmatic approach by juggling their economic and social interests with their religious allegiances. Especially in Holland and Utrecht, Catholic nobles generally remained on their estates and demonstrated their loyalty to the new political regime. As a result of their loyalty to the Republic, Catholic elites were allowed to retain their properties and to continue their lives unmolested.[16]

The moderate structure of repression corresponded to fairly high densities of Catholic populations. Holland and Utrecht had the highest concentrations of Catholics, and also enjoyed a comparable liberality on the part of political authorities, whereas Zeeland, Gelderland, and Overijssel contained much lower numbers and experienced the most severe persecution. It is not possible, however, to distinguish between the causes and effects of persecution relative to Catholic density. Certainly, persecution repressed growth yet, at the same time, high confessional density rendered persecution a political risk for the authorities. Nevertheless, moderate levels of repression, including fines, bribes, recognition money, and occasional crackdowns on priests, engendered a strong sense of commitment among lay Catholics.[17]

This loyal elite gave the Catholic cause its footing in the Netherlands. The presence of ex-regents and nobles faithful to the Republic reassured the authorities of the political fidelity of the entire congregation. In this regard, Catholic elites functioned as mediators between local governments and their citizens who assembled clandestinely and illegally to worship. Elites also provided quite munificent patronage to support priests, maintain seminaries, and pay recognition money.[18] As many Catholic regents and nobles lost political influence because of their religious loyalties, they compensated for this loss of status by assuming firm leadership roles in their local congregations.[19] Thus three factors – shortage of priests, moderate structure of repression, and presence of lay elites – promoted an atmosphere of cooperation to re-establish a Catholic presence in the Netherlands.

Within this political environment, the priorities set by the hierarchy of the Holland Mission established the basic parameters for interaction among priests and laypeople across the United Provinces. The overriding goal of the apostolic vicars was to reconstruct the former church districts in an archdiocesan mould. Apostolic vicars fully exercised pastoral influence over the Northern Netherlands, assuming complete spiritual responsibility for all secular clergy, ecclesiastical districts, chapters, and seminaries, as well as over the administration of all sacraments. The apostolic vicars and other high-ranking officials in the Mission approached the task of church building from an uncompromising diocesan vision. Throughout this period, not only did secular clergy appeal to the Tridentine canons in matters of faith and discipline as English clerics did, but Dutch priests also applied the canons in pastoral ministry.[20]

The Dutch clergy operated from a Tridentine basis, even though by the 1580s no legitimate canonical dioceses or parishes existed in the Northern Provinces.[21] The hierarchy consistently referred to congregations led by secular priests as parishes and steadfastly extolled the centrality of the bishop's office to church reform.[22] Phillip Rovenius maintained in a 1626 treatise directed to the *Propaganda Fide* that diocesan clergy represented the most effective means of returning wayward Catholics and heretics to the Roman Church.[23] According to all the apostolic vicars, a well-ordered diocese, even in the heretical territory of the Northern Netherlands, would produce an abundant harvest of souls.[24] The first aim of the Holland Mission, then, was to re-establish the dioceses laid waste by Revolt and Reformation. Conversely, the reconversion of the Northern Netherlands did not figure as the immediate objective of the Holland Mission. Rather, the leaders of the Mission believed that large-scale reconversion would grow out of a rebuilt and reformed archdiocese, praying all the while for conquest by a Spanish or French army.[25]

The diocesan approach of the Holland Mission carried important consequences for the internal workings of Catholic communities. Apostolic vicars gave utmost priority to the pastoral quality of the clergy, maintained through seminary education and ongoing supervision, rather than recruiting larger numbers of priests to fan out across the Northern Provinces. In fact, apostolic vicars and Haarlem chapter deans spent a great deal of energy trying to keep many priests out of the Northern Netherlands. They fought efforts by religious orders, especially the Jesuits, to bring in more regular priests than were allotted in the various negotiated concordats.[26] From the Jesuit point of view, the apostolic vicars only impeded the work of reconversion through their overweening control over ecclesiastical jurisdictions.[27] But for the leaders of the Mission, such control was essential to a disciplined diocese and, thus, the future of Catholicism in the Northern Provinces.

The diocesan model of reform, however, also perpetuated the highly uneven density of Catholic communities in the seventeenth century. The Mission's insistence on a pastoral ministry composed primarily of trained secular clerics meant that the hierarchy had to take a highly intentional approach in assigning priests to various regions. When dispatching priests, Mission leaders placed primary emphasis on serving higher-density Catholic populations and reaching out from these areas into more sparsely populated districts.[28] Loyal laity in a city, town, village, or region had to reach a certain critical mass before it justified a resident priest.[29] Areas unable to summon a sufficient base had to devise arrangements for an itinerant priest or make do without one. Sizeable communities, particularly those with influential and well-to-do elites, also ensured sufficient financial and political capital to pay a priest and shield him from persecution.[30] Even after seminaries started turning out larger numbers of priests, the pattern of deployment did not change over the course of the seventeenth century. Rovenius noted in 1629 that Holland and Utrecht, provinces with the highest concentrations of Catholics, absorbed 67 per cent of resident priests in the Mission; by 1701 the two provinces claimed 70 per cent of the pastoral corps.[31] Conversely, Overijssel, Groningen, Zeeland, and Drenthe contained the smallest number of Catholics and the fewest priests. The pastoral geography of the United Provinces, therefore, reflected the diocesan perspective of the apostolic vicars and the relative density of lay Catholics.

Given political circumstances and ecclesiastical priorities, the reinvigoration of Catholicism in the Golden Age depended heavily on vigorous lay participation. Leaders in congregations managed many affairs associated with the traditional parish, such as maintaining poor relief operations, caring for local properties, and supporting priests, and assumed new responsibilities, including paying off officials and funding seminary training. Though a diverse assortment of men and women with very different degrees of devotion identified with Catholicism, the leaders in most congregations were well born and well connected. Apostolic vicars boasted on a variety of occasions that the 'best' and 'most honourable' families remained Catholic. The parallel with the centrality of the gentry hall in the English mission is striking.[32] Referred to as curators, lords, ladies, and 'Catholic men', Dutch elites not only protected and provided for priests, but also gave the local community influence in negotiating with senior clerics. The rich correspondence in the archives of the apostolic vicars in Utrecht and the Cathedral chapter in Haarlem reveals the strong commitment of most lay leaders to the priesthood. Laymen and women neither succumbed passively to acculturation nor actively resisted clerical authority in principle. Disagreements and disputes did indeed arise, but they stemmed largely from the standards and expectations laypeople set for the church and its clergy.

The prevalent discourse in correspondence between lay leaders and the Mission hierarchy avowed a commitment to clericalism. In the 1670s, eight elderly people (in their 60s and 70s) in South Holland recalled the powerful sermons they had heard in their youth from Frs Stalpert van der Wiel and van der Uten.[33] Often when lay leaders complained about their priests, they affirmed clericalism as a principle of Catholic religious life. For example, leaders in Leiden protested in the 1680s that their priests 'are not very industrious in their studies', and curators in Harlingen grumbled that their pastor provided 'little direction in the Catholic religion for mindful people'.[34] Apostolic vicars and Haarlem cathedral deans regularly sought out lay views on local clergy by sending commissions to visit various regions and talk with curators. In two visitations in 1633 and 1634, the Haarlem canon J.A. Ban queried curators in districts in north Holland on the quality of pastoral care.[35]

Many laypeople also enjoyed close personal relationships with clergy. Scattered bits and pieces of correspondence with apostolic vicars give some intimation of the extensive social and family networks that connected priests and laypeople in Dutch Catholic communities. The death of a priest and friend in 1599 moved Gerard Coopmans in Oude Tonge to contact Sasbout Vosmeer and declare his affection for the deceased cleric.[36] After a death in the family, a couple in Dordrecht wrote to Vosmeer in 1608, expressing the desire for a personal visit from him.[37] The brother of Anna van den Bossche bequeathed a gold timepiece to Johannes van Neercassel for his friendship over the years.[38] The close, affective relations among many laypeople and priests suggest that any general adversarial relationship based on incompatible objectives and interests, that historians have identified in many parts of Europe, really does not work well for the seventeenth-century Netherlands.

Operating from the model of the traditional parish, lay elites also performed a range of vital functions within local religious communities. Local families provided leadership and, among other things, served as churchwardens and poor relief officers. While men and women undertook a variety of tasks, three responsibilities proved critical to the revival of Catholicism: catechising children, providing patronage, and managing relief efforts.

Prescriptive literature charged priests with responsibility for catechism instruction, though in many places spiritual virgins, or *kloppen*, actually carried out most of the teaching.[39] Though spiritual virgins were not fully lay, they also were not fully religious. Marit Monteiro has argued that they inhabited a middle state between lay and religious vocations. Nevertheless, the virgins' significant presence – over 5,000 women – and their critical work warrant attention.[40] Due to the scarcity of priests, teaching children the rudiments of the Catholic faith fell to the virgins. In areas where there were only a minimal number of clergy, such as Gelderland and Zeeland, virgins assumed complete control over catechism instruction. In regions that contained significantly more priests, as in Holland and Utrecht, virgins still participated in the education of children, though under the supervision of or in collaboration with clergy.[41] Working in conjunction with both secular clergy and Jesuits, spiritual virgins used songbooks and storybooks, in addition to catechisms, to ground Catholic youth in the Roman faith.[42] Consequently, the educational work of women contributed considerably to the renewal of Catholicism in the seventeenth century.

Elite families served as essential bases of patronage for an ecclesiastical institution that had lost all property and assets in the 1570s. Property, in the form of real estate, movable goods, and liquid assets, fuelled the pastoral corps that provided divine grace for Catholics. A treatise from 1640 explicitly stated the problem for Catholics: the loss of revenues to finance a pastorate placed souls in jeopardy.[43] Over the course of the seventeenth century, apostolic vicars, Haarlem chapter deans, seminary presidents, and local pastors worked tirelessly, just as English clerics, to develop a reliable network of generous patrons.[44] The Mission leaned heavily on the munificence of Catholics to finance seminary education and to support priests in the field.

Apostolic vicars in particular cultivated relations with lay patrons and appealed to their religious devotion to raise capital. Van Neercassel, for example, praised the 'outstanding virtue' of mevrouw Boetgreve, who lost her husband in 1679. In the same letter, he gratefully acknowledged a gift from her, promising that the funds would support two seminary burses, which would 'lead to the salvation of others'.[45] Similarly, van Neercassel contacted mevrouw van Kabauw after her husband's death to remind her of the 'great opportunity' she had to bring salvation to the poor.[46] Keenly aware of potential sources of income, he also instructed his priests to pay heed to the declining health of well-heeled parishioners.[47]

As these cases suggest, elite women represented important sources of patronage for the Holland Mission. Similarly, Michael Mullett points out that women played significant roles in 'rescue and support systems' for priests in England.[48] Coming from wealthy families, Dutch spiritual virgins in particular received a great deal of attention from secular and regular priests because of their religious commitments and their personal connections to rich relatives. Priests eagerly sought opportunities to serve as confessors to these women and sometimes allowed them to serve and sing at the altar. Competing for the same sources of patronage, secular priests and Jesuits hurled accusations against one another in the early seventeenth century, the ones charging that the others used influence as pastors to keep virgins from making contact with other priests.[49] Not only did virgins provide financial support for priests, but a number of the women also made significant contributions for student stipends at the seminaries in Louvain and Cologne.[50] In fact, women comprised a majority of the lay patrons, 56.4 per cent (22 out of 39) listed in the *Liber Fundationum* for the Pulcheria seminary in Louvain.[51]

The patterns of patronage for seminary education underscore how familial relations interwove clerics within lay social networks. Gian Ackermans's recent study has shown that the majority of priests, just as spiritual virgins, came from fairly affluent families; 169 out of 298 (56.7 per cent) came at least from the professional and office-holding ranks. Further, a considerable ratio of families produced more than one priest or spiritual virgin. Ackermans's prosopography of the Dutch secular clergy in the second half of the seventeenth century indicates that fully one-third of the priests had one male relative with a religious vocation.[52] Jo Spaans has begun to reconstruct family networks of spiritual virgins in Haarlem and her early results suggest that the same trend possibly holds true for them as well.[53] The structure of patronage reflects the kinship connections among clergy and laity. The *Liber Fundationum* for the Pulcheria seminary in Louvain lists 86 seminary benefactors, of whom 47 (54 per cent) were priests, including senior churchmen such as Albert Eggius, Philip Rovenius, and Johannes van Neercassel. Thus, a significant number of priests came to control at least a share of their family's patrimony and they bequeathed a portion to support future generations in the Dutch priesthood. Almost all benefactors, lay or clerical, gave priority in their testaments to funding any blood relative who entered the priesthood and, failing that, to supporting any seminarian from their native region.[54] Consequently, laity and clergy in the Holland Mission were closely bound together in family and community networks across the Netherlands.[55]

In addition to teaching children and subsidising clergy, maintaining a structure of social provision for needy Catholics became a primary occupation of lay leaders. The basic lines of relief operations corresponded to the institutional forms of charity in the era before the Reformation. That is, the model of the parish continued to inform the ways in which Catholics cared for their own. Just as in traditional parishes, lay leaders, who were still referred to in parochial terms as churchwardens (*kerkmeesters*) and Masters of the Holy Ghost (*Heilige Geestmeesters*), collected and distributed monies to the Catholic poor. In addition, spiritual virgins performed works of mercy to the needy.[56] Congregations established relief networks originally to counter the proliferation of Calvinist diaconates, which tempted poor Catholics to become better acquainted with heretical temples. By the mid seventeenth century, city governments put pressure on all confessional groups to care for their own members, thereby unburdening municipal finances.[57]

By the early 1630s, it appears that most Catholic communities operated some form of provision. In 1628, Rovenius called for three of the 'most principal burghers' of a congregation in Rotterdam to administer relief measures there. Rovenius's appeal to 'principal burghers' reflected the dependence of most local operations on wealthy Catholics to fund and to supervise measures.[58] Judocus Cats observed in 1635 that curators in Schagen followed the salutary practice of drawing up lists of the needy, assessing their circumstances, and meeting with them on a regular basis.[59] Anecdotal evidence intimates that the scale of operations could be relatively extensive. A Jesuit reported a donation of 12,000 florins for the Catholic poor in Rotterdam in the mid seventeenth century and a Jesuit station in Delft at roughly the same time claimed to support 60 families.[60] Yet in the correspondence of the apostolic vicars, complaints, conflicts, and struggles dominate the discourse. After bribing officials and paying priests, lay elites and their congregations surely found it difficult to meet their obligations to their fellow brothers and sisters. Congregations, decrying the abandonment of the poor, often appealed to the apostolic vicar for assistance.[61] In 1683, van Neercassel declared a jubilee indulgence for benefactors who made contributions to charitable agencies, though Catholic poor relief largely remained a burden for local congregations.[62]

Legal proscription and political hostility in the early Dutch Revolt created a crisis in Catholic pastoral ministry, as priests and property almost completely vanished across the Northern Netherlands. As priests began to reorganise in the late sixteenth and early seventeenth centuries, they made common cause with lay elites who remained loyal to Rome, especially those in the relatively dense enclaves in Holland and Utrecht. The unusual dynamics of confessional coexistence in the Netherlands bred a strong commitment to the Roman Church among those who chose to remain loyal and fostered interdependency among clergy and laity. The Holland Mission, a missionary organisation directed by an apostolic vicar, adopted and imposed onto the Catholic communities throughout the Netherlands a staunchly diocesan vision. This approach, among other things, determined that the numbers of priests in the Netherlands would remain small, that they would primarily serve areas with sizeable concentrations of Catholics, and that clerical formation would reflect the post-Tridentine values of the Catholic Reformation.

Alongside this clericalism, a vigorous lay leadership emerged in local Catholic communities. Spiritual virgins taught catechism (as well as serving in other capacities) and, along with other elite women, became important patrons of seminary students and pastoral benefices. Operating from the model of the traditional Dutch parish, women and men managed many other local affairs, not the least of which were poor relief operations. Catholic clergy depended on the laity, just as the laity looked to the clergy for clear and direct spiritual guidance. In difficult matters of discipline and disagreement, the Mission worked assiduously to demonstrate its pastoral concern for the salvation of the laity. All sorts of conflicts between laypeople and priests did occur, but they did so in large part because of a deep commitment to the revival of the Roman Church in the Netherlands.

The international Counter-Reformation came to the United Provinces in the seventeenth century. Because of political and religious circumstances, the adversarial relationship that pitted lay interests against clerical reform programmes across Europe does not adequately capture the collaborative environment in the Northern Netherlands. Rather than a top-down or a bottom-up direction for religious reform, the Dutch case reflects a side-by-side arrangement that can perhaps be best summed up as cooperative confessionalisation.

Notes

1 John Bossy, *The English Catholic Community, 1570–1850* (New York: Oxford University Press, 1976); L.J. Rogier, *Geschiedenis van het katholicisme in Noord-Nederland in de 16e en de 17e eeuw*, 3 vols (Amsterdam: Urbi et Orbi, 1947–48).
2 For critiques of Bossy and Rogier, see Christopher Haigh, 'The continuity of Catholicism in the English reformation', in Christopher Haigh (ed.), *The English Reformation revised* (Cambridge: Cambridge University Press, 1987), pp. 176–208; A.Th. van Deursen, *Bavianen en slijkgeuzen: kerk en kerkvolk ten tijde van Maurits en Oldenbarnevelt* (Assen: Van Gorcum, 1974), pp. 145ff.
3 James D. Tracy, 'With and without the counter-reformation: the Catholic church in the Spanish Netherlands and the Dutch Republic, 1580–1650', *Catholic Historical Review* 71(1985), 547–75. Although there are many excellent arguments for using 'Catholic Reformation', 'Tridentine Catholicism', and 'early modern Catholicism', I opt for 'Counter-Reformation' in this study because of my view that the antagonistic force of Protestantism greatly influenced the development of Catholicism in the seventeenth-century Netherlands. For a discussion of terminology, see John W. O'Malley, *Trent and all that: renaming Catholicism in the early modern era* (Cambridge, MA: Harvard University Press, 2000).
4 See, Gian Ackermans, *Herders en huurlingen: bisschoppen en priesters in de republiek (1663–1705)* (Amsterdam: Prometheus/Bert Bakker, 2003); Xander van Eck, *Kunst, Twist, en devotie: goudse katholieke schuilkerken 1572–1795* (Delft: Eburon, 1994); Willem Frijhoff, *Embodied belief: ten essays on religious culture in Dutch history* (Hilversum: Uitgeverij Verloren, 2002); F.J.M. Hoppenbrouwers, *Oefening in volmaaktheid: de zeventiende eeuwse rooms-katholieke spiritualiteit in de republiek* (Den Haag: Sdu Uitgevers, 1996); R. Po-Chia Hsia and H.F.K. van Nierop (eds), *Calvinism and religious toleration in the Dutch Golden Age* (Cambridge: Cambridge University Press, 2002); Benjamin J. Kaplan, 'Fictions of privacy: house chapels and the spatial accommodation of religious dissent in early modern Europe', *American Historical Review* 107(2002), 1031–64; Marit, Monteiro, *Geestelijke maagden: leven tussen klooster en wereld in Noord-Nederland gedurende de zeventiende eeuw* (Hilversum: Verloren, 1996); Jo Spaans, 'Paragons of piety: representations of the priesthood in the lives of the Haarlem virgins', *Dutch Review of Church History* 83 (2003), 235–46; Marc Wingens, *Over de grens. de bedevaart van katholieke nederlanders in de zeventiende en achttiende eeuw* (Nijmegan: SUN, 1994).
5 For a concise explication of confessionalisation, see Heinz Schilling, 'Confessional Europe', in

Thomas A. Brady Jr, Heiko A. Oberman, James D. Tracy (eds), *Handbook of European history, 1400–1600: Late Middle Ages, Renaissance, and Reformation*, 2 vols (Grand Rapids, MI: William B. Eerdmans Publishing Company, 1996), 2 *Visions, Programs, Outcomes*, pp. 641–82.

6 William Christian, *Local religion in sixteenth-century Spain* (Princeton, NJ: Princeton University Press, 1981), pp. 148–80.

7 Marc Forster, *Catholic revival in the age of the baroque: religious identity in Southwest Germany, 1550–1750* (Cambridge: Cambridge University Press, 2001), p. 19.

8 Forster, *Catholic revival*, p. 61.

9 P.W.F.M. Hamans, *Geschiedenis van de katholieke kerk in Nederland* (Bruges: Uitgeverij Tabor, 1992), pp. 257–8.

10 E. Reusens (ed.), *Documents Relatifs à l'Histoire de l'Université de Louvain (1425–1795)*, vol. 3, *Colleges et Pedagogues* (Louvain: n.p., 1881–85), p. 451.

11 R. Po-Chia Hsia, *The world of Catholic renewal, 1540–1770* (Cambridge: Cambridge University Press, 1998), pp. 43, 56–7, 116–17.

12 Haman, *Katholieke Kerk*, p. 258; R.R. Post, *Kerkelijke verhoudingen in Nederland vóór de reformatie van ± 1500 tot ± 1580* (Utrecht and Amsterdam: Spectrum, 1954), p. 37.

13 See Michael Mullett's essay in this volume, "So they become contemptible": clergy and laity in a mission territory', pp. 33–47. For a few examples of lay appreciation for priests in the Netherlands see Het Utrechts Archief, Apostolische Vicarissen Hollandse Zending en hun Secretarissen, 1579–1728 (hereafter OBC, according to inventory number, correspondents, and date) nr. 8, de Kettler to Vosmeer, 12 November 1607, nr. 226, Hooft to van Neercassel, 9, 13, 20, 30 August, 6, 24 September 1674, nr. 227, Hooft to van Neercassel, 31, March 1676, 6 March 1678, nr. 226, Hop to van Neercassel, 11, 20 August 1674.

14 *Groot Placaet-Boek, Inhoudende de Placaten ende Ordonnantien van de Hoogh-Mog. Heeren Staten Generael der Vereenighde Nederlanden ende vande Ed. Groot Mog: Heeren Staten van Hollandt ende West-Vrieslandt, Mitsgaders van Ed. Mog. Heeren Staten van Zeelandt*, 9 vols ('s-Gravenhage: Weduwe Hillebrandt Iacobsz. van Wouw, 1658–1770), 1:193–4, 199–200, 203–4, 211–13, 219–20, 223–4, 217–18, 227–8; *Nederlandtsche Placcaet-Boeck: Waerinne alle voornaemste placcaten, ordonnatien, accorden ende andere acten ende monumenten, uijt-ghgeven bij EE Hoog-Mogende Heeren Staten Generael der Vereenigde Nederlantsche Provintien*, 2 vols (Amsterdam: Jan Janssen, 1644), 1: 179–82, 344–8, 435–8. For a few examples of persecution, see OBC, nr. 5, Junius to Vosmeer, 9 June 1601, nr. 8, Elreborn to Vosmeer, 18 May 1607, nr. 9, Boucquet to Vosmeer, 12 February 1610, nr. 18, Vosmeer to Vosmeer, 17 July 1610, nr. 20, Vosmeer to Stalpert van der Wiele, 2 July 1613, nr. 249, van Neercassel to de Vanger, 15 March 1679, nr. 253, van Neercassel to Deventer, 4 May 1684, nr. 444, Pethijnus to Vosmeer, 2 January 1603, nr. 343, Petrus Codde, *Priesterlijsten Leeuwarden*, 27 April 1699; G.A. Meijer (ed.), 'Missie-verslagen der Dominicanen bij de Propaganda Fide', *Archief voor de Geschiedenis van het Aartsbisdom Utrecht* (hereafter *AAU*) 49 (1929), 149; A. van Lommel SJ (ed.), 'Kort verslag van den toestand der R.C. godsdienst der voormalige H.Z 1629', *AAU* 13 (1885), 252–3; R. Fruin (ed.), *Uittreksel uit Francisci Dusseldorpii Annales 1566–1616* ('s Gravenhage: Martinus Nijhoff, 1893), pp. xxvii, 100; Rijksarchief van Noord Holland, # 225, Archief van het Kapittel (hereafter Kapittel, according to inventory number, correspondents, and date) nr. 354, Anthonij to Eggius, 29 July 1601, Egbertszoon to Eggius, 9 June 1609.

15 Jonathan Israel, *The Dutch Republic, its rise, greatness, and fall* (Oxford: Clarendon Press, 1995), pp. 379, 383–4; A.J. van Lommel SJ (ed.), 'Relatio seu descriptio status religionis catholicae in Hollandia etc. quam Romae collegit et exhibuit Alexandro septimo et cardinalibus congregationis de propaganda fide, Jacobus de la Torre, Kal. Septembris Anno 1656', *AAU* 10 (1882), p. 188; Wiebe Bergsma, *Tussen gideonsbende en publieke kerk: een studie over het gereformeerd protestantisme in Friesland, 1580–1650* (Hilversum: Verloren, 1999), pp. 140–1; OBC, nr. 10, Foeijt to Vosmeer, 30 March/9 April 1609; Sherrin Marshall, *The Dutch gentry, 1500–1650: family, faith, and fortune* (New York: Greenwood Press, 1987), pp, 88–9.

16 Henk F.K. van Nierop, *The nobility of Holland: from knights to regents, 1500–1650*, trans. Maarten Ultee (New York: Cambridge University Press, 1993), p. 196; Marshall, *Dutch gentry* 81–4;

Benjamin J. Kaplan, *Calvinists and libertines: confession and community in Utrecht 1578–1620* (Oxford: Oxford University Press, 1995), p. 274.

17 For some reports of persecution in Friesland and Zeeland, see A. van Lommel, SJ (ed.), 'Descriptio status in quo nunc est religio Catholica in confoederatis Belgii-Provincii anno 1622', *AAU* 20 (1893), 373–4; A. van Lommel, SJ (ed.), 'Brevis descriptio status in quo est ecclesia Catholica [1616]', *AAU* 3 (1874–75), 220; OBC, nr. 222, *Descriptio visitationis quam institutit Illustrissimus et Reverendissimus D. Johannes Episcopus Castorientus vicarius Apostolicus per Zelandiam et Episcopatum Middelburgesem assumpto Ludolpho ab Heuman suo Archdiacono et Provincio 1664*; Wiebe Bergsma points out that, though the numbers of Catholics varied considerably across Friesland, they numbered only around 10 per cent of the total population in the province in 1663. Bergsma, *Tussen Gideonsbende*, pp. 137–42.

18 Charles H. Parker, *Faith on the margins: Catholics and Catholicism in the Dutch Golden Age* (Cambridge, MA: Harvard University Press, 2008), chapter 6.

19 See for example, OBC, nr. 252, van Neercassel to van Kabauw [van Vrijenhoven], 26 June 1682. For other examples of lay leadership not cited elsewhere, see OBC, nr. 252, van Neercassel to Middelburg, 10 December 1682, nr. 338, Heemskerk to Codde, [1690], nr. 339, Hilversum to Codde, 16/26 March 1691.

20 Mullett, 'Clergy and laity', pp. 34–6.

21 See for example, P. Gerlach, 'Stukken betreffende de opleiding der geestelijkheid in de Hollandse missie', *AAU* 67 (1948), 61; Philippus Rovenius, *Tractatus de Missionibus ad Propagandam Fidem et Conversionem Infidelium & Haereticorum Instituendis* (Louvain: Henrici Hastenii, 1626), pp. 26–7.

22 OBC, nr. 190, *De descriptio ordinis qui est sub vicario apostolico ac pastorum ac diocesorum*, 15–16 May 1623. The 1701 report of Peter Codde does refer to them as stations, but notes that these are 'pastorates or the flock of the faithful in which a sole [priest] or one with an associate missionary is in command'. A missionary usually refers to a regular priest. OBC, nr. 385, *Summarium relationis missionis Hollandiae quam sanctissimo domino nostro Clementi XI. Archepiscopus Sebastianus Apostolicus in illa vicarius, observantia debita exhibuit sub initium anni 1701*; van Lommel, 'Relatio 1656', *AAU* 10 (1882), 95–240, 11 (1883), 57–211; OBC, nr. 90, Rovenius to Twente, 28 August [1607], nr. 89, van Schoonhoven to Rovenius, 11 March [1647].

23 Rovenius, *Tractatus de Missionibus*, pp. 26–7, 42, 44, 47.

24 Parker, *Faith on the margins*, chapter 3.

25 G. Brom (ed.), 'Insinuatio status provinciarum, in quibus haeretici dominantur', *AAU* 17 (1889), 157; van Lommel, 'Relatio 1656', *AAU* 10 (1882), 95–6.

26 OBC, nr. 200, *Memorie van Rovenius aan de Propaganda Fide tegen de Jezuieten* [after 9 May 1624]. For additional concerns, see OBC, nr. 190, Philip Rovenius, *Descriptio ordinis hierarchi cleri Hollandiae*, 15/16 May 1623; Brom, 'Vier missie-verslagen', p. 9; Kapittel #225, nr. 351, *Statuten Rovenii Harlemensis*, 27 September 1618; OBC, nr. 248, van Neercassel to Blockhoven, 7 September 1678, nr. 247, van Neercassel to Nijenbeeck, Grotenhuijsen, and Duistervoorde, 22 October 1676, nr. 250, van Neercassel to Veluwe, 13, 27 October, 22 November 1680.

27 A. van Lommel SJ (ed.), 'Relatio visitationis S.J. in Hollandia a patre Guilielmo 1628', *AAU* 6 (1879), 239; Hamans, *Katholieke kerk*, pp. 261–4.

28 A. van Lommel, SJ (ed.), 'Descriptio status in quo nunc est religio Catholica in confoederatis Belgii-Provincii anno 1622', *AAU* 20 (1893), 360; van Lommel, 'Descriptio status [1616]', pp. 211, 220.

29 OBC, nr. 12, Schagen to Vosmeer, 30 April 1611, nr. 340, van Slingelant to Codde, 9 February 1692.

30 Van Lommel, 'Descriptio status 1622', pp. 358, 366; van Lommel, 'Descriptio status [1616]', pp. 209, 219, 221.

31 Israel, *Dutch Republic*, p. 389. This list does not account for itinerant priests who were not residents nor for religious orders, but represents the pattern of placement for resident pastors.

32 Van Lommel, 'Descriptio status [1616]', pp. 219, 224; van Lommel, 'Descriptio status 1622', pp. 358, 366, 368; van Lommel, 'Descriptio 1656', *AAU* 11 (1883), 99, 126, 132, 172, 179–89,

191, 198, *AAU* 10 (1882), 202, 226, 233; Archief van de Nederlandse Provincie der Jezuiten. Litterae Annuae Missionis Bataviae (hereafter SJ. LA., according to inventory and date) A.C. 2, 1659; Mullett, 'Clergy and laity', p. 36.

33 OBC, nr. 229, Voorburg to van Neercassel, 15 March 1680. See also Kapittel #225, nr 353, Aalsmeer to Zaffius, 1615; OBC, nr. 229, Elst to van Neercassel, 24 March/3 April 1679; OBC, nr. 230, Gramaye to van Neercassel, 14/24 September 1682, nr. 338, Amersfoort to Codde, 19/29 June 1690, nr. 342, Gouda to Codde [January 1697].

34 OBC, nr. 337, Leiden to Codde, 30 May 1689, nr. 230, Harlingen to van Neercassel, 2/12 August 1682. For similar complaints, see OBC, nr. 19, Vosmeer to Schagen, 20 February 1612, nr. 225, Barre to van Neercassel, [1671], nr. 249, van Neercassel to Groningen, 9 February 1680, nr. 252, van Neercassel to Deventer, 19, 22 March, 16 December 1682. For other examples of lay commitment to clericalism, see OBC, nr. 226, Zutphen to van Neercassel, 25 August/4 September 1673, nr. 229, Vlissingen to van Neercassel, 30 March 1679, nr. 242, van Neercassel to Alkmaar, 9 December 1667, nr. 232, van Brakel to van Neercassel, 23 February 1686, nr. 226, Amersfoort to van Neercassel, 17/27 February 1674.

35 Kapittel #275, nr. 131, *Aantekeningen van kanunnik J.A. Ban met betrekking tot Spierdijk, Hoogwoud*, 1633, nr. 132. *Aantekeningen van kanunnik J.A. Ban met betrekking tot een visitatie in N. Holland*, 13 September 1634.

36 OBC, nr. 4, Coopmans to Vosmeer, 4 March 1599.

37 OBC, nr. 9, Willems to Vosmeer, 12 May 1608. Exchanges between Peter van der Dussen and Tilman Vosmeer, brother of Sasbout, give some indication of how well the Vosmeer family was connected across Holland, Utrecht and Cologne. For references, see J. Bruggeman and Y.E. Kortlever (eds), *Inventaris van de archieven van de apostolische vicarissen van de Hollandse zending en hun secretarissen 1579–1728* (Utrecht: Het Utrechts Archief, 2001), p. 367.

38 OBC, nr. 229, van den Bossche to van Neercassel, 30 May, 26 June 1679. Other examples include OBC, nr. 248, van Neercassel to Stalpart, 28 October 1678, OBC, nr. 247, van Neercassel to van Putten, 4 September 1675, nr. 248, van Neercassel to van Andel, 23 June 1677, nr. 8, de Kettler to Vosmeer, 12 November 1607, nr. 226, Hooft to van Neercassel, 9, 13, 20, 30 August, 6, 24 September 1674, nr. 227, Hooft to van Neercassel, 31 March 1676, 6 March 1678, nr. 226, Hop to van Neercassel, 11, 20 August 1674; OBC, nr. 226, Ornia to van Neercassel, 7 August 1672, nr. 250, van Neercassel to Burmania, 22 September 1680.

39 This section on the virgins is indebted to the works of Monteiro, *Geestelijke Maagden*, pp. 49–109; Jo Spaans, 'Paragons of piety', pp. 235–46; Rogier, *Katholicisme*, II: 367–72; Hamans, *Katholieke kerk*, pp. 267–8.

40 Monteiro, *Geestelijke Maagden*, pp. 51–5.

41 For legal measures taken against spiritual virgins, see OBC, nr. 232, Culemborg to van Neercassel, 21 April /1 May 1685, nr. 155, *Staten van Holland tegen de pausgezinden*, December 18, 1635, nr. 158, *Keur van Leiden*, February 10. 1640; *Groot Placaet-Boeck*, I: 212–13; OBC, nr. 50, *Eisch van Nic. Ruychaver, schout van Haarlem, tegen Machtelt Bickers, wegens klopperij* [1593]; Monteiro, *Geestelijke Maagden*, p. 89.

42 Monteiro, *Geestelijke Maagden*, pp. 94–5.

43 OBC, nr. 168, *Cort onderrecht van de heijmelijcke exercitie der Catholijcke Religie in de vereenighde nederlantsche provintien* [1640]; see also Kapittel #275, nr. 92, *De persecutione*, pp. 5–6.

44 For examples not cited elsewhere, see OBC, nr. 11, Janssonius to Vosmeer, 4 May 1610, nr. 252, *Epistola Pastoralis per Amplissimum D. Erkelium prolegenda*, 26 August 1683; Kapittel #225, nr. 354, Petri to Eggius, 14 February [n.y.]. Given where this letter is located in the bound volume, it is likely that the year is 1609. See Kapittel #225, nr. 573, *Akten van transport en andere stukken betreffende de verwerving van beurzen door 'Pulcheria,' 1618–1727. Extracta ex registro seu libro fundationem collegii Pulcherae vulgo collegii Hollandii Louvani; Extracta et notitus manu D.G. Scheppio provisore collegii scriptis et dominus praesidi Melis transmissus in libro fundationem non registratis*. OBC, nr. 245, van Neercassel to Blockhoven, 28 September 1671, nr. 246, van Neercassel to Blockhoven, 8 May 1674.

45 OBC, nr. 248, van Neercassel to Boetgreve, 29 August 1678.

46 OBC, nr. 251, van Neercassel to van Kabauw, 7 September 1681, 26 June 1682, nr. 336, Roos to Codde, 16 June 1688.
47 OBC, nr. 253, van Neercassel to Goes, 26 February, 3 April 1684.
48 Mullett, 'Clergy and laity', pp. 44–6.
49 Gerrit vanden Bosch, 'Pionnen op een schaakbord? De rol van klopjes in de belangenstrijd tussen jezuieten en seculiere priesters in de Republiek omstreeks 1609–1610', Trajecta 9 (2000), 252–83.
50 SJ. LA., A.C. 2, 1659 (Amsterdam); Kapittel #225, nr. 355, Copia litterae Illmi. Nuncii Aplici. Belgii, 3 January 1609; OBC, nr. 10, Foeijt to Vosmeer, 30 March/9 April 1609, nr. 10, Dordrecht to Vosmeer, 5, 15 April 1609, nr. 10, Gorcum to Vosmeer, 24 May 1609; Kapittel #225, nr. 355, Eggius to Vosmeer, 17 March 1/April 1609.
51 Kapittel #225, nr. 572. Liber Fundationum, fols 2–69.
52 Ackermans, Herders en Huurlingen, pp. 54–5, 57.
53 Jo Spaans, 'Faith, family and community: the Catholic community in early seventeenth-century Holland', paper presented at the Sixteenth Century Studies Conference, Toronto, Ontario, October 2004, pp. 4–7.
54 Kapittel #225. nr. 572, Liber Fundationum, 'Formula secundum quam Bursa Collegii D. Pulcheriae fundatur, exceptus specialibus conditionibus quas fundatores paciscuntur'.
55 This analysis of the Liber Fundationum is based on chapter 6 of Parker, Faith on the Margins.
56 Kapittel #225, nr. 358, Paludanus to Catz, 31 October 31 [1618].
57 Joke Spaans, 'Katholieken onder curatele. Katholieke armenzorg als ingang voor overheidsbemoeienis in Haarlem in de achtiende eeuw', Trajecta 3 (1994) 111–12; OBC, nr. 232, Groningen to van Neercassel, [July] 1685, 29 February/10 March 1686.
58 OBC, nr. 90 Rovenius to Rotterdam, 20 July 1628.
59 Kapittel #225, nr. 359, Ordonnances de visite de Judocus Catzius, July 1635.
60 Kapittel #225, nr. 359, Ordonnances de visite de Judocus Catzius, July 1635.
61 For examples, see OBC, nr. 232, Groningen to van Neercassel [July] 1685, nr. 254, van Neercassel to Groningen, 4 August 1685, nr. 232, Groningen to van Neercassel, 16/26 June 1685, nr. 254, van Neercassel to Groningen, 30 June 1685, nr. 232, Groningen to van Neercassel, [July], 6/16 October, 21 November/1 December 1685, nr. 232, Groningen to van Neercassel, 29 February/10 March 1686, nr. 232, Groningen to van Neercassel, 16/26 June 1685, nr. 336, Maassluis to Codde, 3, 30 March, 12 April, 25 May 1688, nr. 14, Vigilius and Dusseldorpius to Vosmeer, 11/21 September 1613, nr. 14, Medenblick to Oirschot (forwarded to Sasbout Vosmeer), 23 January 1613, nr. 378, Visitatierapporten, 1691–1695.
62 OBC, nr. 237, Over inzameling van aalmoezen door religieusen tijdens het jubilee, 8 October 1683.

3

'So they become contemptible':
clergy and laity in a mission territory

MICHAEL MULLETT

The following discussion will explore aspects of relations between priests and people in the post-Reformation English Catholic Church. Attempting to deal with issues concerning the interdependence of clerics and laity and the strategies devised to negotiate their relationships, my study will examine how Catholic priests, both secular and regular, interacted with men and women of the laity, and it will show how clerical prestige, standing and authority – sacramental, ministerial, didactic and moral – were quite drastically adapted to the special conditions prevailing in a missionary Church within Europe, above all to the massive practical and financial dependence of clerics on laypeople. Since the appearance in 1975 of John Bossy's pioneering social history of the English Catholic community in the long post-Tridentine period, other works, including a most valuable collection edited by Marie Rowlands, and my own survey of the situation in the British realms, have also looked into the question of clerical–lay relations in missionary conditions.[1]

The clearest, and in terms of our period the most recent, guidance on the conduct of relations between the Catholic faithful and their priests was given by the Council of Trent. These directions, as we might expect from a synod of pastors overwhelmingly coming from the Mediterranean south, where the traditional formal and legal standing of the parish priest was not disturbed by the events of the Reformation, envisaged the *parochus* as a man securely and episcopally appointed to a local cure of souls carrying with it sufficient maintenance to guarantee him respect, residence, independence and, with them, the freedom to speak out fearlessly as the moral and spiritual mentor of his flock: thus, according to the Council, each bishop was to ensure that no cleric 'shall be promoted to sacred orders unless it be legitimately established that he is in peaceful possession of an ecclesiastical benefice sufficient for a decent livelihood'. From that position of financial independence, the parish priest, formed in the sharpened priestly ideal of the Catholic Reformation, would stand out as a member of the order of Melchizedek, in radical distinctiveness from the lay folk around him, 'that in dress, behaviour, gait, speech and all other things nothing may appear but what is dignified, moderate, and permeated with piety ...'. From his plinth of financial self-sufficiency and security and of moral, educational, sacramental and personal distinction, the priest could act as the candid and, if necessary, severe moral guide to his lay subjects and pupils, impressing on them 'the vices that they must avoid and the virtues they must cultivate in order that they may escape eternal punishment and obtain the glory of heaven'. Indeed, an important reason that the Council gave for priests' being themselves blameless was that this would put them in an unassailable position 'to reprove the lay people for their transgressions ... correct laics'.[2]

So much for the conciliar ideal: the rest of this chapter will be devoted to examining how this blueprint might have worked out, and have been modified, or even discarded completely, in actual practice, within the special conditions prevailing in the English Mission, with particular reference to the English county with the heaviest concentrations of Catholic recusants, Lancashire, and in circumstances on the whole very unlike the vision of combined priestly independence and social authority set up by the Tridentine fathers. The longer history of post-Reformation and pre-Emancipation English Catholicism can be divided into two sub-periods, one of intense, if spasmodic, danger, above all for missionary priests, between c.1580 and c.1680 and second, of easier conditions in the long run up to full Emancipation in 1829. In both of these eras, clerical dependence on, not independence of, the laity prevailed, in the first period largely in terms of the reliance of missionary clerics on the laity for sheer survival, and in the second period, in terms of further dependence for livelihood, if not for life. How did a context of clerical insecurity rather than stability, often of itinerancy rather than fixity of place, of general financial dependence rather than autonomy – all violating the Tridentine model set out above – determine the actual relations of laity and clergy 'in a missionary Church' and, in particular, to what extent were priests able to maintain the notion of priestly guidance and oversight of the laity that the great Council had proclaimed? To what extent, for example, and in terms of the ordinary mechanics of human relations, would a priest forced to rely on lay patrons, either to go on living or to make a living, be able in practice out carry out his Tridentine trust to remind the laity of 'the vices that they must avoid and the virtues they must cultivate ... reprove the lay people ... correct laics'?

The main constraining feature of socio-economic relations between priests and their largely aristocratic clients in post-Reformation England was that of patronage, making it possible, in the first period, for priests to survive, and in the second period, for them to function. And it is, of course, usually difficult – and it certainly would have been in the climate of rigid social relations of deference prevailing in early modern Europe – for protégés to assert didactic authority over patrons. That said, there is clear evidence from the English Mission field of some priests attempting, and with considerable success, to uphold Trent's adamantine norms in these matters. Thus, for example, in the 1620s a particular application of the Tridentine standard of lay obedience to an authoritative clergy was made, amidst the attempt to revive an English episcopal jurisdiction in the person of Richard Smith, bishop of Chalcedon *in partibus infidelium*. The ruling that Smith himself made on the extent of his own clerical power envisaged a rigorous control over laypeople in a highly authoritarian command structure: 'If the Bishop of Chalcedon have all and every power of ordinaries, then sure he hath also power to *command* lay Catholics: and if he hath power to command them they are bound to *obey* him ...' (my emphases).[3] In the same decade, the 'Annual Letter', the yearly and, typically, sanguine progress report of the English Province of the Society of Jesus, recapitulated the situation in Devon in the mid 1620s in which the Tridentine ideal was realised and Jesuits, even though entirely at the mercy of their gentry hosts, nonetheless acted as stern and independent moral censors 'among some families of the gentry in which they lived, instructing them and training them to all piety, repressing bad habits, healing dissention, &c.'.[4]

Priests certainly *expected* to exercise command and control over laypeople, and of all ranks in society. Thus the Elizabethan Jesuit John Gerard recalled, 'While I was in London [1599–1602] the opportunity often presented itself of visiting men of rank, confirming them in the faith, *directing them* ...' (my emphasis), and he repeated his own vocabulary of command when he related the tale of a Catholic squire once lax but becoming 'ensnared in the toils of grace', to such an extent that he appointed two priests 'who would have the *direction* of him and his household' (my emphasis).[5] A particularly vivid incident of the actuality of lay obedience – regardless of the protocols of rank – to priestly direction comes from Bossy's reconstruction of the acceptance by the Lancastrian Lady Molyneux of a clerical command that, in compliance with the Lenten fast, she abandon a roast chicken being prepared for a Sunday dinner in favour of a kipper, perhaps less delicious, but more in line with the rules of the Church.[6]

Clearly, and apart from the canonical issue of priestly status and ordination, there were complex interactions of personality at work, regulating the balance of power between priests and those to whom they ministered, above all within households. Thus, for example, the Franciscan John Wall, executed in 1679, must have made a formidable moral monitor, for his custom was to rebuke immorality (in this instance adultery) wherever it was to be found among the Catholic lay elite:

When need required, he lifted up his voice like a trumpet and, treading St John's steps with a holy indignation and undaunted courage, checked the Herods of his time. A baronet was no more to him than a beggar.... He could not be silent where sin was impudent, even though 'he lost the favour of a great man'.[7]

The foregoing instances, then, are those where the Tridentine ideal of priestly admonition coincided with actuality. It may well be, though, that they were exceptions rather than normalities, for the practical reality of the situation was all too often that, whether or not an individual priest feared to lose the favour of a great man or woman, the whole Mission and its priests, in order to function, depended on the grace and favour of the great, and particularly on the hospitality of their manor houses and halls. It is true that Christopher Haigh indicates a kind of dilemma of choice for the English priestly Mission between an outreach to plebeian Catholics and the adoption of comfortable berths in gentry homes: in the make-or-break period when the possibilities of success confronted those of failure in the narrative of the English Mission, in the crucial decades between the 1580s and the 1630s, 'priests sought comfort and security with rich gentleman rather than risk poverty and danger in the open, and as the wealthy [recusants] were numerous in the Home Counties the priests settled there ... in the relative safety of a manor houses, rather than tramp the cold moors from one hovel to the next'. The orientation of the Mission towards the manor houses had, in its outcome, 'lost opportunities' for its success.[8]

This clear division between the outreach to the halls and the mission to the hovels is, I believe, a false one, for the English Mission did indeed operate *within* gentry homes, but it also fanned out *from* them. First, evidence of the Mission's being based on the recusant manor houses is overwhelming – for example, in the Jesuits' 'Annual Letter' reporting on the situation in Devon, where 'The missioners ... were usefully employed, chiefly among some families of the gentry', while 'Some of the missioners in Yorkshire have no fixed residence, but as necessity requires live with various families of the nobility and gentry ...'.[9] In one Good Samaritanesque scene a Jesuit happens upon a Benedictine missioner, robbed and badly beaten. Naturally, the Jesuit takes the monk, on horseback, to a place of safety and recovery, but this time it is not the inn of the parable in Luke 10, but 'the house of a noble lady where he was most kindly treated until his wounds were healed, and he was then dismissed to buy another horse'.[10]

However, if such accounts confirm the centrality of the gentry hall in the adventure of the English Mission, this was emphatically not an outcome of any deliberate either/or choice of orientation between hall and cottage, for the Catholic manor houses acted in fact as bases from which, especially in the later sixteenth and seventeenth centuries, the wider mission was conducted. Certainly in the 1620s, a decade during which, in 1623, 'the hope of a Spanish match mitigated the persecution for a time' and the Jesuits recorded an astronomic

2,630 changes nationwide 'from heresy to the Catholic faith', the Society's own reports indicate that it was indeed the case that some of the Fathers lived in gentry halls, but the minutes also insisted that they 'are occupied in instructing the poor ... in a perpetual round of labours'. While Yorkshire reported the collection – surely taken up largely from the families of the recusant squires – of 120 gold crowns 'in alms to the poor Catholics', from County Durham it was recorded that 'the richest harvest was gathered in excursions taken for the instruction of the poorer classes ... on long pedestrian journeys and a very poor diet' – doubtless 'tramping cold moors'.[11] We need only add that the use of elite houses in order to disseminate a Catholic Mission at large was in fact the outcome of a deliberate Jesuit strategy of conversion, conducted *d'haut en bas*, broadened out somewhat from a model outlined by John Gerard: 'The way, I think to go about making converts is to bring the gentry over first and then their servants, for Catholic gentlefolk must have Catholic servants.'[12]

The reasons for the ultimate failure of the Church's mission to post-Reformation England as a mass phenomenon must be sought in other factors apart from priests' alleged preferences for creature comforts in the 'Home Counties': we should certainly take into account as a main factor the creeping Protestantisation of English popular culture, alongside the mounting demonisation of 'popery' as the result of a highly effective long-term official propaganda campaign. However, it is clear that, for as long as hopes for a more or less successful relaunch of English Catholicism lasted, especially in the northern counties and during the seventeenth century, its heavy and inescapable dependence on aristocratic patronage, including, especially, reliance on accommodation in aristocratic properties, undoubtedly and inevitably strengthened the already firm hold of the lay gentry and nobility on the Catholic community as a whole, and in particular on its clergy, thereby distorting inexorably the approved canonical relations between the priesthood and the laity, in this case with special reference to the latter's social elite. However, while the large houses owned by, and the continuing deference accorded to, the Catholic aristocracy gave its members an overall precedence in their dealings with clerics of their faith, the wider realities of economic dependence of the priesthood on the English Catholic laity at large had the further effect of skewing the official 'Tridentine model' of clerical mastery and lay tutelage in favour of the laity as a whole. One consequence was an evident distortion in interpretations of the function of the Mass, the monopolistic provision of which was the clergy's most indispensable service to the recusant laity.

The clerical finances of the wider post-Reformation English Catholic community were complicated enough, and there is an overall sense of a system of clerical maintenance more or less cobbled together: there were the separate resources of the religious orders; some priests had private incomes, for example annuities as gentry younger sons; there were some endowments, as well as congregational collections, tantamount to salaries; funding streams were increasingly fed by priestly cooperatives; and the picture towards the end of the eighteenth century is of considerable progress towards a proper payment structure for the clergy. But the wider impression of Catholic clerical funding over much of my period of study is of extensive priestly poverty, compounded, if not created, by an overprovision of often underemployed priests. Although after 1715 a priestly surplus began to turn into a priestly shortage, in the later seventeenth century the small community of about 60,000 nationwide (perhaps up to 18,000 in Lancashire around 1700) was supplied by about 400 priests, a ratio of 1 to 150 (for purposes of comparison, in 2000 the ratio in the English diocese of Lancaster was 1 to approximately 9,870) and it received an average of just under eleven new ordinands per annum during the period 1660–1715, a figure, surely, that any modern Catholic diocese in western Europe or North America would envy. The result of a long spell of priestly overprovision – perhaps even giving rise to a 'clerical proletariat', as during much of late medieval period – was to create precisely the opposite of the Tridentine ideal of priests whose self-sufficient endowment, along with stable residence, was intended to win them respect in their communities: as a seventeenth-century priestly critic of the system wrote, 'these missioners, who have no proper place of residence, are forced either to wander about in other people's [missions] or to fall into want. So they become contemptible, and are considered practically as paid servants; and somebody is always trying to squeeze somebody out of the place he possesses.' An eighteenth-century 'riding priest' added further detail on the penury of many of his colleagues, albeit with admiration for their fortitude rather than 'contempt' for their want: 'The necessities of our brethren can scarcely be imagined. These poor, but zealous labourers, live on a mite, and have not a mite to spare.'[13] Such, I believe, were some of the financial realities – including reliance on lay doles and hand-outs – largely governing lay–clerical relations in Catholic England over much of my period of survey. True, there were serious attempts to address the fundamental problems with trust funds such as the 'Big M' and 'Little M' schemes set up to provide for priests who were elderly and/or unwell, and there were regional bursaries such as the 'Hampshire Hog', fully established in 1683, and the Common Purse of a group of Midland counties set up in 1676.[14] In the end, though, and against the backcloth of a financial structure in which laypeople held the upper hand, fundamental questions that apply to all human relations – 'who's boss?' 'who's in charge?' – were receiving an answer that said, with audible clarity, 'layfolk'.

We may now apply some of those generalisations further, to the actual situation prevailing in England's most strongly Catholic county during the centuries following the Reformation, where we shall in fact find that the inevitable violations of the Tridentine canons on clerical financial self-sufficiency had a dramatic impact on the more strictly religious relations between priests and people, impelling the former into forms of servicing the cultic demands of lay folk that were in clear breach of the decrees of the Council, above all regarding the place of the Mass in the life of the Church.

On account of serious doubts, arising originally from the Chantries Act of 1547, concerning the legality of bequests, in formal wills subject to probate, which left money for Masses, post-Reformation English Catholics developed the convention of leaving 'spiritual wills' which gave more precise instructions (using such a formula as 'my mind and will is ...') to their co-religionist executors as to how exactly they wished their wealth to be disposed of for religious causes. Such instructions can provide fascinating incidental information on Catholic lay religious consciousness in post-Reformation England, some of it conceivably reflecting the increasing hegemony of Protestant doctrine within the wider community, as with the Lancashire testator of 1658 who put his 'Soul into the hands of my Lord & Savior Jesus Christ by whose infinit mercyes & merits I hope to be one of the Elect ...'.[15] At the same time, poignant hopes are expressed that 'Almighty God ... reduce & restore this kingdom to the Catholique Religion ...' or, in a separate formulation, 'for the Conversion of three/these [?] kingdoms to the Catholick faith ...'.[16]

Such hopes and aspirations apart, though, one of the most remarkable threads running through such testaments as these is the prevailing financial, and thus, by extension, more general social attitudes they betray towards a clergy who lacked the kind of free-standing financial maintenance that the Tridentine regulations on the priesthood envisaged. Perhaps there was an underlying tendency, even, in the minds of testators, to pauperise priests, among whom the reality of indigence was in fact extensive – to treat them as 'paid servants', if not as mendicants, and in receipt often of crumbs from tables. Thus the undated will of the Lancastrian George Gillow made provision that the yearly 'profit' – probably about £5 – on a sum to be held in a legally valid trust until his brother Richard's majority 'be given yearly to the Secular Clergy Priest tht shall for tht time officiate & serve in or about great Eccleston in the county of Lancaster'. In a parallel bequest in favour of Richard, should the latter die before reaching his majority, the priest was to receive the interest on £50 'as above directed', but the return on a second sum of £50 was 'to be yearly paid to the poor of little Eccleston'.[17]

A similar tendency to treat priests as recipients of doles is evident in the spiritual will of another Lancastrian, Ralph Gerard, who showed the detectable bias of his Catholic fellow countymen in favour of the secular, rather than the regular, clergy, with his bequest 'to Every Secular Clergy priest in this County twenty shills p priest. & to every Religious Priest within the said County ten shills a priest'. As with other Lancashire Catholic testators of that period, love of locality and shire patriotism dictated the directing of funds to within townships and within the county – these were, after all, *Lancashire* Catholics. They were, of course, also part also of a worldwide Church, wealthy Mr Gerard aiming his massive charity – to the total sum of £1765 – on an extensive European scale, albeit to English Catholic outposts on the Continent, such as the seminaries at Douai and Lisbon, the English Benedictines (also at Douai), the Carthusians at Nieuwpoort and the Poor Clares at Gravelines. But, again, Gerard was a Lancashire man, wanting value for his money, so that donations to Douai and Lisbon, for example, required in return 'to pray Likwise for the Good of my poor Soul'. Perhaps, in the end, few contracts are between parties of exactly equal status, and opulent, munificent Ralph Gerard may have been securing a bit of a bargain when he endowed £5 to a certain priest 'In case he ... continues to officiate in Wiggan Parish & Be willing to offer or cause to be offered up twelve masses for the good of my poor soul as soon as he can conveniently after he heareth of my Death, and Every month after one masse during his Life ...'.[18]

What underlying religious attitudes are revealed in such provisions? Do the religious mentalities at work here belong to the 'medieval' or the 'Tridentine' brand of Catholicism – assuming that there is a real distinction between those poles? Did the financial necessities of priests even coerce them into accepting often egocentric lay religious demands that were out of line with both the spirit and the specific legislation of the Counter-Reformation? It may be fanciful to liken Ralph Gerard's arrangements for requiem Masses to frugal Henry VII's 1509 legacy of £250 for 10,000 Masses for his soul (6d per Mass), and it would certainly be crude to calculate that, on the rough-and-ready assumption that the priest at Wigan would serve for a further twenty years from the time of this bequest, Gerard would be getting over 250 Masses for his £5 (just under 5d per Mass).[19] However, and those, as it were, actuarial calculations apart, there is in these dispositions, surely, something of the pre-Reformation culture of obits, trentals, bede rolls and other mechanisms for investing capital sums for the accumulation of Masses to obtain release from purgatory for individuals, families and sodalities – chantries on the cheap. Despite altruistic elements, which were also present in pre-Reformation testaments of this character – Gerard funding Masses for 'all my Catholick Relations, Benefactours, & all the poor Souls in purgatory' – there is in this will an inescapable air of the solipsistic, with its centring of 'the Good of my poor Soul'. Arguably, the economic straits, or at least the lack of clear financial self-sufficiency, of the post-Reformation English Catholic clergy may have encouraged on the part of some of the laity, not without certain strands suggestive of simony, an impulse, not necessarily fully conscious, to exploit the financial needs of an economically dependent clergy by making them providers of religious personal services.

Certainly, and with particular reference to the relatively stable conditions under which post-Reformation Lancashire Catholics increasingly practised their faith, a complex of what were called 'obligations' were created, emphasising the financial reliance of priests on laypersons and showing the results in terms of priestly praxis of that condition of dependence, as, for example, the late eighteenth-century country priest who recorded 'N.B. My custom has always been to say one Mass yearly for every £10 0s 0d' – one of the 'obligations' being for that most basic and indispensable of sacerdotal requirements, a chalice.[20] And, as time went by, the spread of an advanced speculation economy throughout relatively large swathes of British society seems actually to have fostered an attitude to clerics as, in effect, employees in conditional receipt of alms dependent on the returns upon investments, including those in the state itself. Surely, His Majesty's Treasury was meeting the treasury of merit and the banks of the Jordan ran alongside the Bank of England, when, in 1809, Mary Aspinwall of Ince Blundell, Lancashire, ordered the disposal of the returns of 'Three per Centum Consolidated Bank Annuities' to three priests of the district, on the clear and contractual condition that they 'offer up twenty masses for the benefit of my Soul ... And if ... any of them shall not be complied with, or if any of the said Priests shall refuse to comply with the said Conditions, then ... the Share or Shares of the said Interest Monies in respect of which the said Conditions shall not be complied with shall be paid unto some other Priest willing to comply with such Conditions' – an extraordinary use of nineteenth-century financial capitalism to fund fifteenth-century-style provisions for purgatory.[21] But when patrons pay pipers, they usually want the tunes they like, and perhaps the most notably hard nosed of these take-it-or-leave-it bargains is that of the Lancashire Catholic John Singleton, leaving, in 1808, £2 10s to commission 'six Mases said two for my self, two for my wife, and two for my daughter, Nancy, yearly and every year for ever at the Catholick Chappell in Lea, and in case the Preest of the said chappell shall neglect or refuse to do the same, then at such other Chappell as will execate and perform the said Mases ...'. The market, when 50 shillings would buy Masses 'for ever', was evidently of the buyer's variety.[22]

Yet these transactions went further and deeper than simply indicating an imbalance of power between laity and clergy in the post-Reformation English Catholic community, existing on account of the financial vulnerability of the clerics. Rather, the deals set out above went to the heart of the matter of the doctrine of the faith, with particular reference to an understanding of the Mass, especially as this was set out in the twenty-second session of the Council of Trent, in September 1562. As if intimating that its own attempted distinction between issues of faith and of reform was unreal, the Council dealt with practical issues – including those of simony – in the celebration of the Mass, but it did so, in fact, as a supplement to its guidance on the doctrine of the sacrifice. In other words, in these rulings the Council fathers were in fact doing more than heading off Protestant criticisms of long-standing corruptions and commercialisations in the mode of offering Mass. The specific decree that most closely concerns our present argument had to do with areas in which the benefits of the Mass had, over the course of time, and especially in late medieval Europe, been channelled into a series of private, familial or communal advantages by means of what the Council called 'conditions and bargains': one thinks, for example, of the way that confraternities had acquired, as it were, debentures of Masses. The Council's decrees unmistakably moved on the offensive against the hiving off of the 'fruits' of the Mass to such special accounts by means of 'conditions of compensations of whatever kind, bargains, and whatever is given for the celebration of new masses'; bishops were to suppress 'also those importunate and unbecoming demands ... for alms and other things of this kind which border on simoniacal taint or certainly savour of filthy lucre'. The Tridentine ban on 'any fixed number of masses' might almost have had in mind the kind of accounting procedures evident in the bequests of Ralph Gerard, John Singleton and Mary Aspinwall, all cited above.[23]

Again, the regulations on the avoidance of pecuniary abuse and scandal in the holy sacrifice should be related to Trent's concern not just with corruption and reform – especially the elimination of scandal-accruing simony – in themselves, but with questions of deep theological importance. For it was this Council that determined that the Mass was verily Christ's sacrifice, authentically that of Calvary, 'And inasmuch as in this divine sacrifice which is celebrated in the mass is contained and immolated in an unbloody manner the same Christ who once offered Himself in a bloody manner on the altar of the cross ...'. Further, within the framework of its counter-Lutheran doctrine of salvation, the Council deemed that the sacrifice 'is truly propitiatory and has this effect, that if we, contrite and penitent, with sincere heart and upright faith, with fear and reverence, draw nigh to God, *we obtain mercy and find grace in seasonable aid*'.[24] The Mass, then – Christ's redeeming action ever renewed through time – was crucial to a vision of the redemption that accompanied, throughout their lives on earth, the congregation of the whole people of God enrolled in the Church, assisting their progress, 'contrite and penitent', to their goal of salvation. But just as its doctrine of the Mass was central to Trent's post-medieval Christology, anti-Lutheran soteriology and Catholic ecclesiology, so the individualised and family-centred provisions we have been considering – the contractual 'obligations' entered into by necessitous priests towards the laity for 'the good of my poor soul ... the benefit of my Soul ... six Mases said two for my self, two for my wife, and two for my daughter ...' – violated not only Trent's specific disciplinary canons but also the Council's deeper comprehension of the part that the sacrifice played in the entire salvation of Christians. The Council did not rule out the deployment of the Mass for the benefit 'of the faithful ... departed in Christ ...'.[25]

but it did so within a schema in which it was the holistic salvific benefit of the Mass for the entire people of God that was stressed. While under the tutelage of its mentors John Gother (d. 1704) and Richard Challoner (1691–1781) the English Catholic community was supposedly acquiring a firmer understanding of the faith and spirituality of the Tridentine Catholic Reformation, cases that we have considered suggest that lay appropriations of the rite of the Mass essentially for purposes of separate or family advantage managed, thanks to the financial exigencies of the clergy, to challenge official and conciliar teachings: in other words, it looks as if a deeply embedded ancestral Catholic popular piety, fixated on characteristically late-medieval anxieties over the prospects in purgatory of individuals and family members, was in a position to set aside Tridentine orthodoxies in these matters of doctrine and pious practice.

So there is evidence that imbalances of power, above all economic power, between priests and people in the post-Reformation English Catholic community gave generous scope to the laity's apparently pre-Tridentine conception – patently often a privatised one – of the Church's ministrations. Meanwhile, there is suggestion, too, of some laypeople's exercising devotional leadership, even *vis-à-vis* clerics. In the second half of the seventeenth century the recusant Lancashire gentleman William Blundell kept two Jesuit chaplains in succession. The imperious squire, when acting as the director of his family's devotional routines, might even beckon his chaplain to play a subordinate part in the devotions that he himself orchestrated – even in the priest's proper preserve of religious observance. Thus, in 1667 Blundell recorded

> Upon the eve of the Conception of our Lady, I, being of the sodality with others of my family, proposed to our spiritual director that we might all together say the rosary upon the said feast day. He said he did very well like it, but could not conveniently be present himself, having but weak health and finding that such exercises did spend him. I told him that he might in such a number of persons answer in silence.[26]

So the delicate negotiation with the neurasthenic Jesuit continued, Blundell trying in his journal to mask his irritation with a priest who, while he declined to take part in family prayers – 'But he said that he found that even the noise of others speaking was often troublesome to him' – yet 'spent the most part of the afternoon of that holyday in playing at tables and shovel board in the dining room and in the hall, and at four of the clock and a half retired to his chamber'. Yet although squire Blundell was prepared to make allowances to this 'person of singular virtue and prudence', a 'companion' as well as a 'director', a clear breach had opened up over the resident priest's blank refusal to take part in the devotional sociability of the pious household over which this country gentleman presided. A reversal of religious roles had become acute in this frosty encounter between priest and patron.[27]

In other circumstances, ideological issues beyond the strictly religious might arise to disturb the peace between priests and patrons or, in other words, to provide reminders of where the balance of authority lay between those parties. Thus another Lancashire gentleman, Thomas Tyldesley, took exception in the early eighteenth century to his chaplain's refusal to pray for 'our Master', the Stuart Old Pretender, recalling 'I had occasion to chide Mr Jo Swarbrick for disloyalty'.[28] And if the little spats in which Blundell and Tyldesley were involved with their priests disturbed the supposed deference of laymen to spiritual directors, cruder cases of financial exploitation exposed the realities of relations, while, at their most extreme, bullying and violence might vividly dramatise inequalities of power that were the utter opposite of Trent's proclaimed norms. Such a case disfigured whatever rural idyll existed at the traditional recusant mission at Stonecroft Farm in Northumberland, where the resident Dominican chaplain 'Peter Thompson' reported years of harassment at the hands of the owner, Jasper Gibson, until, finally, the slow burn of harassment burst into an explosion of violence in 1721, when one Sunday morning saw Gibson attack Thompson ' like a hell dog in the presence of his Protestant servants and others that were come to prayers [that is, Mass]', forcing the priest to take refuge elsewhere.[29]

If such incidents indicate some of the tensions and ambivalences existing between clerics and squires living together under the roofs of recusant homes, surely the Tridentine norms of priestly mastery and lay subjection ought to have prevailed in the cases of *female* Catholics, women being, as is well known, considered suitable cases for deference and subjugation in early modern – and perhaps most emphatically in early modern *Catholic* – social thinking. The problem is that two striking anecdotes available to us vividly illustrate a mentoring role towards priests as inhering in women, tutoring priests to return to their own integrity. Take first the case of a surviving Marian priest, James Bell (martyred in 1584) who had conformed to the Church of England and in fact served in its priesthood for thirty years. It was when he returned to his place of birth, Lancashire, that Bell encountered a Catholic gentlewoman who took him to task and 'begane very earnestly and religiously to dehort [dissuade] the old man from that vile and wicked kind of service..... She put him in mind that he was made a priest to say mass and to minister the sacraments after the Catholic use.' The lady proceeded to press home her pedagogy, visiting Bell 'in his sickness and once again exhorted him to remember his state and vocation', finally bringing about his reconciliation to the Church and the renewal of his priestly practice.[30] The Council, having completed its work only a few years earlier, had, clearly, envisaged the role of moral direction as inhering in priests *vis-à-vis* 'laics', but in this case perhaps we might ask '*quis docet ipsos doctores?*'

But it is possible that the very absence of formal ordained capacity in Catholic women actually equipped them as monitors of the standards which the ordained should observe – one thinks, for instance, the role of St Catherine of Siena in the 1370s in directing the papacy to return itself to its only valid centre, Rome. Like the vignette concerning James Bell, an incident in the martyrology of Thomas Maxfield (or Macclesfield), executed in 1616, also suggests the female role of showing forth the standards of constancy and courage to which the priest must rise, the clerics being in both these scenes the recipients of religious instruction from laywomen. In both Bell's and Maxfield's cases the instructors of clerical pupils were ladies of rank, their authority as admonitors clearly underscored by their social standing, though in the dialogue concerning Maxfield even the lady's rank took second place to her reputation for a holiness that conveyed its own charismatic authority. The powerfully dramatic scene depicting her intervention opens with an unknown lady's displaying an extraordinary courage and resource in order to interview the (wavering) martyr:

> Amongst those that made entry into the martyr there was a certaine gentlewoeman who was renowned not so much for the greatness of her gentrie as for her sanctitie of life. She hauing put on a poore habite, assumed for a companion another woeman conscious of her fact [aware of her identity], and soe entered the prison as if she had some husband or father there to bring him some meate. When she was within [,] what by humble entreatie & faire speeches vnto the keepers with liberal bestowing of money vpon them & promising more hereafter, she procured so farr that she wrested a licence to speake to the Martyr.[31]

In the mysterious lady's conduct in Maxfield's terrible cell there are, clearly, pronounced ambiguities of category and status: contemporaneous cultural assumptions might more readily have attributed her courage and resourcefulness to a man, implicitly rebuking the priest's temporary lack of fortitude – and taking on a disguise had become a necessary survival strategy for English priests rather than for laypeople, certainly since the 1580s. Indeed, it was in her adoption of a kind of priestly role in her encounter with Maxfield that the lady visitor most openly challenged accepted boundaries between priests and laity. After outlining some practical measures for his physical well-being, the gentlewoman proceeded to enter on a series of allocutions which displayed her assuming the 'priestly' role, indeed that of the 'ghostly counsellor' and even of the confessor. Her discourses clearly show how stereotypical assumptions about the relative roles of priests and people, and indeed of men and women, in early modern England might be overturned. The lady begins her exordium with almost a pastoral rebuke to her client: 'she sometimes feared least feare of death had layed hould on him & therefore inculcated such motiues as she remembered of contemning death'. The meditations consisted in part of a kind of Christian stoicism mingled with notes from the medieval *artes moriendi* tradition, her homily culminating in a peroration in which she 'willed him' to thinck on the victories of the Martyrs, & imitate the constant faith of them whose tryumphs & rewards he coueted; lastly she said that death was not to be feared vnto which an immortalitie did succeed, for by the shortnesse of a holy death a blessed life should be had in possession, & that which in vs here is a light and momentary tribulation, the same doth worke in heauen an eternal waight of glorie.[32]

Maxfield had as an immediate prospect, at worst, hanging by the neck followed by disembowelment and dismemberment alive, or at best, and as it turned out, a quarter hour of slow and hideous strangulation, albeit without pre-mortem butchering, so his mentor's promise of a 'light and momentary' tribulation may sound in our ears as more in the nature of a spiritual exercise than an accurate prediction. But the priest took her words, restoring his morale and reminding him of his purpose, swiftly and entirely to heart: 'There is cause indeed, renowned Mistresse, why I ought to yield great thanks vnto Almightie God' for his martyr's end.[33] In its human interactions this encounter quite closely resembled an interview between a condemned man and a prison chaplain, only with the *personae* reversed: perhaps that is why Fr Anstruther, who must, surely, have known of the tale of the mystery woman, airbrushed it out of his narration of Maxfield's final hours: Anstruther, the otherwise ever-scrupulous historian of the seminary priests, replaced the account of the laywoman's powerful and assertive role with a minute – one, surely, more seemly from a clericalist point of view – to the effect that Maxfield was visited before his execution by the Dominican chaplain to the Spanish ambassador, who administered the last sacraments.[34] Perhaps Anstruther's intervention in the narrative may actually confirm, as do some of the episodes recounted in this chapter, the extent to which the exigencies and the perils of the English Mission overturned the 'Tridentine' proprieties of relations between clerics and laics – including those between priests and women.

Notes
1 John Bossy, *The English Catholic community 1570–1850* (London: Darton, Longman & Todd, 1975); Marie Rowlands (ed.), *English Catholics of parish and town*, A joint research project of the Catholic Record Society and Wolverhampton University (London: Catholic Record Society, 1999): Michael A. Mullett, *Catholics in Britain and Ireland 1558–1829* (Basingstoke, Hants., and London: Macmillan Press, New York: St. Martin's Press, 1998).
2 H.J. Schroeder, OP, *The Canons and Decrees of the Council of Trent English Translation* (Rockford, IL: Tan Books, 1978), pp. 152, 136–7.
3 A.F. Allison, 'A question of jurisdiction: Richard Smith, Bishop of Chalcedon, and the Catholic laity', *Recusant History* 16:2 (1982), 119.
4 Henry Foley, SJ, *Records of the English province of the Society of Jesus, Volume VII. Part the Second Collectanea Completed;* ... (London: Burns and Oates, 1883), p. 1111.
5 Patrick Martin and John Finnis, 'Tyrwhitt of Kettleby, Part II: Robert Tyrwhitt, a main benefactor of Fr. John Gerard, SJ, 1600–1605', *Recusant History* 26:4 (2003), 560.
6 Bossy, *English Catholic community*, p. 114.
7 Michael Hodgetts, 'The Yates of Harvington 1631–1696', *Recusant History* 22:2 (1994), 167.
8 Christopher Haigh, 'From monopoly to minority: Catholicism in early modern England', *Trans-*

actions of the Royal Historical Society, 5th series, 31 (1981), 145–7.
9 Foley, Records of the English province of the Society of Jesus, VII, II, p. 1111.
10 Ibid., pp. 1110–11.
11 Ibid., pp. 1098, 1111–12.
12 Martin and Innis, 'Tyrwhitt of Kettleby', p. 560.
13 Bossy, English Catholic community, pp. 188–9, 220–3, 229–49; J.A. Hilton, Catholic Lancashire from Reformation to renewal 1559–1991 (London: Phillimore, 1994), pp. 54, 56; Godfrey Anstruther, OP, The seminary priests: A dictionary of the secular clergy of England and Wales 1558–1850 III. 1660–1715 (Great Wakering, Essex: Mayhew-McCrimmon, 1976), p. x.
14 Anstruther, Seminary priests, III, p. 11; Bossy, English Catholic community, pp. 245, 246.
15 L[ancashire] R[ecord] O[ffice]: RCLv: Box 25: Will of Richard Shaw, Gent of Walton-le-Dale, Lancashire, 1658; Ralph Gerard's Will, n.d.
16 LRO: RCLv: Box 25: Spiritual Will of George Gillow, n.d. – late 17th–early 18th century.
17 LRO: RCLv: Box 25: Spiritual Will of George Gillow, n.d. – late 17th–early 18th century.
18 LRO: RCLv: Box 25: Ralph Gerard's Will'; 'Legacies from Mr Ralph Gerards Will'
19 R.S. Nolan, 'Bequests for Masses (England)', The Catholic Encyclopedia, Volume X, online edition; for examples of late medieval transactions for obituary Masses, see R.N. Swanson, Church and society in late medieval England (Cambridge, MA and Oxford: Blackwell, 1993), pp. 296–9.
20 LRO: RCLv: Box 25: Lea Chapel (formerly Salwick Hall), Lancs.: '…assemblage of obligations'.
21 LRO: RCLv: Box 25: Will of Mary Aspinwall…, 1809.
22 LRO: RCLv: Box 25: Will of John Singleton, 1808.
23 Schroeder, Canons and decrees of Trent, p. 151.
24 Ibid., pp. 145–6; emphasis in original, quoting from Hebrews 4: 16.
25 Ibid., p. 146.
26 T. Ellison Gibson (ed.), Crosby Records: A Cavalier's Note Book Being Notes, Anecdotes, & Observations of William Blundell of Crosby, Lancashire … (London: Longman, Green, 1880), p. 133.
27 Ellison Gibson (ed.), Crosby Records, p. 133.
28 The Tyldesley Diary: personal records … 1712–13–14, cited in Mullett, Catholics in Britain and Ireland, p. 85.
29 Leo Gooch, 'Priests and people in the eighteenth century', Recusant History 20:2 (1990), 208–9.
30 Patrick McGrath and Joy Rowe, 'The Marian priests under Elizabeth I', Recusant History, 17:2 (1984), 109–10.
31 J.H. Pollen (ed.), 'The Life and Martyrdom of Mr. Maxfield, 1616 …', Catholic Record Society, Miscellanea III (1906), 38–9.
32 Ibid., p. 39.
33 Ibid.
34 Anstruther, The seminary priests …II. Early Stuarts 1603–1659 (Great Wakering: Mayhew-McCrimmon, 1975), p. 215.

4

Integration vs segregation: religiously mixed marriage and the 'verzuiling' model of Dutch society

BENJAMIN KAPLAN

Few paintings from the Dutch Golden Age are as familiar to so many people as is Rembrandt's group portrait, *The Syndics of the Clothmakers' Guild* (1662) (Figure 4.1). The syndics had the duty of assessing the quality of cloth sold in Amsterdam and ensuring that no shoddy wares were passed off as good. It was a duty with a moral edge, and Rembrandt's painting exudes seriousness. Wearing modest black, with flat white collars, the five syndics, assisted by the hatless servant behind them, appear united in their common endeavour. One would never imagine from this image that they were divided from one another in any fundamental way. Yet we know that these five men belonged to four different confessions. The chairman, seated with the book directly before him, was Calvinist. The second man from the left, half-standing, was a Mennonite of the strict, Old Frisian variety, and probably a deacon of his congregation. The syndic on the far right was Remonstrant. The other two syndics, Jacob van Loon and Aernout van der Mye, were prominent Catholics who had semi-clandestine Catholic churches, so-called *schuilkerken*, in their homes.

Isabella van Eeghen, who in 1957 uncovered the identities of these men, called them 'a group of birds of very diverse plumage, who only in our Republic could sit around one table in so brotherly a fashion in the middle of the seventeenth century'.[1] Thanks to her research, Rembrandt's painting has come to symbolise the religious toleration of Dutch society in its Golden Age, a society where, according to English ambassador William Temple, 'differences in [religious] Opinion make none in Affections, and little in Conversation'; where people of different faiths 'live together like Citizens of the World, associated by the common ties of Humanity, and by the bonds of Peace'.[2] Temple's description of the Dutch religious scene, like Rembrandt's painting, conveys an image of the

Figure 4.1 Rembrandt, *The Syndics of the Clothmakers' Guild* (1662).

Netherlands as a place where men like the syndics do not just coexist peacefully alongside one another, they live and work cooperatively together with one another. United by common interests, they share common tastes and values. Religious differences are relegated to the private sphere, where every individual enjoys freedom of conscience. People worship God as they please, and the people with whom they worship aren't necessarily the same ones they live next door to or do business with.

According to Temple, it was 'the force of Commerce, Alliances, and Acquaintance, spreading so far as they do in small circuits' that made 'conversation, and all the offices of common life, so easie, among so different Opinions'.[3] In other words, in the intimate communities of Dutch towns and villages, people of different faiths got along because they were bound together by a dense net of economic, familial, neighbourly and other ties. Constantly interacting in daily life, they were familiar and comfortable with one another. Temple was hardly the only foreign visitor to suggest that social integration was the key to religious toleration in the Dutch Republic. His countryman James Howell remarked, 'I believe in this street where I lodge, there be well near as many religions as there be houses; for one neighbour knows not, nor cares not much what religion the other is of.' Ellis Veryard delved down from street level to that of the household, suggesting that it was 'very ordinary to find the man of the house of one opinion, his wife of another, his children of a third and his servants of one different from them all; and yet they live without the least jangling of dissension'.[4] It is hard to believe, as Howell claimed, that people normally did not know what faith their neighbours practised, or that most families were really as mixed as Veryard suggested. The authors of such descriptions were trading in a stereotype, one that circulated widely among both foreigners and natives. That stereotype cast Dutch society as religiously both uniquely diverse and thoroughly integrated.[5]

Stereotypes, of course, have no credibility if they do not bear a recognisable relation to truths. Biographies, histories of cities, and other studies have revealed countless instances of people of different faiths having friendly personal relations. They have offered examples of guilds, militias, chambers of rhetoric, and other organisations – even confraternities – whose ranks were religiously mixed. No study so far has found any sharp geographic segregation, with people of different faiths excluded from one another's neighbourhoods. To capture this state of affairs, Willem Frijhoff has long used the term 'omgangsoecumene' – 'ecumenicity of everyday life' – or a similar construction, and this term has been widely adopted by other scholars.[6] In my view, the term is problematic because it departs so far from one of the key meanings of ecumenicity, which is a striving for the resolution of religious differences and the restoration of religious unity.[7] The term 'omgangsoecumene' has been useful, though, insofar as it has helped us articulate the great difference between interfaith relations in practice and in ideology, and on the level of individuals as distinct from groups. As the research of Frijhoff, Pollmann, and others has made clear, personal relations could, in practice, be smooth and even amicable without any lessening of people's ideological commitment to the enmities that were an essential part of so much Christian piety in the confessional age.[8]

In 1995, Simon Groenveld threw down the gauntlet to this historiographic consensus, questioning whether Dutch society remained religiously integrated throughout its Golden Age. In his book *Huisgenoten des geloofs*, Groenveld asked whether, beginning around 1650 and continuing for some hundred years, the Republic was not in fact 'verzuild', that is, 'pillarised'.[9] This is a term commonly used to describe the Netherlands in the late nineteenth century and first half of the twentieth century, when Dutch society was highly segregated, with the adherents of different faiths and ideologies having separate schools, hospitals, clubs, unions, political parties, and other organisations. Catholics, Calvinists, socialists, and (according to some scholars) liberals married, did business, and socialised predominantly among their own kind, forming distinct subcultures which had their own newspapers and other media. Though there are lively debates about its nature, most historians and sociologists agree that *verzuiling* was a fundamental aspect of Dutch society in that later era.[10] By drawing a parallel to modern developments, Groenveld sketched a radically different picture of relations between people of different faiths in the early modern era.

Of course, in some respects Groenveld built upon the work of previous scholars, among them J.A. de Kok, who argued that the decades leading up to 1650 saw Dutch society divide into confessional camps.[11] With the Revolt against Spain and the adoption of Reformed Protestantism as the official faith of the rebel provinces, many Dutch people in the late sixteenth century found themselves betwixt and between. They did not support the intolerant, Tridentine Catholicism championed by Philip II, yet neither were they Calvinists. J.J. Woltjer dubbed these people the 'middle groups', a label which perhaps misleadingly suggests that their beliefs were a compromise, or splitting of the difference, between Calvinism and Catholicism.[12] What is clear is that this group was as heterogeneous as it was large, and that as late as 1620 a majority of Dutch people did not belong as members to any of the churches that emerged as rivals in the young Dutch Republic. Some people were entirely unchurched, while others maintained an affiliation to one or another of the churches that was looser than full membership. De Kok argued that, by 1650, the great majority of Netherlanders had made their choice, and that from that time the Dutch population was effectively divided into Calvinists, Catholics, Mennonites, and adherents of other, smaller denominations. This process of choosing sides Groenveld compared to *verzuiling*.

The century from around 1650 to 1750, then, in his vision, was one of *verzuildheid*, with Dutch society firmly divided into confessional blocks. In this period, the beliefs of each confession shaped not only the core religious activities of its members, they also 'determined ... the character and content of education and charity', which constituted what Groenveld called a 'second circle' of activity surrounding the core. What decisively proved *verzuiling*, however, was the way 'confessionally determined patterns of norms and values' shaped a 'third concentric circle' of social, economic, and cultural activity, determining how people behaved, with whom they did business, what books they read, and much more.[13] Eventually, the churches' grip on the lives of their members loosened, thanks to the influence of the Enlightenment and a new set of values emphasising patriotism and civic virtue. Around 1750, claimed Groenveld, Dutch society entered a phase of 'de-pillarisation' that was to last roughly a century before pillarisation began once again to increase.

Presented in a mere eighty pages, Groenveld's portrait of churches whose norms informed all aspects of their members' lives, and of congregations that formed discrete, even isolated sub-communities, is as extreme as it is sketchy. If it fits any religious groups in the Republic, it would be certain Mennonite ones renowned for their strictness, like the Old Frisians and Old Flemings. Whether it applies generally, though, is very much a question. Implicitly or explicitly, most studies that have appeared since Groenveld's book have rejected its argument. Among these are Gabrielle Dorren's book on Haarlem, Charles de Mooij's on

Bergen op Zoom, Ronald Rommes's on Utrecht, and Wiebe Bergsma's on Friesland.[14] Bergsma even questions the assumption, widely shared, that by around 1650 the Dutch population had divided along confessional lines. He finds that throughout the seventeenth century and into the eighteenth century, roughly a quarter of the inhabitants of Friesland, Groningen, and Drenthe still were not members of any church.[15] Joining this consensus are Willem Frijhoff and Marijke Spies, authors of the synthetic volume *1650: Hard-won unity*. They acknowledge a 'growing segregation' between the confessions, but suggest that it was limited to worship and charity and did not extend even to education, never mind recreation or other spheres.[16] The one concession they make to the *verzuiling* model concerns charity. In a 1997 monograph, Joke Spaans showed that, beginning in the last quarter of the seventeenth century, magistrates and provincial authorities in Friesland encouraged churches to take responsibility for assisting the poor of their faith. Beginning in the 1670s, Frisian authorities made formal agreements with the tolerated churches, granting them tax exemptions and otherwise facilitating their charitable operations. Finally, in the 1750s, the provincial states legally required the churches to operate deaconries, and poor church members were no longer deemed eligible for the municipal charity previously disbursed on a non-confessional basis to all deserving, needy burghers.[17] Dorren and Spaans have described a similar trend in Haarlem, and evidence suggests that the trend may have been general.[18] It did not necessarily result in a comprehensive subdivision of the poor by confession; in fact, in Friesland a majority of the poor continued always to be aided by municipal, not ecclesiastical funds.[19] To the extent, however, that charity came to be segregated along confessional lines, it does constitute a sphere where Groenveld's model seems to fit, at least partly. One should note, though, that the segregation seems scarcely to have begun as of 1650, and there was no reversal of the trend – nothing that might be called depillarisation – after 1750.

In Groenveld's model, one of the most critical spheres where *verzuiling* always manifested itself was that of marriage and family life: in a pillarised society, religious groups did not intermarry frequently. In fact, in all branches of the human sciences, scholars commonly regard whether groups intermarry as a decisive criterion of their integration or segregation. If people of different faiths intermarry, families become mixed and the lines dividing groups are blurred. If they do not, nuclear units remain homogeneous and can serve as the building blocks of discreet subcommunities. Determining rates of interfaith or, as it was then called, 'mixed' marriage in the Dutch Republic seems therefore a useful way to bring hard evidence to bear on this historiographic debate.

In general, scholars have assumed that mixed marriages were frequent in Holland and other parts of the Republic that were religiously mixed, more so than in England or other European lands. As suggested by Veryard's remark, mixed marriages were part of the stereotype of 'Dutch toleration' that circulated during the Golden Age. Contemporaries believed that such marriages were not just a symptom of the religious toleration prevailing in the Republic, but one of its causes, teaching people of different faiths to exercise forbearance toward one another. To be sure, as Groenveld points out, all the major churches condemned mixed marriages and sought to combat them, warning members against them and disciplining those who contracted them. The only group not to adopt such a negative stance were the Waterlander Mennonites. Yet none of the churches declared mixed marriages invalid, nor did any secular laws before the mid eighteenth century obstruct such marriages or punish those who entered into them. Both Reformed ministers and civil authorities were prepared to marry people of different faiths to one another.[20]

Unfortunately, little systematic research has been conducted to determine the actual frequency or patterns of interfaith marriage in the Republic. What follows is a survey of the data available from scattered studies, supplemented by some additional primary source investigations. The data presented mostly concern marriages between Catholics and Reformed Protestants, the two largest religious groups in the Republic. They range from the seventeenth through the eighteenth centuries, in part to reveal long-term patterns but also because the available evidence is simply much fuller for the later period. The result may be a rather abstract, impersonal treatment of marital relations, which, in the early modern era as today, were among the most nuanced and intimate of all human relationships. Nevertheless, it can help us to evaluate competing claims as to how integrated or segregated Dutch religious groups were.

The chief difficulty in determining rates of mixed marriage is a lack of comprehensive, systematic sources, especially for the late sixteenth and first half of the seventeenth centuries. In 1574, a provincial synod of the Reformed Churches meeting in Dordrecht observed 'that many brothers and sisters on all sides are entering into marriage with those who are papist or Mennonite'.[21] Such complaints may fuel a suspicion that mixed marriages were frequent in the early years of the Dutch Republic, but they offer firm evidence only of a perception held by ministers and elders. Almost as problematic are cases in which local consistories subjected Reformed Church members to ecclesiastical discipline for marrying outside the faith. While these cases offer insight into the lives of specific couples, they do not provide a basis for determining actual rates of intermarriage. Reformed Protestants were not subject to ecclesiastical discipline unless and until they became actual members, *lidmaten*, of the church, which many never did, while others did so only as adults. Members married to someone of another faith escaped ecclesiastical censure if their wedding had taken place before they joined the church. Even people who chose spouses of another faith after becoming church members were not always censured.[22]

The principal sources that sometimes allow us to determine rates of intermarriage are local marriage registers. These record (either together or as separate series) the registration (*ondertrouw*) of couples intending to marry, the publication of banns that followed, and finally their weddings. In Zeeland, Drenthe, and the Ommelanden of Groningen, Reformed ministers performed the only legal weddings. In other provinces, as in the Generality Lands, couples could wed in either the Reformed Church or town hall, though civil ceremonies were not available in all locales.[23] Even where they were, some Catholics chose to marry in the Reformed Church, as did some Protestant dissenters. In Bergen op Zoom, one of the chief cities of the Dutch Generality Lands, the large majority of Catholics continued to marry in the Reformed Church even after civil ceremonies were introduced. Here, in the early eighteenth century ministers began to record the religion of the couples who appeared before them. The resulting figures, as calculated by Charles de Mooij, appear in Table 4.1. Overall, at least 11 per cent of all marriages between 1736 and 1796 were religiously mixed. In the late 1720s the figure was almost 15 per cent, declining by the late 1740s to 8.5 per cent, then rising once again to over 14 per cent by the 1780s. Over three-quarters of these mixed marriages, some 8.2 per cent of all marriages, were between a Catholic and a Reformed Protestant.[24] Located in the Generality Land of States-Brabant, Bergen had a population that, in the aggregate over the period in question, was about 33 per cent Reformed, 60 per cent Catholic, and 5 per cent Lutheran. If people had chosen spouses without regard to religion – that is, if there had been no tendency toward endogamy – about 40 per cent of marriages would have joined a Catholic and a Reformed Protestant.

Table 4.1 Bergen op Zoom: percentage of all marriages that were mixed

Years	% mixed, all religions	% Catholic–Reformed
1726–30	14.7	–
1736–40	10.7	8.2
1746–50	8.5	–
1786–90	14.2	5.5

Blanks = No data
Source: De Mooij, *Geloof kan Bergen verzetten*, p. 582; additional raw data provided by Charles de Mooij.

Unlike in Bergen, in most places it was only after the introduction of laws restricting mixed marriages that the religion of couples began to be recorded systematically. These laws reflected the rise among Dutch regents of new concerns and negative attitudes toward certain mixed marriages: not those between

Protestants of different confessions, which none of the laws mention, but those between Protestants and Catholics. Among the earliest was a 1677 ordinance issued by Utrecht's magistrates in response to complaints by the local consistory that the Catholic Church was gaining adherents through mixed marriages at the expense of the 'true Reformed religion'. Utrecht's magistrates stipulated, as a condition of registering mixed couples, that Catholic brides and grooms had to promise to allow their Reformed partners to practise their faith unhindered, and to allow the couple's children to be baptised and raised in the Reformed faith. Those who violated their promise were to be stripped of their citizenship – and thus too, in the case of artisans, of their guild membership and, with it, their livelihood. Violators might even forfeit their right to reside in the city.[25] From this point, one finds in the Utrecht registers, both civil and Reformed, notations such as 'the groom agrees to comply with the resolution of *haar Edele Mogende* [the magistrates], he being Roman [Catholic]'. These notations were infrequent, however, (Table 4.2) and it is likely that many mixed couples were not being registered as such. In 1709, magistrates felt it necessary to reissue the 1677 ordinance, this time insisting that it be strictly obeyed. Already on the rise, the number of couples registered as mixed doubled overnight. As the consistory complained, some Catholics still evaded the law by claiming to be Reformed, but if ever there was a time when authorities achieved something close to a complete

Table 4.2 Utrecht: marriages registered as Reformed–Catholic

Year	Total marriages	Number registered as Reformed–Catholic	% registered as Reformed–Catholic
1680	383	8	2.1
1690	293	10	3.4
1700	346	10	2.9
1710	419	38	9.1
1711	382	21	5.5
1712	403	46	11.4
1713	434	38	8.8
1714	367	25	6.8
1715	337	26	7.7
1720	361	26	7.2
1730	409	16	3.9
1740	318	21	6.6
1750	386	27	7.0
1760	276	17	6.2

Source: Het Utrechts Archief, DTB Registers van de Gemeente Utrecht, inv. nr. 75–77,

registration of Catholic–Reformed couples, it was immediately after 1709.[26] In the next six years, no fewer than 8.3 per cent of all couples were registered as such (Table 4.2). Between 1720 and 1760, a sampling suggests, the figure averaged a little over 6 per cent.[27] Whether this decline from the 1710s reflected laxer registration procedures or changing marriage patterns is unclear.

While the figures derived from Utrecht's marriage registers are problematic, those from Holland are even more so. After all, in Utrecht mixed couples could usually acknowledge their religions without fear of further consequences. True, at least nine couples were prosecuted under the 1677 and 1709 ordinances but, as one of the victims of this persecution (as he viewed it) protested, he 'knew hundreds of people living in this city, who did the same thing as he', that is, raise their children as Catholics, disregarding the promises they had made.[28] The Utrecht ordinance may have sought to regulate the behaviour of mixed couples, but it did not really prevent people from contracting mixed marriages, nor did it penalise Protestants who married Catholics. The first authorities to do that were the States of Holland, who decided in 1737 that Calvinist army officers in Holland's pay were to be dismissed if they married Catholic women. The States General soon adopted this rule for officers throughout the Dutch army, later extending it to all soldiers.[29] In 1739 they excluded Calvinist men married to Catholic women from all political offices in the territories they governed. The States of Holland and Gelderland did the same in the 1750s, a decade that saw a wave of legislation issued to combat what the authorities perceived as a growing problem.[30] From that time, in the affected territories, Protestant youths under a certain age were barred from marrying Catholics outright. The banns for Protestant–Catholic couples had to be published at six-week intervals rather than weekly, delaying the wedding by some four months. And couples who persisted were prohibited in Holland from exchanging a dowry, owning property jointly as husband and wife, or arranging for the longest-living spouse to enjoy usufruct of the other's goods after the latter's death. Authorities anticipated that some couples would try to evade these strictures by one of the partners converting to the other's faith, either sincerely or with the intention of returning to their original faith after the wedding. To prevent such conversions *pro matrimonio*, as they were called, the various States established a probationary period, decreeing that a couple could not register to be married for a year after either partner converted.[31]

As a result of this legislation, magistrates and ministers in Holland, Gelderland, and the Generality Lands were supposed to keep track of marriages between Protestants and Catholics. In Rotterdam, they fulfilled their obligation by keeping a separate register of Reformed–Catholic marriages; in Enkhuizen, where a single register was kept, they noted couples who fell under the terms of the legislation; in Amsterdam, the commissioners for marital affairs began to record the religion of all brides and grooms who, when asked their faith, did not declare themselves to be Reformed. Using marriage registers, Donald Haks calculated the number of Reformed–Catholic marriages in three communities of South Holland between 1755 and 1794 (Table 4.3). He found that even in Leiden, the only city among the three, the number never rose as high as 3 per cent, while in Maassluis and Wassenaar there were hardly any such marriages at all. G.J. Mentink and A.M. van der Woude similarly added up the number of Reformed–Catholic marriages registered in Rotterdam (Table 4.4). Their results were equally meagre – this at a time when Rotterdam's population included about 62 per cent Reformed Protestants and 30 per cent Catholics.[32] The registers of other cities in Holland yield similar results. In Enkhuizen, Reformed–Catholic marriages were fewer than 1 per cent of the total registered in the 1750s, rising to 3 per cent by the 1770s (Table 4.5). The figures are even lower for Amsterdam, where, out of 2,533 marriages in 1760, not a single one was registered as being between a Catholic and a Reformed Protestant. In 1770, eight marriages were so registered, a mere 0.3 per cent of the total; in 1780, six, or 0.2 per cent.[33] These figures are difficult to believe: Catholic–Protestant marriage would have to have been utterly taboo to have been so rare in so large and mixed a city: in 1809 the first national census of religious affiliations found 50 per cent of Amsterdam's more than 200,000 inhabitants to be Reformed Protestants and 20.9% Roman Catholics.

One possibility, then, is that through their harsh legislation the States of Holland achieved their goal of discouraging intermarriage between Protestants and Catholics. Another possibility, though, is that the legislation encouraged people to lie about their faith, producing fraud on a massive scale. According to one Catholic pastor, that is precisely what was going on in Amsterdam, with the acquiescence of the city's marriage commissioners. In response to a query from a colleague in Antwerp in 1789, Father Bartholomeus Alberts explained that 'most marriages of that sort [mixed Reformed–Catholic] are fraudulently contracted', the Catholic partner claiming to be Reformed, and that 'no [pastor] made any difficulty about admitting such persons [who had lied about their faith] to the sacrament [of communion]' subsequently.[34] According to Alberts, it was principally the 'common folk' who lied to the commissioners about their faith, and indeed this group had an opportunity which members of the urban elite may have lacked: commissioners were not likely to know the former, either personally or by reputation. Those of modest resources also had a motive that would have weighed less heavily on elites: a municipal ordinance required the banns of mixed couples to be published at city hall as well as in church, and consequently commissioners charged such couples three times as much to register as they did Reformed couples.[35]

Nowhere else in the Netherlands were the incentives and possibilities for fraud as great as in Amsterdam, so it is hardly surprising that couples of mixed

Table 4.3 Percentage of all marriages registered as Reformed–Catholic in three Holland communities

Years	Leiden	Maassluis	Wassenaar
1755–60	0.7	0	0
1761–70	1.7	0.4	0
1771–80	2.6	0	0
1781–90	2.8	0.2	1.5
1791–94	1.1	0.3	0.9

Source: Haks, *Huwelijk en gezin*, p. 135.

Table 4.4 Rotterdam: marriages registered as Reformed–Catholic (10-year totals)

Years	Total marriages	Number registered as Reformed–Catholic	% registered as Reformed–Catholic
1755–64	4916	47	1.0
1760–69	5174	53	1.0
1765–74	5054	62	1.2
1770–79	5219	77	1.5
1775–84	5682	86	1.5
1780–89	5902	87	1.5
1785–94	5644	100	1.8

Source: Mentink and Van der Woude, *De demografische ontwikkeling te Rotterdam en Cool in de 17e en 18e eeuw*, p. 174. Figures include the suburb of Cool.

Table 4.5 Enkhuizen: marriages registered as Reformed–Catholic

Years	Total marriages	Number registered as Reformed–Catholic	% registered as Reformed–Catholic
1755–59	337	3	0.9
1760–64	383	3	0.8
1765–69	390	8	2.1
1770–73	265	8	3.0

Source: Enkhuizen ondertrouwregisters 1750–1761 and 1762–1773, at http://home.hccnet.nl/j.buisman/genea/menu/index.html (accessed 15 August 2006).

religion elsewhere sometimes fled to that city to escape the obstacles put in their way at home.[36] Yet even with regard to Amsterdam, it is not certain that dissembling has greatly distorted our figures. According to the city's registers, 6.2 per cent of all marriages in 1770 were mixed ones involving one Reformed partner; the other partner might be Catholic or, more commonly, of a different Protestant confession – in 1780, 6.4 per cent of all marriages were of this kind (Table 4.6). Basing herself on other sources, Dini Helmers has found that, of all the couples in Amsterdam who separated or divorced in three years (1769, 1784, and 1804), a very similar number, 6.9 per cent, were religiously mixed.[37] One might suppose that, if anything, religiously mixed couples would be over-represented among those whose relationships had run aground.

Table 4.6 Amsterdam: marriages registered as mixed, with one Reformed partner

Year	Total marriages	Number registered as mixed	% registered as mixed
1700	2504	100	4.0
1710	2268	74	3.3
1720	2400	64	2.7
1730	2908	68	2.3
1740	2432	80	3.3
1750	2485	69	2.7
1760	2533	107	4.2
1770	2427	151	6.2
1780	2307	147	6.4

Source: Gemeentearchief Amsterdam 5001, inv. nrs. 526–604, 700–738. Source for 1780: Simon Hart, 'Enige statistische gegevens inzake analfabetisme te Amsterdam in de 17e en 18e eeuw', *Amstelodamum [Maandblad]* 55 (1968), 3–6. The figures for 1700–50 are based on double registrations, those for 1760–80 on the religion indicated for each individual registered.

Not all cities charged mixed couples higher fees than they did other couples – Enkhuizen, for example, did not – nor did any other city offer people the cover of anonymity to the extent that Amsterdam did. Social control was probably weaker in Amsterdam than it was anywhere else in the Republic, and it is difficult to imagine that much fraud transpired in villages, where everyone knew everyone else. Perhaps that is why other sources and methodologies applied to rural communities have yielded results similar to those of Haks for Maassluis and Wassenaar. In his painstaking reconstruction of the South Holland village of Maasland, D.J. Noordam calculated how many men married women of other faiths, counting marriages between Protestants of different confessions as well as between Protestants and Catholics. Of all the men born in Maasland between 1640 and 1719, only a single one did so. Calculating on a different basis, Noordam found that the number of religiously mixed households in Maasland almost tripled between 1730 and 1800 – from almost none to a meagre 1.7 per cent.[38] A contemporary census of villages in the Noorderkwartier of Holland, compiled in 1742 by Nicolaas Struyck, an early enthusiast for demography, yields similar figures. Struyck recruited schoolmasters, burgomasters, a merchant, a clockmaker, and other inhabitants of the villages in question as informants. Going door to door, they found only 1.1 per cent of all households religiously mixed; at most, 0.4 per cent of all households were mixed Catholic–Protestant.[39]

Of course, not all mixed marriages joined Catholics and Reformed Protestants, and it is instructive to compare, to the extent possible, the frequency of intermarriage between different religious groups. In Bergen, three-quarters of all mixed marriages were between Catholics and Reformed Protestants. That was largely because Protestant dissenters constituted only about 5 per cent of Bergen's population. The same factor explains why over two-thirds of mixed marriages in Maasland (between 1730 and 1800) were between Catholics and Protestants: here, Protestant dissenters constituted fewer than 1 per cent of the population. In the Noorderkwartier, by contrast, where over 20 per cent of the population were Mennonite or Lutheran, three-quarters of mixed marriages were between Protestants (Table 4.7). Relative to their numbers, then, Protestants intermarried with one another far more often than they did with Catholics. Lutherans seem to have been particularly amenable to mixed marriages: in Bergen over half of all Lutherans contracted them, while in Utrecht, according to Rommes, some 41 per cent did so (mostly with Reformed Protestants).[40] Small Protestant minorities had little option but to seek partners of another faith. Thus, in Amsterdam almost two-thirds of Remonstrants who married in 1760, in total a mere eleven persons, were joined to a non-Remonstrant, while almost a third of Mennonites did likewise (Table 4.8). Beginning with Blaupot ten Cate in the nineteenth century, many historians have suggested that intermarriage with Calvinists helps to explain why the number of Mennonites and Remonstrants in the Netherlands suffered such a dramatic decline in the eighteenth century. Apparently, many Mennonites and Remonstrants ceased to view the dogmatic differences between their own churches and the Reformed as significant. Either directly through conversion, or through mixed marriage and the raising of their children as Reformed, they were absorbed into the Reformed majority.[41] Perhaps this is why neither the Reformed Church nor secular authorities showed great concern about such marriages. A similar process sapped the strength of Protestant dissent in Britain and Ireland during the same period.[42] By contrast, most Dutch Catholics were determined to marry within their faith. In Bergen only 7 per cent of Catholics married Protestants, while in Amsterdam in 1760 the registers suggest that fewer than 1 per cent did; even if the registers are skewed by hundreds of per cent, still only a modest number of Amsterdam Catholics would have married Protestants. Their avoidance was facilitated in these communities by their large numbers, which made it easier for them to find suitable partners of their own faith. Obviously, though, there also operated, on both sides of the divide, an aversion to Protestant–Catholic marriages. This aversion had been inculcated by generations of church teaching, cultural differentiation, and appropriation by individuals and families of opposing religious identities. In some communities, the aversion may have been so strong that one can indeed speak of a taboo.

Table 4.7 The Noorderkwartier in 1742: distribution of mixed couples

Religious mix	Number of couples (total 70)	% of all mixed couples
Reformed–Mennonite	25	36
Reformed–Lutheran	18	26
Reformed–Catholic	13	19
Other	3	4
Unknown	11	15

Source: A.M. van der Woude, *Het Noorderkwartier* (Utrecht, 1983), 1:132, 3:689 n. 98, based on Nicolaas Struyck, *Vervolg van de Beschryving der Staartsterren*, 2 vols (Amsterdam, 1753), 2:4–83.

Table 4.8 Amsterdam 1760: marriages to spouses of a different faith (according to registration)

Religious group	Total number of marriages	Number marrying spouse of other faith	% marrying spouse of other faith
Remonstrant	11	7	63.6
Mennonite	32	10	31.3
Lutheran	815	103	12.6
Reformed	3089	107	3.5
Catholic	752	4	0.5

Source: Gemeentearchief Amsterdam 5001, inv. nrs. 603–604, 737–738.

In 1794, Petrus Loosjes, a Mennonite scholar living in Haarlem, observed that '[even] with this [current] toleration … it is still rare, though less rare than in earlier times, that persons of different faiths enter into marriage with one another'.[43] As Loosjes's words imply, rarity is a relative thing, but it would be difficult to call mixed marriage a rare phenomenon in eighteenth-century Bergen op Zoom. In Utrecht too, such marriages were at least common enough that most people would have had personal acquaintance with a mixed couple. The question is whether Loosjes was observing accurately the customs of his native Holland. Was it really rare in the Dutch Republic's reputedly most tolerant province for people of different faiths to marry one another? The marriage registers of Amsterdam, Rotterdam, Leiden, Enkhuizen, Maassluis, and Wassenaar all suggest so. They indicate that marriages between Catholics and Reformed Protestants were extremely rare as of the mid eighteenth century (and in Amsterdam's case, already as of 1700), their number rising by the end of the century to levels that were still lower than Bergen's or Utrecht's. As we have seen, however, the reliability of the registers in this regard, which some historians have assumed, is problematic to different degrees, depending on the size of the community and degree of social control to which couples in it were subjected. More reliable evidence seems to confirm that rural intermarriage rates were low in the eighteenth century, indeed lower than overall intermarriage rates were in the early twentieth century, the period when the Netherlands was classically *verzuild*.[44]

If it is the case that intermarriage between Protestants and Catholics was rare in Holland in the early to mid eighteenth century, had rates been higher previously but then declined? Certainly a suspicion is warranted that this was the case, but unfortunately, problematic as our data are for the eighteenth century, our picture of the seventeenth is more holes than canvas. The dearth of systematic sources is itself telling, as it reflects an apparent lack of concern among secular authorities about mixed marriages. Perhaps such marriages were so common and accepted before the late seventeenth century as to be unremarkable (that is what anecdotal evidence suggests), but for the present this remains only a surmise.[45]

Even if, however, by the eighteenth century certain religious groups in Holland rarely intermarried, that does not mean that society had become thoroughly *verzuild*, as Groenhuis claims. Marriage and family life may have formed, along with charity, a particular sphere in which religious groups became segregated from one another, even as their members continued to rub shoulders in neighbourhoods, guilds, militias, and clubs, to attend one another's weddings and funerals, to be business partners and friends, and in other respects too to live together, as Temple said, 'associated by the common ties of Humanity'. As Alexandra Walsham and William Sheils have pointed out in the English context, integration and segregation were not mutually exclusive, all-or-nothing alternatives.[46] Hopefully, by distinguishing between different spheres of activity and forums of interaction, historians of the Netherlands can go beyond their current debate about 'omgangsoecumene' and 'verzuiling'.

Notes
1. I.H. van Eeghen, 'De staalmeesters', *Jaarboek Amstelodamum* 49 (1957): 65–80, quotation at p. 80.
2. William Temple, *Observations upon the United Provinces of the Netherlands* (London, 1673), p. 182.
3. Temple, *Observations*, p. 183.
4. C.D. van Strien, *British travellers in Holland during the Stuart period: Edward Browne and John Locke as tourists in the United Provinces* (Leiden, 1993), p. 228 n. 70, p. 203.
5. Benjamin J. Kaplan, "For they will turn away thy sons": the practice and perils of mixed marriage in the Dutch Golden Age', in Benjamin J. Kaplan and Marc R. Forster (eds), *Family and piety in early modern Europe*, pp. 115–33 (Aldershot, 2005).
6. Frijhoff used the term as early as 1979 in 'La coexistence confessionnelle: complicités, méfiances et ruptures aux Provinces-Unies', in Jean Delumeau (ed.), *Histoire vécue du peuple chrétien*, 2:229–57 (Toulouse, 1979). Adopted by *inter alia* Christine Kooi, 'Sub Jugo Haereticorum: minority Catholicism in early modern Europe', in Kathleen M. Comerford and Hilman Pabel (eds), *Early modern Catholicism: essays in honour of John W. O'Malley, S.J.*, pp. 147–62 (Toronto, 2001), at p. 159; Gabrielle Dorren, *Eenheid en verscheidenheid. De burgers van Haarlem in de Gouden Eeuw* (Amsterdam, 2001), pp. 134, 166; Charles de Mooij, *Geloof kan bergen verzetten. Reformatie en katholieke herleving te Bergen op Zoom 1577–1795* (Hilversum, 1998), p. 628.
7. See e.g. Wikipedia article 'Oecumene', at http://nl.wikipedia.org/wiki/Oecumene (accessed 15 August 2006).
8. See especially Judith Pollmann, *Religious choice in the Dutch Republic: the reformation of Arnoldus Buchelius (1565–1641)* (Manchester, 1999); Willem Frijhoff, *Embodied belief: ten essays on religious culture in Dutch history* (Hilversum, 2002), ch. 2.
9. S. Groenveld, *Huisgenoten des geloofs: was de samenleving in de Republiek der Verenigde Nederlanden verzuild?* (Hilversum, 1995).
10. While some scholars have questioned how unique *verzuiling* was to the Netherlands, other scholars, finding versions of it in other European lands in the modern era, have questioned how useful the concept is even when applied just to the Netherlands. For reviews of the extensive literature on *verzuiling*, see *inter alia* Piet de Rooy, 'Zes studies over verzuiling', *Bijdragen en Mededelingen voor de Geschiedenis der Nederlanden* 110: 3 (1995), 380–92; Peter van Rooden, 'Studies naar lokale verzuiling als toegang tot de geschiedenis van de constructie van religieuze verschillen in Nederland', *Theoretische Geschiedenis* 20 (1993): 439–54; Staf Hellemans, 'Zuilen en verzuiling in Europa', in U. Becker (ed.), *Nederlandse politiek in historisch en vergelijkend perspectief* (Amsterdam, 1993), pp. 121–50. Some aspects of *verzuiling* in the modern era, especially the political ones, patently do not apply to the early modern era, and Groenveld accordingly omits them from his model.
11. J.A. de Kok, *Nederland op de breuklijn Rome-Reformatie. Numerieke aspecten van protestantisering en katholieke herleving in de noordelijke Nederlanden, 1580–1880* (Assen, 1964).
12. See especially J.J. Woltjer, *Friesland in hervormingstijd* (Leiden, 1962).
13. Groenveld, *Huisgenoten des geloofs*, quotations at pp. 71, 70.
14. Dorren, *Eenheid en verscheidenheid*, pp. 133–4 and 163–7; De Mooij, *Geloof kan bergen verzetten*, especially pp. 628–60; Ronald Rommes, *Oost, west, Utrecht best? Driehonderd jaar migratie en migranten in de stad Utrecht (begin 16e-begin 19e eeuw)* (Amsterdam, 1998), especially p. 191; Wiebe Bergsma, *Tussen Gideonsbende en publieke kerk: een studie over het gereformeerd protestantisme in Friesland, 1580–1650* (Hilversum, 1999), pp. 96–150 and 295–404.
15. Bergsma, *Tussen Gideonsbende en publieke kerk*, pp. 96–150 and *passim*.
16. Willem Frijhoff and Marijke Spies, *1650: Hard-Won Unity* (Assen, 2004), pp. 349–57.
17. Joke Spaans, *Armenzorg in Friesland 1500–1800: publieke zorg en particuliere liefdadigheid in zes*

Friese steden: Leeuwarden, Bolsward, Franeker, Sneek, Dokkum en Harlingen (Hilversum, 1999), pp. 227–366.

18 Joke Spaans, 'Katholieken onder curatele. Katholieke armenzorg als ingang voor overheidsbemoeienis in Haarlem in de achttiende eeuw', *Trajecta* 3 (1994), 110–30; Cornelis Cau *et al.* (eds), *Groot placaet-boeck, Inhoudende de placaten ende ordonnantiën ende edicten van de Doorluchtige Hooghmogende Heeren Staten Generael der Vereenighde Nederlanden, ende vande Edele Groot Mogende Heeren Staten van Hollandt ende West-Vrieslandt, mitsgaders van de Edel Mogende Heeren Staten van Zeelandt*, 9 vols (The Hague, 1658–1797) [henceforth cited as *GPB*], 6:355–6.

19 Spaans, *Armenzorg in Friesland*, pp. 314–15.

20 On attitudes, strictures, and ecclesiastic policies toward mixed marriage, see Kaplan, "For They Will Turn Away Thy Sons".

21 F.L. Rutgers (ed.), *Acta van de Nederlandsche synoden der zestiende eeuw* (Utrecht, 1889), p. 201.

22 Judith Pollmann, 'From freedom of conscience to confessional segregation? Religious choice and toleration in the Dutch Republic', in Richard Bonney and D.J.B. Trim (eds), *Persecution and pluralism: Calvinists and religious minorities in early modern Europe, 1550–1700*, (Oxford, 2006), pp. 123–48 (my thanks to Dr Pollmann for allowing me to read her essay prior to publication); Herman Roodenburg, *Onder censuur. De kerkelijke tucht in de gereformeerde gemeente van Amsterdam, 1578–1700* (Hilversum, 1990), pp. 146–204; Manon van der Heijden, *Huwelijk in Holland. Stedelijke rechtspraak en kerkelijke tucht 1550–1700* (Amsterdam, 1998), pp. 218, 236–7, 275.

23 These civil and Reformed Church registers record the vast majority of weddings, though it is known that in the Generality Lands a few Catholics chose to flout the law and be married only by a priest (W.A.J. Munier, 'Peilingen naar de neerslag van overheidsmaatregelen betreffende de huwelijkssluiting in de DTB-registers van stad en meierij van 's-Hertogenbosch gedurende de Staatse periode [1629–1795]', *Nederlands archief voor kerkgeschiedenis* 76 [1996]: 128–88). The same was probably the case elsewhere as well. To ensure, however, that their property was secure and their children were recognized as legitimate, most Catholics went through the procedure of marrying legally, and had a priest 'remarry' (*hertrouwen*) them, that is, solemnise their union in addition. Like Catholics, Protestant dissenters might be 'remarried' by their own clergy, though from the 1650s Mennonites generally ceased to bother with a separate ecclesiastic ceremony.

24 De Mooij, *Geloof kan Bergen verzetten*, pp. 131–41, 578–83.

25 Het Utrechts Archief [henceforth cited as UA], Stadsarchief II, inv. nr. 77, first pages, extract from resolution of city council dated 15 January 1677.

26 UA, Kerkeraad der Ned. Hervormde Gemeente Utrecht (746), inv. nr. 12: Resoluties en notulen, 10 July 1713.

27 These figures include numerous couples whose Catholic member promised to convert to the Reformed faith. Few reliable figures are available for the religious breakdown of Utrecht's population in the eighteenth century but, as of 1650, it was about 33 per cent Calvinist, 35 per cent Catholic, 7–8 per cent Lutheran, 8–10 per cent Remonstrant, 1–2 per cent Mennonite, and 12–16 per cent unaffiliated with any church. Benjamin J. Kaplan, 'Confessionalism and its limits: religion in Utrecht, 1600–1650', in *Masters of light: Dutch painters in Utrecht during the Golden Age* (San Francisco and Baltimore, 1997), pp. 60–71.

28 UA, Kerkeraad, inv. nr. 12: Resoluties, 17 February 1716.

29 These laws were issued in response to a pattern in which Dutch soldiers stationed in or near the Southern Netherlands were falling in love with Catholic girls and consequently being 'corrupted and seduced into popery'. Clearly, though, officials perceived a more general threat. H.F.W.D. Fischer, 'De gemengde huwelijken tussen katholieken en protestanten in de Nederlanden van de XVIe tot de XVIIIe eeuw', *Tijdschrift voor Rechtsgeschiedenis* 31 (1963), 463–85; *GPB*, 6:238–9.

30 *GPB*, 6:527, 8:537, 539, 541–2.

31 *GPB*, 7:813–15 (States General placard dated 3 June 1750), 8:543–4 (States of Holland placard dated 24 January 1755); J. Drost *et al.*, *Gelderse plakkatenlijst 1740–1815* (Zutphen,

1982), p. 64 (States of Gelderland placard dated 19 May 1752). In December 1751 the States General extended the terms of the 1750 placard to all Protestants who married Catholics; *GPB*, 8:539–42.

32 G.J. Mentink and A.M. van der Woude, *De demografische ontwikkeling te Rotterdam en Cool in de 17e en 18e eeuw* (Rotterdam, 1965), p. 46.

33 S. Hart, 'Enige statistische gegevens inzake analfabetisme te Amsterdam in de 17e en 18e eeuw', *Amstelodamum [Maandblad]* 55 (1968), 5.

34 Noord-Holland Archief, Rooms-Katholiek Bisdom Haarlem (275), inv. nr. 256, letters dated July 1789.

35 Jan Wagenaar, *Amsterdam in zijne opkomst, aanwas, geschiedenissen, vorregten, koophandel, gebouwen, kerkenstaat, schoolen, schutterye, gilden en regeeringe* (Amsterdam, 1767), 7:427

36 Gemeentearchief Amsterdam, Schout en schepenen (5061), inv. nr. 3052: Memorieboek van Commissarissen van huwelijkse zaken.

37 Dini Helmers, *'Gescheurde Bedden'. Oplossingen voor gestrande huwelijken, Amsterdam 1753–1810* (Hilversum, 2002), p. 219. Helmers, who questions the accuracy of the marriage registers, does not phrase her finding thus.

38 As of 1730, Noordam believes, the population of Maasland was about 80 per cent Reformed, 20 per cent Catholic. If people there were marrying without regard to religion, about 32 per cent of marriages would have been mixed.

39 Out of a total 6,590 couples, 70 were mixed, of whom 13 were Reformed–Catholic, another 3 were other Protestant–Catholic, and we do not know the religion of either partner in 11 cases. Nicolaas Struyck, *Vervolg van de Beschryving der Staartsterren, en nader ontdekkingen omtrent den staat van 't menschelyk geslagt, benevens eenige sterrekundige, aardrykskundige en andere aanmerkingen*, 2 vols in 1 (Amsterdam, 1753), 2:4–83, as compiled by Van der Woude, *Het Noorderkwartier*, p. 132. According to Struyck, the households in twenty-two villages were 67.1 per cent Reformed, 11.0 per cent Catholic, 17.4 per cent Mennonite, 3.3 per cent Lutheran, 0.1 per cent Jewish, 0.1 per cent unknown, and 1.1 per cent mixed. If people had married without regard to religion, about half of all marriages would have been mixed.

40 50 per cent of Lutheran men and 30 per cent of Lutheran women entered into mixed marriages, 'usually' with a Reformed Protestant, according to Rommes; these figures do not include a significant number of persons whose choice of partner is unknown. Utrecht's Lutheran community declined from around 8 per cent of the total population at mid-century to 3–4 per cent by 1700. Rommes, 'Lutherse immigranten in Utrecht tijdens de Republiek', in Marjolein 't Hart, Jan Lucassen and Henk Schmal (eds), *Nieuwe Nederlanders. Vestiging van migranten door de eeuwen heen* (Amsterdam, 1996), pp. 35–53; Rommes, *Oost, west*, pp. 58, 189 (where he gives a figure of over 40 per cent for Lutheran women).

41 See *inter alia* S. Blaupot ten Cate, *Geschiedenis der Doopsgezinden in Friesland* (Leeuwarden, 1839), pp. 248–9; S. Groenveld, J.P. Jacobszoon and S.L. Verheus (eds), *Wederdopers, menisten, doopsgezinden in Nederland 1530–1980*, 3rd edn (Zutphen, 1993), pp. 198–9.

42 Michael Watts, *The Dissenters*, vol. 1 *From the Reformation to the French Revolution* (Oxford, 1978), 330; for the example of Quakers in Ireland, see Kevin Herlihy, *The Irish dissenting tradition, 1650–1750* (Dublin, 1995), pp. 94–5.

43 Adriaan Loosjes, *Beschrijving van de Zaanlandsche dorpen* (The Hague, 1968, orig. edn 1794), p. 288; quoted in Van der Woude, *Het Noorderkwartier*, p. 132.

44 In 1914, the overall rate of mixed marriage for the Netherlands was 11.2 per cent, while by 1956 it had risen to 16.2 per cent: John Hendrickx, 'The analysis of religious assortative marriage. An application of design techniques for categorical models', Ph.D. dissertation, Katholieke Universiteit Nijmegen, 1994, pp. 144–53. For modern intermarriage rates see also 'Volkstellingen 1795–1971', www.volkstellingen.nl/nl/volkstelling/images/pdf/VT_1971_A2_H2.pdf/VT_1971_A2_H2.pdf (accessed 7 Sept 2006); Dienke Hondius, *Gemengde huwelijken, gemengde gevoelens. Aanvaarding en ontwijking van etnisch en religieus verschil sinds 1945* (Den Haag, 1999), pp. 57–65; Rooden, 'Studies naar lokale verzuiling', summarising nineteenth-century figures for Naaldwijk and Hoorn.

45 One possible difficulty with this conclusion is if our figures, reflecting the sources on which they are based, represent religious allegiances as being firmer and more fixed than they really were. Was every person registered as Reformed, for example, a devoted, consistent adherent of the Reformed faith? How did people register who were uncertain of the truth, or in search of it, or who found truth in the teachings of more than one church, or of none, or who regarded ecclesiastical affiliation as secondary to personal piety? Despite the claims of Kok, Groenveld and others, it is by no means certain that this amorphous group, so large and prominent in the early years of the Republic, disappeared entirely after 1650. This is a crucial but complex issue requiring fuller treatment than is possible here.

46 Alexandra Walsham, *Charitable hatred: tolerance and intolerance in England, 1500–1700* (Manchester, 2006), pp. 207–14; William Sheils, "Getting on" and "getting along" in parish and town: Catholics and their neighbours in England', in this volume.

5

'Getting on' and 'getting along' in parish and town: Catholics and their neighbours in England

WILLIAM SHEILS

In a celebrated lecture Patrick Collinson suggested that, while England, unlike many of its European neighbours in the century following the Reformation, did not experience a major religious war or any successful rebellion in the name of religion, its religious and political life was characterised by a series of cultural conflicts at the parochial level which were rooted in religion. These conflicts took place within mainstream Protestant opinion concerning competing visions of the commonwealth and the place of church and clergy within it.[1] The argument suggested, in contrast to the prevailing historiographical orthodoxy which interpreted early modern English society in terms of social tension between the better-off members of parish society and their poorer neighbours, that the religious language used in these conflicts was more than a reductive response to socio-economic stress.[2] This argument has recently been taken up for the early years of the Reformation by Ethan Shagan, who sees religious change not as the source of local conflict but as an opportunity for local groups to exploit the more general crisis of authority occasioned by religious division in pursuit of a variety of other local rivalries. Thus Shagan focused on divisions within conservative, or Catholic, opinion about how best to negotiate with a heretical regime in the 1550s.[3] In both analyses religious change brought with it conflict within confessional groupings concerning the proper means of engagement with prevailing political authority.

Paradoxically, against these histories of internecine religious turmoil Margaret Spufford and her students have posited an essentially integrationist account of the way local communities coped with the stress of religious change. Based on detailed reconstructions of local communities, their careful studies of religious outsiders on the radical end of the Protestant spectrum revealed much interdenominational cooperation at the parish level in facing the hazards of everyday life, from marketing produce to writing a will.[4] Their work suggests that religious outsiders could function effectively within their rural and urban communities and, even more importantly, were entrusted with and prepared to assume parochial social and political responsibilities. This 'ecumenism of everyday life', to borrow Willem Frijhoff's phrase, is reflected also in work during the past decade on confessional interaction in France and the Netherlands, which has revealed a high degree of mutual, if sometimes grudging, acceptance of religious minorities within localised contexts. How far it was extended to Catholic communities in England remains to be seen.[5]

But first, a word about language. The subtitle of a 2006 study of religious pluralism in early modern England incorporates the language of toleration, 'tolerance and intolerance', and much work since the 1990s on Europe has employed the language of coexistence and confession.[6] Each deploys the terminology of an essentially socio-religious discourse, using a language of differentiation that implies relationships between recognised and recognisable religious communities. Such language has been deployed to good effect when discussing the leadership of religious groups but, when studying those whose religious identity is most frequently adduced not from considered statements of belief but from brief court appearances, incidental listings by a usually hostile authority, or fleeting references in the correspondence of their elite co-religionists, it may be helpful to employ less obviously religious terminology. 'Getting on' and 'getting along' deploy the language of neighbourliness and commonality rather than that of religion and difference, and the use of such 'ordinary language' as a mode of description has been acknowledged by social theorists from at least the 1970s. These two related phrases describe the key social priorities of groups and individuals at this, or any other, period: how to both 'get on' – that is to say, to improve one's social, political and cultural standing in society – and how to achieve this while also 'getting along' – that is to say, maintaining good relations – with the dominant group. These terms, therefore, appear to capture the dilemma of the laity of below-gentry status and offer a means of understanding the variety of responses which were adopted in pursuit of those desired, but not always mutually realisable, ends. As we will see, the strategies adopted by English Catholics in their local communities were responsive to context, and were adjusted according to shifts in power and authority at both local and national level.

Whatever may have been the ambitions of their religious leaders, the strategies adopted by the individuals, households and communities which figure in this paper were probably chiefly aimed at survival in the beginning, followed by a measure of acceptance and, by the eighteenth century, recognition in some cases of their social contribution to their neighbourhoods. The story, however, was far from linear, and varied from place to place, and its complexity is best understood through consideration of case studies. This paper will examine lay Catholics in two rural areas, one crossing parochial boundaries on the northern edge of the moorlands of North Yorkshire and the other in the parish of Madeley in Shropshire, and in two urban communities where Catholics were well represented, the metropolis of London and the regional capital of York.[7]

The rural uplands: Egton

The North York moors lay at the extremity of ecclesiastical power within the huge archdiocese of York; separated from the cathedral city by extensive and sparsely populated uplands, the area proved resistant to Protestant evangelisation for much of the sixteenth century, and with a long coastline to the North Sea it provided several safe landing places for missionary priests when they started to arrive in the mid 1570s.[8] The port of Whitby, with its Catholic lords of the manor, lay at the centre of this recusant community which spread in numbers across three inland parishes and chapelries, Lythe, Egton and Fylingdales, as well as at Brotton, a coastal community to the north.[9] During the later sixteenth century the support of the Cholmleys, lords of Whitby and local magistrates, was crucial to these communities, and they were supported by other minor gentry households, like the Smiths at Egton, whose social power was far less but who could provide protection for newly arrived priests. From the early seventeenth century, however, following the defection of the Cholmleys to the established church, leadership of the community fell to the substantial farming families of the area. This had become apparent from the 1610s when, at Egton, where prosperous farming households such as those of the Hodgsons and Pearsons were identified as recusant in the visitation returns, almost a third of the households in the dispersed chapelry contained at least one Catholic member. These returns represent the chapelry's own assessment of its inhabitants, and consideration of them raises interesting questions about local power and authority. The episcopal visitation of 1615 took place in the context of a vigorous enforcement of the Oath of Allegiance, used by government in the hope of exploiting divisions between those Catholics willing to sign up to it and their more intransigent co-religionists.[10] The returns reveal a sophisticated response on the part of the parochial authorities; they reported on Catholics in considerable numbers, reflecting the well-established reputation of the region, but the names they offered to the authorities included a high proportion of the elderly, women and young single men, not yet householders. This may, of course, have reflected the community but, as recusancy rendered individuals liable to fines and also excluded them from holding local office, it is more likely that the churchwardens presented those whose identification was least disruptive to the smooth working of local institutions. In parishes like Egton, with high proportions of Catholics – about a third of the adult population and including substantial farmers and tradesmen – the smooth running of the community and the fulfilling of parochial responsibilities such as poor relief and law enforcement, required that Catholics share in the burdens of local office. The well-being of the whole community depended upon the inclusion and cooperation of these families.[11] Pragmatism dictated that, where there were significant numbers of Catholics and no strong Protestant leadership, 'getting along' was vital, not only to the Catholics but also to their Protestant neighbours, in order to maintain the local institutions of government, whatever official policy may have desired.

Protestant leadership arrived at Egton, belatedly, in the late 1670s, by which time the local Catholics had formed a settled community of over one hundred individuals, dispersed both socially and geographically throughout the community. They had enjoyed the ministry of a locally born priest for a number of years, and may even have given expression to their sense of local security in the erection of a moorland chapel. That may have encouraged Protestant activism, as, when it was expressed in the 1670s, it came not from the clergy but from the laity, at a time when fear of popery and suspicion of royal policy figured strongly in national affairs, producing popular anti-Catholic demonstrations which coalesced into the alleged Popish plot. At Egton it focused on the maladministration of the chapelry, precipitating a lengthy tithe dispute. The parochial tithes were held by a local gentleman suspected of popish sympathies who, since the mid 1670s, had failed to provide an adequate clergyman, or indeed any clergyman, for the congregation. The dispute rumbled on for fifteen years during which the long-serving Catholic priest in the chapelry, Nicholas Postgate, had been executed at York in the frenzied atmosphere of the Popish Plot; but by 1689, following a petition from the parochial Protestants that 'many of the meaner part of the inhabitants within our said chapelry, wanting a spiritual guide and pastor, were in danger to be seduced and betrayed by popish emissaries and Romish priests lurking amongst us', more stable arrangements were made for providing Protestant ministers. Even at this time, however, relations across confessional lines remained cordial and supportive at the individual and household level, for a number of households themselves contained adherents of differing religious persuasions. However, although the patterns of neighbourly support; witnessing of wills, serving as executors and standing surety for each other in legal and property matters, were not seriously disrupted, it is undeniable that, between 1676 and 1689, the community became polarised in ways which it had not experienced before, with the emergence of two distinct communities, Anglicans and Catholics, of roughly equal size.[12]

At first glance the turbulence of these years did not have much impact on the local community; the number of Catholics remained stable and they were still to be found among the leaders of the local community, filling parochial offices. Numbers alone are not the only test of confessional strength, however, and while the community continued to be led by farming families in the early eighteenth century, the poor and families and individuals from beyond the area, attracted by Egton's reputation and the availability of the sacraments, figured more prominently within the community. In consequence, the eighteenth-century community was very different from its predecessor. It was not the static, introverted community of traditional historiography but a constantly changing one, to a degree that caused concern to clergy, both Catholic and Protestant. This was especially so over the question of intermarriage, which both saw as harmful to confessional stability, and the priest, at least, was right to be concerned: the marriage register of the chapelry shows that a high proportion of marriages recorded towards the end of our period were between partners of different religious persuasions but, significantly, none of these names appears in the detailed list of recusants produced in 1753, suggesting that, at this date, inter-marriage led to Protestantism.

It would seem that, by the 1720s, the relations between the recusant community at Egton and its neighbours had changed somewhat, and the boundaries between the groups had become more clearly marked. Although the Catholic community still retained a core of prosperous farmers contributing to the political and economic life of the parish, it now contained greater numbers of the poor and of incomers.[13] As such, it was probably less well integrated but, if so, probate evidence indicates that, as in other upland regions, ties of kinship continued to be as strong if not stronger than ties of religion, with collateral kin from across the confessional divide being frequently remembered and acknowledged by testators.[14] Nevertheless, by the mid eighteenth century the Catholics of the chapelry had emerged as a more distinct quasi-denominational presence than their forebears had been, and the mixture of accommodation and separation which this entailed was manifest not only among the living, but also in the churchyard where, as the curate of nearby Whitby reported to the archbishop in 1735, 'the papists have a particular part of the churchyard assigned to them for the interment of their dead, and they are married, baptized and interred without his (the curate's) knowing anything of the matter until afterwards, that they come to pay him his fees'.[15]

The manufacturing Midlands: Madeley

Leaving the isolated moorlands of the North for the Midlands, the parish of Madeley in Shropshire was very different from Egton, though it shared its characteristic of dispersed settlement. At the centre of a waterborne distribution network covering much of the midland and western counties and situated in an industrialising part of the country, it was well placed to participate in the modernisation process taking place in English society. With coalmining recorded from the middle of Elizabeth's reign and ironworks established in Coalbrookdale by 1615, new settlements emerged in the parish, doubling its population in the course of the seventeenth century.[16] The parish was dominated by the Brooke family, well-known Catholic recusants who owned the manor and almost all the parochial land, giving the parish the character of a 'closed parish' in which seigneurial power gathered around it a tenantry of co-religionists, protecting them from harassment by authorities, both ecclesiastical and secular.[17] And so it seems, for such evidence as we have for Catholicism before the 1640s is indirect and derives from the names of those who refused to pay church rates or fill parochial offices, or who failed to sign the Protestation Oath in 1642. Among these were leading figures in the community, such as William Webb and Francis Woolf, agents for the Brooke family. This seigneurial protection ended with the imprisonment in the Tower of Sir Basil Brooke in 1641, and the outbreak of Civil War opened up the parish to external scrutiny, which local Protestant gentry were keen to exploit. Even so, relations between Catholic and Protestant within the parish remained relatively cordial, at least in the face of external pressure. They joined together successfully in the mid 1640s to petition their imprisoned landlord to appoint a local man to the vacant vicarage, while in 1648 a group of tenants, led by the new vicar, resisted the attempt by neighbouring Protestant gentry to seize the sequestered industrial workings of the Brooke family. Even under the pressure of civil war, and with an imprisoned Catholic landlord, neighbourly relations proved strong enough to resist the aggressive ambitions of local outsiders to gain control of the economic resources of the community.[18]

After the Restoration of 1660, Catholicism at Madeley became a matter of public record through regular presentments before the church courts and quarter sessions, with 135 individuals accused between 1664 and 1686. The Brooke family continued to offer some protection and probably ensured the absence of any record of Catholics at Madeley in the Compton census of 1676, but their subsequent departure from the manor house and the tensions surrounding the Popish Plot brought confessional rivalries into the open. In 1682 at least thirty-three parishioners, the highest number presented in any year, were brought before the courts. Taxation and parochial records allow us to identify the social status of many of these post-Restoration Catholics, who were distributed throughout the community, The Brookes and their servants stood at the apex, with a scattering of lesser landowners and yeoman farmers, almost equal in numbers to their Protestant peer group, but Catholics were most heavily represented among the skilled workers and craftsmen employed in the ironworkings at Coalbrookdale. The only sector of the parish in which Catholics remained poorly represented was the mining community at Madeley Wood. Madeley Catholics exhibited similar social relations, as did their co-religionists at Egton; although the gentry families tended to seek marriage partners with Catholic families in the neighbourhood, intermarriage was the most common experience among families of lower social status. For some of these, as at Egton, intermarriage tended to result in the family returning to the established church, but the evidence remains equivocal, as the careers of the children of John and Mary York, married in 1680, indicate. Of their six surviving children three were recorded as being baptised by the vicar, the others presumably being baptised by a priest, but even of those baptised by the minister two were noted as Catholics in later life, suggesting that, as at Egton, the recording of baptism in the parish register was that and no more. Further support for this is provided by the survival of benefice accounts for the years between 1672 and 1686 which give receipts for churching after childbirth, a socio-religious rite denounced by the more Calvinist clergy. The rite was performed at Madeley during these years, and even those Catholics who had not had their children baptised by the minister sought its benefits, and were willingly admitted to it.[19] Similar accommodation was also recognised in the matter of burial, where even the two priests dying at this time were received into the churchyard, notwithstanding the existence of a traditional burial ground used by local Catholics ten miles away on the Staffordshire border, in the former nunnery of Brewood.[20]

At Madeley, as at Egton, relations between Catholics and their neighbours, though exacerbated by shifts in national politics, remained robustly supportive, and this extended to the secular sphere. Catholics leased houses from Protestants and even sent their sons to be schooled by the vicar, and each group witnessed and acted as executors to the other's wills. Catholics also fulfilled their parochial duties, several of them serving as overseers of the poor, even at the height of the Exclusion Crisis, and so crucial were they to the running of the parish that, in 1695, six of the sixteen Trustees of the Poor, an incipient parish vestry, were Catholic. It is clear that, as in Egton, parochial life could not be sustained fully without the acceptance and cooperation of the leading Catholic families. Most surprising of all, perhaps, were the contributions which the wealthier Catholic residents made to the fund for the extension of the parish church in 1711, needed to accommodate the growing numbers of coalminers and ironworkers in the rapidly expanding industries. This no doubt reflected a long history of harmonious relations and, perhaps, the presence of a Protestantism sympathetic to the more traditional customs of religion; but it also demonstrates that for leading Catholics, as much as for their Protestant neighbours, confessional rivalries needed to be put aside in order to provide for the pastoral and social benefits of a well-ordered community.

The examples of Egton and Madeley provide essentially integrationist models of local religion, despite their differences; one an isolated moorland parish with no significant resident gentry presence, the other a growing, industrialising community led by a resident Catholic gentry family which participated in county politics. Each exhibited strong leadership among the farming community and skilled craftsmen which survived the periodic upheavals of national politics and whose members participated in parochial office holding and were required to do so by their Protestant neighbours. They forged social, economic and kinship links across confessional boundaries, and though their clerical leaders expressed concern about kinship in particular, this did not threaten the overall survival of the community, even if it did result in some individual losses. Neither parish appears to have been evangelised vigorously by Protestant clerics: the isolation and poverty of the living at Egton made this difficult, and the presence and patronage of the Catholic Brookes at Madeley no doubt kept radicals out. That fact, and the consequent presence of substantial numbers of Catholics in each place, may also have contributed to the survival of more traditional cultural forms, whether the extended kinship connections acknowledged in the Egton wills or the practice of churching at Madeley. It seems that these experiences do not so much demonstrate a model of toleration or of coexistence, each of which implies an emphasis on difference, but more a culture of neighbourliness, in which the survival and advancement of individuals, households and communities were best served by recognition of what was needed to maintain local stability and common prosperity.[21] These imperatives were held to even in those difficult times when national politics emphasised conflict or their clerical leaders preached steadfastness and suffering.

Metropolis and city: London and York

The experience of rural Catholics needs to be placed alongside that of their co-religionists in the towns and cities of the realm. Urban Catholic experience, in which parochial institutions expressed political and social networks less obviously, is poorly chronicled in comparison to the countryside, yet London contained the densest concentration and possibly the largest number of Catholics in the kingdom, though, like the city itself, they were divided and broken up into several overlapping communities and jurisdictions. Catholics were found in sizeable numbers at the Inns of Court from Elizabeth's reign, congregated round the town houses or lodgings of Catholic gentry throughout the period, and lived at court or close to the embassy chapels from the early seventeenth century, while the prisons contained clergy and laity at all times and proved effective arenas for proselytising.[22] What is difficult to measure is the impact of this cosmopolitan, clerical and gentrified Catholicism on those who lived and worked in the metropolis. What is clear is that effective leadership at civic level collapsed quickly after the early years of Elizabeth's reign, when Catholics were removed from office.[23] They continued to participate in parochial government for longer, especially in those parishes like St James, Clerkenwell in the western suburbs, where Catholics were among the more substantial residents, but even here they had either conformed or been removed from office by the early decades of the seventeenth century.[24]

In terms of local leadership and relations with other groups, most London Catholics did not enjoy the patronage or mediation of well-established residents so crucial to their rural co-religionists. How did they survive, and where did they live? The number of recusants recorded in the city wards between 1581 and 1629 was small, the largest presence being 24 in Aldgate, a ward close to the Inns of Court. London Catholics generally lived in the suburbs, and especially the western ones, such as St Andrew's, Holborn and St James, Clerkenwell, also close to the Inns.[25] This suggests that the protection offered by the jurisdictional privileges of the Inns of Court and the support provided by Catholic gentlemen studying at them were crucial factors in the religious geography of the capital. There were also a number of town houses and lodgings in these and adjacent parishes used by Catholics visiting the capital on business. These were also populous parishes with a regular influx of immigrants and a plethora of extra-parochial jurisdictions, which added to the problems of detection and prosecution of offenders and offered cover to religious dissidents, just as the populous eastern suburbs around Hackney did for Puritan radicals.[26] In these expanding communities small groups of Catholics could survive under the cover of a constantly changing population or, like the nine or so recusant families who lived south of the river, in Montague Court, Southwark, under the protection of a Catholic landlord who claimed the area was exempt from local jurisdiction.[27] Elsewhere local officials were not always assiduous in pursuing Catholics, especially in parishes like St Martin's in the Fields, where a number of Catholic gentry had lodgings. During the agitation surrounding the proposed Spanish match in the early 1620s both the public rhetoric from the pulpit of St Martin's and entries in the parish records display strong anti-Catholic sentiments, yet prior to that the local justices had dealt very leniently with Catholics who had failed to take the Oath of Allegiance, and in 1627 the parish officers were pressured by the diocesan officials to be more assiduous in presenting recusants.[28]

If the western suburbs can be said to have had communities of Catholic tradesman and servants, servicing the court and the gentry households of the area, they did not participate in the formal structures of parochial life or establish significant supra-parochial links with their co-religionists. These were found elsewhere. The contacts of a prosperous merchant such as John Tailor, a grocer living in Fleet Street, were citywide; he provided a point of contact for new arrivals in the city and conveyed letters as well as goods to priests, ambassadors and visiting gentry,[29] but he was an exception and for many of the capital's ordinary Catholics London's prisons provided the best opportunity for access to priests and the sacraments, for contact with fellow Catholics, and for hearing news and acquiring books.[30]

Prior to the late seventeenth century London's Catholics were not a recognisable community, but existed in a number of fluctuating congregations excluded from local power structures within a rapidly growing metropolis. As such, they remain elusive to the historian, and were equally shadowy to their contemporaries. This bred suspicion, which was not allayed by the problematic nature of the institutions which sustained Catholic life: the prisons carried the taint of criminality and the suspicion of clerical conspiracy, the jurisdictional privileges of the Inns of Court were viewed by hostile observers as dens of disloyalty protecting young Catholic gentlemen, and the embassy chapels added xenophobic fears to those already mentioned. In such circumstances popular anti-Catholic feeling lay below the surface of the capital's life and could be whipped up at times of political tension. This was true in 1623 in the aftermath of the abortive Spanish match negotiations, when the collapse of a floor in Blackfriars Hall, where three hundred Catholics were assembled to hear a sermon, produced an angry mob that harassed the survivors so violently that even Protestant observers were appalled at its vehemence. The violence was short lived, but the affair produced cheap pamphlets and engravings that revived popular anti-Catholicism.[31] On the eve of the Civil War the local justices moved vigorously against Catholics, prosecuting over 1,400 in 1640, and a year later, in the wake of the Irish massacres, the anti-Catholicism of the London mob was exploited effectively by the parliamentarian John Pym, so that an intimidated monarch left his capital.[32]

Catholic numbers in the capital declined during the Civil War and Interregnum, following the withdrawal of the court and most Catholic gentry, but numbers revived after the Restoration, especially around the embassy chapels and the royal chapels of Henrietta Maria and, from 1662, Catherine of Braganza. By 1670 it was claimed that these chapels could not hold all those Catholics who wished to worship there, and in 1680 it was said that between two and three hundred, mostly women, attended the queen's chapel, though of course many of these would be temporary residents of the capital. The Compton census of 1676 listed 2,069 Catholics in the diocese of London, and in 1680 a list of suspected recusants contained 1,582 names. Numbers then were much as they had been in 1640 and the residential pattern also remained the same, with few living in the city itself and the great majority in the western suburbs; but in contrast to the earlier period, Catholics in the capital now included over three hundred independent tradesmen and craftsmen, including thirty doctors, surgeons or apothecaries, and others associated with luxury trades and services.[33] By the end of the century the capital's Catholics were no longer a shadowy presence, but had emerged as a distinct denominational group, especially in the suburbs. They remained, however, subject to periods of harassment and popular suspicion, as in 1665 when the Great Fire occasioned anti-Catholic and anti-French riots in the capital and elsewhere. During the agitations of 1679–81 London witnessed extravagant pope-burning processions which attracted huge numbers: that at Temple Bar on 17 November 1679 was said to have had 200,000 spectators, and there were other smaller and less-organised examples of popular harassment of Catholics throughout the 1680s.[34] Relations between Catholics and Protestants in the capital were a continuing source of mistrust but, in the aftermath of the Popish Plot, how to deal with Catholicism was also a major source of disagreement within Protestant ranks, between Whig and Tory, Anglican and Dissenter. By the early eighteenth century anti-Catholicism came to be a defining issue within Protestantism as much as a source of interconfessional conflict.[35]

London was, of course, at the heart of national politics and growing exponentially, and the experience of Catholics there may not have been representative of cities generally. York, the regional capital of the North, also felt the force of national politics, but it experienced little structural or demographic change over the period and so may provide a contrasting case study.[36] The city and region were conservative in religion at the start of the period and traditional civic ritual survived into the 1570s, the performance of the *Pater Noster* play in 1573 providing a focus for a major dispute between conservatives and reformers on the Council.[37] By that date the few local Protestants had not received strong support from central authority but, following the arrival of Edmund Grindal as archbishop and the queen's cousin Henry, Earl of Huntingdon as President of the Council of the North,[38] an active policy of prosecuting local Catholics was embarked upon, revealing a sizeable community of about ninety in the city. About two-thirds of these were women, some of them married to conformist husbands from the city's professional classes – doctors and lawyers, or civic office-holders. In addition there were about twenty others, men and women, who were freemen of the city, those who served minor civic office on the common council or in their craft guild and also participated in parochial government as churchwardens, constables or trustees of the poor.[39] Some of these, like the butcher John Clitheroe or the draper George Hall, were substantial tradesmen with citywide connections, and at the end of the 1570s Catholics in the city counted among their numbers two wives and a widow of recent lord mayors. Unlike in London, York Catholics were well connected with the civic elite and living in the heart of the city, but the 1580s witnessed their gradual removal from civic office and a series of ordinances designed to restrict their freedoms; the fine for non-attendance at church was doubled to two shillings and enforced, and all civic officials were banned from attending traditional social events, such as weddings where the blessing of 'bridebeds' took place.[40] The corporation, urged on by Huntingdon, was determined not only to remove Catholics from civic influence but also to strike at their cultural identity, and this policy was extended in the 1590s to the parishes of the city when, in 1593, the corporation, unable to rely on parochial officers, appointed 'honest men' to report those who failed to attend public worship. Implementation was piecemeal and even the central government agencies such as the High Commission and the Council of the North remained compromised by officials with Catholic sympathies or relations. Nevertheless, faced with this concerted policy, Catholicism in the city declined in numbers between 1580 and 1640 to about sixty individuals, surviving within the households of the few remaining professional or prosperous trading families, like the Vavasours.[41] The more stringent policy also filled the prisons with Catholics from city and county and, as in London, these became centres for worship and mission.[42]

For those who did remain Catholic, however, the years after the death of Huntingdon, in 1595, were marked by some mitigation in prosecution as the Council of the North fell under the less energetic purview of Lords Sheffield (1601–12) and Scrope (1612–28), the latter suspected of Catholic sympathies himself. Civic officials took their lead from these two and, while the reply of the schoolmaster John Thorne, threatened with imprisonment for recusancy in 1603, may have been exceptional in its tone, it does reveal the ways in which local Catholics could deploy their contacts to avoid the penalties of the law: 'I will send for Mr Lancelot Turner, for I know he will bring me fower of the best Aldermen in York to be surety for me, And if this will not serve, I know if I were before Mr Buck, he would give his word for me and bid me go home ... some gentlemen in York owes me sixscore and ten pounds ... so that I need not lye in the bottom of Kidcote'.[43] That confidence derived from the interconnectedness which some leading York Catholics had with their Protestant neighbours, who often stood surety for them when they faced arrest, and by the early seventeenth century may also have grown in response to the increasing numbers of Catholic gentry who rented town houses or resided in suburbs like Naburn and Heworth.[44] By this date recusants could be found in small numbers in most parishes of the city, but overall numbers remained modest, hovering around the sixty to eighty mark, and women continued to be heavily represented.

There is no evidence that the establishment of godly rule in York following the siege of 1644 made life any more difficult for the city's Catholics, and the general breakdown in parochial institutions may have made their lives easier, notwithstanding the public stance of the corporation and its preachers.[45] The Restoration of 1660 marked a further break. The failure to restore the regional agencies of central government meant that local institutions were no longer under their scrutiny. In consequence, the corporation records are devoid of references to ordinances against papists, even for the years of the Popish Plot. In 1670 the system of ward searchers was reintroduced, but it was deployed chiefly against dissenters, especially Quakers, rather than Catholics. The only list of recusants produced dates from 1674, clearly in response to the Test Act, and the modest number of recusants in the city did not attract hostile attention from their neighbours. Some of them had good friends among the governing class; Thomas Constable, alderman in 1676 and mayor in 1680, who was closely linked to the East Riding Catholic gentry family of the same name, acted as trustee for other Catholic families seeking to evade exactions on their properties and, in 1673, was one of the trustees for the funds belonging to the Yorkshire Brotherhood, the body of secular priests working in the North. The wife of Thomas Moseley, sheriff in 1679, was from a well-known Catholic county family, and the widows and descendants of Sir Robert and Sir William Belt, respectively mayor and recorder during the Interregnum, both converted to Catholicism. Among the lawyers in York were three Catholics, while two others, including one advocate in the ecclesiastical courts, had Catholic wives, and the medical profession also retained its Catholic connections through Peter Vavasour, Stephen Tailor and the exotically named Alexius Vodka.[46] Clearly the professional services and social connections of these men were not confined to their co-religionists, although by this date there was a growing Catholic constituency for such services.

Between 1660 and 1688 thirty-five Catholic gentry families set up residence or temporary lodgings in the city, which was now benefiting from the commercial expansion of the nation and developing a social season around its administrative and judicial functions.[47] To provide for the spiritual needs of these Catholics, mass was said in a variety of temporary locations and there was no shortage of priests: as many as twenty-two sat down to dinner in 1672 and similar meetings are recorded at other dates. The city was normally the residence of the vicar-general, who organised the Yorkshire mission in 1676, and it is clear that a regular system of roving priests ensured the sacraments to the city's Catholics, whether citizens or visiting gentry.

Socially secure within the city, Catholics were not unduly disturbed during the Popish Plot and may have been protected by their neighbours: only three were reported and no action was taken against them and, while a number of individuals from the county were tried for treason at York assizes, all save two priests were acquitted. According to a priestly observer, even those imprisoned were allowed to lodge beyond the prison walls and only called in when the political temperature of the city rose.[48] Even in these years, anti-Catholicism was not a significant feature of civic politics, but that was to change following the restoration of Catholicism under James II, during whose reign Catholic worship went public with the establishment of a number of chapels. The Governor of York, Sir

John Reresby, estimated the number of Catholics in the city at about sixty and recorded that five rooms were publicly used for Mass, not including that at the convent recently established beyond Micklegate Bar. Schools were also set up and in 1687 the Catholic Bishop, John Leyburne, visited the city, confirming over 240 people, including a number of neighbouring gentry.[49]

There were a few examples of crowd violence against these public expressions of Catholicism, and on Shrove Tuesday 1688 the chapel in Minster Yard was stoned. The arrival of William of Orange later that year, however, occasioned large-scale anti-Catholic activity in the city; Reresby observed that 'the militia troops and some of the gentlemen that were volunteers ... ransacked several houses which belonged to papists (or where they laid) for priests, arms and horses', a view later confirmed by James Torre, who added that the people 'also fell a plundering several private houses of papists'.[50] Following this flurry of activity a Whig hegemony settled on the city, ensuring that no one with Catholic connections penetrated its governing circles, but this was as far as things went. The prohibition on Catholics becoming freemen of the city was never implemented and Catholics, like their Protestant dissenting neighbours, settled into a denominational life style alongside but somewhat apart from the Protestant establishment; their numbers grew to around two hundred in the 1720s and they continued to offer their services to Catholic and Protestant alike, but they also began to develop their own social and welfare institutions with the support of their gentry co-religionists.[51]

Conclusion

The experience of Catholics in London and York differed in some respects. Although Catholics in both places were excluded from formal political power, the leading members of the York community, unlike their co-religionists in the capital, retained access to local political elites. Even the institutions of central government in the North were liable to influence by Catholics. But London and York shared many other characteristics. Both communities relied on gentry support and each was subject to sporadic and sometimes violent outbursts of anti-Catholicism, usually in the wake of national political uncertainty. It seems that politics disturbed popular interconfessional relations more easily in cities than in the countryside, albeit sporadically and without enduring local consequences. Provincial experience in both parish and city produced a local leadership of settled and moderately prosperous lay Catholics that was absent from the capital. The conclusion here is that Catholics and Protestants in local society, when left to themselves, opted to 'get along', and that it was national political concerns, whether real or imagined, which upset this relationship. It was during such breakdowns that the language of religion, in this case that of intolerance, was deployed, and by the end of the period the issue of Catholicism was as much a source of division within local Protestant elites as between Protestant and Catholic. In such circumstances the secular language of neighbourliness describes this relationship more effectively than the religious language of toleration, as consideration of the alternative to 'getting along' suggests.

Our example of the alternative strategy is from York: the case of Margaret Clitherow, executed in 1585 as a result of defiantly refusing to 'get along'. Margaret was well connected to the civic leadership, her stepfather was soon to be mayor and her husband was a prosperous and well-connected butcher, and she was also related to officials of the Council of the North and other government institutions. Hers was a classic case in which it would have been relatively easy to sustain a quiet religious independence had she so wished. Her decision not to 'get along' had profound consequences not only personally but for both communities, Catholic and Protestant. Not only did her trial disturb relations between Catholic and Protestant at a time of heightened tension nationally, but it greatly exercised her Protestant accusers, who did their best to try and find cause not to exact the full penalty of the law, and it also disrupted relations within the local Catholic community, not all of whom endorsed her stand and the implications it had for social and domestic relations.[52] In Margaret's case not 'getting along' was just as disruptive to intraconfessional relations as to interconfessional ones. In such circumstances it is not surprising that for much of the period lay Catholics usually opted for the neighbourly virtues of civil society over those of the confessional state, and that they were supported in this by their Protestant neighbours. Breakdowns occurred and tensions were endemic, but for both Catholic and Protestant laity daily confrontation with the religious other demystified it and made it, if not always likeable, at least bearable, and part of their 'pragmatic adaptation to reality'.[53]

Notes

1 P. Collinson, 'Wars of Religion', in his *The birthpangs of Protestant England* (London, 1988), pp. 127–55.
2 See K. Wrightson and D. Levine, *Poverty and piety in an English village: Terling c1525–c1725*, 2nd edn (Oxford, 1996).
3 E. Shagan, *Popular politics and the English reformation* (Cambridge, 2003), pp. 197–232 and his 'Confronting compromise: the schism and its legacy in mid Tudor England', in Shagan, *Catholics and the Protestant nation: religious politics and identity in early modern England* (Manchester, 2005), pp. 49–68, esp. p. 54.
4 M. Spufford, *The world of rural dissenters, 1520–1725* (Cambridge, 1995), esp. essays by Plumb, pp. 103–32 and Stevenson, pp. 360–87.
5 See above pp. 48–66; for the Netherlands, R. Po-Chia Hsia and H. van Nierop (eds), *Calvinism and religious toleration in the Dutch Golden Age* (Cambridge, 2002).
6 A. Walsham, *Charitable hatred: tolerance and intolerance in England* (Manchester, 2006); G. Hanlon, *Confession and community in seventeenth-century France: Protestant and Catholic co-existence in Aquitaine* (Philadelphia, 1993).

7 The paper does not address the situation of Catholics where they existed in very small numbers, where gentry support was crucial to continuity: for examples of this see H. Aveling, *Northern Catholics* (London, 1963), pp. 87–102 and D. MacCulloch, *Suffolk under the Tudors* (Oxford, 1986), pp. 320, 341–2.
8 Aveling, *Northern Catholics*, pp. 94–6.
9 Emma Watson, "A Stiff-necked, willful and obstinate people": the Catholic community on the North York Moors c.1559–1603', *Yorkshire Archaeological Journal* (2006), 181–204; W.J. Sheils, 'Catholics and their neighbours in a rural community: Egton chapelry, 1590–1780', *Northern History* 34 (1998), 109–33.
10 W.J. Sheils, 'Household, age and gender among Jacobean Yorkshire recusants', in Marie Rowlands, *Catholics of parish and town 1558–1778* (Catholic Record Society, 1999), pp. 131–53; J.P. Sommerville, 'Papalist political thought and the controversy over the Jacobean Oath of Allegiance', in Shagan, *Catholics and the Protestant nation*, pp. 162–83.
11 Sheils, 'Household, age and gender', p. 149, and idem, 'Catholics and their neighbours', pp. 109–33.
12 Sheils, 'Catholics and their neighbours', pp. 123–5; *ODNB* see Postgate, Nicholas.
13 Sheils, 'Catholics and their neighbours', pp. 126–33. There appears to be a greater sense of denominational identity from the early eighteenth century, noticed by Bossy in the drift to the towns, J. Bossy, *The English Catholic community 1570–1850* (London, 1975), pp. 282–87; for marriage and denominationalism see Kaplan, above pp. 62–3.
14 For kin see J. Thirsk (ed.), *The agrarian history of England and Wales*, vol. 4 (Cambridge, 1967), p. 9; M. James, *Family, lineage and civil society* (Oxford, 1974), p. 4.
15 Quoted in Sheils, 'Catholics and their neighbours', p. 109
16 M. Wanklyn, 'Catholics in the village community, 1630–1770', in Rowlands, *Parish and town*, pp. 10–37, the following paragraphs are based upon Professor Wanklyn's work.
17 Bossy, *English Catholic community*, pp. 168–81.
18 For discussion of Catholics between 1640 and 1660 see W.J. Sheils, 'English Catholics at war and peace', in C. Durston and J. Maltby, *Religion in revolutionary England* (Manchester, 2006), pp. 138–57.
19 W. Coster, 'Purity, profanity and Puritanism: the churching of women in England c.1500–1700', *Studies in Church History* 27 (1990), 377–88.
20 *Victoria County History, Shropshire*, 2, pp. 83–4; perhaps significantly, the burials noted by Wanklyn were of female recusants, 'Madeley', pp. 221, 224.
21 K. Wrightson, *Earthly necessities; economic lives in early modern Britain, 1450–1750* (New Haven, 2000), pp. 75–8.
22 For the Inns see G. de C. Parmiter, *Elizabethan Popish recusancy at the Inns of Court* (London, 1976) for the chapels, C. Hibbard, *Charles I and the Popish Plot* (Chapel Hill, NC, 1983) for prisons, see below, n. 30.
23 I. Archer, *The pursuit of stability: social relations in Elizabethan London* (Cambridge, 1991), pp. 45, 257.
24 A. Dures, 'The distribution of Catholic recusants in London and Middlesex, c1580–1629', *The Essex Recusant* 10 (1968), 70; J. Larocca, *Jacobean Recusant Rolls for Middlesex* (Catholic Record Society, 1997).
25 Dures, 'Distribution', pp. 77–8.
26 P. Lake, *The boxmaker's revenge* (Manchester, 2001), pp. 179–85.
27 J. Boulton, *Neighbourhood and society: a London suburb in the seventeenth century* (Cambridge, 1987), pp. 266, 284; M. Questier, *Catholicism and community in early modern England* (Cambridge, 2006), pp. 515–18. After the departure of the Montagues in 1625 Catholics were regularly presented to the justices.
28 Julia Merritt, *The social world of early modern Westminster; abbey, court and community 1525–1640* (Manchester, 2005), pp. 333–5.
29 L. McClain, *Lest we be damned: practical innovation and lived experience among Catholics in Protestant England, 1558–1642* (London, 2004), pp. 159–60.

30 For prisons see *ibid.*, pp. 144–7 and M. Questier, *Conversion, politics and religion in England, 1580–1625* (Cambridge, 1996), pp. 199–200.
31 A. Walsham, *Providence in early modern England* (Oxford, 1999), pp. 272–78.
32 M. Gandy, 'Ordinary Catholics in mid-seventeenth century London', in Rowlands, *Parish and town*, p. 168. This number was over five times larger than any presentment in the previous three years. J. Walter, *Understanding popular violence in the English Revolution* (Cambridge, 1999), pp. 201–34.
33 J. Miller, *Popery and politics in England 1660–1688* (Cambridge, 1973), pp. 22–5.
34 *Ibid.* pp. 103–5; T. Harris, *London crowds in the reign of Charles II* (Cambridge, 1987), pp. 103–6, 183.
35 M. Knights, *Politics and opinion in crisis, 1678–81* (Cambridge, 1994), pp. 219–26.
36 C. Galley, *The demography of early modern towns:York in the sixteenth and seventeenth centuries* (Liverpool, 1998).
37 J.C.H. Aveling, *Catholic recusancy in the City of York, 1558–1778* (Catholic Record Society, 1970), p. 43. One could argue that, until the end of Elizabeth's reign, the region reflected the character of one with a 'Catholic' majority, like Ireland or the Southern Netherlands, see above pp. 158–65, 171–8.
38 P. Collinson, *Archbishop Grindal 1519–83: the struggle for a reformed Church* (London, 1979), pp. 187–215.
39 Aveling, *York recusancy*, pp. 38–44, for links with office-holders see pp. 330–9. Much of the following discussion is based on material in Aveling's book, though his concerns were generally with the internal history of the recusant community.
40 *Ibid.*, pp. 44, 53–4, 193.
41 *Ibid.* pp. 48–85, this excludes the gentry households living in the suburbs, which probably doubled the number of Catholics in the neighbourhood. R. Rex, 'Dr Thomas Vavasour', *Recusant History* 20 (1990), 436–54.
42 Aveling, *York recusancy*, pp. 59–65; Questier, *Conversion, religion and politics*, pp. 50, 159–61, 165.
43 Quoted in Aveling, *York recusancy*, pp. 82.
44 The families of Palmes at Naburn, Thwenge at Heworth each contained priest members.
45 For godly rule in York at this time see W.J. Sheils, 'John Shawe and Edward Bowles: civic preachers in peace and war', in K. Fincham and P. Lake (eds), *Religion and politics in post-Reformation England* (Woodbridge, 2006), pp. 209–23.
46 Aveling, *York recusancy*, pp. 92, 97–8.
47 *Ibid.* pp. 96–7; for York's economy in this period see P.M. Tillott (ed.), *Victoria County History, City of York*, pp. 198–200.
48 Aveling, *York recusancy*, pp. 99–102.
49 A. Browning (ed.), *Memoirs of Sir John Reresby* (2nd edn, Royal Historical Society, 1991), pp. 581–2.
50 Reresby, *Memoirs*, p. 531; Torre, quoted in Aveling, *Catholic recusancy*, p. 103. Leyburne's confirmation listed is printed at pp. 254–6.
51 Aveling, *Catholic Recusancy*, pp. 108–30, figures at p. 122. As Catholics settled into denominational status it is possible that their own social provision created a greater separation after 1700 than had been the case before, especially over marriage; see Kaplan above, pp. 62–3 and Sheils, 'Catholics and their neighbours', p. 125: and Bossy, *English Catholic community*, pp. 132–44.
52 P. Lake and M. Questier, ' Margaret Clitherow, Catholic nonconformity, martyrology and the politics of religious change in Elizabethan England', *Past and Present* 185 (2005), 43–90, esp. pp. 60–7, 84; K.M. Longley, *Saint Margaret Clitherow* (Wheathampstead, 1986), pp. 54–7, 106–11.
53 Hanlon, *Confession and community*, p. 280.

6

Burying the dead; reliving the past: ritual, resentment and sacred space in the Dutch Republic

JUDITH POLLMANN

What was it that suddenly made Reformed minister Paulus Arleboutius feel uneasy, that autumn day in 1633? Had he remembered that it was 1 November, the Feast of All Saints, an important date in the Catholic calendar? Had he perhaps detected a smirk on the faces of the villagers who had come to ask him for the key to the church, claiming that they needed to bury one of their dead? Whatever it was that made him leave his home, when he arrived at the church he found that his misgivings had been entirely justified. The church door was barred from the inside, and once he managed to break it open, he was appalled to see that his place on the pulpit was occupied by an unknown monk who stood preaching to a considerable crowd of people. Forcing his way forward through the crowd, Arleboutius commanded him to stop, 'saying that he had done enough to breach the commandments of their most noble Lords the States' and warning him that that he was filling his 'begging bowl' at the peril of the congregation, who might well get into trouble over this.[1] The monk, unfazed, retorted that it was too cold and wet to preach in the cemetery and sarcastically remarked that, since the States were known as the 'merciful', they probably would not be too hard on the people. As Arleboutius began to argue that the priest should have used a private home, the crowd began to stir. 'Women [were] clinging to my body with tears in their eyes', the minister recalled later, while their menfolk began to threaten him.

Arleboutius was lucky that some people of rank in the crowd intervened and protected him, urging him not to inflame the people further and to let the preacher finish his sermon. Yet while he was prepared to hear the sermon out, when the monk began to prepare for Mass the minister felt that he had to take a stand. Ripping away the altar cloth and throwing it on the floor, Arleboutius sat himself down on the altar, physically preventing the priest from proceeding, until the latter finally gave up and left. It took a while before the 'peasants' in the crowd tired of mocking and threatening the minister, but finally they also departed. At last Arleboutius could relock the door. When he got home he found three concerned colleagues from other villages who had come for a visit and who had been to the church to look for him, only to hear the crowd screaming 'kill him, kill him'. Not being of Arleboutius' heroic mould, they had at that point thought it wiser to return to their colleague's lodgings and pray for his safe return.[2]

The incident on All Saints' Day was one among many that Paulus Arleboutius had to contend with in the few months that he served in the Brabant village of Tilburg. As one of a small group of ministers who were charged with bringing the Reformation to the territories that had just been conquered from the Spanish Netherlands, he had made his entry into the village in early August, escorted by the High Sheriff and a company of two hundred horsemen. No one had been able to find the key to the church, not the chaplain, nor the sexton, nor the churchwardens. Half the afternoon was spent in breaking open the locks and replacing them, before there could be a solemn handover of the key to Arleboutius: 'and then the trumpets sounded, the cavalry left and, finding myself alone among so many impassioned papist peasants, I left for my boarding house'.[3]

Three days later the minister had his first clash with Augustinus Wichmans, the Catholic parish priest who had previously served in the church. Wichmans had begun preaching in the cemetery, while his followers hassled anyone who showed enough temerity to go inside and listen to Arleboutius' competing offerings.[4] In the following months, the minister fought an uphill struggle for control over his new church. Young men kept sneaking into the tower to ring the bells on saints' days of local importance; the cobblers' apprentices did not want to let the day of their patron, St Crispin, pass without hearing the bells rung, while the 'beasts' from the guild of St Barbara also found their way to the bell chamber. Then, on 21 December, the Feast of St Thomas, the church locks were smashed and pastor Wichmans simply hijacked the church. He was apparently trying to force Arleboutius to share the space (perhaps because he knew that such *simultaneum* arrangements existed elsewhere), but because he also reintroduced images and other Catholic paraphernalia into the church the building was becoming virtually unusable for Reformed worship.[5] When Arleboutius complained, the States General confirmed that he had sole rights to the use of the church, but it conveniently left it up to him to negotiate with the guilds and others about the removal of the imagery that offended him.[6] The stalemate was still unresolved when, by May 1634, the military tide turned and Arleboutius was arrested by Southern Netherlandish troops in retaliation for the arrest of a Catholic priest by the States. He spent fifteen months in prison before he was released.[7]

The conflicts surrounding the parish church of Tilburg exemplify how important the possession of church space was for Netherlandish Catholics. This was an emotive issue not just in the years immediately after the Reformation, when the Catholics who had been displaced from their churches had to find alternative locations to conduct clandestine services, but also remained so for centuries to come, long after Catholics had secured alternative spaces in which to worship. Willem Frijhoff is undoubtedly correct in saying that for Netherlandish Catholics regaining the churches became 'a *pars pro toto* for political emancipation'.[8] Yet, although it is easy enough to understand why Catholics should have longed for an end to their position as second-class citizens, it is less obvious why it should have been the issue of church space, more than any other of form of discrimination that Catholics experienced, which remained the focus of their anger. In this chapter I will try to offer an explanation for this phenomenon, arguing that it was, in fact, because Catholics were not completely excluded from their former churches that their stake in this space remained so high.

When Catholic churches were first requisitioned in the rebellious provinces in the 1570s, scenes such as those at Tilburg were rare. In Holland and Zeeland, at that time neither believers nor their priests had the stomach to offer resistance to measures of which no one could predict the duration and the exact outcome. Local authorities who supported the Revolt at that stage either backed the Reformation wholeheartedly or were, at the very least, unwilling to fight for the old Church.[9] By comparison, the behaviour of the Tilburgers and their priest shows not only that five decades of Counter-Reformation activity in Brabant had created a much more conscious and militant willingness to defend the church, but also that the villagers and the Catholic clergy were aware that the minister lacked political backup in the local community, so that they could risk defying the laws laid down by their new overlords in faraway The Hague.[10]

Yet even in places where there had been little open resistance to the coming of the Reformation, Netherlandish Catholics were not easily ousted from the space that they considered sacred and that they believed was theirs. Decades after they had been dispossessed, there were reports of Catholics praying in their former parish churches, at graves and spaces where there had once been altars.[11] The ruins of former churches, and places where important relics and images had once been housed, also continued to attract the devout. In 1598, for instance, it proved difficult to stop women from venerating a cross that had been erected in the ruins of Utrecht's Chapel of the Holy Cross. When the cross was removed, they simply shifted the focus of their worship to the ruins of the altar.[12] A Marian shrine at Heiloo continued to function as a place of pilgrimage long after its holy image had been removed and the chapel had been demolished. In 1653, the Amsterdam furrier and wine merchant Herman Verbeeck ignored the derision of his kinsmen and claimed that his ailing wife benefited much from a visit to

RITUAL, RESENTMENT AND SACRED SPACE

Figure 6.1 Funeral near the ruin in Eikenduinen (1729). Engraving in Jacob de Riemer, *Beschryving van 's Graven-Hage* (1730).

the ruins. The discovery in 1713 of a miraculous well nearby whose water had the power to cure animals further increased the popularity of Heiloo as a sacred site, even among Protestants.[13] In Eikenduinen near The Hague, too, believers continued to worship at the place where there had once been a miraculous image of the Virgin and a relic of the Holy Cross. On Good Friday 1762, almost two centuries after the destruction of the sacred objects that had once been housed there, five or six hundred believers visited the ruins, carrying prayer books and rosaries and unperturbed by the fact that there were no longer any objects to serve as the focus of their devotion (Figure 6.1).[14]

Figure 6.2 Gerrit Pietersz. de Jong, *Portrait of a family in front of the ruins of the chapel of Our Lady of Succour in Heiloo* (1630).

As Alexandra Walsham has shown in her work on Wales, such cults associated with ruins, wells and other elements of the sacred landscape did not simply signify the 'survival' of pre-Reformation practices but were also the result of a conscious Counter-Reformation effort to reappropriate space and to 'mobilise such locations as living links with the holy history of these territories'.[15] That priests in the Netherlands were also interested in reinvesting the landscape with sacrality is evident from the work of the priest and hymnodist Joannes Stalpart van der Wiele (1579–1630). In his hymn on Saint Engelmundus of Velsen he deplored the loss of an opportunity to pray at the saint's tomb, which now lay empty and desecrated, but recommended that the faithful should seat themselves at the nearby brook 'clear and chaste, that once took [the saint's] prayers in its flow', so as to 'find peace before returning to their *steden*'. Since *steden* can mean both 'homes' or 'towns' Stalpart van der Wiele may have wanted to emphasise the contrast between town life and the stillness and holiness of the natural landscape near the brook; in any case, he clearly thought that there were spiritual benefits to be derived from seeking out a landscape that bore the imprint of holiness.[16] Laypeople apparently shared this sentiment; in 1630 a Catholic family had itself portrayed amid the ruins of the shrine in Heiloo, surrounded by those who sought to access the sacred there (Figure 6.2). As Walsham observed for England, the rosary beads in this picture function as a marker of Catholic identity.

In the meantime, however, most of the ritual life of Catholics had shifted to new sites. Compared to their English counterparts, Netherlandish Catholics had found it relatively easy to rebuild some form of ritual life. The Dutch authorities, while denying Catholics their freedom of worship, recognised their 'freedom of conscience' and did not try to force Catholics to attend the Reformed church, or to make them choose between citizenship in the Republic and allegiance to Rome. Certainly in Holland it was more or less accepted that, at home, people should be free to do as they wanted, which meant that it became possible to organise worship in private homes and eventually for such gatherings to grow into sizeable congregations. Arleboutius' advice to the friar who had climbed his pulpit, to hold his sermons in a private home, clearly derived from this practice, even if he was thereby also encouraging him to break the law.

Outside the major towns of Holland and Utrecht the main problem for Catholics was primarily a shortage of priests rather than a shortage of locations. In the countryside and smaller towns people were often unable to see a priest for years on end, so that they had to confess 'in their own heart'. The chances that someone could be given Last Rites on time were often remote indeed. Not many Catholics in the Republic had the opportunity to attend Mass every day or to take frequent communion, practices that were gaining popularity elsewhere in Catholic Europe. Even the devout *kloppen* (lay sisters) of Haarlem could not receive the Sacrament of Confirmation, which had to be administered by a bishop, until the Twelve Year Truce made it safe for them to travel to Brabant.[17] Yet, like their English counterparts, Dutch Catholics proved very good at adjusting to changing circumstances.[18] As Wingens has noted, many important relics were moved and moved again, as military and political circumstances changed, without notable loss in appreciation from Catholics in the Republic, who were prepared to travel far to worship these displaced relics. Pilgrimage sites moved and shifted with time and with political and military fortunes, and believers moved with them. As in England, some images from the churches were given a sanctuary in private homes. In Helmond, a statue of St Peter was kept in the same house and displayed once a year on the saint's feast day right up until the late nineteenth century.[19] Laypeople, and especially the *kloppen*, displayed considerable creativity in forging alternative forms of worship. In the late sixteenth century some lay believers worked simply by themselves to keep the fire burning, going from house to house to read to people and to pray with them. Others gathered relatives and servants to sing and pray together.[20] New sodalities were organised and were encouraged to set up their own house chapels and to shield priests.[21] An inventive *klop* who had visited Ghent and witnessed the devotion to the Stations of the Cross there found a barn on her return home, 'wet and windy' but sizeable enough for such a devotion, which was soon extended with indoor processions for the mysteries of the Rosary.[22] Fictional forms of sacred space were created in print: the *Berch der geestelijcker vreughden* of 1618 guided believers through a programme of songs, meditations and exercises that allowed them to reach the summit of the 'mountain of spiritual joy'.[23] Vernacular singing, sometimes from devotional songbooks specially written for this purpose, was a key element in the many religious gatherings where laypeople met without a priest. This practice apparently became such a central part of religious life in the mission that it encroached on the liturgy and had to be banned by the apostolic vicars.[24]

However, there were dangers involved in clandestine worship. In Friesland, in around 1600, the Jesuits found they had to work exclusively at night-time and could never stay at the same place for more than a day; even by 1650 there were still places in Friesland where priests could not risk wearing vestments while saying Mass. In the Generality Lands, as Charles de Mooij reminds us in his chapter in this book, such precautions were still necessary in the third quarter of the seventeenth century.[25] As in England, the zeal with which local authority figures implemented legislation against illicit religious gatherings differed from place to place and followed the ebb and flow of political developments. But, unlike England, the Republic had no court whose authority extended beyond the individual provinces, and in the myriad of provincial and local jurisdictions it was almost impossible to implement any legislation systematically. As in England gentlemen and nobles could, in practice, often do as they liked on their own estates, so in many parts of the Netherlands they could also openly and successfully defend the *ius patronatus* that gave them the means to maintain the Catholic faith and offer protection and hospitality to Catholics from neighbouring areas.[26] On the eastern and southern borders Catholic enclaves were often not too far away, while in Holland and Utrecht decisions from local courts often carried little weight in neighbouring lordships and towns. Where there was persecution, flight was normally an option, and legal obstruction often a possibility; outside the Generality Lands, anti-Catholic action tended to be haphazard and take the form of harassment, which at its worst could still lead to long periods of imprisonment for priests, but which usually resulted in occasional fines and unenforceable bans.

From the early seventeenth century, moreover, it became increasingly common for sheriffs and Catholic communities to reach a financial settlement by which Catholics paid 'recognition money' in return for being left in peace. As a result of such arrangements, in the early seventeenth century the cities of Holland and Utrecht, especially, saw the emergence of *huiskerken*, permanent spaces for Catholic worship, mostly in private houses that were refurbished for that purpose. The Amsterdam church that is now known as 'Our Lord on the Attic' but that used to be called 'Het hart' (The Heart) is one of the most famous and spectacular surviving examples of such a building. The conversion of the top floors of two houses into a major church was undertaken in 1661 by the merchant Jan Hartman, who planned it for use by his son, who was studying to become a priest. In the event, Hartman's family fell on hard times and had to sell the building, but its Protestant owners were prepared to rent it out to Catholic priests and the Catholic community felt secure enough not just to develop institutionally (by 1700 they had begun to keep a baptismal register and had set up a confraternity) but also to invest heavily in decoration and refurbishing.[27] As Xander van Eck has shown, Catholics throughout Holland were spending lavishly on their *huiskerken*. One of the Catholic 'house churches' in Gouda, for instance, was in 1643 found to contain many paintings, a large silver crucifix, several altars, silver candlesticks and lamps, as well as a beautiful organ.[28] Of course, *huiskerken* were almost always small. If Amsterdam had twenty-six places of Catholic worship in 1681, this was largely because most of them could accommodate no more than a few dozen believers. This put a strain on personnel and priests kept having to ask for dispensation to celebrate Mass more than once a day.[29] It is no surprise that Catholics welcomed the French invasion of 1672, which promised to grant them religious freedom, with immediate attempts to repossess the medieval parish churches. By the eighteenth century, however, the authorities had accepted the presence of secular priests and recognised their *staties*. In more and more towns it was now possible to erect what were really purpose-built, good-sized churches. As long as they were numerous enough to

Figure 6.3 Pieter Saenredam, Interior of the Cathedral of St Jan at Den Bosch (1646).

pay for it, Catholics, certainly outside the Generality Lands, could create church space that was adequate to perform the liturgy and to ensure that a reasonably regular ritual life could take place.

Yet the continuing hold that their former places of worship had on the Catholic imagination suggests there was more at stake than a practical need for space.[30] Just as in England, some Catholics staked their claims on paper. In the late 1580s the young Catholic Arnoldus Buchelius produced meticulous descriptions of Utrecht's ravaged churches in an effort to preserve their past splendour for collective memory. In 1713 the Gouda priest Ignatius Walvis still dedicated the whole of the second volume of his history of Gouda to a description of the medieval churches, their altars, and their donors and the Masses they had founded there, while Van Heussen's monumental *Batavia Sacra* (1714) and its revised Dutch translation aimed to use church history and meticulous descriptions of lost church space to show that 'the Batavian church has not collapsed and not been buried under its own rubble ... but has stood upright'.[31] Others had their concerns expressed in paint. Thus, some patrons of the painter Pieter Saenredam commissioned church interiors in which Catholic objects and symbols were present, thus fictionally repossessing the spaces for Catholic worship. His view of the south aisle of the Reformed Church of St Bavo in Haarlem of 1633, for instance, shows a Catholic priest in full vestments waiting to receive a party who are bringing him a child for baptism. Similarly, while Saenredam had made a drawing of the church of St Jan of Den Bosch after it had been purged of its imagery, in 1646 he painted an interior of the church that showed the space in full Catholic splendour and all decked out for Mass, including an altarpiece that had never been in the building. Clearly a Catholic customer wanted to see the church not as it was, nor even as it had once been, but as it ought to be (Figure 6.3).[32] Frijhoff found examples in the eighteenth century of Catholics who would literally dream of seeing their priests say Mass in the churches that had been in Reformed use for a century and a half, while in Catholic prophecies, too, the return of the churches was a central element.[33] Even after Emancipation, Catholics were so obsessed by the hope that some of their churches would be returned to them that it took until the later nineteenth century before a Catholic ecclesiastical building boom really got under way.[34]

It is important to note, though, that the attitude of Dutch Catholics towards their lost sacred space was also very ambiguous. While on the one hand they considered their former buildings to have been desecrated, on the other it seems that, to Catholics, the medieval churches somehow retained their sacrality – even though they had been stripped of imagery and sacramentals and were now used by heretics. Interestingly, it was the Calvinist Arleboutius who had qualms about preaching in a church that contained images and where 'horrors' were being committed, whereas Tilburg's Catholic village priest did apparently not object to saying Mass in a place that was tainted by heresy.[35] As the continued worship in places like Heiloo and Eikenduinen suggests, destruction and iconoclasm were seemingly not considered to be 'pollutants'. Even in the feverish atmosphere of June 1734, when Catholics in some parts of the Republic were prophesying a bloody day of reckoning that would lead to the repossession of their churches, a comment by a zealous milkmaid that the Franeker church would need a good scrub before it was fit for Catholic use was apparently only prompted by concern about dirtying her skirts if she had to kneel down there.[36] Given that historians have found much evidence for a fear of 'pollution' in the ritual behaviour of both Catholic and Protestant participants in the French Wars of Religion and other religious conflicts (not to mention the house-proud reputation of Dutch housewives), the Catholic indifference to the polluting effects of the desecration of sacred space by Protestants seems quite remarkable.[37] As Walsham shows in her contribution in this volume, English Catholics who were forced to attend Protestant services developed a much greater sense that their parish churches were contaminated by Protestant worship.

Netherlandish Catholics did not have to attend Protestant services, but neither could they afford to completely divorce themselves from the space that had been appropriated by the Reformed. We know that some attempted it: the Utrecht chantry priest Wouter Brock locked himself into his house in 1580 in protest against the Reformation and spent the next thirty-two years indoors, uncontaminated by the new religious and political realities in his society.[38] Yet Wouter Brock's segregation from the Reformed came to an end at his death, as there was no choice but for him to be buried in ground that was shared with believers of all denominations. With a few exceptions, there were no separate burial places for Catholics in the Republic. Although the churches had been appropriated for exclusive liturgical use by the Reformed, the ministers were charged with offering the services of what contemporaries called the 'public church' to all comers. Anyone, regardless of whether he or she was baptised in or a communicant member of a Reformed congregation, could be married and buried in the church and have their children baptised there. In England, recusants could be refused burial in the cemeteries of the Church of England, while Catholics in any case often had to be buried at night, and the issue remained contentious until the emergence of a fixed special fine in the eighteenth century. In contrast, Catholic dead in the Netherlands continued to be welcome both in the cemeteries and in the 'public church', which is why the villagers' request to Arleboutius to give them the key to the church to bury one of their dead had seemed perfectly normal.[39]

At such a funeral, the minister's presence was not required. The Reformed Church in the Netherlands stuck to strict Calvinist notions about burial and the holiness of space. Since it did not believe in intercession for the dead, it did not offer any rituals to accompany burials (even the funerary sermons that became such a feature of Protestant life elsewhere were the exception rather than the rule) and, since it rejected traditional notions about the holiness of consecrated space, it had no theological objections to the burial of Calvinists with non-Calvinists.[40] Moreover, it was not actually the Reformed consistories that decided about church space. In the Netherlands, churchwardens were traditionally city or village officials who operated independently from the consistories and who also ran their finances separately. Since the income from graves was one of their main sources of revenue, they had a vested interest in maintaining church burials for all denominations. Although the Reformed consistories formally disapproved of burials in church, the importance of maximising income for the maintenance of the churches meant that this was a battle they never stood any chance of winning. In any case, Reformed believers retained a strong predilection for church burials, preferably around the time of the Sunday sermon, and graves near the pulpit fetched prices that matched those of the traditionally popular choir location.[41]

Formally, of course, Catholics did not consider the earth of the public church to be sacred; the graves of Catholics had to be sanctified by the addition of some consecrated earth to the coffin in the safety of their homes, where the coffin would also be sprinkled with holy water. Yet, inevitably, the presence of their dead there made it emotionally impossible for Catholics to treat the rest of the church as a contaminated space. Many of them still prayed there, on the graves of their kin, though perhaps not normally during the Reformed Sunday sermons, as the Catholic women of Stolwijk did in 1613.[42] Others wanted to share in the commemorative culture that developed in church spaces during the Golden Age: wealthy Catholic families, like their Protestant counterparts, would commission tombstones and hang up hatchments with their coats of arms in the church. Moreover, the churches were also important civic spaces. Dutch heroes were commemorated on tombstones and churches were widely used for perambulations and socialising, with towns providing organ music and artificial lighting for the entertainment of the public. When the Amsterdam Beguine Cornelia Arens announced that she wanted to be buried 'in the gutter' rather than in the vault that the Beguines retained in their former church on the Begijnhof, this was not, therefore, because she rejected burial in a space that had been defiled by the worship of the English Protestant community who had been granted its use. Rather, she wanted to offer her humble funerary arrangements as a form of penance for those of her kin who had converted to Protestantism. When she died in 1654, the Beguines nevertheless decided to bury her in the vault inside the church, but three times her coffin was interred only to be found standing in the gutter the next morning. Only then was it accepted that her wishes were to be respected; her grave can still be seen in the pavement today.[43]

While the continued burial of Catholics in the public church and its cemeteries was thus never a matter of controversy, the implications of this practice may have been more significant, and more paradoxical, than is usually acknowledged. As long as Catholics buried their dead there, they retained an important physical and spiritual stake in the churches, which meant that resentment at their dispossession could not abate. In all likelihood this was aggravated by the fact that the obligation to bury the dead in a public church or its cemetery placed a considerable constraint on the performance of funerary rituals. Wingens has argued that pilgrimages and processions to the Catholic lordships that were embedded in the territory of the Republic, allowed Catholics briefly to manifest themselves publicly in processions and provided an important form of release for them.[44] Funerals actually presented a much more frequent occasion than did pilgrimages for Catholics to manifest themselves as such in the public sphere and, moreover, to do so fully in front of non-Catholics. Quite how much this was the case is evident from the legislation that the Reformed town government of 's Hertogenbosch drew up in an attempt to root out such public displays of Catholic funerary ritual. In 1630, just after the conquest of the town, the Reformed legislators started by banning crosses and candles in funeral processions, while the white funeral cloths that were used for children and virgins were also prohibited. A tax was levied on the crowns of real or paper flowers that were traditionally placed on the coffins of children and when people started to substitute them with embroidered crowns these, too, were taxed.[45] Even so, in 1637 the consistory of the French-speaking Reformed Church or *ÉgliseWallonne* in Den Bosch could still list a whole range of other Catholic burial customs that offended their sensibilities. In the homes of the deceased, Catholics continued to burn candles and to close doors and windows. Bareheaded girls in white, some of them carrying flowers, still often walked at the head of the funeral processions. And in the churches and the cemeteries themselves, all sorts of undesirable kneeling went on, while prayers were also said in public. That the authorities responded by imposing a blanket ban on all such practices was unusually draconian; no town in Holland would have dreamed of interfering with burning candles at home, for instance. There is some evidence that this legislation was enforced. In 1682 a miller was fined a hefty 25 guilders for having shut windows and doors, and having stopped his windmill. But reports of experiences elsewhere in the Generality Lands suggest that eventually the authorities may have been forced to accept that some public Catholic practices could not be rooted out.[46]

That this was certainly the case in the more tolerant Holland is evident from details of local and confessional burial practices recorded by the physician and ethnographer Johannes Le Francq van Berkhey in the third part of his massive work, *Natuurlyke Historie van Holland* of 1776.[47] At that time, in villages in

South Holland Catholics indicated the death of someone in the house by standing a board with a cross on the doorstep (Protestants fixed ribbons to the door). As in Den Bosch, Catholic children or adults who died as virgins were decked out with crowns of herbs and flowers, which were buried with them.[48] While the main funeral cloths in Holland, too, were black, a length of white cloth was draped across the coffin of anyone who had died a virgin. Catholic corpses were carried round the church or cemetery two or three times; the dead of other denominations only once, if at all.[49] Biers or burial cloths were left over open graves for some days or sometimes weeks – Berkhey thought because this allowed Catholics to cover the grave with a cross in lieu of the wooden crosses that were no longer permissible.[50] Catholics could not hold their liturgy for the dead in public, but they were 'extremely committed to the ringing of bells for the dead', and apparently they were given the scope to do so. After an initial Reformed ban on bell-ringing – which was traditionally believed to fend off the devil and therefore considered superstitious – Holland's Reformed synod had in 1585 allowed its reintroduction on the grounds that it served to call mourners to the funeral.[51] In Catholic practice this was extended to include bell-ringing to announce a death, on days when a corpse was lying in state, and for several hours on the day of the funeral. Berkhey's own city of Leiden catered for this potentially controversial demand by ringing the bells every day between 1.30 p.m. and 2.30 p.m., the most popular and affordable time to bury one's dead (nocturnal funerals being all the rage and therefore very expensive). In other towns, bell-ringing was arranged individually. Although Berkhey noted that, in Amsterdam, it could become quite expensive if one wanted bells rung on every day that a body was not yet buried, it was clearly perfectly usual to invest in some ringing.[52] The two and a half hours of bells that accompanied Hermannus Verbeeck's funerary arrangements in 1681 were not excessive.[53]

Yet, while funerals presented an occasion for Catholics ritually and publicly to manifest themselves as 'different' from people of other faiths, it seems unlikely that these occasions were experienced as a form of 'release', in the sense of the pilgrimages that Wingens studied. None of the public funerary rituals that Catholics succeeded in salvaging was sacramental, and their priests were excluded from them, while the rituals that were essential for the souls of the dead had to be performed in the privacy of Catholic homes. Moreover, funerals were multi-confessional affairs. Perhaps because the Reformed Church had never formulated an alternative to the funerary sociability of the pre-Reformation era, both neighbours – sometimes formally organised in *gebuurten* – and guilds continued to play an enormous, and often legally defined, role in funerals.[54] Since there was never any strict spatial confessional segregation in Dutch cities, and since guilds, too, were confessionally mixed, Catholics were likely to be accompanied to their last resting places by people of different denominations. In all likelihood, neighbours would come to pay their last respects at the home of the dead, while in many areas they were also involved in the last hours of life, and probably helped lay out the corpse for the funeral. In this way, non-Catholics took part in, or at least showed respect for, rituals that might not be sacramental but that were most certainly distinguishable as Catholic. Conversely, this obliged Catholics not to flaunt their rituals in front of their neighbours. When, in 1625, the Reverend Schevenhusius found crosses standing around the grave of a young woman to whose funeral he had been invited, he destroyed them himself.[55] It would be interesting to know whether Protestant neighbours were tactfully excused from obligations that would involve them in 'superstitious' practices, or whether they objected to the presence of candles and rosaries used when laying out the corpses of their Catholic neighbours, for instance.[56] It is more likely that they accepted and perhaps even copied such customs. Berkhey noted several instances of rituals, like the use of flowers for the virginal deceased, which were 'mostly' in use by Catholics but which also had their Protestant adherents. On the other hand, when Utrecht Catholics were given freedom of worship during the French occupation of 1672–73, and so could bury their dead with all the ritual required, this immediately led to frictions with the Reformed consistory, who decided that their members were now being exposed to 'superstitious practices'. For the first time, the city council found it necessary to stipulate that the pallbearers should be of the same religion as the deceased.[57]

Recent research has shown that, in everyday life, Catholics in the Dutch Republic were constantly forced to engage with non-Catholics, and mostly did so peaceably.[58] The multiconfessional character of funerals may serve as yet another illustration of what Frijhoff has called *omgangsoecumene*, or 'social ecumenicity'. Yet funeral rituals also represented a frustrating compromise in which the ritual repossession of space was surreptitious and only temporary and was always constrained by rules and traditions that forced both Protestant and civic characteristics onto what, to Catholics, was an occasion of religious and salvific significance. Although priests were allowed to be buried in the churches, for instance, they were never given tombs that would express their role as priests. The many surviving painted portraits of priests on their deathbeds served as substitutes for befitting tombs, but a painting was definitely second best.[59]

Burials, therefore, reminded Catholics more of the world they had lost than of the opportunities they retained in a multiconfessional society. It is not surprising that many of those who could do so preferred to carry their dead from the multiconfessional atmosphere of the cities to the old, sacred sites which only had meaning for Catholics. Many of the Catholic dead of The Hague were buried at the ruined shrine at Eikenduinen; Jansenist priests were buried in a vault under the ruined choir of the church in Warmond; while by the late eighteenth century Leiden's wealthiest Catholics had their dead taken by boat to be buried at a site in Oegstgeest that was associated with St Willibrord.[60] If burying the dead had to mean reliving the past, it was preferable to do so without any nasty reminders of the present. Yet such burials were not for all; many places had no consecrated ground nearby and, since transportation involved the payment of fees at both ends of the journey, the expense was considerable.[61] Most Catholics had no alternative but to take their dead to spaces that for them were both sacred and desecrated, and in a manner that asserted their otherness but that did not allow them to express its full spiritual significance. Faced with such ritual picking at the scabs of the past, it is perhaps no wonder that it was sacred space, more than anything else, which kept the wound of dispossession open.

Notes
1. Paulus Arleboutius, 'Cort verhaal van het gedenk-waardigste 't welk is gepasseert omtrent mijnen dienst tot Tilborgh anno 1633', in [W.J.F. Juten and G.C.A. Juten], 'Invoering der hervorming de Tilburg', *Taxandria. Tijdschrift voor Noordbrabantse geschiedenis en volkskunde* 15 (1908), 200–20, at p. 206.
2. Arleboutius, 'Cort verhaal', p. 206.
3. *Ibid.*, p. 203.
4. See Frans Hoppenbrouwers, 'Augustinus Wichman. Zielenherder te Tilburg in crisistijd (29 november 1632–11 januari 1643), *Tilburg. Tijdschrift voor geschiedenis, monumenten en cultuur* 14 (1996), 3–14, also available at www.historietilburg.nl/tijdschrift/15/431.htm.
5. W.A.J. Munier, *Het simultaneum in de landen van Overmaas. Een uniek instituut in de Nederlandse kerkgeschiedenis* (1632–1878) (Leeuwarden, 1998).
6. Transcripts of the resolutions of the States General about the situation in Tilburg at http://lopabo.fontys.nl/jan_prive/Resoluties_RVS/RRS.175.doc.
7. Arleboutius, 'Cort verhaal'.
8. Willem Frijhoff, 'Katholieke toekomstverwachting ten tijde van de Republiek. Structuur en grondlijnen tot een interpretatie', *Bijdragen en mededelingen betreffende de geschiedenis der Nederlanden* 98 (1983), 430–59.
9. On this lack of resistance see e.g. Judith Pollmann, 'Countering the Reformation in France and the Netherlands. Clerical leadership and Catholic violence, 1560–1585', *Past and Present* 190 (2006), 83–120.
10. Very similar scenes occurred in the Lands of Overmaas, see Munier, *Het simultaneum*, pp. 55–9.
11. See e.g. J.J. Graaf, 'Uit levens der "Maechden van den Hoeck"', *Bijdragen voor de Geschiedenis van het Bisdom Haarlem* 18 (1892), p. 61; A.Th. van Deursen, *Mensen van klein vermogen. Het kopergeld van de Gouden Eeuw* (1978–81; this edn Amsterdam 1992), pp. 274–5; Willem Frijhoff and Marijke Spies, *1650. Hard-won unity, Dutch culture in a European perspective 1* (Basingstoke and Assen, 2004), p. 384.
12. Arnoldus Buchelius, *Commentarius rerum quotidianarum in quo ... occurrent exempla*, University Library Utrecht Ms. 798, 2 vols, II, fols 233 r–v.
13. Peter Jan Margry, 'Heiloo, O.L. Vrouwe ter Nood', database Bedevaartplaatsen at www.meertens.knaw.nl; Hermannus Verbeeck, *Memoriaal often levensraijsinghe*, ed. Jeroen Blaak, egodocumenten 16 (Hilversum, 1999), pp. 95–6.
14. Jan van Herwaarden, 'Eikenduinen. Heilig Kruis/O.L. Vrouw van Eikenduinen', both in the database Bedevaartplaatsen at www.meertens.knaw.nl. For similar examples in the Generality Lands, see e.g. Marc Wingens, *Over de grens. De bedevaart van katholieke Nederlanders in de zeventiende en achttiende eeuw* (Nijmegen, 1994), p. 49.
15. Alexandra Walsham, 'Holywell. Contesting sacred space in post-Reformation Wales', in Will Coster and Andrew Spicer (eds), *Sacred space in early modern Europe* (Cambridge, 2005), pp. 211–36, citation from p. 220.

16 Cited and discussed in Charles van Leeuwen, *Hemelse voorbeelden. De heiligenliederen van Joannes Stalpart van der Wiele, 1579–1630* (Nijmegen, 2001), p. 264.
17 Graaf, 'De levens der "maechden", p. 17.
18 Alexandra Walsham, 'Translating Trent? English Catholicism and the Counter Reformation', *Historical Research* 78 (2005), 288–310, at pp. 300–8.
19 Wingens, *Over de grens*; A.M. Frenken, 'Nog enige bijzonderheden betreffende de parochiekerk van Helmond', *Bossche bijdragen* 8 (1926–27), 77–102, at p. 93.
20 H.J. Oldenhof, *In en om de schuilkerkjes van Noordelijk Westergo. Katholiek leven in Frieslands Noordwesthoek onder de Republiek (1580–1795)* (Assen, 1967), p. 119.
21 Frijhoff and Spies, *1650*, p. 378.
22 Graaf, 'De levens der "Maechden", p. 108.
23 Ludovicus Makeblijde, *Den berch der geestelycker vreughden, vol hemelsche hoven ende melodieuse lof-sangen: tot voorderinghe der christelicker Deughdtsaemheyt* (Antwerp, 1618). Published in Antwerp, it was aimed specifically at readers in the Republic. On the Catholic use of songs see Charles van Leeuwen, 'Zang als wapen van de contrareformatie', in Louis Grijp et al. (eds.), *Een Muziekgeschiedenis der Nederlanden* (Amsterdam, 2001), pp. 232–8 and Judith Pollmann, 'Hey ho, let the cup go round! Singing for reformation in the sixteenth century', in Heinz Schilling and István György Tóth (eds), *Religion and cultural exchange in Europe, 1400–1700, Cultural Exchange in Europe I* (Cambridge, 2006).
24 Van Leeuwen, *Hemelse voorbeelden*, pp. 160–8.
25 Oldenhof, *In en om de schuilkerkjes*, pp. 127–8.
26 John Bossy, *The English Catholic community, 1570–1850* (London, 1975), pp. 149–94.
27 Marco Blokhuis, Guus van den Hout et al., *Vroomheid op de Oudezijds. Drie Nicolaaskerken in Amsterdam: de Oude Kerk, Ons' Lieve Heer op Solder, de Sint Nicolaaskerk* (Amsterdam, 1988). On the tradition of *huiskerken*, see Benjamin J. Kaplan, 'Fictions of privacy. House chapels and the spatial accommodation of religious dissent in early modern Europe', *American Historical Review* 107 (2002), 1031–64.
28 Xander van Eck, *Kunst, twist en devotie. Goudse katholieke schuilkerken, 1572–1795* (Delft, 1994). See also Xander van Eck, 'From doubt to conviction. Clandestine Catholic churches as patrons of Dutch Caravagesque painting', *Simiolus. Netherlands Quarterly for the History of Art* 22 (1993–94), 217–34.
29 Oldenhof, *In en om de schuilkerkjes*, p. 197.
30 Judith Pollmann, 'The cleansing of the temple. Church space and its meanings in the Dutch Republic', in José Pedro Paiva, *Religious ceremonials and images. Power and social meaning (1400–1750)* (Coimbra, 2002), pp. 177–89; Frijhoff, 'Katholieke toekomstverwachting'.
31 M. Aston, 'English ruins and English history. The Dissolution and the sense of the past', *Journal of the Warburg and Courtauld Institutes* 36 (1973), 231–55; Judith Pollmann, *Religious choice in the Dutch Republic. The reformation of Arnoldus Buchelius (1565–1641)* (Manchester, 1999), pp. 60, 84–6; J.W.[Ignatius Walvis], *Beschrijving der stad Gouda, bevattende een verhaal van de stads grondlegginge ... en beruchte vrome mannen*, 2 vols (Gouda and Leiden, 1713); Hendrik van Heussen, *Batavia Sacra* (Brussels, 1714). The words are those of his translator, H. van Rhijn, cited in P. Polman, *Katholiek Nederland in de Achttiende Eeuw*, 3 vols (Hilversum, 1968), I, pp. 238–49, 356.
32 Gary Schwartz and Marten-Jan Bok, *Pieter Saenredam. The painter and his time* (London, 1990), pp. 74–5, 79, 89, 204–6, argue that the commissioning of the view of St John in Den Bosch may have related to the controversy over the survival of the sodality of Our Lady, which had a chapel in the church. However that may be, it was clearly not intended as an exact record of the past. We do not know who commissioned it, but its first recorded owner was a Catholic. For another example of such fictions in paint see Xander van Eck, 'Dreaming of an eternally Catholic Utrecht during Protestant rule: Jan van Bijlert's Holy Trinity with Sts Willibrord and Boniface', *Simiolus* 30 (2003), 19–33, at pp. 27–8.
33 Frijhoff, 'Katholieke toekomstverwachting', p. 447.
34 Blokhuis, Van den Hout et al., *Vroomheid op de Oudezijds*.

35 Arleboutius, 'Cort verhaal', pp. 209–10.
36 Oldenhof, *In en om de schuilkerkjes*, p. 356.
37 First discussed with reference to the French wars of religion by Natalie Z. Davis, 'The rites of violence. Religious riot in sixteenth-century France', *Past and Present* 59 (1973), 51–91, and see e.g. Penny Roberts, 'Contesting sacred space. Burial disputes in sixteenth-century France', in Bruce Gordon and Peter Marshall (eds), *The place of the dead. Death and remembrance in late medieval and early modern Europe* (Cambridge, 2000), pp. 131–48. On notions of purity and cleanliness in the Dutch Republic see Simon Schama, *The embarrassment of riches. An interpretation of Dutch culture in the Golden Age* (London, 1987).
38 Cornelis Cornelisz, 'Utrechts Kronijkje', in J.J. Dodt van Flensburg (ed.), *Archief voor kerkelijke en wereldsche geschiedenissen, inzonderheid van Utrecht*, 7 vols (Utrecht, 1838–48), VI, pp. 9–134, at p. 65.
39 Bossy, *The English Catholic community*, pp. 140–4; Will Coster, 'A microcosm of community. Burial, space and society in Chester, 1598–1633', in Coster and Spicer, *Sacred space in early modern Europe* (Cambridge, 2005), pp. 124–43, 136; David Cressy, *Birth, marriage and death. Ritual, religion and the life-cycle in Tudor and Stuart England* (Oxford, 1997), pp. 465–6.
40 Pim den Boer, 'Naar een geschiedenis van de dood. Mogelijkheden tot onderzoek naar de houding ten opzichte van de dode en de dood ten tijde van de Republiek', *Tijdschrift voor Geschiedenis* 89 (1976), 161–201; C.A. van Swighem, *Een huis voor het woord. Het protestantse kerkinterieur in Nederland tot 1900* (The Hague and Zeist, 1984). For a helpful discussion of notions of holiness and space in Calvin see Christian Grosse, 'Places of sanctification. The liturgical sacrality of Genevan Reformed churches, 1535–1566', in Coster and Spicer, *Sacred space*, pp. 60–80, and for discussions of attitudes to burial in other European Calvinist churches, the essays by Spicer, Roberts and Murdock in Gordon and Marshall (eds), *The place of the dead*.
41 Van Swighem, *Een huis voor het woord*, p. 255; Marcel Portegies, *Dood en begraven in 's Hertogenbosch. Het Sint Janskerkhof, 1629–1858* (Utrecht, 1999), p. 108.
42 A. Th. van Deursen, *Bavianen en sleukgeuzen. Kerk en kerkvolk ten tijde van Maurits en Oldenbarnevelt* (Assen, 1974), pp. 394–5.
43 Ger van Dijk, *Van 'der beghinenlande' tot begijnhof. De geschiedenis van het begijnhof van 1307 tot heden* (Amsterdam, 2004), pp. 33–5.
44 Wingens, *Over de grens*.
45 Portegies, *Dood en begraven*, pp. 60–1, 97, 113, 121.
46 Ibid., pp. 51, 121, 126. These complaints are very similar to those noted in England, Cressy, *Birth, marriage and death*, pp. 401–2. For the survival of such practices elsewhere in the Generality Lands, see e.g. Frenken, 'Nog eenige bijzonderheden', p. 87.
47 Johannes Le Francq van Berkhey, *Natuurlyke Historie van Holland*, 9 vols (Leiden and Amsterdam, 1769–1811), vol. 6, part III-3.
48 Ibid. p. 1848.
49 Ibid. p. 1908.
50 Ibid. pp. 1881, 1914.
51 Portegies, *Dood en begraven*, p. 52.
52 Berkhey, *Natuurlyke historie*, III-3, pp. 1903–6.
53 Verbeeck, *Memoriaal*, p. 25.
54 Den Boer, 'Naar een geschiedenis van de dood', pp. 182–4; Portegies, *Dood en begraven in 's Hertogenbosch*, pp. 51, 102.
55 Van Deursen, *Mensen van klein vermogen*, p. 274.
56 H.L. Kok, *De geschiedenis van de laatste eer in Nederland* (Lochem, 1970), pp. 154–77, but note that he is often hazy on the recorded date of the customs he is describing. Berkhey, *Natuurlyke historie*, pp. 1848, 1903.
57 Utrechts archief, Archief van de hervormde kerkeraad, minutes of the consistory, vol. 10, 14 March 1573; Utrechts Archief, SA II, Stadsbestuur, vol. 121-8, fol. 233v, resolutie of 23 July 1673. I am most grateful to Dr Bertrand Forclaz for sharing his notes on this material with me.

58 For current thinking on this issue see H.F.K. van Nierop and R. Po-Chia Hsia (eds), *Calvinism and religious toleration in the Dutch Golden Age* (Cambridge, 2002).
59 Paul Dirkse, '"En ging gerust te bedt, om vrolijck op te staen in 't ander leven". Doodsportretten van Noord-Nederlandse katholieke geestelijken', in Bert Sliggers, *Naar het lijk. Het Nederlandse doodsbedportret 1500–heden* (Haarlem, 1998), pp. 116–47, at p. 143, notes that in the Southern Netherlands the genre was almost unknown.
60 Van Herwaarden, 'Eikenduinen'; Berkhey, *Natuurlyke historie*, 1994–5; Adriaan Wittert, *Lijkreden op het zalig afsterven van den zeer eerweerdigen heere Franciscus Dominicus Meganck* (Leiden, 1775).
61 Berkhey, *Natuurlyke historie*, III-3, p. 1960.

7

Beads, books and bare ruined choirs: transmutations of Catholic ritual life in Protestant England

ALEXANDRA WALSHAM

Late medieval Christianity has aptly been described as 'a ritual method of living'.[1] It hinged upon the solemn performance of rite and revolved around the assumption that the sacraments dispensed by a spiritually elite caste of priests were conduits of an invisible grace that was essential to individual salvation. Underpinned by the conviction that the material world was a touchstone of holiness, it was also a religion of immanence that engendered a vast repertoire of holy objects and a dense and complex geography of sacred places. The advent of Protestantism in England presented an acute theological and practical challenge to this system of practice and belief. Monasteries, convents and shrines were dissolved, destroyed, and allowed to decay into ruin and the churches and cathedrals in which congregations had prayed for centuries were appropriated and iconoclastically purged of 'abominable idols' to befit them for reformed services. Hearing Mass was prohibited upon pain of a crippling fine and the missionary priests whose activities were vital to the spiritual health of the faithful were hunted down, tortured and executed. In 1585 harbouring and helping them became a treasonous crime for which laypeople themselves could pay the ultimate price. Although the intolerance of the Elizabethan and Stuart state was tempered by the combination of connivance and charity that typified interconfessional relations at the grass roots, the fact remains that English Catholic ritual life in the late sixteenth and the seventeenth centuries was severely constrained. Catholicism's clandestine existence as an underground church forced it to dispense with much of the ceremony and apparatus that had hitherto shaped liturgical experience and inhibited its ability to mimic the rich baroque culture of worship that was evolving in Italy, Spain and southern Germany.

Drawing on comparative material from other parts of the British Isles, this essay examines the subtle and creative transmutations in devotion and piety that took place against the backdrop of both Protestant repression and the programme for the renewal of the Church of Rome encapsulated in the decrees of the Council of Trent. As we shall see, orthodox practices were reconstituted in ways that allowed them to survive and indeed to thrive as emblems of anti-heretical defiance, but also sometimes brought them into tacit conflict with Tridentine priorities, not least because they were conducted in arenas and spaces which instinctively evaded ecclesiastical oversight, notably the home and the natural environment. Close attention to these processes illuminates the mixture of cooperation and tension that marked relations between the Catholic clergy and laity and sheds incidental light on the extent and nature of interaction between the members of competing faiths in English society, who co-inhabited a landscape that remained encrusted with potent memories of the nation's Catholic past.

During the first decade of Elizabeth's reign, some committed Catholics found it possible to maintain the central ritual aspects of their faith without too much difficulty. Time-serving Marian priests contrived to ensure that the parish communion resembled the Mass, despite the revised wording and rubrics of Cranmer's liturgy, while those ejected from their livings celebrated the traditional rite for the conservative in private. By the 1570s and 1580s, however, these muddled compromises were disappearing as a reformed ministry began to emerge from the universities and a new breed of Counter-Reformation missionaries entered the country. Despite the relative scarcity of the men who could perform the miracle of transubstantiation, this holy mystery remained the chief focus of lay devotion. Those who had greatest access to it were the members and retainers of wealthy families like the Meynells and Treshams who played such a significant role in sheltering the beleaguered priesthood. In these devout households it was quite possible to adhere to the pattern of frequent reception of the Eucharist recommended by the fathers of Trent, and to do so in settings that sought to emulate the ornate splendour of Continental oratories. At Battle in Sussex, for instance, the secular priest Richard Smith said Mass for his mistress, Lady Magdalen, Viscountess Montague three times a day in a sumptuous chapel complete with an elevated altar and separately carved pulpit and choir.[2] The fervent penitential piety Dorothy Lawson practised at St Anthony's, near Newcastle-upon-Tyne, in the 1620s combined frequent, searching examination of conscience with formal weekly sessions with her resident chaplain and confessor, William Palmes. Ironically, it was perhaps in the devout households in which Catholicism found asylum in Protestant countries, rather than the conventional unit of the parish and diocese, that the early modern clergy may have had the best opportunity to nurture habits of rigorous internal scrutiny.[3]

Londoners, meanwhile, could resort to foreign embassies and to prisons in

CATHOLIC RITUAL LIFE IN PROTESTANT ENGLAND 105

which captured priests were incarcerated, sometimes with a surprising degree of licence and freedom.[4] By contrast, country Catholics outside the orbit of aristocratic and gentry enclaves had to make do with occasional visits from peripatetic missionaries. In the Welsh Marches, Mass was said at secret locations under cover of night, the equipment being conveyed in 'mails and cloak-bags', and in early seventeenth-century Lancashire the Benedictine Ambrose Barlow could be found performing it in humble farms, cottages and barns.[5] Such circumstances were difficult to reconcile with the strict regulations regarding the administration of the sacrament formulated by the Council of Trent, not least its explicit ban on celebrating the Eucharist in private, domestic dwellings. The casuistry manuals studied by trainee priests in the seminaries afford a glimpse of the ceremonial concessions and dispensations that had to be made in this environment: Mass could be said on portable altars, without proper vestments and using tin chalices and old missal books, provided that the 'superstitious' rubrics were systematically deleted. It was permissible to perform it in any location 'except at sea or on a river' – indeed the 'prudent' missionary would 'not even shrink from a bridal chamber' if this was 'the most suitable place' available, 'because it is not polluted since it is not a church'.[6]

For many ordinary Catholics, access to the sacraments must nevertheless have remained a rarity. This did not necessarily mean a slow drift into the arms of the Protestants; the determined found ways of compensating for what the Jesuit Robert Southwell called the 'sacred hunger' that afflicted them.[7] One method was the path of mental contemplation: deprived of the physical experience of seeing and eating the host, some reproduced it mystically and inwardly, receiving the spiritual benefit of the sacrament without recourse to human intermediaries. Jan Rhodes reminds us that this trend owed as much to the proliferation of printed texts and the burgeoning culture of reading as it did to the Reformation, but such tendencies were arguably intensified where qualified priests were in short supply.[8] Devotional practice also found ways of counteracting the danger of remaining in a state of mortal sin for several weeks or months. John Radford conceded that in an emergency Christ ('who ... is not so bound to his Sacramentes but that without them he can give his grace') might directly grant absolution to penitents who displayed 'perfecte contrition, and sorrow', even if they had not confessed to a priest.[9] It is easy to see how anxious individuals might latch on to an exception and stretch it to become an everyday rule, and how pastors sensitive to the real fears of their flocks could condone a process that simultaneously had the potential to erode their sacerdotal role.

Attention should also be drawn to the development of confraternities of the rosary. Energetically promoted by the Jesuits, these congregations were envisaged as a 'spiritual safe haven' for humble Catholics who had no other means of protecting their souls against the pains of purgatory. Emphasising the benefits of the papal indulgences attached to membership of them, Henry Garnet presented such sodalities as 'a most holesome medicine, and comfortable sanctuary', as well as a mechanism for invoking the aid of the Virgin Mary for 'rooting out heresie' from their native country: 'the beades must be to our afflicted brethren, in steed of all maner of armour or weapons'.[10] Whether founded by missionary initiative or springing up independently, local cells of recusants and church papists were mutually supportive prayer groups led by literate lay teachers. As in the Netherlands, the circumstances of persecution compelled zealous laypeople to play a more active part in directing and organising worship than they could in contexts where Catholicism was dominant.[11] The very feature of these voluntary societies that troubled some Counter-Reformation bishops on the Continent – their capacity to compete with the parish and to encourage popular participation in a kind of supplementary liturgy – was, paradoxically, a positive asset in England.[12]

The rosary also provided scope for a form of individual devotion that was easy to conceal in a hostile Protestant climate. Small, mobile and readily hidden in a pocket or fold of one's clothing, it could be recited in a variety of locations, including roads, woods and fields. Neither night, nor blindness, nor illiteracy precluded its fruitful use. Presented by missionaries as 'the unlearned mans booke', it was also an aspect of the solitary piety exercised by devout ladies and gentlemen in their chambers and closets.[13] Uniting traditional practice with a vibrant new Tridentine variety, for many it became 'a manifest badge or token of the Romane Religion': 'when she walked abroad, by her beads or cross which she use to wear about her neck', Lady Magdalen Montague defiantly 'professed herself to be a Catholic, even to whatsoever heretical beholders'. For others too, it was symbol of subversive resistance to Protestantism. In the Tower of London, John Gerard fashioned rosaries from orange peel with his tortured hands and passed them to his fellow prisoners wrapped in paper onto which he had written invisible messages with citrus juice.[14]

Along with medallions, crucifixes and Agni Dei, the rosary fell into the technical category of the sacramental. The efficacy of this class of blessed objects was not automatic (as for the sacraments) but dependent on the disposition of the recipient, and the difficulty they had always presented was that, once consecrated by the clergy, they could be removed and employed by the laity in ways that defied institutional control. Seminary priests might stress that they should be used as an aid to inner contemplation, but laypeople often treated them superstitiously, as direct gateways to the sacred. In an effort to contain these tendencies within the boundaries of orthodoxy, the Jesuits introduced their own approved brand in the guise of Ignatius water.[15] However, the tensions that surrounded items that functioned, in Bob Scribner's words, as 'a kind of popular Catholic version of the priesthood of all believers' can only have been enhanced where

CATHOLIC RITUAL LIFE IN PROTESTANT ENGLAND 107

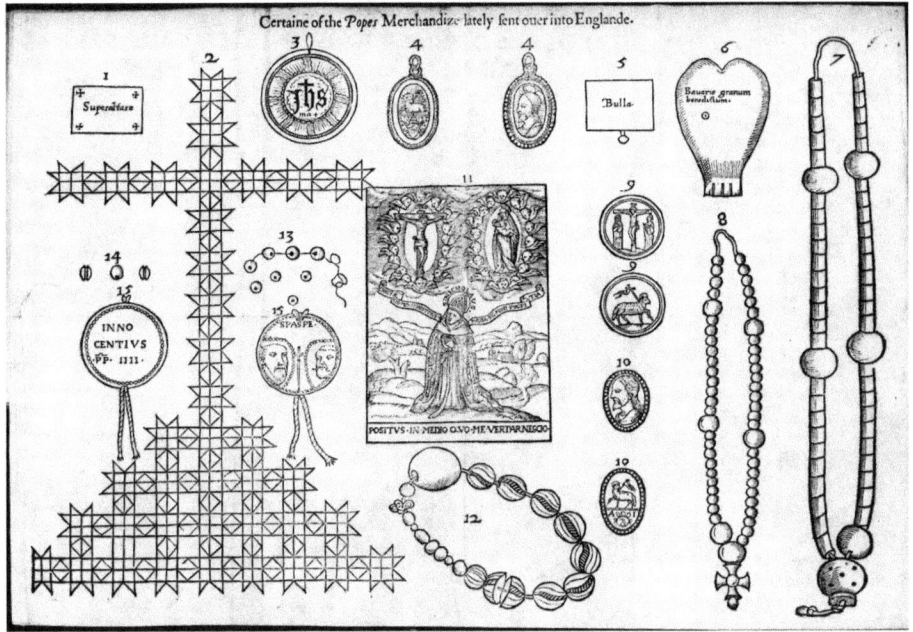

Figure 7.1 B[ernard] G[arter], *A newe yeares gifte dedicated to the popes holiness and all the Catholikes addicted to the sea of Rome* (London, 1579).

Rome became a subjugated minority faith.[16] Described (and perhaps inadvertently advertised?) in detailed diagrams that taught Protestants how to identify 'the Popes wares and merchaundize' (Figure 7.1),[17] the temptation to regard such emblems as quasi-magical talismans was evidently hard to resist, and not just among the rural peasantry. The inventory of suspicious items found in the London house of George Brome and his sisters Elizabeth and Bridget in 1586, which included sacred grains, a long paper painted with the name of the Virgin in red and yellow letters, and 'a box with peces of massinge cake', hints that even the well-informed laity may have seen them as a potent arsenal of supernatural power.[18] In some circles, it may be suggested, post-Reformation English Catholicism was a religion less reliant on sacraments than it was on sacramentals.

The ever-expanding reservoir of relics presented similar problems for ecclesiastical discipline. Too numerous to bring neatly under clerical supervision, fragments of medieval saints saved from ransacked churches and monasteries were supplemented by the possessions and body parts of recently martyred priests such as Edmund Campion and Henry Garnet gathered from the foot of the gallows. Preserved and exploited by laity for thaumaturgic purposes, the 'holy radioactivity' they emanated had a disturbing tendency to engender secondary relics. After one of the nails that had allegedly fastened Jesus to the Cross was

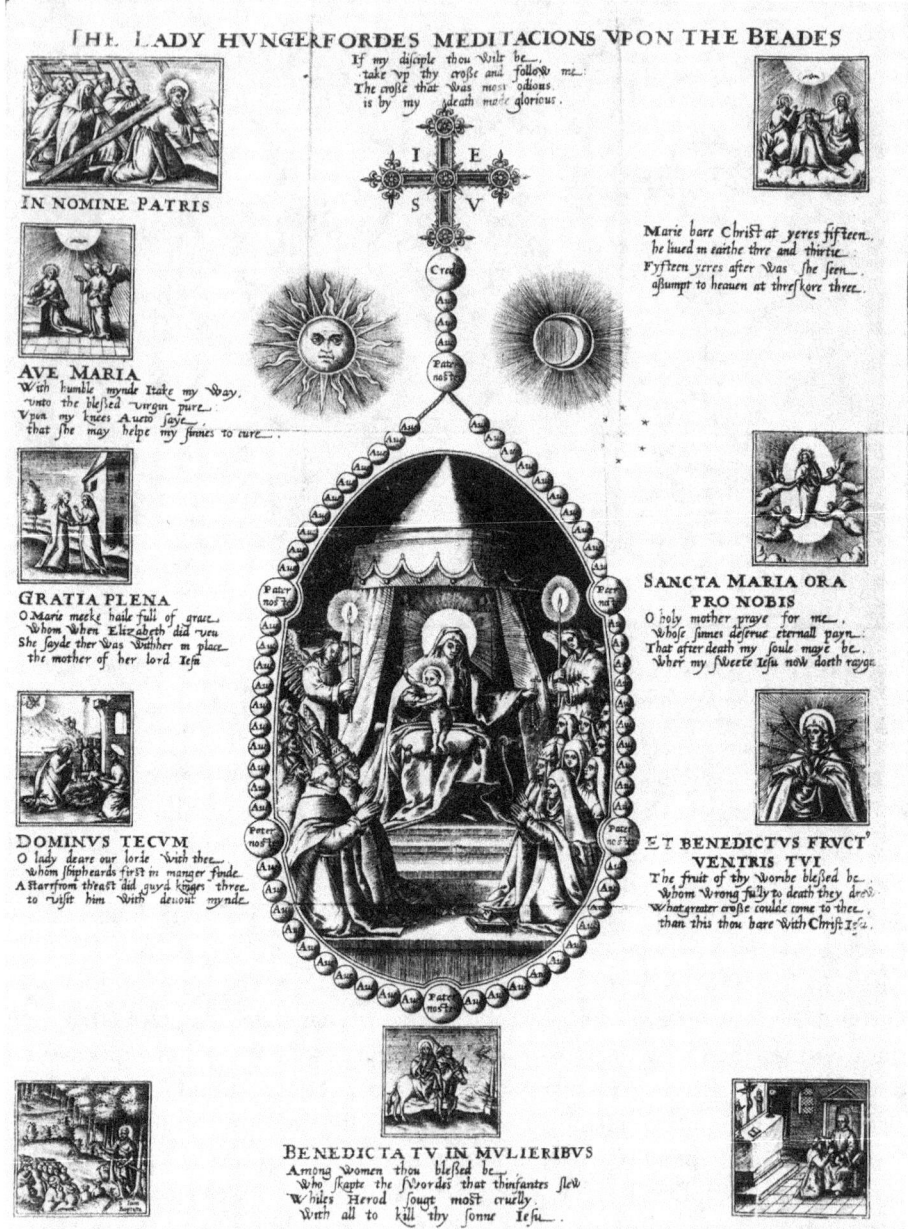

Figure 7.2 John Bucke, *Instructions on the Use of the Beades* (Louvain, 1589).

confiscated by Bishop John Jewel, the empty linen case in which a faint impression of it was preserved began to work wonders. The spontaneous proliferation of unauthorised ritual objects provided many opportunities for the development of religious practices that hovered precariously on the edges of, if not outside, the official liturgy.[19]

Sacramentals and relics operated in symbiosis with pictures and books, from which they cannot always be sharply distinguished. Medieval images of piety still remained usable, even when the attached indulgences had been crossed out, and engravings of the rosary, such as the one John Bucke incorporated in his *Instructions* (1589), might function just as well as real strings of beads where these were unobtainable (Figure 7.2).[20] More generally, texts were vital in securing the survival of a Church under the cross. The English missionaries made clever use of books as 'dumb preachers' and surrogate pastors and they undoubtedly played a critical part in shaping the devotional lives of Catholic laypeople. The York matron Margaret Clitherow delighted in reading the Rheims New Testament and Thomas Kempis's *Imitation of Christ* and mimicked the religious by learning Our Lady's Matins in Latin; in prison Philip Howard bestowed many hours on the sacred task of writing and translating works of piety as well as on perusing tracts by Luis de Granada and the Holy Scriptures.[21] Lower down the social scale, pocket-sized manuals of prayers contributed to creating real and virtual textual communities.[22] Though they were envisaged as a mechanism for cultivating an obedient and orthodox laity, they too could be interpreted and appropriated in ways that liberated men and women from deference to the clergy. Liturgical books designed to guide believers through the Mass could end up functioning as a partial substitute for it and hagiographical works could likewise be put to inappropriate uses: copies of Pedro de Ribadeneira's *Life of Ignatius Loyala* effected so many miracles in early Stuart England that it was reported that even illiterate persons had begun to purchase it.[23] Texts assumed a key role in a ritual culture in which devout interiority was often curiously intertwined with crypto-materialist piety.[24]

These transmutations need to be examined alongside distinctive forms of behaviour that developed in response to the Elizabethan Settlement. First and foremost is the rite of studied refusal that was recusancy. Official spokesmen like Sir William Cecil may have insisted that the demand for outward conformity did not amount to an intrusion into the conscience, but for Catholics taught that external actions could materially affect their fate in the afterlife, this claim must have seemed transparently specious. No less of a predicament for the loyal majority was the fact that, in an Erastian state, church attendance had ineluctable political overtones: it was a gesture of allegiance to the monarch and nation.[25] By contrast with the situation in the Dutch Republic, where membership of the Calvinist Church was only voluntary, this inevitably transformed recusancy into a confessional act, 'a peculiar signe distinctive betwixt religion and religion', in the words of Robert Persons.[26] To conform, on the other hand, was to be branded with the mark or livery of the heretical Antichrist, '*character bestiae*'.[27] The fiscal penalties and stints in prison suffered by those who deliberately withdrew from Protestant services served to nurture in them 'a caste-like consciousness of superior purity'.[28] This bold ritual of omission was both buttressed by and in turn served to reinforce the notion that the spaces in which the reformed liturgy was celebrated were contaminated and contaminating. Catholics were warned that they exposed themselves to the 'peril of infection' by entering Protestant churches. Polluted by the use of the Prayer Book, these were places where the souls of the faithful were in danger of being poisoned by the speech and company of false teachers: the preaching of the heretics, declared the seminary priest Richard Bristow, was liable to 'creepe upon you like a canker'.[29] The case of the Norfolk gentleman Francis Wodehouse reveals that for some recusants the very buildings in which Protestants held their 'pestilential meetings' became a place of psychological torment. Tempted to submit after many years of stalwart nonconformity, upon entering the church he was seized with such agony that he seemed to be 'carrying within himself an unendurable hell'.[30]

Recusancy, of course, coexisted with partial or occasional conformity. Representing an attempt to reconcile religious principle with patriotism and spiritual purity with self-preservation, church papistry persisted not only despite the strictures of the clergy but also with their tacit approval. Schismatics often expressed their dissent even while participating in Protestant worship. Chief among these was ritual refusal to receive the fraudulent sacrament of the reformed Eucharist. Others mentally or physically withdrew into their pews and perused devotional books, muttered prayers or fingered their rosaries. At Etwall in Derbyshire, Sir Nicholas Gerard chanted psalms when the parson commenced the liturgy; in Suffolk Sir Thomas Cornwallis sat reading while others knelt, in a provocative inversion of the rubrics; the Hereford brewer John Vicars walked up and down the outer aisles of the cathedral to avoid having to listen to the proceedings.[31] As magistrates in Lancashire lamented in 1590, the presence of such Catholics in church 'dothe more hurte, then theire absence did'.[32] Interestingly, at least some of these compromises rested on the assumption that the ecclesiastical structures usurped by Protestants had not been so sullied that they were rendered illegitimate as locations for Catholic devotion. As in the Netherlands, where we find occasional cases of women praying in quiet corners of churches even after they had been transformed into the 'caves of murderers',[33] many Catholics seem to have believed that these medieval buildings still, in some sense, belonged to them. In England, this may have been reinforced by the residues of 'popish superstition and idolatry' left behind by the imperfect Reformation which so aggrieved the Puritans. Protestants worshipped in buildings filled with many reminders of the old religion: stained glass windows, funeral monuments, medieval fonts, stone crosses, roof angels, and even statues of the saints. As Richard Bristow remarked, 'the very forme & fashion' of churches, chapels, sepulchres and chancels was a testimony to the Catholic faith: are they not, he asked, 'our cognisance and badges?'[34]

This attitude is also apparent in the answers that some casuists offered in response to queries about whether the faithful could contribute towards the repair of their parish churches or decorate them for seasonal festivals. This was permissible because 'the use of consecrated churches by schismatics and heretics for their sermons and other filthy practices does not prophane them'; erected and endowed by their ancestors, they remained 'the property of Catholics'. 'As long as there is the slightest hope of England returning to its original faith and religion', it was their duty to 'stop them falling into ruin' so that in due course they could be rededicated to true liturgical use.[35] It is clear from these examples that Catholics and Protestants in England did not live in a completely segregated landscape: they competed to define the meaning of spaces with pre-existing religious associations.

Similar ambiguities emerge in relation to rites of passage. Here the process of separation from parish churches lasted well into the eighteenth century. There were several incentives for consenting to an officially recognised christening. High infant mortality might mean that an infant could die unbaptised if one had to wait too long for a visit from a priest and the problem was compounded by the Tridentine drive to ensure that the ceremony was carried out as swiftly as possible. Bringing one's children to be sprinkled in a Protestant church could also stave off allegations of illegitimacy and prevent attendant legal wrangles, though some split hairs by bribing their local vicars to enter their sons and daughters in the register.[36] Catholics also continued to be married by reformed ministers. The clergy were struggling to eliminate this solution to 'the unpleasantness of being suspected of adultery' in the 1580s, but it was still common among the 'inferior sort' as late as 1760, when Bishop Richard Challoner lamented that many went 'through the whole ceremony of the Common Prayer Book, either for want of instruction ... or for want of resolution'.[37] The determination of recusants to be interred in the consecrated ground of their parish churches and churchyards was even more pronounced. While some were prepared to tolerate Protestant solemnities to secure this, others adopted the strategy of forcing entry into church buildings and sacred enclosures. In the North-West, Catholics persisted in performing traditional customs at home and pausing at wayside crosses before conveying the corpse to the church, where they hastily buried it themselves, entreated the minister to omit the office, or departed before it was read.[38] Elsewhere, burials were more surreptitious and nocturnal events. In 1631, the church of Holton in Oxfordshire was broken into by a group of parishioners (both Catholic and Protestant) and a grave dug for the body of an excommunicated recusant, Mrs Elizabeth Horseman, under the communion table.[39] At Allensmore in Herefordshire, a yeoman's wife called Alice Wellington was buried before sunrise in Whitsun week 1605: from his bedroom window the vicar saw a procession of some forty or fifty persons carrying bells, crosses and burning tapers, but the body was laid to rest before he had time to dress and put a stop to the illicit funeral.[40]

Sometimes, though, neither guile nor violence was necessary, because Catholic burials occurred by discreet arrangement with the Protestant incumbent.[41] Writing of seventeenth-century Ireland, where Catholics also continued to seek to be interred in parish churches used for reformed worship and even erected their own mortuary chapels directly adjacent to them, Clodagh Tait remarks perceptively on the irony that for stalwart recusants this 'in effect meant eternal attendance at Protestant service'.[42] It was as if they were laying posthumous claim to spaces that had been unjustly annexed by the heretics. Perhaps some shared the sentiment of the Dutch priest Petrus den Hollander, who cried out with joy, when he heard on his deathbed that he was to buried in the church at Rhoon, 'My dry bones will shout that the church occupied by the uncatholics belongs to the Catholics!'[43]

These phenomena underline the neighbourly accommodations and mutual manifestations of tolerance that so often softened confessional divisions and enmities in both Britain and the Netherlands.[44] There is, though, evidence of a stronger impulse for separation on the Catholic side and of greater rigidity on the part of Protestants. Many preferred their children to be christened by priests, like the Welsh mother who carried her infant to the disused chapel of a Cistercian monastery at Margam and had the rite performed by the missionary Morgan Clynnog in 1591.[45] Private baptism was clearly on the rise by the 1590s, when a draft bill drawn up by William Cecil, Lord Burghley proposed levying £100 on every person who suffered their children to be baptised illicitly by the Catholic clergy. This finally became law in 1606, when it was also made an offence for papists who were *not* excommunicates to be buried outside their parish graveyards – a measure that reinforced the intermingling of the bodies of the members of competing faiths.[46] Instances in which contumacious recusants were refused plots in hallowed ground induced the Lancashire gentleman William Blundell to enclose a piece of his own estate so as to provide a resting place for the blessed dead. Over eighty persons were buried there between 1611 and 1631, when the High Sheriff arrived with a posse of men to destroy the walls, deface the stone crosses and dig up some of the graves.[47] Others reappropriated neglected former chantry and nunnery lands.[48] Weddings too were increasingly conducted outside church precincts – in fields and under trees, as well as in private houses – and not always in the presence of the priesthood. Extra-sacramental espousal was widely accepted as valid and necessity often outweighed the efforts of the Counter-Reformation Church to eliminate clandestine marriage.[49] Catholic ritual life in the post-Reformation period was thus shaped by a triangular matrix of forces:

the priorities of Catholic renewal, the exigencies of Protestant oppression and the trials of lay intransigence.

An underlying thread of the preceding discussion has been the way in which persecution compelled the faithful to create a new geography of the sacred centred on the household and the landscape. Ejected from parish churches, as Frances Dolan has remarked, Catholics developed 'a tactical and fluid relation to space'.[50] This theme may be explored further by considering how far the practice of pilgrimage proved able to survive the shock of the Reformation. Protestantism's mocking attack on the credulity and corruption that underpinned the tradition of undertaking ritual journeys to national and local shrines precipitated a phase of humanist caution and restraint with the Catholic Church which lasted until the final quarter of the sixteenth century. Gradually, however, this gave way to a renewed Counter-Reformation enthusiasm for pilgrimage a form of 'spiritual medicine for heretical poison'. Assisted by the patronage of the papacy and powerful rulers like the Wittelsbachs and Habsburgs, sites like Altötting in Bavaria, Loreto in Ancona, and Halle and Scherpenheuvel in the Spanish Netherlands became compelling symbols of baroque exuberance and confessional bellicosity.[51]

English recusants of wealth and status had both the opportunity and the means to participate in this resurgent international culture of religious tourism, but how did Catholics of lesser rank satisfy the combination of spiritual yearning and recreational release for which the liminal experience of pilgrimage had long proved such an effective solution? Firstly, they continued to make visitations to abandoned chapels and crumbling monastic buildings. The 'bare ruined choirs' immortalised in William Shakespeare's lyrical phrase remained the focus of much covert devotion. For northern Catholics, the Holy Island of Lindisfarne was a favoured destination,[52] while in Somerset, the dissolved Benedictine Abbey and Tor at Glastonbury exerted a magnetic attraction. In 1586 an old man who lived a mile from Brandon Hill, the place where Joseph of Arimathea and his companions had reputedly chosen to settle, could be found visiting the decaying foundations, climbing up to the summit on his knees and carrying with him a reliquary rescued from the monastery as an amulet 'against the molestation of spirits'.[53] In 1614, the High Commission prosecuted thirty recusants from Yorkshire who had been caught praying on the eve of the Virgin's feast day at the ruined Lady Chapel situated on a bare hill above the former Carthusian priory of Mount Grace. Despite the fact that it was roofless and exposed to high winds, people could be found there in silence for hours on end.[54] In Elizabethan Wales, papists frequented ancient chapels linked with holy wells 'in heapes' and 'very superstitiously' on their patronal saints' days, 'by great journeys barefoot'.[55]

The same activities troubled Protestant officials in Ireland and Scotland, where, as at Heiloo in the United Provinces, Catholics circumambulated the

Figure 7.3 Pilgrimage to the ruined chapel of Our Lady of Runxputte near Heiloo. Engraving by Frederik de Wit, first published Amsterdam c. 1690.

shrines, or the sites on which they had once stood, all visible trace of the sacred structures themselves having long since disappeared (Figure 7.3).[56] In Peebles, local Calvinist elders and magistrates lay in wait at the ruined Cross kirk for those who visited it solemnly at Beltane, and Lady Aboyne undertook an annual thirty-mile pilgrimage to the Chapel and Well of Grace in the parish of Dundurcas in the Scottish Highlands, walking the last two without shoes.[57] Where buildings had been demolished, it was not uncommon for devotion to be displaced onto revered spots in the natural landscape. The pattern at Hasselt, where pilgrims reverted to the sacred field (*heilige stede*) after the chapel dedicated to the Holy Sacrament was destroyed and the site turned into a dunghill, can be found replicated at Fernyhalgh in Lancashire: here the faithful assembled at the nearby Lady Well, the former chantry itself having been torn down during the reign of Edward VI.[58] Churchyard and wayside crosses were other landmarks with powerful associations with the medieval Church. In Jacobean Yorkshire the ecclesiastical courts made sporadic efforts to stop people praying at the mere stumps of vandalised monuments left behind by zealous iconoclasts.[59]

Much of the activity carried out at neglected locations was private and unsupervised, but other activities were deliberately harnessed by the missionary priesthood as a polemical tool and given official sanction by the grant of papal indulgences. In 1676, for instance, Clement X promised complete remission of sin to those who resorted to the chapel of St Michael the Archangel on Skirrid-Fawr near Abergavenny, a mountain supposedly cleft by the earthquake that occurred at the moment of Christ's crucifixion, and prayed for 'the extirpation of heresies and the exaltation of Holy Mother Church'. Mass gatherings at Michaelmas were still being noted in the 1750s.[60] Two sites with medieval traditions of pilgrimage, however, stand out from the rest: St Winifred's Well in North Wales and St Patrick's Purgatory in Lough Derg. Eagerly promoted by the Counter-Reformation clergy as important rallying points for a Catholic Church under fierce assault, both drew large and increasingly audacious crowds during the course of the period, despite recurrent efforts to suppress them.[61]

Such places were emblematic of doctrines vehemently condemned by the Protestant establishment: the cult of the Virgin Mary and saints and the notion that the living could make intercession for the dead and speed their path through purgatory. They were also evocative reminders of a version of British history that Reformation propagandists were busily rewriting to support their claim that a pure and uncorrupted brand of Christianity had been planted in these islands long before St Augustine's arrival in the seventh century. The memory of hallowed locations that bore mythical witness to the triumphs and tribulations of indigenous Celtic and Anglo-Saxon saints like Patrick, Ninian, Winifred, Mildred, Piran and Neot was preserved not only by priests anxious to recolonise this past and by recusants like Nicholas Roscarrock who compiled their lives in manuscript, but also by the remembered rites carried out by pilgrims in a form which Willem Frijhoff calls 'embodied belief'.[62] A similar revival of native founding saints seems to have occurred simultaneously in the northern Netherlands, where the Apostolic Vicar Sasbout Vosmeer encouraged veneration of Saints Willibrord and Boniface.[63]

Iconoclastic attacks on these medieval sacred sites appear to have increased rather than discouraged devotion to them. Both Holywell and St Patrick's Purgatory were the target of repeated spasms of symbolic violence but, as at the battle-scarred shrine of Scherpenheuvel, the architectural martyrdom they suffered did more to spur than to stem the flow of pilgrims. An early eighteenth-century clergyman commented of Irish Catholics that 'when any Superstitious place is defaced or demolished, they repair it, and seem to be more inclined to Resort to it than formerly. They account it Meritorious to adhere obstinately to a Practice prohibited by Hereticks, and if any Punishment be inflicted upon them for it, they believe they suffer for Righteousness sake'.[64] Reformed rites of desecration and destruction also helped to stimulate the creation and circulation of miracle stories with a distinctly anti-Protestant flavour, such as the divine judgement that befell one scoffing heretic who defiled St Winifred's Well with his muddy boots.[65] Along the same lines was the rumour that the water of the holy well at Heiloo cured best when mixed with the blood of the Beggars.[66]

Nevertheless, it was difficult for the Catholic clergy to channel lay devotion in theologically acceptable directions. It was hard enough where priests had the backing of ecclesiastical law and the civil magistrate: at Scherpenheuvel Bishop Matthias Hovius eventually had the oak tree in which the miraculous image of the Virgin hung chopped down in an attempt to stop pilgrims stripping bark from its trunk and employing this in a manner that smacked of paganism.[67] In contexts that lacked a proper episcopal hierarchy, let alone political support, it was even more difficult to restrain popular enthusiasm within orthodox parameters. This was also true of the new holy places that sprang up in connection with contemporary martyrs. The site that held most allure for English Catholic pilgrims was Tyburn, where dozens of priests were hung, drawn and quartered for treason. By 1616, it had become customary to adorn the gallows with garlands, branches and flowers and to strew the ground beneath with herbs at midnight on the evening preceding an execution.[68] Ten years later, Queen Henrietta Maria openly displayed reverence to the place where so many had sacrificed their lives in defence of her faith, kneeling and praying there for 'the space of five *pater nosters*'.[69] Margaret Clitherow and other female recusants similarly travelled on bare feet to Knavesmire, near York, under the cover of darkness to venerate the spot where several missionaries were hung in 1582.[70] In Oxford many rushed to a spring said to have burst forth where one of the mangled quarters of the priest George Napper was displayed in 1611, in the hope of healing wonders, until it was stopped up by order of the Vice-Chancellor of the University.[71] Some of these sites were discovered and promoted by the Catholic clergy: for example, a holy well in County Clare, identified by a vision of St Michael the Archangel which appeared to a pious lady, was carefully managed by her confessor. But initiatives on the part of individual priests could also evoke the unease of their superiors, as in the case of the self-proclaimed Irish thaumaturge Father James Finnachty, who blessed several springs and proclaimed they had therapeutic powers.[72]

This example points to another side effect of the circumstances in which English Catholicism found itself: the extreme dangers faced by priests who defied the law in order to dispense soul-saving sacraments fostered a tendency to regard them as living saints. Commenting on the crowds who travelled to the prison in Wisbech, where many captured missionaries were incarcerated, William Weston recalled how they 'came from every part of the kingdom, some as to a holy place, undertaking a kind of pilgrimage'. Mrs Jane Wiseman, who brought her two daughters to be blessed before they entered convents abroad, 'did repent that she had not gone barefooted thither'.[73] The very spaces where the holy fathers who took terrible risks to succour the faithful had lived, visited, or been held captive had the capacity to become foci for cultic devotion. In the Tower of London John Gerard took comfort from the fact that he inhabited the same cell in which the Blessed Father Henry Walpole had once been locked and tortured and which Walpole had made into a miniature oratory by chalking up the names of the orders of the Angels and of Mary, Christ and God the Father (in the three sacred languages of Latin, Greek and Hebrew).[74] The Jesuits seem to have had particular charisma in the eyes of the laity. Upon her first meeting with a member of the Society, Mrs Wiseman begged him to let her kiss his feet: when he refused, she instead kissed the floor on which he was standing.[75] It is hardly surprising that the secret hiding places Catholics constructed for priests in their houses were revered by later generations as hallowed receptacles.[76]

These episodes point to a final aspect of the reconfiguration of Catholic sacred space in the wake of the Reformation, and that is the sanctification of the home itself. The rooms in which altars were erected and the Eucharist celebrated may have had a special aura of holiness, but a sense of religious intensity suffused many recusant houses in general. Although hardly invulnerable to the rude intrusions of pursuivants, these were spiritual refuges from a hostile world which some chose to consecrate to God and the saints. The Vaux household at Harrowden was dedicated to the Blessed Virgin Mary of Loreto.[77] Dame Dorothy Lawson not only placed her home under the patronage of St Michael and St Anthony, but caused the exterior gable to be decorated with the holy name of Jesus, to provide a visible symbol of hope to local mariners guiding their ships out to sea. Modelling her own conduct on that of St Catherine of Siena, who lived a life of cloistered perfection within her father's house, she turned her own residence into a kind of personal convent, praying and meditating as she traversed it.[78] This was in keeping with the recommendation of Jesuits like Robert Southwell, whose *Short Rule of Good Life* (1596–97) described how the devout could make their homes 'in a maner a paradise' by mentally or physically designating rooms to moments in Christ's life and passion. He also advised them to take walks in their gardens and orchards, 'as it were shorte pilgrimages to visit such Saints as are patrons of the place'.[79] Some sacralised these spaces by placing statues or images in them. Others did so through ritual: in the absence of cathedrals and churches, gardens could be suitable arenas for the processions that marked great ecclesiastical festivals like Corpus Christi.[80] In many respects, private houses became a substitute for the ecclesiastical buildings sequestered by their confessional enemies, counterparts of the semi-tolerated *schuilkerken* in Dutch cities – churches concealed behind the façade of domestic residences.[81] If the Counter-Reformation hierarchy regarded household religion with a degree of suspicion in those parts of Europe where the Church of Rome was triumphant,[82] in Britain and the Netherlands it had to recognise, albeit with some reluctance and reservation, that this was one of the keys to Catholicism's very survival.

The ritual life of Catholics in post-Reformation England, then, had several notable features. It was often clandestine and nocturnal; it centred on the home and evocative places in the landscape; and it relied as much, and sometimes more, on books, beads and blessed objects as it did on the priestly sacraments of penance and the Mass. The foregoing discussion has also highlighted the negotiations between Tridentine theology and policy and the lived experience of the laity at the grass roots. It has shown how rite and space were confessionalised in a context where Catholicism lacked the muscle of the state and how, paradoxically, its minority status may have provided it with some unique opportunities to reform devotion in accordance with new priorities. It has illustrated that relations between priests and the people to whom they ministered were frequently cooperative but equally often fraught and that it was not always easy or possible to police the sacred effectively. A high degree of lay independence coexisted with enormous respect for the missionaries who endangered their lives merely by entering the country. Such tensions and contradictions were, of course, present throughout the Catholic world, but the condition of being a minority faith surely accentuated them. Finally, even as they clashed with Protestants about spaces and ceremonies, these were spheres of activity that draw attention to moments at which Catholics compromised with and were tolerated by the heretics – sometimes in the very places that had been seized from them and violently desecrated in the first phases of the Reformation.

Notes
1 Keith Thomas, *Religion and the decline of magic* (Harmondsworth, 1973 edn), p. 88.
2 A.C. Southern (ed.), *An Elizabethan recusant house comprising the Life of the Lady Magdalen Visountess Montague (1538–1608)* (London, 1954), pp. 43, 47.
3 William Palmes, *Life of Mrs Dorothy Lawson, of St Anthony's, near Newcastle-upon-Tyne*, in Northumberland, ed. G. Bourchier Richardson (Newcastle-upon-Tyne, 1851), pp. 33–5. This argument is pursued in greater detail in my 'Translating Trent? English Catholicism and the Counter Reformation', *Historical Research* 78 (2005), 288–310, esp. p. 297.
4 See respectively, Benjamin J. Kaplan, 'Diplomacy and domestic devotion: embassy chapels and the toleration of religious dissent in early modern Europe', *Journal of Early Modern History* 6 (2002), 341–61, and Peter Lake and Michael Questier, 'Prisons, priests and people', in Nicholas Tyacke (ed.), *England's Long Reformation 1500–1800* (London, 1998), pp. 195–233.
5 Philip Caraman (ed.), *The other face: Catholic life under Elizabeth I* (London, 1960), p. 52; W.E. Rhodes (ed.), 'The apostolical life of Ambrose Barlow, O.S.B.', *Chetham Miscellanies* NS 2 (1909), p. 11.
6 P.J. Holmes (ed.), *Elizabethan casuistry*, C[atholic] R[ecord] S[ociety] 67 (1981), pp. 18–25, 78–86, at p. 23.
7 J.H. Pollen (ed.), *Unpublished documents relating to the English martyrs, vol. I 1584–1603*, CRS 5 (1908), pp. 313–14.
8 See Lisa McClain, *Lest we be damned: practical innovation and lived experience among Catholics in Protestant England, 1559–1642* (New York and London, 2004), ch. 4, esp. pp. 136–7, though some of the claims made in the book are mistaken and/or inadequately substantiated. J.T.

Rhodes, 'The Body of Christ in English Eucharistic devotion c. 1500–1620', in Richard Beadle and A.J. Piper (eds), *New science out of old books: studies in manuscripts and early printed books in honour of A.I Doyle* (Aldershot, 1995), pp. 388–419.

9   John Radford, *A directorie teaching the way to the truth in a briefe and plaine discourse against the heresies of this time* ([English secret press], 1605), pp. 104–5.

10 Anne Dillon, 'Praying by number: the Confraternity of the Rosary and the English Catholic community, c. 1580–1700', *History* 88 (2003), 451–71, at p. 468. See also Lisa McClain, 'Using what's at hand: English Catholic reinterpretations of the rosary, 1559–1642', *Journal of Religious History* 27 (2005), 161–76 and *Lest we be damned*, ch. 3, esp. pp. 90–6. Henry Garnet, *The societie of the rosary. Newly augmented* ([London secret press], 1596–7), sig. A5r–v, 68–9.

11 Mathieu G. Spiertz, 'Priest and layman in a minority church: the Roman Catholic Church in the Northern Netherlands 1592–1686', in W.J. Sheils and D. Wood (eds), *The ministry: clerical and lay*, Studies in Church History, 26 (Oxford, 1989), pp. 287–301, at p. 297.

12 John Bossy, 'The Counter-Reformation and the people of Catholic Europe', *Past and Present* 47 (1970), 59–60.

13 Garnet, *Societie*, p. 3 and see pp. 84–5, 183–4. See also John Bucke, *Instructions for the use of the beades* (Louvain, 1589), esp. pp. 84–5.

14 Garnet, *Societie*, p. 179; Southern (ed.), *Elizabethan Recusant House*, p. 44; John Gerard, *The Autobiography of an Elizabethan*, ed. and trans. Philip Caraman (London, 1951), pp. 117–20.

15 For some examples, see Henry Foley (ed.), *Records of the English Province of the Society of Jesus*, 7 vols in 8 (London, 1877–84), ii, p. 17; iii, pp. 125, 267; v, p. 212; vii (ii), pp. 1141, 1179. Trevor Johnson, 'Blood, tears and Xavier-Water: Jesuit missionaries and popular religion in the eighteenth-century Upper Bavaria', in Bob Scribner and Trevor Johnson (eds), *Popular religion in Germany and Central Europe, 1400–1800* (Basingstoke, 1996), pp. 183–202. For further discussion, see my 'Miracles and the Counter-Reformation mission to England', *Historical Journal* 46 (2003), 779–815, at pp. 797–9.

16 R.W. Scribner, 'Cosmic order and daily life: sacred and secular in pre-industrial German society', in his *Popular culture and popular movements in Reformation Germany* (London–Ronceverte, 1987), pp. 1–16, at p. 12.

17 Bernard Garter, *A new yeares gifte, dedicated to the popes holinesse, and all Catholikes addicted to the sea of Rome* (London, 1579), sig. H2r–3r and fold-out diagram.

18 British Library, London, MS Lansdowne 50, fol. 164r.

19 Gerard, *Autobiography*, pp. 110–11. The phrase 'holy radioactivity' is Ronald Finucane's: *Miracles and pilgrims: popular beliefs in medieval England* (London, 1977), p. 26. See also Walsham, 'Miracles', pp. 794–7.

20 See Martha W. Driver, *The image in print: book illustration in late medieval England and its sources* (London, 2004), ch. 6; Bucke, *Instructions*.

21 John Mush, 'A true report of the life and death of Mrs Margaret Clitherow', in John Morris (ed.), *Troubles of our Catholic forefathers*, 3 vols (London, 1872–7), iii, pp. 393–4; Caraman (ed.), *Other face*, pp. 168–70. This theme is developed fully in my "Domme Preachers"? Post-Reformation English Catholicism and the culture of print', *Past and Present* 168 (2000), 72–123.

22 E.g. *Godly contemplations for the unlearned* ([Antwerp, 1575]).

23 Foley (ed.), *Records*, vii (ii), pp. 1142–3.

24 Cf. Eamon Duffy's comments on late medieval piety: *The stripping of the altars: traditional religion in England c.1400–c.1580* (New Haven, 1992), p. 256.

25 See my *Church Papists: Catholicism, conformity and confessional polemic in early modern England* (Woodbridge, 1999 edn).

26 Robert Persons, *A brief discours contayning certayne reasons why Catholiques refuse to go to church* ([London secret press], 1580), fols 15r–18r, at fol. 17v.

27 Gregory Martin, *A treatise of schisme* (Douai [English secret press], 1578), p. 17.

28 John Bossy, *The English Catholic community 1570–1850* (London, 1975), p. 109, and ch. 6 passim.

29 Richard Bristow, *A briefe treatise of diverse plaine and sure ways to finde out the truthe in this doubtful*

and dangerous time of heresie (Antwerp, 1574), fol. 140b. See also Persons, *Brief discours*, fols 6r–9r.
30 William Weston, *The Autobiography of an Elizabethan*, ed. and trans. Philip Caraman (London, 1951), pp. 148–52.
31 Adrian Morey, *The Catholic subjects of Elizabeth I* (Totowa, NJ, 1978), p. 159; *Victoria County History, Derbyshire*, ii, ed. William Page (London, 1907), p. 24; Patrick Ryan (ed.), 'Diocesan returns of recusants for England and Wales 1577', in *CRS Miscellanea XII*, CRS 22 (1921), p. 79.
32 F.R. Raines (ed.), 'The State, Civil and Ecclesiastical of the County of Lancaster, about the Year 1590', in *Chetham Miscellanies V*, Chetham Society OS 96 (1875), p. 3.
33 A.T. Van Deursen, *Plain lives in a golden age: popular culture, religion and society in seventeenth-century Holland*, trans. Maarten Ultee (Cambridge, 1991), p. 301.
34 Bristow, *Briefe treatise*, fol. 143a.
35 Holmes (ed.), *Elizabethan casuistry*, pp. 25, 110–11. A harder line was, however, taken by William Allen and Robert Persons.
36 Bossy, *English Catholic community*, pp. 132–44.
37 Holmes (ed.), *Elizabethan casuistry*, pp. 117–18. Challoner quoted in Marie B. Rowlands, '1767 – religious life', in Rowlands (ed.), *Catholics of parish and town 1558–1778*, CRS Monograph Series 5 (1999), p. 271.
38 Raines (ed.), 'State, Civil and Ecclesiastical', pp. 5–7.
39 David Cressy, 'Who buried Mrs Horseman? Excommunication, accommodation and silence', in his *Travesties and transgressions in Tudor and Stuart England* (Oxford, 2000), p. 132 and pp. 116–37 *passim*.
40 *The late commotion of certaine papists in Herefordshire. Occasioned by the death of one Alice Wellington, a Recusant, who was buried after the popish maner* (London, 1605).
41 Bossy, *English Catholic community*, p. 142.
42 Clodagh Tait, *Death, burial and commemoration in Ireland, 1550–1650* (Basingstoke, 2002), p. 79.
43 Van Deursen, *Plain lives*, p. 301.
44 See my *Charitable hatred: tolerance and intolerance in England 1500–1700* (Manchester, 2006), ch. 5.
45 British Library, London, MS Harley 6998, fols 3r–v.
46 Caraman (ed.), *Other face*, p. 283; Statutes of the Realm, 3 Jac. I, c. 5.
47 Philip Caraman (ed.), *The years of siege: Catholic life from James I to Cromwell* (London, 1966), p. 28; F.O. Blundell, *Old Catholic Lancashire*, 3 vols (London, 1925–41), i, pp. 32–7.
48 See Rowlands, '1767 – religious life', p. 280; Tait, *Death*, p. 78.
49 Bossy, *English Catholic community*, pp. 136–40.
50 Frances E. Dolan, 'Gender and the "lost" spaces of Catholicism', *Journal of Interdisciplinary History*, 32 (2002), 641–65. See also Lisa McClain, 'Without church, cathedral or shrine: the search for religious space among Catholics in England, 1559–1625', *Sixteenth Century Journal* 33 (2002), 381–99, and *Lest we be damned*, chapter 2.
51 See Philip M. Soergel, *Wondrous in his saints: Counter-Reformation propaganda in Bavaria* (Berkeley, 1993); Marc R. Forster, *Catholic revival in the age of the Baroque: religious identity in South-west Germany, 1550–1750* (Cambridge, 2001), chapter 2; Luc Duerloo and Marc Wingens, *Scherpenheuval: Het Jeruzalem van de Lage Landen* (Leuven, 2002); Craig Harline and Eddy Put, *A Bishop's tale: Mathias Hovius among his flock in seventeenth-century Flanders* (New Haven, 2002), chapter 6.
52 'The Journal of Sir William Brereton 1635', in *North Country diaries (second series)*, Surtees Society 124 (1915), pp. 21–3.
53 Weston, *Autobiography*, pp. 111–12, 15.
54 Borthwick Institute of Historical Research, York, High Commission Act Book 16 (1612–1625–6), fols 31v, 38r–v; M.C.E. Chambers, *The life of Mary Ward (1585–1645)*, 2 vols, ed. Henry James Coleridge (London, 1882–5), ii, pp. 478–9. See also Anthony J. Storey, *Mount*

CATHOLIC RITUAL LIFE IN PROTESTANT ENGLAND   121

   Grace Lady Chapel: an historical enquiry (Beverley, 2001).
55 British Library, London, MS Lansdowne 111, fols 10r–v.
56 For Ireland, see Gillespie, *Devoted people*, pp. 91–2, and Michael P. Carroll, *Irish pilgrimage: holy wells and popular Catholic devotion* (Baltimore–London, 1999), though some of the claims of the latter should be treated with caution. For Scotland, see Margo Todd, *The culture of Protestantism in early modern Scotland* (New Haven, 2002), pp. 205–9. There are many references to such pilgrimages in the kirk sessions records. For Heiloo, see Willem Frijhoff, 'The function of the miracle in a Catholic minority: the United Provinces in the seventeenth century', in his *Embodied belief: ten essays on religious culture in Dutch history* (Hilversum, 2002), pp. 115–16, 126–8.
57 Margaret B. Sanderson, 'Catholic recusancy in Scotland in the sixteenth century', *Innes Review* 10 (1959), 87–107, at p. 104; James Murray McKinlay, *Ancient church dedications in Scotland: scriptural dedications* (Edinburgh, 1910), p. 112.
58 Willem Frijhoff, 'The holy shrine of Hasselt: Forms, values and functions of a revived pilgrimage', in his *Embodied belief*, pp. 235–73; Blundell, *Old Catholic Lancashire*, Appendix I, esp. pp. 169–72.
59 Borthwick Institute of Historical Research, York, Visitation Court Book 1615, fol. 31r.
60 M.R. Lewis, 'The pilgrimage to St Michael's Mount: Catholic continuity in Wales', *The Journal of Welsh Ecclesiastical History* 8 (1991), 51–4; James Joel Cartwright (ed.), *The Travels through England of Dr Richard Pococke, successively Bishop of Meath and of Ossory during 1750, 1751, and later Years*, Camden Society, NS 42, 44 (1888–9), ii, p. 216.
61 See my 'Holywell: contesting sacred space in early modern Wales', in Will Coster and Andrew Spicer (eds), *Sacred space in early modern Europe* (Cambridge, 2005), pp. 211–36; Bernadette Cunningham and Raymond Gillespie, 'The Lough Derg pilgrimage in the age of the Counter-Reformation', *Éire-Ireland*, 39 (2004), 167–79.
62 Roscarrock's 'Lives of the Saints' is Cambridge University Library, MS 3041; Frijhoff, 'Holy shrine', p. 241. For Catholic versions of British ecclesiastical history, see Robert Persons, *Treatise of three conversions*, 3 vols (1603–4) and Richard Broughton, *The ecclesiastical historie of Great Britaine* (Douai, 1633).
63 Spiertz, 'Priest and layman', pp. 289–93; Van Deursen, *Plain lives*, p. 301.
64 John Richardson, *The great folly, superstition and idolatry of pilgrimages in Ireland* (Dublin, 1727), sig. B3r.
65 Gerard, *Autobiography*, p. 47.
66 Frijhoff, 'Function of the miracle', p. 129.
67 Harline and Put, *Bishop's tale*, p. 106. For the similar difficulties experienced at the Jesus Oak in the Soniën Woods, see Craig Harline, 'Miracles and this world: the battle for Jesus Oak', *Archiv für Reformationsgeschichte* 93 (2002), 217–38.
68 J.H. Pollen (ed.), 'The Life and Martyrdome of Mr Maxfield, Priest, 1616', in *Miscellanea III*, CRS 3 (London, 1906), p. 43.
69 British Library, London, MS 39288, fol. 6, in Caraman (ed.), *Years of siege*, p. 96.
70 Morris (ed.), *Troubles*, iii, pp. 395–6.
71 Michael Questier (ed.), *Newsletters from the Archpresbyterate of George Birkhead*, Camden Society, 5th ser. 12 (1998), p. 99.
72 Raymond Gillespie, *Devoted people: belief and religion in early modern Germany* (Manchester, 1997), pp. 159–60, 92 respectively, and see pp. 67–8, 70, 161.
73 Weston, *Autobiography*, pp. 167, 176.
74 Gerard, *Autobiography*, p. 105.
75 *Ibid.*, pp. 30–1.
76 Michael Hodgetts, '*Loca Secretoria* in 1581', *Recusant History* 19 (1989), 386–95; Hodgetts, *Secret hiding places* (Dublin, 1989).
77 Gerard, *Autobiography*, p. 163.
78 Palmes, *Life of Mrs Dorothy Lawson*, pp. 34, 42; Dolan, '"Lost" spaces of Catholicism', pp. 662–3.
79 Robert Southwell, *A short rule of good life* ([London secret press, 1596–7]), pp. 128–33.

80 As recorded by Henry Garnet, 1605: Foley (ed.), *Records*, iv, p. 141.
81 Benjamin J. Kaplan, 'Fictions of privacy: house chapels and the spatial accommodation of religious dissent in early modern Europe', *American Historical Review* 107 (2002), 1031–64, esp. 1050–1.
82 Bossy, 'Counter-Reformation', p. 68.

8
The Southern Netherlands connection: networks of support and patronage

PAUL ARBLASTER

For Calvinists and Catholics in seventeenth-century England, the United Provinces and the Habsburg Netherlands were models of how things should, ideally, be at home, or examples of just how awful things might be. In the one people could be prosecuted for selling gingerbread on the feast of St Nicholas, in the other for demonstratively failing to kneel when a priest passed by carrying the blessed sacrament.[1] One group in England surreptitiously imported Middelburg Psalms (complete with the rubrics for a Reformed order of service), the other Plantin missals, breviaries and primers. Both sent young men to fight in the Low Countries, or to study, but on opposite sides of the confessional/political divide. And at least during the reign of the Archdukes, admiration for the Habsburg Netherlands was not limited to English Catholics. For the Catholics of Scandinavia, north-western Germany, Scotland, Ireland and the United Provinces, the Habsburg Netherlands was a primary source of structural support, and a point of contact with the wider Catholic world.[2]

I would like to suggest points of comparison, of similarity and of difference, for the ways in which this was true of the Dutch and of those from the Three Kingdoms. In order to do so, I would first distinguish four senses in which the Habsburg Netherlands provided a 'point of contact'. The first is as part of a common but divided homeland. In spite of all anachronism, this sense will be called 'Great Netherlandish'. It only applies to those whose provinces had once been part of the Habsburg (or even Burgundian) complex of territories in the Low Countries, not in any way to the English, Scottish and Irish. The 'Great Netherlandish' attitude applies particularly for those from provinces that were still largely or partly under Habsburg rule, such as Flanders, Brabant, Limburg and Gelderland, which were also areas in the ecclesiastical province of Mechelen rather than Utrecht. It could, however, also play a role for those from further north, and not only for Catholics. There was little reason why somebody from Utrecht or Amsterdam should consider Flanders any more foreign than Friesland, especially if their parents were southern refugees, and even more so if there was some southern inheritance they might hope to recover. As the cartographic exhibition Eenheid op Papier showed a few years ago, in spite of the formal division of sovereignty in 1648 there was a feeling that the Low Countries formed some sort of unity, however divided, right up to the Belgian Revolution of 1830.[3] In this sense the relationship between Dutch Catholics and the Habsburg Netherlands was unique.

A second sense, one in which the Habsburg Netherlands was not unique, was that in which they were geographically convenient. To obtain a Catholic education, to receive ordination, to respond to a religious vocation, or simply to practise the Catholic religion without fear of harassment, the Habsburg Netherlands was easier and cheaper to get to than most other Catholic territories. However, the same was true, for the English and the Scots, of France, and for the Dutch, of Germany, while for the Irish it may at times have been easier to get to Spain than to Flanders. In general terms, the Habsburg Netherlands was the most important point of contact, but they were never the only such point.

A specific aspect of geographic convenience for Catholics in border areas of the Dutch Republic was that they could cross the border on a Sunday to hear Mass – a characteristic that the Habsburg Netherlands shared with German principalities and with a number of enclaves or feudally 'sovereign' lordships scattered through and around northern and north-eastern Brabant. The Catholic rulers of these exceptional jurisdictions were tied to the Habsburg interest through political favours and honours, in a few cases including the Golden Fleece, particularly during the rule of the Archdukes Albert and Isabella in the Southern Netherlands (1598–1621). Again, the relevance of border crossing applies particularly to Flanders, Brabant, Limburg and Gelderland. A Catholic in Haarlem might as well have been in Aberdeen for all the difference that border crossing could make to weekly attendance at Mass, although local conditions could make a considerable difference in other ways.

The third and fourth senses are two aspects of a single fact: the Habsburg Netherlands in many ways exemplified a Tridentine ideal of what a Catholic society should be like. This made it a congenial place for confessionally committed Catholics (sense number three: the Habsburg Netherlands as an attractive model), although it could be alienating for those of a more conservative cast of mind.[4] It also meant that there was a greater local willingness to support religious refugees and foreign missions than there might be elsewhere (sense number four: the Habsburg Netherlands as a sympathetic host). In neither sense was the Habsburg Netherlands unique; but in the first decades of the seventeenth century both senses appear to have been much stronger there than anywhere else. It is this double sense of the Habsburg Netherlands as attractive and welcoming that will now be considered more closely.

The Tridentine Netherlands

In the Low Countries, Catholic reform in the spirit of Trent was initiated almost before the Council had concluded.[5] This newly Tridentine Church was militant, certainly, but also traumatised. The monumental buildings and baroque art replaced churches, convents and artworks vandalised, sometimes repeatedly, in the course of the 1560s, 1570s and 1580s. The slaughter of priests at Oudenaarde was less dramatic than at Briel, Roermond or Enkhuizen but not essentially different.[6] Customary processions and devotions had often been interrupted, contested, in several cities suppressed. This, more than anything, turned Catholic opponents of royal policy away from the Revolt. When such processions and devotions were reintroduced it was with a self-conscious appeal to tradition, not unaccompanied by invented traditions and open innovations.[7] If the Habsburg Netherlands was a sympathetic host, it was partly because it knew what Catholics from more northern areas had gone through.

Nor was Trent the only source of the new characteristics of Catholic revival. The relationship between church and state had been transformed in the second half of the sixteenth century with the erection of fourteen new dioceses, a new primatial see at Mechelen and the elevation of the existing dioceses of Cambrai and Utrecht into archdioceses. An area formerly subject to four suffragan sees of French and German metropolitans became a national church in three provinces (in modern terms corresponding very roughly to Dutch, Flemish and Walloon) with a total of eighteen bishops.[8] Rights of episcopal nomination were held by the sovereign, subject to papal approval. The great abbeys, whose superiors were the lords spiritual of the provincial states and the Estates General, were brought under the control of these bishops. Under the new bishops, seminaries were opened to train a Tridentine parish clergy, and leading figures in government, including Philip II himself, founded new colleges at Leuven and Douai for the education of a higher clergy to fill the dignities newly reserved to graduates in theology or canon law. Being a decent chap and somebody's nephew was no longer sufficient qualification for a prebend. The functioning of this new system, especially when it had to be rebuilt almost from scratch within a few years of first being implemented, posed tremendous human resource challenges in terms of headcount, qualifications and motivation.[9] English, Scottish and Dutch refugees, and at a slightly later date Irishmen, made some contribution to meeting these challenges, while the more numerous missioners who trained in the Habsburg

Netherlands to return home at the risk of dungeon and gallows provided an inspirational example.[10] This was another reason for the hospitality extended: the Habsburg attempt to build a 'national' and reformed Church in the Low Countries stood to gain directly and indirectly.

It was a new system that still relied on the stick as much as on the carrot, but after a series of massive persecutions in the decades 1540–80 the suppression of dissent had become relatively low-key.[11] By the seventeenth century, anyone reluctant to kneel to the blessed sacrament could always nip down a side street. This softer approach to the application of pressure on nonconformists was probably part of the attraction for those whose hope for eventual Catholic triumph in their own homelands included a realisation that things had gone well past a stage where harsh measures might be helpful, if in hindsight they ever had been. The few additions to the Dutch Reformed martyrology from the later 1580s are of those who died of insanitary prison conditions or were hanged for breaching the terms of their banishment.[12] The church courts continued to impose rituals of public shaming, penitential pilgrimages, fines or beatings on those breaching established moral or doctrinal norms;[13] but the civil authorities did not fully relinquish jurisdiction over heresy until mid century, when the business of identifying and confiscating lands abandoned by Protestant refugees was finally winding down.

There was a flourishing Catholic press, which was vital to the production of Catholic books in English, and even more so in Irish: the history of Irish-language printing, with Irish type, effectively begins in Leuven.[14] For Dutch Catholics, Flemish presses were important, but less so and less directly. By the seventeenth century clandestine and even open printing of Catholic works was common in Holland. The indirect importance was economic: Antwerp was a massive centre for the production of cheap editions of catechisms, prayer books, lives of saints – and of course images of saints.[15] Dutch buyers could obtain books that would never have been printed – or would have cost a lot more – without the wider market of the Habsburg Netherlands. The first English and Dutch translations of Francis de Sales's *Introduction à la vie dévote* were printed in the Habsburg Netherlands only three years apart; but the English was intended for clandestine export, the Dutch, in the first instance, for a readership in the Southern Netherlands itself.[16]

Control of the press through formal censorship was in law comprehensive, but in fact somewhat haphazard.[17] Special exemptions from the general press laws were granted for books intended for the use of Catholics in Protestant territory, allowing anonymous and pseudonymous publishing. Censors of books, appointed by the bishops, had to be university graduates. For books in English or Irish, censors could delegate to someone who knew the language. Censorship should not itself be seen as too monolithic a phenomenon. It restricted the range

NETWORKS OF SUPPORT AND PATRONAGE 127

of views that could be openly published but was itself a site of contestation in the ecclesiastical squabbles of the seventeenth century. It was not unheard of for ecclesiastics to seek the suppression of a work that had been published with the approbation of members of a rival clerical faction. Just which censor a book was submitted to, and how fulsome they were in their approval of it, can be one indication of networks of alliance and support.

Missionary foundations

It was the combination of the four factors outlined: historical ties, geographic convenience, a model of reformed Catholic society and the willingness to provide a refuge, which meant that the Habsburg Netherlands was the obvious place for Catholic exiles from north-western Europe to congregate. This does have to be put into perspective, though: the first generation of English Catholic refugees began arriving in the Low Countries in 1559, but during the period 1570–90 the dislocations caused by rebellion and war were such that English Catholic exiles were fleeing from Flanders, mainly to France. The English College at Douai was relocated to Rheims; the English Bridgettines fled from Mechelen to Rouen; numerous English Catholics were seeking patronage in France – where Scottish Catholics, due to the dynastic connection, were already well ahead of them.[18]

Holland had seen the first official steps against Catholicism in 1573 (after a series of notorious murders and robberies in 1572); even so, Haarlem and Amsterdam were Catholic until 1578; the suppression of Catholic worship throughout the United Provinces was decreed only in 1581. This was twenty years after the same had happened in England, and in a piecemeal manner that English historians would more readily associate with the 1530s and 1540s, perhaps even the 1560s, than with the 1580s. 'Reformed' ministers who continued to provide Catholic sacraments on the sly were a problem up to, perhaps even after, 1600.[19] Those pensioned off, rather than taken on, by the new religious establishment might eke out their living as hedge priests – an embarrassment as much to the Tridentine clergy as to the Calvinist authorities. But a crypto-Catholicism with reluctant and token conformity – also attested in early modern England, Scandinavia, the Balkans and Japan – in the long run always transmuted either into comfortable and full conformity, or into fiercely maintained local or family traditions devoid of any sense of catholicity, unless a living link to the wider church was provided by missionary priests.

The slowness with which Sasbout Vosmeer realised this was undoubtedly due, in part, to the relative strength of the Catholic position in the Netherlands, and in part to the unclearness of the future situation. In England the whole nation was delivered over to a state church and the one brief revival of public Catholic worship was in those areas under rebel control during the few weeks of the Rising of the North in 1569. The only options for Catholic practice in England, not mutually exclusive, were a missionary priesthood and regime change.[20] In the Northern Netherlands revivals of public Catholic worship were going on all the time, depending on the military situation, most importantly at Groningen from 1580 to 1594, Maastricht 1580–1632, Breda 1581–90 (and again 1625–37), Nijmegen 1586–91, and Deventer and Zutphen 1587–91. It was only after 1590, the Revolt having survived William of Orange's assassination and his son, Maurice, leading its armies back onto the offensive, that a clandestine seminary was set up inside the country, with a handful of students lodged and tutored in a private house. At about the same time, the Dutch Church formally became a Mission, Clement VIII delegating wide powers to the papal nuncio in Cologne, who sub-delegated them to Sasbout Vosmeer as vicar apostolic.[21] In 1596 the Cologne nuncio was moved to Brussels, keeping his powers over the Dutch Mission and adding the English Mission to his portfolio.[22]

When Catholicism was suppressed in Haarlem in 1578, the cathedral had a bishop – who was out of town – and thirteen canons. The bishop went to Germany and ended his days as an auxiliary bishop of Münster; the dean went to Leuven, becoming president of Viglius College; two canons fled to Cologne, one to Lille, and it is not clear what became of three more; one accepted a pension from the States of Holland; and five remained in Haarlem, forming one of the kernels around which the Dutch Mission began to take shape in the 1580s and electing new members (now without prebends) as vacancies came up.[23] It was not until 1703 that the so-called 'chapter of Haarlem' was officially declared defunct. There was no comparable survival in England, much though secular priests and Benedictines liked to suggest there had been, and consequently no comparable canonical institutional framework already in place.[24] There were numerous localised sites of resistance in England, but the English mission as a coordinated undertaking in the first instance had to be organised from abroad – in the event, from Douai in Flanders. Despite the great resilience and internal resources of Dutch Catholicism there was still an exile diaspora, but initially this was centred on Cologne, followed at some distance by Münster, Mainz and Trier. Those who fled to Habsburg territory did so as individuals, perhaps having personal or family connections to benefit from, but not as part of an exile community.

Even after 1590, when the situation in the Habsburg Netherlands was improving, Spain and Rome became alternative locations for English, Scottish and Irish foundations, although not for the Dutch. As late as 1604, despite the urgings of the Brussels nuncio, Sasbout Vosmeer decided that Cologne would be the best location for the Dutch Mission's first missionary college, founded to replace the now failing clandestine seminary.[25] In the decades after 1621 a number of factors made the Habsburg Netherlands even less exclusively attractive. Perhaps the most important was the renewal of war – with the Dutch until 1648; with the French (a few intermissions aside), in effect, from 1635 to 1715. The centre of gravity of the English and Scottish Catholics in the Low Countries was at Douai, which went to France by conquest in 1668. Then there was the increased attractiveness of France itself, with the delayed development there of an alternative model of reformed Catholicism and a desire on the part of Louis XIII and Louis XIV to be seen as, if not more Catholic than the pope, at least more Catholic than the Habsburgs.[26] In contrast, the Irish and Dutch centre of gravity was not Douai, but Leuven. The Dutch presence in Leuven was increased in the 1660s when the college founded in Cologne in 1604 was moved there, where a second college for the Dutch Mission had already been opened in 1617.

From the 1610s onwards clerical networks of mutual support were built up that linked Catholic clergy from all parts of the Low Countries, North and South, and the university was one of the central nodes of these networks, both as an institution with its own powers of patronage and preferment and as a place where individuals could forge friendships that lasted into later life. Later in the century these networks came to include Irish academics, figures such as John Sinnich, professor at Leuven and canon of Bruges. The English and Scottish clergy, operating virtually autonomously from colleges of their own nations, were somewhat free of these entanglements (although they had entanglements enough of their own at home). The Jansenist troubles that literally tore the Dutch Church apart, and severely tested the Irish, largely passed the English Church by, except as a variant of the mud-slinging name-calling that went on in jurisdictional disputes between regulars and seculars. It may well be that there is a very simple explanation for this – in the two words 'Douai' and 'Leuven'. The vast bulk of the English clergy was trained at a university where Jansenism was a minority interest, while many of the Dutch and Irish clergy were trained in the birthplace and bastion of the heresy. In this respect, as in many others, the ecclesiastical politics of the Dutch Mission and the English exile communities were inextricably tied up with those of the Habsburg Netherlands.

Ecclesiastical jurisdictions were no more firmly fixed than royal government. From 1622 the Congregation of Propaganda claimed authority over the Northern missions, and stimulated the education of missionaries in Rome as well as in Flanders; from 1657 to 1669 some Dutch priests at Propaganda's college in Rome were taught by Oliver Plunket, later archbishop of Armagh and martyr. In the 1630s jurisdiction over the English and Scottish missions was transferred from the Brussels nuncio to his counterpart in Paris, while the pope's representative in Brussels was downgraded from a nuncio with full legatine powers to an internuncio. The external structures of support and patronage to which Catholic minorities and diasporas could turn, whether in national or institutional terms, were constantly changing; it would be simplistic to consider any of them a fixed element. The greatest continuity was provided by the exile colleges themselves: foundations that remained a fixed point of reference despite the changes in royal and ecclesiastical jurisdictions.

Catholic diasporas

Seminaries were not the only such exile foundations. English and Irish Catholics established an amazing array of religious houses in exile, many of them in the Habsburg Netherlands.[27] Very often houses in France or elsewhere were daughter institutions of foundations in Flanders. Most untypically, the Institute of the Blessed Virgin Mary, an English order founded in Flanders, lost all its Flemish houses but went on to flourish in Germany, Bohemia and Hungary.

There was only one exile house specifically for Northern Netherlanders: the Abbey of Berne in Vilvoorde. Almost uniquely, the Premonstratensian Abbey of Berne had survived the suppression of institutional Catholic life in the Dutch Republic, thanks to its traditionally close association with the barons of Breda, who also happened to be princes of Orange. During the First Stadholderless Period, coinciding with William III's minority, the position of the monastery in the barony of Breda became untenable and in 1657 the community relocated to Vilvoorde, just north of Brussels. It retained some lands in the barony, visiting them for administrative and pastoral purposes, but the community's life of monastic observance was maintained at Vilvoorde until the death of the last abbot in 1799, and throughout this time the monastery continued to recruit from the largely Catholic population of the Generality Lands. Of eleven abbots during the period 1657–1799, only two were Southern Netherlanders. Although not Dutch exile institutions, two other Premonstratensian abbeys in royal Brabant, Postel, a recent abbey right on the border, and Tongerlo, a medieval foundation with some landholdings and customary rights over the border, were engaged in the Dutch Mission, providing priests and recruiting novices in the Generality Lands.

Dutch participation in Flemish conventual life has never been studied, but a glance at the lists of superiors in the *Monasticon Belge* reveals a scattering of Dutch monks and nuns in leading positions in Southern houses. Louisa Truits, a native of Leiden, was elected abbess of the Cistercian monastery of Spermalie in 1649.[28] It would take extensive prosopographical prospecting to get any idea of how many ordinary nuns travelled from the Northern to the Southern Netherlands in response to a religious vocation. Given how much easier it would have been for them than for English or Irish Catholics, the numbers could be surprisingly high. The Jesuit missioner Adriaan Boom was confessor to at least one *klop* in Haarlem, Maria Jacobs, who thought that it was an option worthy of serious consideration.[29] This also throws light on the question of whether the state of life of *kloppen* – pious women living alone or in unenclosed communities under a simple vow of chastity, devoting their lives to the corporal and/or spiritual works of mercy – was a vocation in itself or just a compromise solution for those who felt the pull of a religious vocation but could not respond to it fully.[30] Consideration of whether *kloppen* were would-be nuns has never examined just how many actually could be nuns.

Dutch men with a contemplative vocation could also travel south to fulfil it. In 1605 the prior of the Charterhouse of Scheut, in Anderlecht, had a coadjutor from Delft.[31] Five years later, the new prior was from Zaltbommel. He had already served as prior in Lier and Leuven and went on to serve in 's-Hertogenbosch, and seems to have been moved from house to house to instil a bit of Dutch fervour in the difficult days of rebuilding community life. When the abbey of Affligem was reinstituted as a house of the reformed congregation of Bursfeld, the Dutch prior Benedictus van Haeften marked the occasion by inviting the Dutch theologian Cornelius Jansenius to deliver a lecture.[32] Van Haeften's work as a reformer of monastic discipline was carried through into the dependent priories of Bornem and Basse Wavre by Michel de la Porte (or Vander Poorten), a native of Breda who had become a monk of Affligem in 1603, at the age of twenty.[33] The rebuilding and reform of Affligem, the first member of the first estate in the States of Brabant, was paralleled at an abbey of similar historical importance, St Pieters in Ghent, by Arsenius Schaeyck, abbot 1615–31, who had been born in Utrecht and served as a priest there from 1569 to 1578 before moving south and discerning a monastic vocation. It was Schaeyck who introduced Tridentine enclosure to the abbey, in line with the newly strict interpretation of the Benedictine vow of stability and, with the aid of the bishop, Antoine Triest, gradually withdrew members of the community from pastoral commitments outside the monastery. While it is currently fashionable to consider Tridentine enclosure (and resistance to it) from a gender perspective, no consideration is given to the men who belonged to orders that were more strictly enclosed. This is an area where thoughtful comparative study might provide a more nuanced view of gender, and of religious life.

Dutch and British Catholics in the Southern Netherlands could also find forms of support that did not rely on ecclesiastical networks. Laypeople of a certain social rank might seek appointments at court, in the army, in the civil administration. If they obtained such positions this created support for wider circles of servants and dependents, and hopefully also social obligations from well-placed figures in the exile's homeland. There is little sense in which men from States Flanders, Brabant, Limburg or Gelderland who obtained positions in the administration of royal Flanders, Brabant, Limburg or Gelderland can be considered exiles, although the epitaph of Joannes vanden Velde, a former alderman of 's-Hertogenbosch who became a member of the Council of Brabant in Brussels, does state that he left his city when it fell to the Dutch, out of loyalty to the Catholic King.[34] They are perhaps best seen as internally displaced persons – and as the example shows, there could be considerable compensations for the loyalty their displacement demonstrated.

Those from north of the great rivers might more reasonably be thought of as exiles, although perhaps for them too the 'Great Netherlandish' perception of the Low Countries made serving Habsburg sovereigns seem natural. When Catholic worship was suppressed in Utrecht, the archdeacon of Utrecht was already a councillor and master of requests of the Brussels Privy Council, and soon afterwards became chancellor of the Order of the Golden Fleece. This was simply a continuation of patterns of patronage going back to Burgundian times – unlike later court appointments given to English, Irish, Scottish and even French exiles. In the seventeenth century the handful of northerners in government service in the South includes figures such as Jacob Pijnssen van der Aa, *rekenmeester* of the Council of Domains in royal Brabant and the husband of Catharina Francesca de Robiano. His cousin, the magistrate and man of letters Pieter Cornelisz Hooft, was writing to him in October 1639 for help with an inheritance question – an entailment that Hooft's wife might be able to claim if she were recognised as neutral in the Revolt, rather than a fugitive whose rights in Brabant were forfeit; but in this case no sense of obligation was created. Unfortunately for Hooft, Van der Aa died within weeks of being enlisted in the cause, and the case dragged on until after the Treaty of Münster.[35] Earlier in the century, the Moesenbroeks and the Drenckwaerts, notable families of Dordrecht, provided the archdukes with a chancellor for Overijsel, Drenthe, Twente and Lingen (parts of which were either under their control or under contribution), and a receiver-general of the treasury.

Provincial councils were on their guard against royal appointments of 'foreigners', meaning those born in other provinces, but Dutchmen and Burgundians could be appointed in the central administration in Brussels. The court and the army, like the university and the great collegiate churches, were places where appointments could be even more cosmopolitan, and included English musicians and priests, and Irish and Scottish guards and ladies in waiting, as well as Netherlanders, Spaniards, Italians, Germans and even the occasional Hungarian or Pole. In the words of one of James I's emissaries, Brussels was 'verie populous, of all nations that are Catholick and civill'.[36]

The pension lists of the Brussels court contain a few clearly Dutch names, such as those of Willem Janssen Benninck and Jacob Jacobsen Wolf, hydraulic engineers taken into the service of the court in 1626; and of Veronica Hetzema, widow of a corporal of the guard of halberdiers, or Clémence de Hoytema, widow of privy councillor Igram Van Achelen.[37] With Oudegeest, Otten, Blom or Willemssen one might hazard a guess, but with greater reluctance. Most names, however, are much less determinate. Here again is a field lying wide open to cultivation.

More ordinary laypeople also moved to the Habsburg Netherlands, although the extent to which they did so for reasons of religion is extremely difficult to gauge. Most famous, perhaps, are the forty teenagers expelled from the orphanage of 's-Hertogenbosch for refusing to take part in Protestant services, and found places in Brussels by the Infanta.[38] The registrations of English refugees in Brussels in 1597 include that of Anthony Stampart, who had been in the service of a number of exile gentlemen and was currently procurator for the students of the English College in St Omer.[39] Occasional comments in letters reveal English craftsmen at work in the Habsburg Netherlands: John Thursby, a buttonmaker; Richard Mainwaring, a drawer of gold and silver wire.

Registrations of new citizens are another source for relatively ordinary people. While full citizens were part of a broad urban elite, it is difficult to deny entirely the ordinariness of a grocer from Nijmegen, a waffle-baker from Goes, or an innkeeper from Aberdeen. The requirement for citizenship was usually something along the lines of a year's residence, proof of financial self-sufficiency, swearing loyalty to the city and the king (which implied willingness to serve in the watch if called upon to do so), and declaring adherence to the Catholic faith. We don't know how pro forma this last declaration was.

There must, however, be a strong presumption, at least during years of war and hardship, that the main attraction of Bruges and Antwerp to Dutch and British settlers was the open practice of Catholicism, combined with relatively easy intercourse with compatriots and the homeland. In the years 1585–89, when thousands were leaving Antwerp, ten new citizens from Holland, Friesland and Utrecht were registered there, and three from Scotland. We cannot know how many more arrived as residents without enrolling as citizens, and citizenship in Antwerp was somewhat more exclusive than in most cities. In 1616 the bishop of Antwerp was concerned that 240 Catholic families had moved to the North for economic reasons, while that same year four craftsmen and a surgeon from Holland requested, and gained, citizenship. There are all sorts of reasons why they might have done so. No economic movement is all one way, and these may just be eddies of perceived benefit in the prevailing current. This is clearly the case with the influxes of Dutch and Scottish fishermen, merchants and skippers seeking neutral citizenship during the Anglo-Dutch wars. Other motives might be familial or marital. In Bruges, one Zeelander was awarded citizenship gratis, because he was going to support a widowed mother of three children, taking them off the public purse. Another possibility to consider is that some, at least, of these registrations could have been attempts to safeguard inheritances from refugee parents which might have been lost if the claimants had been formally identified as fugitives. There is only one case where we can be sure of motivation without further research. On 16 June 1627 the city of Bruges, by royal order, awarded citizenship to the Fleming Martyne Verbeele and her husband and stepchildren, 'all from Vlissingen, reconciled by the same Martyne'.[40] The historiography of the Dutch and English Missions has only recently moved beyond ecclesiastical history; that the study of the Catholic diaspora should take some time to follow suit is only natural.

The existence of established exile communities in the Habsburg Netherlands that included married laypeople meant that there were second-, even third-generation English, Scottish, Irish etc. Catholics who might identify with the land of their birth, rather than of their ancestry. Some priests born in the English Catholic diaspora had high-flying ecclesiastical careers. George Chamberlain, born in Ghent, studied at the English colleges in Spain and Rome but became a canon of Ghent cathedral, graduated licentiate of canon law from Leuven, and ended up as bishop of Ypres.[41] Caesar Clement, born in Leuven, became chaplain-general to the Army of Flanders and dean of the chapter of St Gudula's in Brussels.[42] The only parallel among priests born in England is William Gifford, an alumnus of Leuven and the English College in Rome, who made it as far as dean of the chapter of St Peter's in Lille (where his fellow English exile John Martiall also held a prebend) before being expelled from the Habsburg Netherlands for espionage in 1606.[43] He did go on to surpass Chamberlain or Clement by becoming archbishop of Rheims. Some English merchants in Antwerp had sons who entered the Flemish provinces of religious orders, and not necessarily as a means of avoiding the rigours of missionary life. One such, Lionel Aynscombe SJ, died at sea en route to China in 1658; another, Robert Collimore OP, ended his days on the Dutch Mission at Leiden in 1661.[44]

Other second-generation English exiles identified with the exile community and its religious institutions, rather than with the host country, but the distinction was not always clearly cut. William Ward, a lieutenant in Sir William Stanley's regiment, had three children, all born in Antwerp; of these one daughter married another English exile, a military contractor in Austrian Habsburg service, while Ward's son, Francis, became a priest, and assistant confessor to the English Benedictine nuns in Brussels.[45] The English merchant Lionel Wake arrived in Antwerp on business as a Protestant but settled there a Catholic.[46] He had eleven children baptised in the city.[47] One of his sons studied in Leuven and Rome, eventually becoming a priest on the English Mission.[48] Of Wake's daughters, one married within the English community at Antwerp; another married an Antwerp merchant, Peeter Stevens (Van Dijck painted matching portraits of the couple, which are now in the Mauritshuis); one daughter became a *klop*.[49] The one most interesting here is Mary Margaret of the Angels, born and baptised in Antwerp as Margaret Wake, who in 1634 became a Teresian nun in the English Carmel in Antwerp, making her profession between the hands of the first English Teresian, Venerable Anne of the Ascension (who had made her profession to Blessed Anne of St Bartholomew; who had made her profession to St Teresa of Avila herself). Mary Margaret was in time elected prioress, governed her community in perfect accordance with the rules and constitutions of the order, and died in 1678 at the age of sixty.[50] Almost forty years after her death, in 1716, her tomb was opened and her body was found to be incorrupt. A crowd of locals forced its way into the church to venerate her, on the grounds that a saint born in Antwerp was a gift of God to the whole city. It seems that members of a foreign community could be naturalised even after death.

Conclusion

There are important similarities in the Dutch, English, Irish and Scottish experience of dependence on the Southern Netherlands as the prime point of contact with Catholic Europe, and on Brussels as the most direct source of diplomatic support and patronage. The most obvious similarity, but far from the only one, is the location in the Southern Netherlands of missionary seminaries for each of these nationalities. Laypeople from each of these countries were to be found in some numbers in Brussels, Antwerp and Bruges, and occasionally elsewhere – some of them Catholics of convenience, some of them happy to find a haven of conscience, others forming a more activist diaspora. Among the last were those that provided funds and leverage for missionaries, and sons and daughters as recruits to religious endeavours.

For each nation, however, the timing and the nature of dependence differs. The Southern Netherlands became more important for the Dutch and the Irish in the second half of the seventeenth century, the very time it was becoming less important for the English and the Scots. The different locales of contact (Douai for the English and the Scots, Leuven for the Irish and the Dutch) may have been even more significant, judging by the different responses to Jansenism. Another factor in the different ways in which the Southern Netherlands were important was just what support and patronage was available elsewhere, be it France, Spain, Italy, Germany, even Austria or Hungary. But most important were the differences in the relations between the Habsburgs and each of the different countries of origin – the various provinces of the Republic, the various kingdoms of the British Isles. To a large extent this determined what sorts of patronage could be provided, and variations in the inclination to provide them.

Notes

1. Hans van de Mortel, *Criminaliteit, rechtspleging en straf in het Hollandse drosambt Heusden, 1615–1714* (Tilburg, 2005), p. 161; Marie Juliette Marinus, *De contrareformatie te Antwerpen(1585–1676). Kerkelijk leven in een grootstad* (Brussels, 1995), pp. 238–9.
2. Paul Arblaster, 'The Archdukes and the Northern Counter-Reformation', in Werner Thomas and Luc Duerloo (eds), *Albert and Isabella, 1598–1621. Essays* (Turnhout, 1998), pp. 87–92.
3. Jan Roegiers et al. (eds), *Eenheid op papier: de Nederlanden in kaart van keizer Karel tot Willem I* (Leuven, 1995).
4. As shown in Judith Pollmann, *Religious choice in the Dutch Republic: the Reformation of Arnoldus Buchelius, 1565–1641* (Manchester, 1999).
5. See e.g. E. de Moreau, *Histoire de l'Eglise en Belgique. 5: L'Eglise des Pays-Bas 1559–1633* (Brussels, 1952); Alain Lottin, *Lille, citadelle de la contre-réforme? (1598–1668)* (Dunkirk, 1984).
6. Honoré Staes, *De martelaars van Oudenaarde: verhaal uit den tijd der Beeldstormers (1571–1572)* (Bruges, 1912).
7. See for instance Margit Thøfner, *A common art: urban ceremonial in Antwerp and Brussels during and after the Dutch Revolt* (Zwolle, 2007); cited with gratitude to the author.
8. M. Dierickx, *De oprichting der nieuwe bisdommen in de Nederlanden onder Filips II, 1559–1570* (Antwerp and Utrecht, 1950).
9. On some of these challenges see Craig Harline and Eddy Put, *A bishop's tale. Mathias Hovius among his flock in seventeenth-century Flanders* (New Haven and London, 2000).
10. Jean Chifflet, *Palmae cleri Anglicani, seu Breves narrationes eorum, quae in Anglia contigerunt circa mortem, quam pro Religione Catholica VII. Sacerdotes Angli fortiter oppetiere* (Brussels, Jean Mommaert, 1645); Gerrit Vanden Bosch, 'Over de doden niets dan goeds? Zeventiende eeuwse elogia en necrologia van jezuïeten in de Hollandse Zending als bronnen voor religieuze mentaliteitsgeschiedenis', *Trajecta* 6:4 (1997), 334–45.
11. Aline Goossens, *Les inquisitions modernes dans les Pays-Bas Méridionaux (1520–1633)*, vol. 2 (Brussels, 1998), pp. 122–3.
12. [Adriaan van Haamstede et al.], *Historien der vromer Martelaren*, vol. 2 (Dordrecht: Joris Waters, 1612).
13. Jozef De Brouwer, *De kerkelijke rechtspraak en haar evolutie in de bisdommen Antwerpen, Gent en Mechelen tussen 1570 en 1795*, 2 vols (Tielt, 1971–72).
14. E.W. Lynam, 'The Irish character in print, 1571–1923', *The Library: Transactions of the Bibliographical Society* 4:4 (1924), 293–6; Dermot McGuinne, *Irish type design: a history of printing types in the Irish character* (Blackrock, 1992).
15. Alfons K.L. Thijs, *Van geuzenstad tot katholiek bolwerk. Maatschappelijke betekenis van de Kerk in contrareformatorisch Antwerpen* (Turnhout, 1990), pp. 97–106.
16. *An introduction to a devoute life*, trans. John Yaxley ([Douai], 1613); *Aen-leydinghe oft Ondervvijs tot een devoot godtvrughtigh leven*, trans. Adriaan van Meerbeeck (Antwerp, 1616).
17. On some aspects of the censorship laws and their operation see Paul Arblaster, 'Policy and the press in the Habsburg Netherlands, 1585–1690', in Brendan Dooley and Sabrina A. Baron (eds), *The politics of information in early modern Europe*, Routledge Studies in Cultural History 1 (London and New York, 2001), pp. 179–98; Paul Arblaster, '"Dat de boecken vrij sullen wesen". Private profit, public utility and secrets of state in the seventeenth-century Habsburg Netherlands', in Joop W. Koopmans (ed.), *News and politics in early modern Europe (1500–1800)* (Leuven, 2005), pp. 79–95.
18. Peter Guilday, *The English Catholic refugees on the Continent 1558–1795* (London and New York, 1914), esp. pp. 19–20; John Antony Bossy, 'Elizabethan Catholicism: the link with France', unpublished doctoral thesis (Cambridge, 1960), esp. pp. 43, 53, 59.
19. Paul H.A.M. Abels, '"Misbruycken ende papistischen superstitiën": Hollandse bemoeienis met de Utrechtse kerk rond 1600', *Oud-Utrecht* 77:4 (2004), 99–106.
20. Michael E. Williams, 'William Allen: the sixteenth century Spanish connection', *Recusant History* 22:2 (1994), 123–40.
21. L.J. Rogier, *Geschiedenis van het katholicisme in Noord-Nederland in de zestiende en zeventiende eeuw*,

5 vols (Amsterdam and Brussels, 1964), pp. 516, 495.
22 Louis Van Wassenhove, *Ottavio Mirto Frangipani, nuntius van Vlaanderen en de Engelsche katholieken (1596–1606)* (Baasrode, 1925).
23 Rogier, *Geschiedenis* (1964), pp. 229–30, 550–1.
24 See Bernard Ward, 'The Old Chapter', *Catholic Encyclopedia*, vol. 11 (New York, 1911) s.v.; Hugh Farmer, 'Historical influences on the early development of the EBC', *English Benedictine History* 7 (1981), 1–8; Edward Maihew, *Congregationis Anglicanae Ordinis Sanctissimi Patriarchae Benedicti Trophaea* (Rheims, 1619); Clement Reyner, *Apostolatus Benedictinorum in Anglia* (Douai, 1626).
25 Rogier, *Geschiedenis* (1964), p. 518.
26 René Taveneaux, *Le Catholicisme dans la France classique, 1619–1715*, 2 vols (Paris, 1980).
27 Guilday, *English Catholic refugees* (1914); Pascal Majérus, *Ordres mendiants anglo-irlandais en Belgique* (Brussels, 2001); Claire Walker, *Gender and politics in early modern Europe. English convents in France and the Low Countries* (Basingstoke and New York, 2003).
28 *Monasticon Belge*, tome 3, vol. 2 (Liège, 1966), p. 470.
29 Gerrit Vanden Bosch, 'Pionnen op een schaakbord. De rol van klopjes in de belangenstrijd tussen jezuïeten en seculiere priesters in de Republiek omstreeks 1609-1610', *Trajecta* 9:3 (2000), 252–83, at p. 270.
30 The most important of the many works on the subject are E.E.A.J.M.Theissing, *Over klopjes en kwezels* (Utrecht, 1935); Marit Monteiro, *Geestelijke maagden* (Hilversum, 1996); D. van Heel OFM, 'Rotterdamse klopjes', *Neerlandica Seraphica* 13 (1939), 327–9. The first basis of the historiography is J.J. Graaf, 'Uit de levens der Maechden van den Hoeck te Haarlem', *Bijdragen voor de geschiedenis van het bisdom Haarlem* 17 (1891), 231–302; 18 (1893), 61–149; 19 (1894), 140–59, 287–313; 20 (1895) 110–159, 321–402.
31 *Monasticon Belge*, tome 4, vol. 6 (Liège, 1972), pp. 1413–16, 1482.
32 Herman Verleyen, *Dom Benedictus van Haeften, proost van Affligem 1588–1648: bijdrage tot de studie van het kloosterleven in de Zuidelijke Nederlanden* (Brussels, 1983).
33 *Monasticon Belge*, tome 4, vol. 1 (Liège, 1964), pp. 123–4.
34 *Basilica Bruxellensis pars altera, sive Appendix* (Mechelen: Laurentius Vander Elst, 1743), p. 56.
35 H.W. van Tricht (ed.), *De briefwisseling van Pieter Corneliszoon Hooft*, vol. 3 (Culemborg, 1979), pp. 181–3, 201–17 passim.
36 Sir George Chaworth's diary of his embassy to Brussels in 1621, in Alfred John Kempe (ed.), *The Loseley Manuscripts* (London, 1836), p. 456.
37 J. Proost, *Inventaire ou table alphabétique & analytique des noms de personnes contenus dans les registres aux gages & pensions des chambres des comptes* (Brussels, 1890), pp. 19, 37, 8, 26.
38 Rogier, *Geschiedenis* (1964), p. 895.
39 Brussels, Algemeen Rijksarchief, Audiëntie 1398/7: registration of English and French residents in Brussels, 1597.
40 A. Jamees, *Brugse Poorters*, vol. 3 (1990).
41 Louis Jadin, 'Procès d'information pour la nomination des évêques et abbés des Pays-Bas, de Liège et de Franche-Comté d'après les Archives de la Congrégation Consistoriale. 1re partie: 1564–1637', *Bulletin de l'Institut Historique Belge de Rome* 8 (1928), 69, 118, 122, 136, 148, 161, 202–6. These processes provide many valuable details of the professional networks of the higher clergy.
42 *ODNB*, s.v. 'Chamberlain, George', 'Clement, Caesar'.
43 Leo Hicks, 'The exile of Dr William Gifford from Lille in 1606', *Recusant History* 7 (1963–4), 214–38.
44 Alfred Poncelet, *Nécrologe des Jésuites de la province Flandro-Belge* (Wetteren, 1931), p. 77 n.10; Dominican obits in *Verzameling der graf- en gedenkschriften van de provincie Antwerpen. Arrondissement Antwerpen*, vol. 5 (Antwerp, 1873), p. 127.
45 Brussels, Algemeen Rijksarchief, Audiëntie 1398/7.
46 On Wake's business activities see Roland Baetens, *De nazomer van Antwerpens welvaart. De diaspora en het handelshuis De Groote tijdens de eerste helft der 17de eeuw*, vol. 1 (Gemeentekrediet, 1976),

pp. 208, 230–1, 247; P. Voeten, 'Bijdrage tot de geschiedenis van het handelsleven te Antwerpen tijdens de eerste jaren van het Twaalfjarig Bestand (1609–1612)', unpublished licentiate thesis (Leuven, 1954), p. 98; Ben Broos, *Meesterwerken in het Mauritshuis* (The Hague, 1987), pp. 119–21.

47 Broos, *Meesterwerken* (1987), pp. 121–4.

48 A. Schillings (ed.), *Matricule de l'Université de Louvain*, vol. 5 (Brussels, 1962), p. 151; Anthony Kenny (ed.), *The Responsa Scholarum of the English College, Rome. Part Two: 1622–1685* (CRS 55; 1963), p. 406; Dominic Aidan Bellenger, *English and Welsh priests 1558–1800. A working list* (Bath, 1984), p. 118.

49 Arthur K. Wheelock, Jr, Susan J. Barnes and Julius S. Held, *Van Dyck. Peintures* (Washington, 1990), pp. 196–7; Thomas Hunter, *The Life of Catharine Burton, Mother Mary Xaveria of the Angels, of the English Teresian Convent at Antwerp. Collected from her own writings and other sources*, [edited by Henry J. Coleridge] (London, 1876), p. 278.

50 Joannes Diercxsens, *Antverpia Christo nascens et crescens seu Acta Ecclesiam Antverpiensem*, vol. 7, 1607–1700 (Antwerp, 1773), p. 415; Anne Hardman, *English Carmelites in penal times* (London, 1936), p. 54. The author would like to express his appreciation to Fr. Ian Dickie, former archivist of the Archdiocese of Westminster who in 1997 identified the comparative study of the Dutch and English Missions as a lacuna in current scholarship.

9

Priests, nuns, presses and prayers: the Southern Netherlands and the contours of English Catholicism

CLAIRE WALKER

In 1622, Elizabeth Godwin, a young gentlewoman from Wells, made her religious profession in the English Augustinian cloister of St Monica's in Leuven. The house's chronicle account of her conversion and path to the convent includes a tale about the supernatural power invested in rosary beads. A physician who had encouraged her vocation related that one day he happened upon the devil in the form of a black crow and that he 'took out his beads and flung them at him', whereupon Satan vanished, leaving an uprooted plum tree and 'filthy stink' in his wake. The chronicle did not attribute Godwin's desire to be a nun nor her choice of Leuven to this story; rather it was recorded 'because it shows the power of beads and other hallowed things against the devil'.[1] Related by a man who 'had lived among the Jesuits', Godwin's miraculous tale confirms the complex interactions between English and Tridentine Catholicism, and the collaborative role of both missionary priests and laity in importing and disseminating Counter-Reformation reforms and piety. Boys and men left England to be educated in schools abroad or trained as priests, they then returned to their homeland and imparted Continental Catholic ideas and devotions to their kin and associates or, if they were clerics, to their flock, some of whom then chose to travel abroad to become priests and nuns, yet likewise remained in contact with their families and friends, either directly if priests on the mission, or indirectly through letters, literature and visits by their associates.

The single and multiple passages of men and women between England and the Continent, commonly the Southern Netherlands, did much to shape the contours of English Catholicism. This was acknowledged by John Bossy in his seminal study, *The English Catholic community*. Yet although Bossy's thesis hinged upon the role of the Mission in defining post-Reformation Catholicism, he focused on the community in England rather than the institutions that produced the missionaries.² Subsequent scholarly debate became embroiled in the 'survival versus revival' argument that arose from Christopher Haigh's critique of Bossy.³ Various historians have criticised the insularity of this literature, arguing that it disconnected Catholic from 'mainstream' English history.⁴ It similarly discouraged comparative studies with Welsh, Scottish and Irish Catholicism. Tadhg Ó hAnnracháin has pointed out that, despite shared political, ethnic and linguistic links, there 'is a sense of mutual isolation and relative lack of cross-fertilization between the various communities of scholars'.⁵

Perhaps even more glaring, given the many expatriates and the religious houses, is the dearth of scholarship on connections with Continental Catholics. Peter Guilday provided the most extensive coverage of the colleges, seminaries and monastic establishments in exile. Highly subjective, and by the early twenty-first century very dated, his *English Catholic refugees on the Continent, 1558–1795*, nonetheless drew on a wealth of archival research in Britain and Europe and revealed the scale of the émigrés' activities and the support they received from Rome, Spain, the Southern Netherlands and other Catholic states.⁶ Numerous books and articles published by the successors to the Continental religious houses and the Catholic Record Society offered insights into individual and institutional efforts to assist the exiled English Catholics. Partisan and often hagiographic, this material was principally more interested in the providential and the spiritual than in assessing foreign political and religious influence. There have been notable exceptions but until the final decades of the twentieth century the study of English Catholicism remained as insular geographically as it was historiographically.⁷

Since the 1990s the debate has moved forward and begun to contextualise English Catholicism within the wider religious, political and cultural research on early modern Europe. Michael Questier and Peter Lake have explored the sites where competing political and religious cultures met to challenge the neat juxtapositions that characterised previous debates and assumptions.⁸ Alexandra Walsham's research has both revised formerly narrow definitions of 'Catholic' and positioned the English mission and the piety it transmitted as products of the Continental Counter-Reformation.⁹ Walsham and others have also considered the significance of the vast body of Catholic devotional and controversial literature, much of it published abroad, to show that printing was a vital element of missionary activity.¹⁰ Alison Shell's work on 'imaginative writing' has investigated the political nature of poetry and drama written by Catholics in England and abroad. Shell's analysis of the ways drama performed in colleges and seminaries abroad might instil a martyrological ideal into the boys and young men educated there, with obvious consequences for their ministry in England, makes abundantly clear the significance of the exiled religious houses in shaping English Catholic *mentalités*.¹¹

Drawing upon the research and insights of this new generation of scholars, who have done much to reorientate the history of post-Reformation English Catholicism so as to encompass wider disciplinary and international boundaries, this paper will consider the importance of the exiled Catholic diaspora in the Southern Netherlands, in particular the religious communities of men and women which were essential for both Catholic survival and the transmission of Tridentine ideas and practices. As schools, seminaries, powerhouses of prayer, respectable retreats, refuges from persecution, tourist sites, intellectual hubs and centres for political activism, the colleges and cloisters nurtured existing and future generations of Catholics both directly and indirectly. After an overview of the religious institutions and their activities, I will focus on ways by which they shaped piety in their homeland, looking in particular at the popular Counter-Reformation devotion, the rosary.

Exile in the Southern Netherlands: the religious houses and Catholic renewal

Geographically, the Southern Netherlands was one of the places most likely to prove attractive to exiles from England, given the ease of passage from ports on either side of the Channel. However, the Spanish territories proved a popular destination for Catholics who decided to absent themselves from their homeland, largely as a result of the political support they received from Spain during the reign of Elizabeth. Initially, other than priests and laymen who were compelled to depart England owing to their opposition to Elizabeth's accession, scholars were one of the first identifiable groups to establish themselves abroad. British students had frequented Continental universities before the Reformation and their established links with several institutions made these suitable refuges in times of religious and political uncertainty. Peter Guilday noted that within a year of Elizabeth's succession more than a hundred scholars left Oxford and Cambridge, most relocating to Leuven, which was the intellectual centre for Catholic exiles before the English College was established at Douai in 1568.[12] Lay Catholics followed and by 1561 their numbers in towns like Antwerp, Leuven, Brussels, Bruges and Ghent were so great that the regent of the Low Countries, Margaret of Parma, lobbied Philip II for assistance in the form of pensions for the impecunious English nobles and gentry, and religious establishments for the clergy.[13]

Spanish support enabled the phenomenal profusion of religious institutions for the émigrés. Between 1568 and 1700 over thirty establishments were founded in the Southern Netherlands alone, most during the governorship of the Archdukes Albert and Isabella (1598–1633).[14] The numbers of men and women entering these religious houses are not precise but it has been estimated that between 1598 and 1642 some 5,000 took their vows across the Continent.[15] My research on English nuns counted 1,057 professions in nine cloisters between 1590 and 1710, seven of which were in the Spanish Netherlands.[16] Reports from English government agents abroad regularly warned of the dangers posed by the tide of Catholic exiles. A list of religious houses in the Southern Netherlands from the reign of Charles I noted 1,101 seminarians, priests, monks and nuns in twenty-five English, Irish and Scots establishments.[17] In 1708, the spy John Macky reported twenty-two English houses in Flanders and one college of Scots Jesuits, containing 610 nuns, 303 priests and innumerable students, seminarians and novices.[18] Although these figures were inaccurate, Macky nonetheless insisted that his list 'will plainly show Her Majesty from whence such a growth of popery in England proceeds and why it must increase upon us every day if not prevented'.[19] Indeed, from the outset the existence of the religious institutions and the numbers joining them were sufficient to elicit a legislative response from the English government, which, from Elizabeth's reign, sought to restrain not only those who became priests from returning to English soil, but also the exodus of young men and women to the Continent for education and the constant flow of books and devotional objects into England.

For good reasons, the government took note of the political tenor of these religious institutions. From 1574 a steady stream of priests, first from Douai, then Jesuits from the English College in Rome, and ultimately the other secular, Jesuit, Benedictine, Franciscan and Dominican establishments abroad, made their return journeys across the Channel to clandestine ministry and possible death at the gallows. The numbers of clergy and their distribution have elicited considerable scholarly debate.[20] Yet priests' memoirs suggest many performed a diverse ministry that combined household chaplaincy with preaching missions to less well-serviced regions. Thus, the Jesuit John Gerard, while resident at William Wiseman's house in Essex, also went on 'missionary journeys' as far afield as Lancashire.[21] While there is no question that some areas suffered from a lack of clerical and therefore liturgical sustenance, the colleges and seminaries imported more than simply human resources into England. The Counter-Reformation in all its militancy and practical piety crossed the Channel too, and it was arguably this legacy of English religious exile on the Continent that sustained Catholics, more than the personal ministry of priests.

Geographic convenience and Spanish support may have attracted English émigrés to the Low Countries, but they were also encouraged to settle there by its rulers, in particular the Archdukes Albert and Isabella who, between 1598 and 1633, 'consciously reshaped the Catholic Church in the Tridentine image'.[22] In addition to overseeing reform in their own territories, which included investment in several new religious institutions, they provided significant support to embattled Catholic minorities in the Protestant states of northern Europe. With the backing of Spain they patronised the exiled religious institutions and well-connected lay émigrés, and via direct political and diplomatic channels endeavoured to secure toleration for Catholics in the British Isles.[23] Their assistance to English religious houses included financial and political support for the seminaries at Douai and Leuven, the Jesuit College at St Omer, and various women's cloisters, including Mary Ward's controversial attempt to establish a female version of the Society of Jesus. As well as providing pensions, they lobbied others to subsidise the houses, generously contributed towards devotional items, intervened in external and internal political matters, and regularly visited their favoured establishments.[24]

The English Benedictine abbey in Brussels was one such place. Advocates of the cloister from the outset, Albert and Isabella participated in the clothing and profession of the eight founding nuns, providing a banquet for them and their guests afterwards. In subsequent years, the Infanta offered similar support to other novices and she visited the nuns many times. Despite language barriers, she consoled sick nuns and inspired the sisters with her sincere piety.[25] Others associated with the archducal court at Brussels likewise proffered their aid. Isabella's confessor, Andrés de Soto, acted as commissioner-general of the English Franciscan province and oversaw the foundation of the Third Order Regular cloister of Franciscan nuns in Brussels in 1621. Significantly, the new convent was to commemorate Isabella's own decision to become a Franciscan tertiary upon Albert's death and it was dedicated to St Elizabeth, her patron saint.[26]

Albert and Isabella also assisted lay émigrés. The Infanta's entourage included Irish and Scots women, while various aristocrats were welcome at court and attained pensions and honours from Spain through the assistance of their hosts in the Low Countries.[27] Other, less well-connected but powerful exiles were also recipients of the archdukes' favour. In 1612 a consortium of English Catholic merchants in Antwerp was granted a concession allowing it to circumvent new protectionist laws on the import of cloth. As Paul Arblaster observed, the merchants funded the English mission and facilitated travel to and from the Continent, as well as being the fathers of the next generation of nuns and priests. Thus, this was a shrewd move because exiled individuals and families did much to further the archdukes' missionary ambitions.[28] Although not a direct recipient of the rulers' patronage, men like the prolific Catholic publisher John Heigham contributed greatly to the Catholic cause. Heigham, who had spent time in prison in England before settling in Douai in 1603 and then St Omer in 1613, commissioned works from local printers for the clandestine Catholic book trade in England. He married a woman from Artois, and two of their children entered the religious life. Both Heigham and his wife smuggled consignments of books into England, and he is known to have arranged the passage of students for the English College at St Omer. He acted as a guide for English visitors to St Omer and discussed religious issues with Protestant dinner guests.[29]

Men like Heigham formed an émigré community with their clerical and monastic compatriots, attending religious services in the churches and chapels of the British cloisters, patronising them and often giving their children to them initially for education but later perhaps as seminarians and novices. Thus, in the late sixteenth and early seventeenth centuries we find families like the Babthorpes of Osgodby in Yorkshire. The staunch recusant Lady Grace Babthorpe (c.1563–1635), who had spent time in York Castle, and her husband, Sir Ralph (1561–1618), settled in Leuven in 1613 to avoid imprisonment and the forfeiture of their estates. Of their four sons and three daughters, Robert became a Benedictine monk, Ralph and Thomas entered the Society of Jesus after studying at the English colleges at St Omer and Rome, and Barbara (after initially entering the Brussels Benedictines) joined Mary Ward's Institute, where she became superior. After Sir Ralph's death in 1618, Grace Babthorpe was professed among the English Augustinians in Leuven in 1621 with her granddaughter, Frances Babthorpe. Frances' father, Sir William, the recusant heir, eventually lost the family estates. Penniless, he joined the Spanish army in the Netherlands in 1633 and died fighting the French in 1635. Several of his other children also joined the religious orders abroad.[30]

Émigré families like the Babthorpes, whose own exile necessitated links with local religious and civic authorities, were instrumental in the foundation of many religious houses. The beginning of the English Augustinian cloister of St Monica's in Leuven offers a case in point. The founding nuns who came from the town's Flemish convent, St Ursula's, were assisted by kin, like Thomas Worthington, who lobbied the archbishop on their behalf, even offering to support them financially, as well as locating a suitable dwelling. Others, like the generous 'Mr and Mrs Liggons', an English couple living in Leuven who provided food, found them a servant and even offered to sell them their house, and the English student who provided money to purchase a sanctuary lamp for the chapel, were simply pious Catholics who wanted to extend their charity to their co-religionists.

The nuns' clerical assistants reinforce the complex web of connections between the women, their kin, the wider exiled diaspora and their Spanish patrons. St Monica's first chaplain, the Oxford-educated exile John Fenn, had served as chaplain in Sir William Stanley's regiment in the Spanish army and translated devotional books before his first links with the Flemish St Ursula's in 1601. He helped to secure the appropriate permission for the new house and offered to serve the nuns for no stipend.[31] Other Masses were said by a poor Irish priest studying in Leuven, and by the Irish Franciscans who had just established their college in the town but had nowhere suitable to celebrate the sacrament.[32] Caesar Clement, nephew of the former prioress Margaret Clement, who was educated at Douai and ordained in Rome, and who had been a chaplain at the court in Brussels and vicar-general of the Spanish army in Flanders before his appointment as dean of St Gudula's at Brussels in 1617, also assisted and sent them food. In many instances these patrons were lifelong friends of the cloister and, like Thomas Worthington and Fr Fenn, were buried there on their deaths. Caesar Clement left legacies to St Monica's, the English Benedictine nuns in Brussels and the English College at Douai.[33] Kinship, a shared experience of exile and the desire to restore Catholicism in their homeland bound the disparate émigrés together in their adopted country and inspired them to revive Catholicism at home.

They worked towards this goal in a variety of ways. Most obviously, the seminaries trained the missionaries whose pastoral ministry to Catholics in their homeland and occasional political intrigues enacted their Continental patrons' ambitions for the British Isles. Here I want to look at the less-confrontational means by which those who remained in the Spanish Netherlands ensured Catholic survival and renewal, in particular, the transmission of reformed Catholicism by nuns and priests in the cloisters and towns inhabited by the émigrés. Through schools, boarding facilities and occasional hospitality, the religious houses had ample opportunity to proselytise and catechise their lay compatriots.

Most establishments had schools where English children could receive a Catholic education. Many were small enterprises, like the Franciscan convent in Bruges that in 1668 had fifteen scholars, and the Dominican college for boys near Antwerp that opened in 1660 with six students, and between 1671 and 1672 had only five.[34] Others, however, operated on a much larger scale. The popular Jesuit College at Douai had an average annual enrolment of over a hundred during the seventeenth century – at its peak in 1635 there were two hundred boys, and twenty-five fathers teaching them. The Benedictine college of St Gregory in the same town operated on a smaller scale, with thirty to forty students between 1620 and 1670 and just under sixty by the end of the century.[35] Some of the larger girls' establishments had up to thirty pupils by the eighteenth century.[36] The boundaries between future permanent inmates and temporary residents were often blurred, and some students would have been encouraged to enter the novitiate. Yet most lay pupils returned to lay society, principally in England. In 1663 Sir Philip Skippon was told about the Ghent Benedictine nuns' school where the girls were 'at liberty to return home when they please'.[37] It is estimated that three-quarters of the Jesuit school at St Omer's pupils apparently remained laymen.[38]

The function of the exiled education facilities was clear. Scholars were schooled in academic subjects and gender-specific skills, and gained a good spiritual grounding. The latter would serve them well should they join the cloister, but was equally suitable for those who would become the next generation of recusant spouses and parents.[39] The rules of the Augustinian canonesses' school in Bruges aimed to train the scholars 'to play their part as "Christian gentlewomen"'.[40] The Ghent Benedictines reputedly taught 'young gentlewomen to sing, &c'.[41] Although the school registers of cloisters like the Benedictines of Cambrai overlap with postulant records, of the seventy-five women or so who entered and left between 1623 and 1710, some went to other cloisters, a few remained single, but most presumably married, like Elizabeth Plumpton, who arrived as a twelve-year-old 'pensionnar' in 1703 but subsequently wed twice and would have passed on something of her upbringing abroad to her children.[42] Generations of families like the Haggerstons of Northumberland were educated abroad, and while several individuals entered the religious life, their siblings returned to England to marry and produce further children for education and religious profession.[43] School registers that contain successive generations of families like the Bedingfields, Blundells, Yates and Carylls attest to the significance of the educative institutions abroad in forming the intellectual, moral and religious core of the Catholic minority.

Not only the young had an opportunity to frequent the religious houses and imbibe something of their spiritual culture. The exiled communities also had boarding facilities and guesthouses for mature visitors who required temporary or longer-term accommodation. Some, like Ann Hall, the widowed mother of the Benedictine abbess, who arrived at Cambrai in 1674, retired to cloisters and led semi-monastic lives for their final years. In 1693 the widowed Lady Bridget Crossland settled at Cambrai with her two granddaughters, only one of whom subsequently became a nun.[44] Other boarders were transitory, like the dowager duchess of Buckingham, who in the 1640s spent around twelve months with the Ghent Benedictines,.[45] During periods of religious and political uncertainty at home, religious houses might be overwhelmed with kin seeking refuge, their inhabitants forced to give up their own beds to accommodate the refugees.[46] Although they usually only associated with the community for a few months or a year or two, these guests lived in close proximity to their hosts and interacted with them both socially and during religious services. Thus, there was ample opportunity to acquire something of the reformed devotions practised by the nuns that might then be imparted to kin and associates outside the cloister.

Travellers were also welcome for even briefer encounters. During Sir Philip Skippon's 1663 visit to Leuven, he stayed in the Augustinian canonesses' guest facility and was shown around the university by some of the English students who lodged there on a more permanent basis.[47] In 1694 the Catholic Earl of Perth and his wife dined with the English Carmelite nuns in Hoogstraten and were housed for the night in the confessor's lodgings.[48] Seventeenth-century tourists, both Catholic and Protestant, used British clergy as guides in the towns they visited. Thus the Scottish divinity student James Fraser noted on his 1559 return journey from Rome that he had met 'several Scotch and Irish fathers' in Ghent and that 'I owe indeed much of my information of this place to F. Gray', a Carmelite.[49] Although these were not standard tourist sites mentioned in the popular seventeenth-century guidebooks, by the early eighteenth century visits to the exiled religious houses were a common element in the British Grand Tour and travel accounts recorded visits to cloisters, conversations with priests and nuns, and their hospitality.[50]

The interaction at monastery guesthouses, parlours and tourist sites provided a Continental point of contact between the religious exiles and their co-religionists (and, indeed, Protestants) in England. While the clergy might offer their services as tour guides, the enclosed nuns welcomed visitors curious about life behind convent walls and the women immured there. Indeed some travellers' accounts suggest that the women's communities consciously displayed their wares in a bid to attract visitors. Nuns from aristocratic families and beautiful younger sisters and novices were sent to the grate to persuade even the most sceptical guest of the merits of the monastic state they had chosen.[51] Visitors not only talked to the clerics and nuns, but they also attended religious services. In 1694 the Earl of Perth attended compline in the Bruges Augustinian nuns' chapel.[52] Others acquired spiritual souvenirs and advice about places of religious significance. In 1663 Sir Philip Skippon was given a printed account of the miraculous cure in 1660 of Mary Minshull, whose lameness and other ailments were healed with oil from the sanctuary lamp in Our Lady of Succour's chapel in Brussels. Two days later he visited the chapel where the miraculous cure had occurred. The Dunkirk Benedictines advised him to visit St Omer, where he would find the bodies of some English saints.[53]

The alacrity with which the émigré religious houses welcomed guests, despite the prescriptions of enclosure, suggests that this hospitality was too important to forgo. There was certainly a pecuniary element involved, as visitors represented a source of patronage. Other visits were principally family reunions in which relatives stayed with their kin who had left home and country. However, the cloisters' ready acceptance of their status as tourist attractions and their preparedness to appeal to laypeople's prurient curiosity implies that they viewed visits as an opportunity to proselytise to 'heretics' and to satiate their Catholic guests' thirst for the elaborate religious ritual and pious conversation denied them at home. Thus the religious houses in the Southern Netherlands not only supplied priests for the British Isles, they supplemented the mission by providing an external point of contact where their co-religionists (and Protestants) might access the Counter-Reformation. Something of the spiritual intensity and life abroad inevitably found its way back across the Channel in the travel diaries, souvenirs and memories collected along the way. Moreover, travellers and even those who were never able to leave Britain's shores gained access to the renewed devotional vigour of their faith as it was being reformed and practised on the Continent, through the wealth of printed matter which made its way from presses in the Southern Netherlands.

Literature and devotion: Continental presses, cloisters and the contours of piety

It is impossible to identify precisely the number of 'Catholic' books produced between 1558 and 1700. Allison and Rogers identified 932 items in English printed abroad or clandestinely in England between 1558 and 1640.[54] For the period 1641 to 1700, 1,333 Catholic-related publications covering all of the British Isles have been listed.[55] Obviously not all this material originated in the Spanish Netherlands, but some of the most significant English presses were located there. In particular, the Jesuit press at St Omer is thought to have produced around 275 works in the 150 years from its establishment in 1608, mostly during the first half of the seventeenth century.[56] Douai, the centre for the training of English, Irish and Scots priests, was another publishing powerhouse. Between 1603 and 1613, it was the base for Roger Heigham, the second-most prolific publisher of English Catholic material after the St Omer press. He produced an average of three books a year between 1615 and 1631.[57]

The content of this literature ranged from liturgical and devotional material, to catechetical and instructional, to controversial and political items. Thomas Clancy's analysis of books published between 1615 and 1714 found that manuals for mental prayer and pious devotions like the rosary comprised nearly a quarter of all output.[58] Although some of this literature catered for the exiled religious houses' needs, the laity had access to a broad range, much of which was imbued with reformed Catholic principles. The regular reissue of certain items, like the *Jesus Psalter*, which was reprinted forty-one times between 1570 and 1640, and the popularity of enormously influential works, like Loyola's *Spiritual Exercises*, which not only appeared in abridged formats but also inspired a range of other educational manuals on mental and vocal prayer, the correct way to hear and participate in the sacraments and how to live a pious life, are a testament to the market among lay Catholics as well as members of religious orders. Most were translations of popular Continental texts, and they appeared predominantly in English, but some catered for native speakers in Wales, Scotland and Ireland too.[59] Other texts were produced with the illiterate in mind. Illustrated books, like *A Methode, to Meditate upon the Psalter, or the Great Rosarie of our Blessed Ladie*, combined text for the literate with pictures and verse for those who could not read.[60]

Evidence that the Continental literature found its way into domestic libraries comes from the 1584 search of a Buckinghamshire woman's house which uncovered a cache of pious Catholic books, along with various sacramental and devotional objects. Sources also indicate the circulation of texts by clergy, among Catholics and even into prisons and Protestant hands.[61] In 1677 Anne Hanne was professed as Dame Gertrude in the Paris Benedictine cloister. Already forty years old, Hanne had previously served Alethea Fairfax, who, with her mother, Abigail Fairfax, and aunt, Appolonia Yate, provided her monastic dowry. They furnished more than financial support, however. Lady Abigail Fairfax, who was noted for her piety, had lent Hanne copies of Gertrude More's *Confessiones Amantis* and Augustine Baker's *Sancta Sophia*, which confirmed her desire to enter a cloister.[62] The influence of these books, written in the Cambrai Benedictine cloister, published abroad and clandestinely sent into England, evidently encouraged devotion in the Fairfax household and ultimately spawned a monastic vocation. The Protestant authorities viewed such texts as seditious, so Catholic literature, along with relics and other holy objects, was the object of searches of suspected Catholic premises and, once, located was ritually incinerated in public places.[63]

The government's concern about the subversive power of literature was not unfounded. Alexandra Walsham has shown vividly the ways in which it might function as 'domme preachers' when priests were not available or, at the very least, supplement the oral ministry of those on the Mission.[64] Like texts, prayers and rituals performed similar functions. Lisa McClain's study of the creative ways post-Reformation English Catholics adapted to the new religious landscape, with its absence of churches and shrines and a dearth of clergy to administer the sacraments, makes this abundantly clear.[65] While priestly influence and lay inventiveness were important fashioners of English devotion, the Spanish Netherlands also played a central role. As a consequence of the kinds of encounters in Continental religious houses outlined above, reformed piety invariably filtered across the channel to be appropriated and enjoyed by Catholics in the houses, gardens, barns, prisons and places of execution where they practised their faith. One of the most versatile and popular devotions was the rosary.

The miraculous story tangentially inserted into Elizabeth Godwin's biography in the Leuven Augustinians' chronicle highlights its continued importance. Studies have shown how the Society of Jesus revised the observance, made popular in the fifteenth century by the Dominicans in accordance with Counter-Reformation ideals, and promoted rosary confraternities in missionary territories.[66] From the outset, the English exiles acknowledged its utility in their efforts to return their homeland to the Catholic fold. Following the example of the Jesuits in Rome, the English college at Douai instituted its own confraternity. William Allen wrote that the seminarians were 'most carefully instructed in … the way of using the Blessed Virgin's rosary with the mediations attached to it, in order that by understanding these things themselves they may be more fit to explain them hereafter to the simple people'.[67] The Jesuit Henry Garnet wrote a manual for the English rosary confraternity in which he stated that recitation of its prayers and corresponding meditation was useful in imparting the teachings of the New Testament and Catholic doctrine. He wrote 'everie devoute Catholicke, dailye when he saieth his beades, doth as it were in a booke read and reverentlye laieth before his eies' the central Church teachings on the lives of Christ and his mother.[68] Priests practised what they were taught. Imprisoned in the Tower and tortured, the Elizabethan Jesuit John Gerard fashioned rosaries out of orange peel to exercise his damaged fingers.[69]

The devotion was widely used in the convents too, both as part of formal religious observance and as personal prayer. Its popularity is evident in the dedication of rosary manuals to individual nuns. The 1620 English translation of Francis Borgia's *The Practise of Christian Workes*, which included *Certaine Pious Meditations Upon the Beades*, was dedicated to the Abbess of the Poor Clares at Gravelines by the supervisor of the Jesuit press at St Omer. He wrote that the text would encourage the pious to prayer and hoped that 'your, & the devotions of your holy family, wil give it new force'.[70] John Fenn, chaplain to the Augustinian nuns in Leuven, had translated Gaspare Loarte's *Instructions and Advertisements, How to Meditate the Misteries of the Rosarie of the Most Holy Virgin Mary* before assuming spiritual care of nuns. The women undoubtedly benefited from his work, as the rosary was a regular devotion in the cloister. Moreover, upon his death he left his library to the convent.[71] Other nuns developed their own contemplations. The saintly Carmelite prioress at Lier, Margaret Mostyn, who was especially devoted to the Virgin Mary, composed her own way of meditating through the mysteries of the rosary. The document was included in her hagiography by her confessor, Edmund Bedingfield, as instructions Mostyn had received in a Marian vision.[72]

Nuns employed the rosary in a variety of ways. Apart from its inclusion in formal communal prayer, sisters meditated on its mysteries during the Mass. In 1711, the decorative painter Sir James Thornhill enjoyed the 'delicious music' of a service in the Ghent Benedictine nuns' chapel and peeped through the grate to witness several of them 'telling their beads'.[73] Some cloisters subscribed to Marian sodalities. The Cambrai Benedictine nuns possessed a document outlining the indulgences attained by membership of one confraternity, suggesting that they practised a modified version of it.[74] When the Lier Carmelite house was 'beset by devils' which tormented Margaret Mostyn, the nun's beads were miraculously blessed by the infant Jesus and thereafter employed effectively against evil spirits.[75] Individuals were noted either for their devotion to the rosary or for their practical use of it during periods of spiritual desolation or distracting work. Anne Bromfield at St Monica's in Leuven suffered much desolation of mind and spirit and she found the rosary particularly useful when it came to easing her anguish.[76] Indeed, the Ghent Benedictine nuns who earned much-needed income from a craft industry that kept many sisters from the formal hours of prayer recited the rosary as they worked on the silk flowers.[77]

The rosary's utility and efficacy made it easily transmittable to the laity beyond the religious houses. Just as its practice was instilled into the Douai seminarians, so too was it passed on to the children in monastic and convent schools. In the Bruges Augustinian cloister, the girls in the school were required to 'say their beads walking with their Mistresses' daily at 10 a.m. They were encouraged to sleep with their rosary beads on their wrist, so that if they woke during the night they might 'adore God with some short aspiration'.[78] In 1760 Charles Neville, at school at St Omer, informed his father than he had been admitted into the college's Marian sodality.[79] Other religious sent their kin rosaries. The Benedictine Anthony Batt sent his sister in England a set of beads and instructions on how to use them. He said that the rosary was 'well knowne to most Catholikes' and that it was 'a most acceptable service and devotion' to God, the Virgin Mary and the 'Court of Heaven', while conversely it would cause 'a great confusion' to the devil, 'chasing him out of our hearts'.[80] The Jesuit Sabine Chambers specifically dedicated his rosary manual to the 'devout Catholike laity of England'.[81] The reception of such advice is evident by its prominence in devotion. Magdalen, Viscountess Montague said the rosary thrice daily and even wore her beads publicly to profess herself a Catholic.[82] The convert Augustinian nun Catherine Holland obtained rosary beads when attracted to the faith and would secretly say them on her knees at bedtime.[83] In the 1660s the Lancashire Catholic William Blundell formed a small family sodality of the rosary.[84] Scottish Catholics did likewise, and in 1788 Irish archbishops sought Rome's approval for what amounted to a national confraternity of the rosary.[85] Moreover, there are various stories of priests throwing their beads from the scaffold before execution and the crowd below surging to obtain the relics.[86]

As Lisa McClain and Anne Dillon have argued, the rosary was a badge of Catholicism that clearly identified a possessor of beads as Catholic. Yet, it was also an eminently versatile devotion that could be performed clandestinely – some conforming Catholics even said it during Church of England services – and, importantly, without the need for church or priest. Henry Garnet argued that it did not require any 'more knowledge then to say the *Pater noster*, and *Ave Maria*, nor any more charge then the price of a paire of Beades, nor any choice of place or situation of body, but as it shall like the partie'.[87] Thus, like books as 'domme preachers', the rosary was a kind of 'domme sacrament' which post-Reformation Catholics used to compensate for other, unavailable rituals. Given the reform of devotion in which its practitioners repeated the set prayers while meditating on the lives of Christ and Mary, English Catholics familiarised themselves with the aspects of Christocentric and Marian devotion promoted by the Tridentine Church. Thus, what on the surface seemed like a mindless repetitive prayer for the illiterate might well reinforce Catholic doctrine for all devotees, from the 'simpler sorte' for whome Garnet argued 'the beades are the unlearned mans book' to the educated gentry and aristocracy, and indeed the spiritually literate nuns and priests abroad.[88] Devotions like the rosary furthermore enabled Catholics in England to absorb some sense of the rich religious culture enjoyed by their kin on the Continent. Like the priests and lay travellers who made the journey from Dover to Douai and back to England, the rosary, popularly practised and disseminated by the exiled cloisters of the Southern Netherlands, imported elements of the Counter-Reformation and assisted the survival and indeed renewal of English Catholicism.

Notes
1. Adam Hamilton (ed), *The Chronicle of the English Canonesses Regular of the Lateran, at St Monica's in Leuven ... 1625–1644* (Edinburgh and London: Sands & Co., 1906), vol. I, pp. 247–52.
2. John Bossy, *The English Catholic community 1570–1850* (London: Darton, Longman & Todd, 1975).
3. Christopher Haigh, 'The fall of a Church or the rise of a sect? Post-Reformation Catholicism in England', *Historical Journal* 21 (1978), 181–6; Haigh, 'The continuity of English Catholicism in the English Reformation', *Past and Present* 93 (1981), 37–69; Haigh, 'From monopoly to minority: the Catholics in early modern England', *Transactions of the Royal Historical Society* 31 (1982), 129–47; Haigh, *English reformations: religion, politics and society under the Tudors* (Oxford: Clarendon Press, 1993); Haigh, 'Catholicism in early modern England: Bossy and beyond', *Historical Journal* 42 (2002), 481–94. For a good overview of this literature see Andrew R. Muldoon, 'Recusants, church papists, and "comfortable" missionaries: assessing the post-Reformation English Catholic community', *The Catholic Historical Review* 86 (2000), 242–57.
4. Ethan Shagan, 'Introduction: English Catholic history in context', in Shagan (ed.), *Catholics and the 'Protestant nation': religious politics and identity in early modern England* (Manchester and New York: Manchester University Press, 2005), pp. 6–8.
5. Tadhg Ó hAnnracháin, 'Catholicism in early modern Ireland and Britain', *History Compass* 3 (2005) B1 143, 1.
6. Peter Guilday, *The English Catholic refugees on the Continent, 1558–1795* (London and New York: Longmans, Green & Co., 1914).
7. Caroline Hibbard, *Charles I and the Popish Plot* (Chapel Hill, NC, University of North Carolina Press, 1983); Hibbard, 'Early Stuart Catholicism: revisions and re-revisions', *Journal of Modern History* 52 (1980), 1–34; Albert J. Loomie, *The Spanish Elizabethans: the English exiles at the court of Philip II* (London: Burns & Oates, 1963); Loomie, *Spain and the Jacobean Catholics*, 2 vols (London, Catholic Record Society, 64, 68, 1973–78); Loomie, 'Oliver Cromwell's policy toward the English Catholics: the appraisal by diplomats, 1654–1658', *The Catholic Historical Review* 90 (2004), 29–44; Thomas M. McCoog, *The Society of Jesus in Ireland, Scotland, and England 1541–1588: 'Our way of proceeding?'* (Leiden: Brill, 1996); McCoog, 'The English Jesuit mission and the French match, 1579–1581', *The Catholic Historical Review* 87 (2001), 185–213; Paul Arblaster, *Antwerp and the world: Richard Verstegan and the international culture of Catholic reformation* (Leuven: Leuven University Press, 2004); Claire Walker, *Gender and politics in early modern Europe: English convents in France and the Low Countries* (London and New York: Palgrave Macmillan, 2003); Pascal Majérus, *Ordres Mendiants Anglo-Irlandais en Belgique* (Brussels, 2001).
8. Peter Lake and Michael Questier, 'Agency, appropriation and rhetoric under the gallows: Puritans, Romanists and the state in early modern England' *Past and Present* 153 (1996), 64–107; Lake and Questier, 'Puritans, Papists and the "public sphere" in early modern England: the Edmund Campion affair in context', *Journal of Modern History* 72 (2000), 587–627; Lake and Questier, 'Prisons, priests and people', in Lake and Questier, *The Antichrist's lewd hat: Protes-*

tants, Papists and players in post-Reformation England (New Haven and London: Yale University Press, 2002).
9 Alexandra Walsham, *Church Papists: Catholicism, conformity and confessional polemic in early modern England* (Woodbridge: Boydell, 1993); Walsham, 'Miracles and the Counter-Reformation mission to England', *Historical Journal* 46 (2003), 779–815; Walsham, 'Translating Trent? English Catholicism and the Counter Reformation', *Historical Research* 78 (2005), 288–310.
10 Alexandra Walsham, '"Domme Preachers"? Post-Reformation English Catholicism and the culture of print', *Past and Present* 168 (2000), 72–123; Walsham, 'Unclasping the book? Post-Reformation English Catholicism and the culture of print', *Journal of British Studies* 42 (2003), 141–66.
11 Alison Shell, *Catholicism, controversy and the English literary imagination, 1558–1660* (Cambridge: Cambridge University Press, 1999), 226–7; Shell, '"Furor Juvenilis": Post-Reformation English Catholicism and exemplary youthful behaviour', in Shagan (ed.), *Catholics and the 'Protestant nation'*, pp. 185–206.
12 Guilday, *Catholic refugees*, pp. 4, 9–10. See also Bossy, *Catholic community*, pp. 12–13.
13 Guilday, *Catholic refugees*, p. 7.
14 Guilday, *Catholic refugees*, pp. 1–40; John J. Silke 'The Irish abroad, 1534–1691', in T.W. Moody, F.X. Martin and F.J. Byrne (eds), *A new history of Ireland, III, early modern Ireland 1534–1691* (Oxford: Clarendon Press, 1976), pp. 615–24; Paul Arblaster, 'The Archdukes and the Northern Counter-Reformation', in Werner Thomas and Luc Duerloo (eds), *Albert and Isabella 1598–1621: Essays* (Turnhout: Brepols, 1998), p. 90; R. Po-Chia Hsia, *The world of Catholic renewal 1540–1770* (Cambridge: Cambridge University Press, 1998), p. 87.
15 Walsham, '"Domme Preachers"?', 94.
16 Walker, *Gender and politics*, p. 20.
17 National Archives, Kew, Public Record Office (hereafter PRO) SP Flanders 77/8, fols 117–18, A List of the Semminaries, Monasteries, Cloisters, and Colledges ... in the Provinces of the Netherlands, Under the King of Spaines Obedience. It incorrectly calculates 1,103 people.
18 J.D. Alsop, 'John Macky's 1707 Account of the English Seminaries in Flanders', *Recusant History*, 15 (1981), 338–40. The Scots Jesuits had only twenty priests and few scholars. The article uses old style dating.
19 Alsop, 'Macky's 1707 Account', pp. 340.
20 Haigh, 'Continuity', pp. 197–202; Haigh, 'From monopoly', pp. 132–47; Patrick McGrath, 'Elizabethan Catholicism: a reconsideration', *Journal of Ecclesiastical History* 35 (1984), 414–28; Thomas M. McCoog, 'Sparrows on a rooftop": "How we live where we live" in Elizabethan England', in T.M. Lucas (ed), *Spirit style story: essays honoring John W. Padburg, S.J.* (Chicago, Jesuit Way, 2002), 237–64.
21 John Gerard, *The Autobiography of an Elizabethan*, trans. Philip Caraman (London: Longmans, Green & Co., 1951), p. 32. See also Philip Caraman, *Henry Morse: priest of the Plague* (London: Longmans, Green & Co., 1957), p. 33.
22 James D. Tracy, 'With and without the Counter-Reformation: the Catholic Church in the Spanish Netherlands and the Dutch Republic, 1580–1650', in Tracy, *The Low Countries in the sixteenth century: Erasmus, religion and politics, trade and finance* (Aldershot: Ashgate Variorum, 2005), p. 547.
23 Arblaster, 'The Archdukes', pp. 87–92; see also Eddy Put, 'Les Archiducs et la Réforme Catholique: Champs d'Action et Limites Politiques', in Thomas and Duerloo, *Albert and Isabella*, pp. 257–60.
24 Arblaster, 'The Archdukes', pp. 88–90.
25 PRO SP Flanders 77/6, fol. 73; Paul Arblaster, 'The Infanta and the English Benedictine nuns: Mary Percy's memories in 1634', *Recusant History* 23 (1997), 521–3.
26 Cordula van Wyhe, 'Court and convent: the Infanta Isabella and her Franciscan confessor Andrés de Soto', *Sixteenth Century Journal* 35 (2004), 420, 423–4. For other instances of his intervention, see Arblaster, 'The Archdukes', p. 89.
27 Arblaster, 'The Archdukes', pp. 90–1.
28 Arblaster, 'The Archdukes', p. 90.

29 *Oxford Dictionary of National Biography* (hereafter *ODNB*); A.F. Allison, 'John Heigham of S. Omer (c.1568–c.1632), *Recusant History* 4 (1957–8), 228–33, 236.
30 Hamilton (ed.), *Chronicle of St Monica's*, vol. 1, pp. 203–13; *ODNB*.
31 Hamilton (ed.), *Chronicle of St Monica's*, vol 1, pp. 39–40, 59–75: A.F. Allison and D.M. Rogers, *The contemporary printed literature of the English Counter-Reformation between 1558 and 1640: an annotated catalogue, vol. 2 Works in English* (Aldershot: Scolar Press, 1994), pp. 55–6.
32 Hamilton (ed.), *Chronicle of St Monica's*, vol 1, pp. 71–2.
33 *ODNB*; Harry R. Hoppe, 'Dr Caesar Clement, Chaplain to the Archduke Albert', *Recusant History* 7 (1964), 263–4.
34 Poor Clare Convent, Arundel, Franciscan MS Annals, fol. 44; A.C.F. Beales, *Education under penalty: English Catholic education from the Reformation to the fall of James II 1547–1689* (London: Athlone Press, 1963), pp. 182–3.
35 Beales, *Education under penalty*, pp. 166–7, 178–9.
36 Walker, *Gender and politics*, p. 93.
37 P. Skippon, 'An Account of a Journey Made thro' Part of the Low Countries, Germany, Italy and France', in A. and J. Churchill (eds), *A Collection of Voyages and Travels*, 3rd edn (London, 1744), vol. 6, p. 384.
38 Beales, *Education under penalty*, p. 169.
39 For an account of the regime in the English Augustinian canonesses' convent at Bruges, see C.S. Durrant, *A link between Flemish mystics and English martyrs* (London: Burns Oates & Washbourne, 1925), pp. 417–30. Also Beales, *Education under penalty*, pp. 159–66, 178–9; Caroline Bowden, "For the Glory of God": a study of the education of English Catholic women in convents in Flanders and France in the first half of the seventeenth century', *Paedagogica Historica, Supplementary Series*, vol. 5, Ghent, C.S.H.P. (1999), 81–5; B. Elliot, 'Some notes on Catholic education abroad, c.1760, from the correspondence of the Nevills of Holt', *Recusant History* 7 (1964), 249–62.
40 Durrant, *Flemish mystics*, p. 424.
41 Skippon, 'Account of a Journey', p. 384.
42 Joseph Gillow (ed.), 'Records of the English Benedictine nuns at Cambrai (now Stanbrook), 1620–1793', in *Miscellanea VIII* (London: Catholic Record Society 13, 1913), pp. 38–63.
43 M.B. Joyce, 'The Haggerstons: the education of a Northumberland family', *Recusant History* 14 (1977), 182, 188–9.
44 Gillow (ed.), 'Benedictine nuns at Cambrai', pp. 52–3, 56.
45 Annals of the English Benedictines at Ghent. Now at St Mary's Abbey, Oulton in Staffordshire (Oulton: Private Publication, 1894), p. 23.
46 Walker, *Gender and politics*, p. 94.
47 Skippon, 'Account of a Journey', p. 391.
48 *Letters from James Earl of Perth to his Sister, the Countess of Errol*, ed. William Jerdan (London: Camden Society 23, 1845), p. 39.
49 C.D. Van Strien, 'Recusant houses in the Southern Netherlands as seen by British tourists, c. 1650–1720', *Recusant History* 20 (1991), 498. See pp. 501–2 for more examples.
50 van Strien, 'Recusant houses', pp. 500–7.
51 Skippon, 'Account of a Journey', p. 377; *Letters from James Earl of Perth*, pp. 40, 42–4; van Strien, 'Recusant houses', pp. 500, 504–6.
52 Letters from James Earl of Perth, pp. 43.
53 Skippon, 'Account of a Journey', pp. 384, 387, 377. For another example of relics, see p. 376.
54 Allison and Rogers, *Contemporary printed literature*, vol. 2; Walsham, '"Domme Preachers"?', p. 83.
55 Michael Mullett, *The Catholic Reformation* (London and New York: Routledge, 1999), p. 176.
56 Mullett, *Catholic Reformation*, p. 176; Thomas H. Clancy, 'A content analysis of English Catholic books, 1615–1714', *The Catholic Historical Review* 86 (2000), 259.
57 Allison and Rogers, *Contemporary printed literature*, vol. 2, p. 220; *ODNB*; Clancy, 'Content analysis', p. 259.

58 Clancy, 'Content analysis', pp. 261–4, 272. Just under 24 per cent.
59 Walsham, '"Domme Preachers"?', pp. 93–4; Raymond Gillespie, *Devoted people: belief and religion in early modern Ireland* (Manchester and New York: Manchester University Press, 1997), pp. 151–2; Mullett, *Catholic Reformation*, pp. 178–9; Bernadette Cunningham, 'Culture and ideology of Irish Franciscan historians at Leuven 1607–1650', *Historical Studies* 17 (1991), 11–30.
60 *A Methode, to Meditate upon the Psalter, or the Great Rosarie of our Blessed Ladie* (Antwerp, 1598).
61 Lisa McClain, *Lest we be damned: practical innovation and lived experience among Catholics in Protestant England, 1559–1642* (New York and London: Routledge, 2004), pp. 49, 53.
62 'The English Benedictine Nuns of the Convent of Our Blessed Lady of Good Hope in Paris, now at St Benedict's Priory, Colwich, Staffordshire. Notes and Obituaries', ed. Joseph Hansom, in *Miscellanea VII* (London: Catholic Record Society 9, 1911), pp. 372–4; Michael Hodgetts, 'The Yates of Harvington 1631–1696', *Recusant History* 22 (1994), 163.
63 Walsham, '"Domme Preachers"?', pp. 85–8.
64 Walsham, '"Domme Preachers"?', pp. 93–4.
65 McClain, *Lest we be damned*.
66 Anne Dillon, 'Praying by number: the Confraternity of the Rosary and the English Catholic Community, c. 1580–1700', *History* 88 (2003), 456–62; McClain, *Lest we be damned*, pp. 90–6. For Europe, see Louis Châtellier, *The Europe of the devout: the Catholic Reformation and the formation of a new society*, trans. Jean Birrell (Cambridge: Cambridge University Press, 1989).
67 Cited in Dillon, 'Praying by number', p. 462.
68 Henry Garnet, *The Societie of the Rosary. Newly Augmented* [London, 1596–7], pp. 8–9.
69 Gerard, *Autobiography*, pp. 116–17.
70 Francis Borgia, *The Practise of Christian Workes ... Certaine Pious Meditations Upon the Beades* ([St Omer], 1620), sig. *5.
71 Gaspare Loarte, *Instructions and Advertisements, How to Meditate the Misteries of the Rosarie of the Most Holy Virgin Mary* (London, 1597); *ODNB*; Hamilton (ed.), *Chronicle of St Monica's*, vol. 1, pp. 152–3.
72 Anne Hardman, *Mother Margaret Mostyn: Discalced Carmelite 1625–1679* (London: Burns Oates and Washbourne, 1937), pp. 119–22.
73 van Strien, 'Recusant houses', pp. 503–4.
74 Archives Départementales du Nord, Lille, MS 20 H 33, fols 47–56, Fragments [Privileges for a Confraternity].
75 Hardman, *Margaret Mostyn*, pp. 42–5.
76 Hamilton (ed.), *Chronicle of St Monica's*, vol. 2, pp. 181–2.
77 M.J. Rumsey (ed.), 'Abbess Neville's annals of five communities of English Benedictine nuns in Flanders, 1598–1687', in *Miscellanea V* (London, Catholic Record Society 6, 1909), p. 25.
78 Durrant, *Flemish mystics*, pp. 245, 257.
79 Elliot, 'Notes on Catholic education abroad', p. 259.
80 Anthony Batt, *A Poore Mans Mite. A Letter of a Religious Man of the Order of Saint Benedict, unto a Sister of his, Concerning the Rosarie or Psalter of Our Blessed Ladie, Commonly called the Beades* ([Douai], 1639), pp. 3, 14, 17–18.
81 Sabine Chambers, *The Garden of Our B. Lady. Or a Devout Manner how to Serve her in her Rosary* ([St Omer: English College Press], 1619), sig. *2.
82 Richard Smith, *An Elizabethan Recusant House, Comprising the Life of the Lady Magdalen Viscountess Montague (1538–1608)*, ed. A.C. Southern (London: Sands & Co, 1954), pp. 44, 47.
83 Durrant, *Flemish mystics*, p. 277.
84 Michael Mullett, *Catholics in Britain and Ireland, 1558–1829* (Basingstoke and London: Macmillan, 1998), p. 85.
85 David McRoberts, 'The rosary in Scotland', *Innes Review* 23 (1972), 83–5; Mullett, *Catholics in Britain*, pp. 114–15, 185.
86 Dillon, 'Praying by number', p. 454; McClain, *Lest we be damned*, p. 105.
87 Garnet, *Societie of the Rosary*, p. 5.
88 Garnet, *Societie of the Rosary*, [sig. A6].

10

Second-class yet self-confident: Catholics in the Dutch Generality Lands

CHARLES DE MOOIJ

On the evening of Sunday 29 November 1648, shortly after he had taken possession of the church at Boxtel (Figure 10.1), which had been evacuated by the Catholics, the Reformed minister Johan Aelstius got the scare of his life. At 10 p.m. a large crowd appeared in front of his house, dancing and yelling, kicking and pounding his door, and shouting dissolute words; they even fired a bullet through his window. Nor was this all, for they returned the following day. The minister reported to the classis that he feared for his life. This was not the first time that the Catholic inhabitants of the Brabantine village had given vent to their displeasure about the presence of the Reformed. Four weeks previously, the Sunday after the Feast of St Crispin, patron of cobblers and leather-workers, a large mob of uncouth men had entered the church while hymns were being sung after the sermon. They played the fiddle and danced, smoked their pipes and disturbed the divine service, claiming to do so in honour of St Crispin, and they threatened – very apt for leather-dressers – that they would cut to straps all those who converted to the Reformed religion.[1]

Events like those at Boxtel were legion in the southern part of the Dutch Republic after 1648. The acts of the classis often report on such ritually tainted forms of popular anger. Yet, in these cases the offenders were not those who had the political, legal, or military powers at their side. Indeed, the Catholics had recently been reduced to second-class citizens, and had been robbed of their traditional rights and possessions in the process. The behaviour of these men does not appear to be in accordance with their subordinate position; their self-confidence contrasts strongly with the fear displayed by the representatives of the new order. The title of this chapter about Catholics in the Generality Lands, then, might as well have been 'Suppressed yet feared'.

CATHOLICS IN THE DUTCH GENERALITY LANDS

Figure 10.1 Jan de Beijer, *The village church of Boxtel* (1740).

This chapter will explore the extraordinary situation of Catholics in the southern areas of the Dutch Republic during the seventeenth and eighteenth centuries: a Catholic majority brought into a subservient position by a Reformed minority. It deals with the Flemish, the Brabanters, and the inhabitants of the Lands of Overmaas, who – cut off from their co-religionists and compatriots in the South as a result of the military successes of the States General's army – were now regarded, because of their religion, as second-class subjects of a foreign ruler.[2] The areas in which they lived had formerly been part of the provinces that had remained under Habsburg sovereignty. Torn away from their natural centre, these territories were called the Generality Lands: States Flanders, States Brabant, and States Lands of Overmaas.[3]

In 1648 Spain and the Dutch Republic had agreed at the Peace of Münster that each would retain possession of the areas it possessed at the time of the conclusion of the peace. This implied that sovereignty over the northern areas of the county of Flanders and the duchy of Brabant, over half of Maastricht (a town which owed allegiance to two lords: the duke of Brabant and the prince-bishop of Liège), and part of the Lands of Overmaas was formally ceded to the States General. A measure of self-government was out of the question. The seven northern provinces argued that they had conquered the southern territories by force of arms. They hence regarded them as Generality Lands, as 'possessions' of the generality. Their sovereignty over the Generality Lands entitled the States General henceforth to decide on religious policy in these areas.[4]

In 1648 the religious composition of the population varied enormously in different parts of the Generality Lands. These variations were mainly the result of the war, which had lasted almost eighty years. In the towns and areas that had been controlled by the States General before the Twelve Year Truce (1609–21), and had remained so thereafter, the Protestant Reformation had been successful almost without exception; the majority of the population here was Reformed. However, this area covered only a limited part of the Generality Lands, namely the largest part of States Flanders and the north-western corner of States Brabant with the town of Bergen op Zoom.

In contrast, in the towns and areas that had remained under the rule of the archdukes and the king of Spain until the end of the Truce – that is, the major part of the Generality Lands – the inhabitants remained Catholics, even after the States army conquered their places of residence. After 1648 Catholics formed the majority here. With the Catholic Reformation – well under way by the end of the sixteenth century – being largely successful, the quiet and security brought by the archducal government resulted in a certain attachment to ancient forms. In addition, the Catholic religion was closely intertwined with popular culture and daily life, while the religion of a foreign ruler was almost by definition unpopular.[5] It should be pointed out that in those towns where the Reformation had been successful before the Truce, the new religion, instead of having been thrust upon the population by foreign rulers, had been introduced on the initiative and with the active support of the local population.

Particularly during the period before the Truce, the States rulers had been rather pragmatic in their attitude towards religious services. The reformation of church and society in the conquered territories was an important goal, yet those who carried political responsibility – in contrast to the ministers – were not oblivious to its practical feasibility. This implied, in practice, that the States General had the Catholic churches closed in every town they conquered and the priests sent away, but that the churches in the surrounding villages were left alone. Town-dwellers were allowed to go to church in the nearby villages without meeting major problems. The States government no longer went to extremes with the reform of government bodies. Reformed regents and high officials in the towns generally replaced Catholic ones, but the latter's colleagues in the countryside and lesser officials remained in post.[6]

This policy changed during the last phase of the war. More and more often the States General – partly on the initiative of ministers and Reformed synods – restricted the activities of Catholic clergy and had Catholic places of worship in the countryside closed. Yet the wartime conditions made it difficult for the

States authorities to enforce compliance with the rules. This changed only after the peace of 1648. A few weeks after the proclamation of the peace, the States General had all Catholic places of worship closed that were still in use in States Flanders and States Brabant; they sent Catholic clergy into exile and replaced Catholic officials with Reformed ones. At that time, there had been no complete agreement at Münster about the division of the Lands of Overmaas; therefore a *simultaneum*, or simultaneous use of parish churches by Catholics and the Reformed, was reintroduced in this territory, based on a previous local arrangement dating from the war. This exceptional arrangement resulted in numerous quarrels, yet remained in place in some areas for two centuries.[7] The situation was exceptional in the town of Maastricht, which had two overlords, and where, on the basis of the 1632 capitulation treaty, the public exercise of both the Catholic and the Reformed religion had been permitted and both religious groups disposed of the same political rights.[8]

At the same time church assemblies were being organised in the various parts of the Generality Lands that made a start with the appointment of Reformed ministers, schoolmasters, sextons, precentors, and readers, so as to promote the rise and flowering of new congregations. The keystone of the States General's Reformation of the Generality Lands was the introduction of regulations aimed at ending the influence of the Catholic Church in favour of the Reformed Church in the fields of education (1655), marriage (1655), poor relief (1659), and policy and justice (1660). From now on teaching was restricted to Reformed schoolmasters, legal marriages could only be concluded before a minister or a bench of aldermen, while overseers of the poor, just as all officials engaged in administration and justice, henceforth had to be of the Reformed persuasion.[9]

To replace Catholic office holders with men who were members or 'sympathisers' of the Reformed Church was not always a simple matter. In the first instance, vacancies were filled by the Reformed who lived locally or by citizens who had returned from religious exile after the takeover by the States. Yet many of the most prominent Protestant citizens had left for States territory decades earlier. The consequence was that candidates from the North were being appointed. In States Brabant this was not straightforward, since Brabant's privileges demanded that Brabanters alone would be appointed to posts related to government and justice. Because of past promises, the States General therefore preferred to appoint Reformed men who could prove that they or their parents or grandparents were Brabanters who had sought religious exile in the North. When appropriate candidates were lacking, the States General and the princes of Orange either accepted far-fetched Brabantine connections or appointed Reformed individuals from Holland, Zeeland, Utrecht, or Gelre, who were subsequently naturalised as Brabanters.[10]

The influx of Reformed from the North would continue until the end of the *ancien régime*. One of its consequences was that, whereas the Catholic elite remained focused on the Southern Netherlands, Reformed patrician families from Brabant continued to be oriented towards the Northern provinces, especially when it came to finding marriage partners. Yet the demand that office holders should be Brabantine also committed the Reformed elite to its Brabantine identity. This helps to explain why differences between Catholics and non-Catholics in seventeenth- and eighteenth-century Brabant never took on an 'ethnic' colour.

In spite of all the new legislation, the regulations, and the replacement of Catholic office holders by the Reformed, there was never any question of a large-scale reformation in the Generality Lands. The one to two hundred ministers who worked in States Flanders, States Brabant, and States Limburg after 1648 served what were generally very small communities, consisting of a few dozen members. Larger congregations were only found in the cities, in States Flanders, as well as in the north-western corner of States Brabant. For all the efforts at reformation, the large majority of the population remained Catholic and did everything to be able to exercise their Catholic faith. But how did they do so?

At the command of the States General, the familiar parish churches had been shut or had been granted for use by what was often no more than a handful of the Reformed. Their takeover of the churches had in many cases been accompanied by a considerable military show of force, so as to convince Catholics that resistance would be pointless. In most cases real resistance was indeed absent – although there were instances when priests personally dragged a minister from the pulpit.[11] As the example from Boxtel shows, Reformed churchgoers would sometimes also personally experience the disaffection of the Catholics. Church services were disturbed, ministers and churchgoers were abused and assaulted, there was vandalism, people threw rubbish and excrement, and there were many threats.[12] Yet, however frightening this was for the Reformed concerned, it mainly illustrated the powerlessness of the Catholic majority.

In the mean time, Catholic believers were forced to seek out other spaces to celebrate Mass: private homes, workshops such as breweries, or remote farm buildings. Just before the taking of 's-Hertogenbosch, Bishop Ophovius had been farsighted enough to consecrate 125 altar stones so that, where church space became unavailable, the Eucharist could be celebrated in private homes. Twelve years later the town had no fewer than eighteen locations where clandestine Masses were being said from time to time.[13]

The situation differed from place to place. But everywhere, believers, fearing fines or the arrest of their priests, tried to avoid discovery. They changed the location of their gatherings, which sometimes also took place by night; believers were only informed at the last minute, and men kept watch during

Mass. Upon discovery by the sheriff or soldiers, the churchgoers would take flight, but sometimes believers would also opt for confrontation, so that a disturbance of the Mass would lead to a considerable fight. This made the guardians of law and order more circumspect, and they subsequently took even more care when disturbing Masses and would eventually, for the sake of keeping the peace in the city or the countryside, often prefer a financial settlement where fines were paid in advance by the Catholic community.[14]

Undoubtedly, because of the bans and restrictions imposed by the States authorities, some Catholics in the Generality Lands were unable to fully meet their religious duties. But the drive to hear Mass and receive the sacraments was strong; if it was impossible in their own environment, people sought alternatives. To some of the Catholics in the Generality Lands, a solution was offered by the relative proximity of the border. On Sundays and holidays they would cross on foot or by wagon into the Spanish Netherlands, into lands belonging to Liège or Cleves or into the free imperial lordships to worship freely. But while they were willing to undertake long walks or drives, the distance to churches on

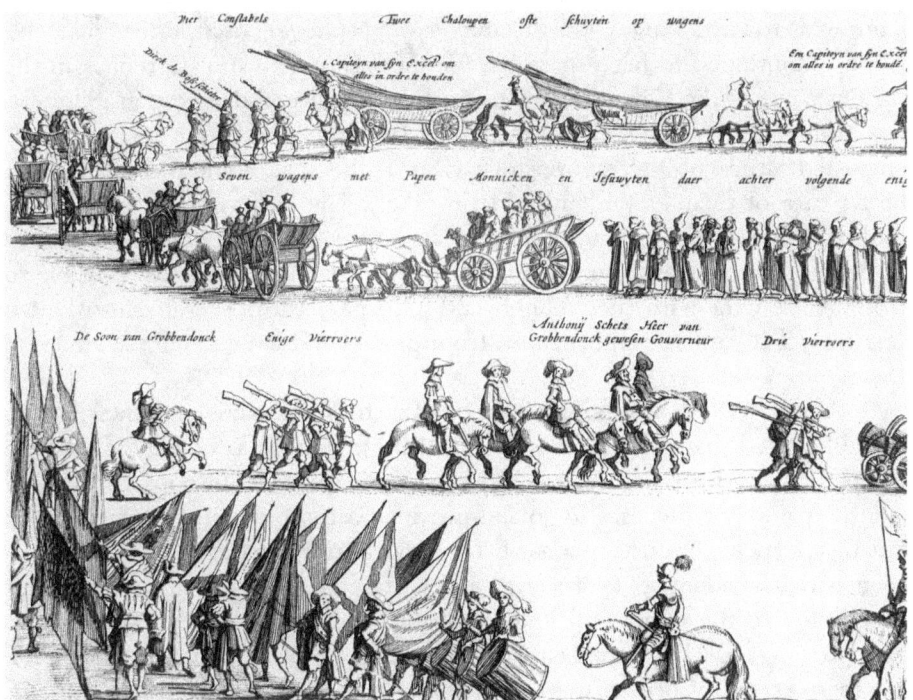

Figure 10.2 Anonymous, *Departure of the Roman Catholic clergy and the royal garrison from 's-Hertogenbosch on 17 September 1629, after the capitulation in favour of Frederik Hendrik, Prince of Orange* (1629).

the other side of the border was sometimes prohibitive. For that reason, small churches and chapels were built just across the borders of these territories, with the support of their rulers. There, in simple conditions, but freely, Mass could be heard.[15]

For Catholics in the Generality Lands, the contacts with co-religionists across the border were invaluable. Those contacts had, in any case, always been intensive; people traded, intermarried, and migrated, and took part in each other's fairs and guilds of marksmen (*schuttersgilden*) festivals. After 1648, moreover, Catholics from the Generality Lands could exercise their religion freely on the other side of the border. They attended Mass and other services there, received the sacraments, and took part in processions and pilgrimages.[16] They also used the ecclesiastical infrastructure across the border. Their bishops resided there, this was where their priests were trained, where their children could receive a Catholic education, enter an abbey, convent, or *beguinage*, and where their orphans would be raised in their parents' faith.

We must realise that the ecclesiastical zoning of Flanders and Brabant and the Lands of Overmaas, despite their division into Dutch and Spanish parts, remained unchanged after 1648. The bishops of the dioceses in question – namely, from west to east, Bruges, Ghent, Antwerp, 's-Hertogenbosch, Roermond, and Liège – continued to be responsible for the pastoral care of Catholics in the various parts of the Generality Lands. It should be noted that responsibility for the bishopric of 's-Hertogenbosch, which lay largely in Dutch territory, was entrusted after 1647 to an apostolic vicar. To be sure, some bishoprics took better care of their Dutch faithful than others. The bishops of Bruges undertook hardly any attempts to reach the dispersed Catholics of western States Flanders.[17] By contrast, the bishops of Antwerp tried in every way possible to maintain contact with their Dutch faithful, sent pastors secretly into Dutch territory, and gathered information from priests and laity about the situation there.[18]

After 1648, the bishops of the Southern Netherlands and their Dutch faithful agreed that their main aim should be to restore as quickly as possible the parochial infrastructure that had been destroyed. The bishops encouraged priests from their dioceses to go and provide pastoral care in Dutch territory. For this purpose they used primarily the services of Franciscans and Jesuits. For their part, the abbots of Norbertine and Cistercian abbeys in Spanish Brabant sent clergy to the villages of States Brabant, where their abbeys had in times past provided pastoral care. But for the restoration of an intensive church life the mere arrival of priests was insufficient. As a result of the changed circumstances, the active support of the faithful was indispensable. The parish churches, *pastories*, church lands, and funds had become Protestant property; the faithful had to provide new church buildings, living accommodation and incomes for their pastors, and they had to play a more active role. Male and female laity were given new or enhanced responsibilities that they had not had previously, both on a material level and in respect of religious practice.[19]

With the prohibition of the public practice of the Catholic religion and banishment of priests, 1648 marked a low point in the religious practice of Catholics in the Generality Lands. Thereafter the faithful and priests gradually succeeded in restoring parochial life. The tempo of restoration varied from place to place, depending on diverse factors. In cities and villages where the Catholic majority could depend on the support or sympathy of a highly placed figure, like the military governor or a local lord, restoration got off the ground within a few years. In the city of Breda, for example, dominated by the House of Orange, where successive princes of Orange had always adopted a tolerant attitude toward the Catholic population, the newly established Catholic Church Council was able to hire a space for use as a church as early as 1652 – and with support from the Reformed city government.[20]

It has often been pointed out that the traumatic experiences of 1672, the 'year of disaster', and in particular the French invasion of the Republic, led to a changed stance with regard to Catholics. The (temporary) restoration of public Catholic worship in conquered places such as Utrecht, Maastricht, and Grave, led Dutch authorities to reconsider their attitude toward their Catholic subjects in general. This changed attitude can be clearly observed also in the Generality Lands. The strict placards against Catholic worship were no longer enforced, clergy could move about more freely and, slowly but surely, so-called *schuurkerken* (barn-churches) were built in villages and cities where previously this had been impossible – all this, to be sure, at the cost of substantial payments to Reformed officials.[21] This does not mean that Catholics obtained complete freedom of action. When Reformed consistories or authorities took too-great offence at so-called *paepsche stoutigheden* (papist insolences), or when the position of the Reformed Church seemed threatened, severe anti-Catholic measures were still taken. When it was deemed necessary, heavy fines were imposed, churches closed, and priests imprisoned or banished. Above all, when Catholic clergy were suspected of playing a role in the apostasy of Reformed men and women, the authorities acted forcefully: the Catholic drive to convert those of other faiths was apparently the most serious threat Reformed authorities could conceive of.[22]

At the beginning of this chapter there was mention about the fear which Reformed inhabitants of the Generality Lands felt *vis-à-vis* the Catholic majority and about the frustrations of the Catholics with regard to the Reformed minority. Those fears and frustration greatly influenced relations between the two religious groups. On the Reformed side, there existed a deep distrust with regard to the Catholics of the Generality Lands. It was doubted whether Catholics were loyal subjects of the States General. Although Catholic burghers sometimes emphasised how much their ancestors had risked for the cause of the Revolt,[23] Reformed people remembered rather the many treasons attempted in the fortified cities of the South; time after time, Catholics and sometimes also priests had been involved in those plots. Notorious, for example, was the failed 'Betrayal of Maastricht' in 1638, in which a secular priest, a Franciscan, and three Jesuits had played roles.[24]

After 1648 various new, sensational cases seemed to prove the unreliability of Catholics. One such case was the conversion in 1658 of princess Louise of the Palatinate, daughter of the former king of Bohemia, who, with help from the Catholic marchioness of Bergen op Zoom, had fled to Antwerp and there become a Catholic. This affair led to a large-scale investigation by the States General into the reliability of Catholics in the western part of States Brabant. Accusations were made about Catholic abuses of power, violations of laws, religious excesses, the illegal opening of city gates, Catholic possession of weapons, etc.[25] It seems the accusations were baseless or greatly exaggerated, but it is not surprising that the States General took such complaints seriously. With their important military lines and fortified cities, the Generality Lands formed a buffer between the heart of the Republic and neighbouring lands to the south and east. The reliability or unreliability of the Catholic inhabitants of fortified cities such as Hulst, Bergen op Zoom, Breda, 's-Hertogenbosch, and Maastricht, and of many smaller strongholds in the South was a matter of national interest.

In turn, Catholics in the Generality areas seemed to do everything to feed the distrust of the Reformed. Most made no secret of the fact that they would have preferred to remain under the authority of the Spanish king. The armed guilds of marksmen in the villages bore the Burgundian cross on their standards and had new members swear that they were Catholic and would remain so – this despite the fact that cross and oath had been forbidden by the States General in 1659. New rumours circulated time and again about impending rebellions in which the Reformed in the Generality Lands would be put to the sword. Prophecies about the arrival of the Catholic French and the restoration of Catholicism contributed nothing to mutual trust either, especially since France seemed an increasingly dangerous enemy and French armies actually penetrated the territory of the Republic. Incidentally, the arrival of the French was no picnic for the inhabitants of the Generality Lands: although Catholicism was restored in some places after their 1672 invasion, that restoration was only of short duration and enthusiasm for it did not weigh as heavily as the sorrow caused by the enormous damage done by French 'liberators'.[26]

Although Catholics in the Generality Lands resigned themselves out of sheer necessity to the preferential treatment of the Reformed and their church, both juridically and financially, there was much dissatisfaction about the hindrance of their own worship. The many laws and regulations issued by the States General that were supposed to prohibit Catholic practices (the papist insolences) were regarded by Catholic inhabitants of the Generality Lands as unjust. They were, accordingly, violated on a large scale. Although in many cases this occurred after payment of a bribe to the official charged with investigation, the frequent violations of the law were, for many of the Reformed, a precise confirmation of Catholics' unreliable character.

In parts of the Generality Lands where enough Reformed persons lived, they constituted the personnel of the government. That was particularly the case in cities where members of the city government and most municipal functionaries were Reformed. But in villages in the countryside of States Brabant and the Lands of Overmaas, there were often simply not enough Reformed persons to comply with the regulation that aldermen and governmental functionaries had to be of the Reformed religion. Often the Reformed communities consisted of just a few families – sometimes just the families of the minister, the schoolmaster, and an official.[27] In such villages, public life was dictated by the Catholic community; Reformed inhabitants had a choice between social isolation with regular harassment on the one hand, or acceptance of Catholic customs and adjustment to the ways of the Catholic population on the other. The reports of Reformed Church classes contain countless examples of either alternative. There are often complaints about Reformed Church members whose front door had been fouled with excrement or whose well had been ritually polluted with the corpse of a dead animal. Here the message was 'piss off'. Conversely, one can also read of a church member who had joined a Catholic marksmen's guild or of a schoolmaster who, to please his pupils' parents and not lose customers, taught from Catholic books. Such conformist behaviour was not appreciated either by classis or by consistory.[28]

That Catholics formed a majority of the population in the Generality Lands doubtless influenced the way they could function as an ecclesiastical community. For political–strategic reasons the Dutch government felt compelled to keep Catholics in check through strict laws; their numeric predominance and their presumed lack of loyalty made a dangerous combination; moreover, the region in question was conquered, and thus subject territory. On the other hand, the same government had to prevent dissatisfaction from leading to rebellion. That meant that the laws that in principle were supposed to restrict Catholic worship could not, in the long run, be enforced too strictly. One could say that, over the long term, there was a certain balance between the different denominations in the Generality Lands: over and against the numeric predominance of Catholics stood the governmental predominance of the Reformed. And although Catholic burghers could not fill any governmental functions and were restricted in their worship, civil authorities made sure that their other rights as individuals continued to be safeguarded.[29] That was one of the reasons why – countless incidents notwithstanding – society in the Generality Lands was never torn apart by religious differences.

Notes

1. P.H.A.M. Abels and A.P.F. Wouters (eds), *Acta Conventus Sylvae-Ducensis extra-ordinarii 1648 [...], ofwel Notulen van de grote kerkelijke vergadering van 's-Hertogenbosch in 1648*, 2 vols ('s-Hertogenbosch: Rijksarchief in Noord-Brabant, 1985 [1986]), II, pp. 233–4; Gerard Rooijakkers, *Rituele repertoires. Volkscultuur in oostelijk Noord-Brabant 1559–1853* (Nijmegen: SUN, 1994), pp. 227, 230.
2. The emphasis in this paper lies on the largest of the three Generality Lands, States Brabant: see Charles de Mooij, 'Verschuivende grenzen', in R. Van Uytven et al. (eds), *Geschiedenis van Brabant, van het hertogdom tot heden* (Zwolle: Waanders, 2004), pp. 371–88; Charles de Mooij, 'Reformatie tegen wil en dank', in Van Uytven et al. (eds), *Geschiedenis van Brabant, van het hertogdom tot heden*, pp. 398–409. For Catholicism in States Flanders, see Th.B.W. Kok, *Dekenaat in de steigers. Kerkelijk opbouwwerk in het Gentse dekenaat Hulst 1596–1648* (Tilburg: Stichting Zuidelijk Historisch Contact, 1971); for the Overmaas-area, see P.J.H. Ubachs, *Handboek voor de geschiedenis van Limburg* (Hilversum: Verloren, 2000), pp. 214–19, 285–7. For Catholicism in the Generality Lands during the eighteenth century, see P. Polman, *Katholiek Nederland in de achttiende eeuw. Derde deel: Buiten de Hollandse Zending 1700–1795* (Hilversum: Uitgeverij Paul Brand, 1968).
3. Nowadays these regions are part of the Dutch provinces Zeeland (States Flanders), Noord-Brabant (States Brabant) and Limburg (States Lands of Overmaas). Small parts of the former States Lands of Overmaas now belong to Belgium and Germany.
4. De Mooij, 'Verschuivende grenzen', pp. 374–81; De Mooij, 'Reformatie tegen wil en dank', p. 403.
5. Rooijakkers, *Rituele repertoires*, p. 121.
6. De Mooij, 'Reformatie tegen wil en dank', pp. 398–402.
7. W.A.J. Munier, *Het simultaneum in de Landen van Overmaas. Een uniek instituut in de Nederlandse kerkgeschiedenis (1632–1878)* (Leeuwarden: Eisma, 1998).
8. P.J.H. Ubachs, *Twee heren, twee confessies. De verhouding van Staat en Kerk te Maastricht, 1632–1673* (Assen/Amsterdam: Van Gorcum, 1975).
9. H.Th.M. Roosenboom, *De dorpsschool in de Meierij van 's-Hertogenbosch van 1648 tot 1795* (Tilburg: Stichting Zuidelijk Historisch Contact, 1997); M.J.H.A. Lijten, 'Het Echtreglement en de naleving daarvan gedurende de periode circa 1700 – circa 1750 in Stad en Meierij van 's-Hertogenbosch', in Th. E.A. Bosman et al. (eds), *Brabandts recht dat is ...* (Assen/Maastricht: Van Gorcum, 1990), pp. 165–79; W.M. Lindemann, 'De bemoeienis van de Staatse Raad van Brabant met de uitoefening van de katholieke godsdienst in de gebieden van de Generaliteit', in Bosman et al. (eds), *Brabandts recht dat is ...*, pp. 181–91.
10. De Mooij, 'Verschuivende grenzen', pp. 383–5.
11. Munier, *Het simultaneum*, pp. 84–5.
12. Rooijakkers, *Rituele repertoires*, gives many examples.
13. P.Th.J. Kuijer, *'s-Hertogenbosch, stad in het hertogdom Brabant, ca. 1185–1629* (Zwolle: Waanders Uitgevers, 2000), p. 642; Anton van de Sande en Aart Vos, 'Een verdeeld huis. Godsdienst en cultuur', in Aart Vos et al. (eds), *'s-Hertogenbosch. De geschiedenis van een Brabantse stad, 1629–1990* (Zwolle: Waanders Uitgevers, 1997), p. 129.
14. De Mooij, 'Reformatie tegen wil en dank', p. 407. Cf. the situation in 's-Hertogenbosch, Breda and Bergen op Zoom: Van de Sande en Vos, 'Een verdeeld huis', p. 129; J.L.M. de Lepper, 'De Katholieke Kerk', in V.A.M. Beermann et al. (eds), *Geschiedenis van Breda. II. Aspecten van de stedelijke historie 1568–1795* (Schiedam: Interbook International, 1977), pp. 186–7, 206–7; Charles de Mooij, *Geloof kan bergen verzetten. Reformatie en katholieke herleving te Bergen op Zoom 1577–1795* (Hilversum: Verloren, 1998), pp. 408–11, 459–63.
15. Polman, *Katholiek Nederland*, pp. 6–8; De Mooij, 'Reformatie tegen wil en dank', p. 406.
16. For pilgrimages across the border, see Marc Wingens, *Over de grens. De bedevaart van katholieke*

Nederlanders in de zeventiende en achttiende eeuw (Nijmegen: SUN, 1994).
17 For the distinction in the efforts of the bishops of Ghent and Bruges, cf. L.J. Rogier, *Geschiedenis van het katholicisme in Noord-Nederland in de 16e en de 17e eeuw*, 3 vols (Amsterdam: Urbi et Orbi, 2nd edn, 1947), II, pp. 622–9.
18 Kok, *Dekenaat in de steigers*; P.M. Toebak, *Kerkelijk-godsdienstig leven in westelijk Noord-Brabant, 1580–1652. Dekenale visitatieverslagen als bron*, 2 vols (Breda: Gemeentearchief, 1995); De Mooij, *Geloof kan bergen verzetten*, pp. 467–71.
19 Polman, *Katholiek Nederland*, pp. 112–15; De Mooij, 'Reformatie tegen wil en dank', pp. 407–8.
20 De Lepper, 'De Katholieke Kerk', pp. 188–9.
21 See note 14.
22 De Mooij, 'Reformatie tegen wil en dank', pp. 408–9.
23 De Mooij, *Geloof kan bergen verzetten*, pp. 430–1.
24 Ubachs, *Twee heren, twee confessies*, pp. 314–34.
25 De Mooij, *Geloof kan bergen verzetten*, pp. 419–36.
26 W. Frijhoff, 'De paniek van juni 1734', *Archief voor de Geschiedenis van de Katholieke Kerk in Nederland*,19 (1977), 170–233; Rooijakkers, *Rituele repertoires*, pp. 278–9; De Mooij, *Geloof kan bergen verzetten*, pp. 628–34. A. Vos, *Burgers, broeders en bazen. Het maatschappelijk middenveld van 's-Hertogenbosch in de zeventiende en achttiende eeuw* (Hilversum: Verloren, 2007), pp. 367–76.
27 Ubachs, *Handboek voor de geschiedenis van Limburg*, pp. 285–7; De Mooij, 'Reformatie tegen wil en dank', pp. 403–4.
28 Rooijakkers, *Rituele repertoires*, pp. 202–21, 445, 528; De Mooij, 'Reformatie tegen wil en dank', p. 409.
29 Vos, *Burgers, broeders en bazen*, pp. 45–51, 106–8, 178–81, 375–6.

11

Between conflict and coexistence: the Catholic community in Ireland as a 'visible underground church' in the late sixteenth and early seventeenth centuries

UTE LOTZ-HEUMANN

Ireland from the Middle Ages to the seventeenth century

In consequence of the Anglo-Norman conquest of 1169–71, late medieval Ireland was ethnically and culturally divided between the indigenous Gaelic Irish population on the one hand and the medieval Anglo-Norman colonisers, the so-called Anglo-Irish, on the other hand. The Anglo-Irish consisted essentially of two groups: the aristocracy, many of whom frequently intermarried with the Gaelic Irish nobility and who were thus gradually integrated into the social and political structure of Gaelic Ireland; and the gentry and burghers in the English Pale and the Anglo-Irish towns. The Pale – the region around Dublin – and the towns, most of which were situated in the east and south-east of Ireland, were the only areas effectively under English government control in the fifteenth and for most of the sixteenth centuries. The Anglo-Irish gentry and burghers retained a firm, separate identity, seeing themselves as upholders of English culture in Ireland.[1]

In the early sixteenth century, as part of Henry VIII's and Thomas Cromwell's 'Tudor Revolution in government',[2] Ireland came under direct rule from England, that is, government by Anglo-Irish noblemen was replaced by government by English-born lord deputies and other English officials. In 1541, the Irish Parliament declared Henry VIII King of Ireland, thereby superseding the title 'Lord' granted by Pope Adrian IV in 1155. Subsequent efforts at building a state and commonwealth in Ireland after the model of the English kingdom foundered. English policy toward Ireland was not systematic and consistent, but vacillating. While the aim of creating a unified 'Irish kingdom' remained unchanged, policies varied considerably – from peaceful integration of Gaelic and Anglo-Irish lords to military campaigns.[3] When, in the sixteenth century, Gaelic and Anglo-Irish lords rebelled against English efforts at state formation, the English administration responded by deploying a standing army and by opting for the policy of plantation – of settling New English planters on the confiscated lands of defeated Gaelic and Anglo-Irish lords.[4]

The religious and cultural make-up of Ireland was also changing dramatically at this time. A 'political Reformation', the establishment of an independent state church with the English monarch as head of that church, took place under Henry VIII. Under his daughter Elizabeth, the formal institutionalisation of a Protestant state church in Ireland approximately paralleled developments in England. In 1560 the Irish Parliament passed the Acts of Supremacy and Uniformity. Thus, in terms of church government and state–church relations, Ireland was theoretically comparable to England: the monarch was supreme governor of the state church.[5]

But up to the 1580s or even the 1590s, the Church of Ireland was not able to penetrate the country.[6] Medieval Catholic religious practices continued to be exercised in what was effectively a confessional and ecclesiastical vacuum. The state church was unable to establish a religious monopoly. In the late sixteenth century it was then confronted with a Catholic Mission.[7] In consequence, both the Protestant and the Catholic churches entered processes of confession building, of becoming clearly defined confessional churches,[8] and both churches competed for the religious allegiance of the inhabitants of Ireland. The Catholic Mission gradually developed into an institutionalised Tridentine Church, with bishops, secular and regular clergy residing in Ireland. Catholicism was embraced by both the Gaelic Irish and Anglo-Irish communities. In contrast, Protestant confession building was dominated by the New English, with regard to the clergy as well as the laity.

Thus, Protestant and Catholic confession building were remarkably coterminous processes in Ireland, and this contributed to a state of intense confessional rivalry and a social process which I have elsewhere described as 'dual confessionalisation'.[9] By the middle of the seventeenth century there were two rival confessional churches present in Ireland: the majority, and therefore often 'visible', but illegal, Catholic 'underground' church on the one hand and the minority, but legal, Protestant state church, the Church of Ireland, on the other hand.

The late Protestant Reformation which the English state tried to spread in Ireland was thus a failure in that it did not manage to embrace the majority of the population. The Church of Ireland became the church of the New English planters and officials, who had been Protestants before they came to Ireland.[10] Thus, the English state did not succeed in enforcing the principle of *cuius regio, eius religio* in Ireland. In fact, throughout the sixteenth century the presence of the English state in Ireland was so weak that it was not able to assist Protestant confession building. On the contrary, the close connection and identification of the Protestant Church with the English state, its officials and its plantation projects discredited the Reformation in the eyes of the majority of the population. As part of the process of dual confessionalisation, the Anglo-Irish and the Gaelic Irish Catholic communities developed a variety of 'internal and external survival strategies' – to use the terminology suggested by Willem Frijhoff.[11]

In the case of many Anglo-Irish and Gaelic lords, their political and military resistance to English intervention in Ireland converged with their religious opposition to the Protestant state church. As a result, they looked to Spain, France and the papacy for military and political aid to overthrow English rule in Ireland. This political and international aspect of the Counter-Reformation cannot be discussed in detail here, but it was an important part of the 'external' factors that contributed to the survival of – as well as the dangers to – Catholicism in early modern Ireland.

Most of the politically loyal Anglo-Irish gentry and burghers also refused to accept the religion of their monarch. This group actually split along confessional lines: only a minority accepted the Protestant state church, whereas the great majority became Catholic. They adopted a complex identity, embracing Tridentine Catholicism and mounting a formidable parliamentary opposition to the political programmes of successive English lord deputies on the one hand, but professing enduring loyalty to the English crown on the other hand. In order to stress their difference from the Protestant New English, they called themselves the 'Old English' from the late sixteenth century onwards. However, the Old English continued to see themselves as culturally superior to the Gaelic Irish.[12]

Even this short overview of developments makes clear that a narrative of early modern Ireland has to be accompanied by constant differentiations and caveats. In terms of the groups mentioned above, it is in fact necessary to speak of communities within communities: the Catholic community, for example, was not only ethnically and culturally divided between the Gaelic Irish and the Old English, it was also divided between the laity and the clergy, and the clergy were divided between the seculars and the regulars, and so on. In the following, I will focus more on the Old English than on the Gaelic Irish, as the Old English were regarded – and regarded themselves – as loyal to the English monarch and were thus expected to accept Protestantism. As a result, their choice of Catholicism was regarded by both Protestants and Catholics as pointing the way for the religious future of Ireland.

The framework of confessional conflict and coexistence: demands and reactions, negotiations and compromises

The framework in which the Catholic community in Ireland had to operate and develop its survival strategies was set, above all, by the Protestant state and state church. The process of dual confessionalisation in Ireland resulted in a kind of stalemate. Although Catholicism could not be suppressed, the Protestant Church of Ireland never formally acknowledged the religious allegiance of the majority of the population or the permanent presence of the Catholic Church. Even though it was clear by the early seventeenth century that the Church of Ireland would not be able to realise its aim of establishing a confessional monopoly in Ireland,[13] it clung tenaciously to this aim and to its status as state church.

For the Catholic Church, Queen Elizabeth's status as supreme governor was of course unacceptable. After Pope Pius V had excommunicated Elizabeth and released her subjects from their oath of allegiance in 1570, Catholics in Ireland reacted to this in different ways. While the majority of the Gaelic Irish elite rejected the ecclesiastical supremacy as well as the secular power of the English crown, the Old English distinguished between the two: without accepting either the state church or church government by the English monarch, they did accept the English crown's secular authority.[14]

On this basis the English government saw room for compromise with the Catholic Old English when Ireland – as England's back door – was politically threatened from outside. In 1627–28, when war with Spain seemed imminent, Charles I and the Old English negotiated the so-called graces, a set of concessions including, for example, the abolition of recusancy fines.[15] The full implementation of the graces would have meant legally codified toleration for the Catholic Old English, a situation that would have been comparable with the status of the Huguenots in France after the Edict of Nantes. But the graces were never implemented in full and were never transformed into an Act of Parliament. The agreement between the king and the Old English met with fierce resistance from the Protestant New English and, when the Spanish threat was over in 1629/30, the crown itself lost interest in the agreement.

However, there developed a certain *modus vivendi* between the government and the Old English Catholic community: the crown was willing to exercise practical toleration toward the Old English because – as regional and local office holders – they were still essential for the functioning of the Irish kingdom.[16] While the Old English lost their political influence in the Dublin Privy Council and the Dublin administration, they were able to retain their political influence – and often this meant resistance to the central administration – in Parliament and on the regional and local levels of administration, particularly in the towns.[17] In the sixteenth century it was mostly the Gaelic Irish who were affected by dispossession, plantation and expulsion after rebellions. However, in the seventeenth century English and New English Protestants increasingly equated Catholicism with disloyal and rebellious behaviour, so that the landed property as well as the economic privileges (such as urban tax and duty privileges) of the Old English came under attack from the state.[18]

From the end of the sixteenth century onwards, the contradiction between the claim of the Protestant Church to have a confessional monopoly and the actual presence of a Catholic majority in Ireland became more and more glaring. Theoretically, all monasteries had been dissolved, but in fact Catholic religious orders took possession of old monasteries in the more remote parts of Ireland, or the Catholic community at least continued to use the old monastic burial grounds.[19] Theoretically, the state church had a minister in every parish, but in fact most ministers had accumulated several benefices and resided where most or all of the parishioners were New English Protestants, whereas the other parishes were left to the Catholic clergy.[20] The institutionalisation of the illegal Catholic Church in the early seventeenth century made even more obvious the contradiction between the theoretical claim of the Church of Ireland to be an all-embracing state church and the reality of a struggle between two rival confessional churches.

The development of the institutions and instruments of church government illuminates the relationship between the Catholic community and the Protestant state church. The central institutions and instruments of Protestant Church government, especially the High Commission of Ecclesiastical Causes and the regal visitations, as well as the institutions and control mechanisms of the state church on the regional and local levels (for example, church courts, recusancy fines and excommunication) failed to produce the desired results; conformity with the state church could not be enforced, and the majority of the population did not convert to Protestantism.[21] The Old English and Gaelic Irish Catholic communities used their social networks in order to resist these attempts to control and discipline them. The institutions and control mechanisms of the state church were thus transformed from instruments of church government and church discipline into instruments of 'spying', of recording the activities of the confessional rival. Unwittingly, they ended up merely antagonising Catholics and widening the confessional gap. As Bishop Bedell remarked about excommunication: 'To excommunicate them [the Catholics] for not appearing or obeying, they being already none of our body, and a multitude, it is no profit, nay, rather makes the exacerbation worse.'[22] How could it have been otherwise, when, at the parish level, even the office of churchwarden could often not be filled with a Protestant? As the commissioners of the regal visitation of 1622 reported: 'Churchwardens in most places there are none, but such as are recusants themselves, and being parties in the cause [i.e. recusancy], the service [of presenting recusants] is not well performed by them ....'[23]

Oaths – traditional means of enforcing confessional conformity – have to be seen in the same context: they were a demand of the Protestant state to which Catholics were forced to react. The Oath of Supremacy was, in many ways, a hidden confessional oath because it explicitly rejected the spiritual and ecclesiastical authority of the pope, clearly stated the break with Rome and stressed the role of the monarch as supreme governor of the Church of Ireland.[24] Thus, swearing the Oath of Supremacy was implicitly incompatible with membership of the Catholic Church.

This is why the oath increasingly created problems for the Old English when the confessional divide hardened in the early seventeenth century. While the state put more and more pressure on the Old English to conform by insisting that office holders swear the Oath of Supremacy, the Old English increasingly regarded it as a problematic formula that mingled religion and politics. As a consequence, the Oath of Supremacy often threw individuals into severe conflicts. If an Old English man swore the oath – possibly with the help of a *reservatio mentalis* – he was often sharply condemned by the Catholic clergy. If he refused to swear the oath, he was no longer appointed to government positions.[25] In fact, when more and more potential office holders – for example, government lawyers, mayors and city councillors – refused to swear the Oath of Supremacy in the early seventeenth century, it became difficult to fill positions because there were not enough New English Protestants to take their place.[26] In the first half of the seventeenth century several attempts were made to draw up an oath of loyalty to the English crown that Catholics could swear without inner conflicts. However, this oath of allegiance foundered because, in a confessional age, it was very difficult, or perhaps even impossible, to formulate an exclusively secular oath that had no religious implications.[27]

In connection with the discussions and conflicts about the oaths of supremacy and allegiance, the Catholic clergy in Ireland also became active in order to ensure the continued loyalty of their flock to the Catholic faith. They drafted a kind of counter-oath in order to place Catholic laymen under an obligation to profess their faith openly and make no compromises with the state. For example, the Protestant bishop of Cork and Ross, William Lyon, was informed by a leading Catholic citizen of Waterford 'that he was sworn to the league that he should never come to the [Protestant] church, nor obey any of her Majesty's ecclesiastical laws concerning the same'.[28]

Catholic survival strategies in Ireland: agency, networks and infrastructure

Catholic lawyers and teachers became important pillars of the Old English Catholic community and its visible underground church. Catholic lawyers who had been removed from positions in the central administration concentrated on local administration as mayors or city councillors and/or they defended Catholic interests as members of Parliament. Moreover, they acted as private legal advisors and arbitrators in cases of conflict within the Catholic community, whose members often shunned the official law courts.[29]

Catholic teachers built up secret schools or worked as private tutors in order to educate the children of the Catholic community and to prepare them for university studies on the Continent.[30] The most famous Catholic school in Ireland was that of Peter White in Kilkenny. In his tract *De Rebus in Hibernia Gestis*, Richard Stanyhurst, who had been educated at White's school, compared it to a Trojan horse, from which the best (Catholic) scholars of the country had emerged.[31] In fact, several of the leading missionaries who returned to Ireland from the Continental universities around the turn of the century had been educated at White's school.[32] The existence of Catholic schools in Ireland was a matter of great concern for the Protestant authorities. Thus, Sir John Dowdall reported to Lord Burghley in 1595: 'Every town is established with sundry schools where the noblemen and gentlemen's sons of the country do repair; these schools have a superstitious or an idolatrous schoolmaster, and each school overseen by a Jesuit, whereby the youth of the whole Kingdom are corrupted and poisoned with more gross superstition and disobedience than all the rest of the Popish crew in all Europe.'[33]

On the one hand, Catholics succeeded in establishing secret Catholic schools that were supplemented by private tutors in the households of the wealthy. On the other hand, the English state and the Church of Ireland succeeded in establishing a Protestant monopoly over university education in Ireland by founding Trinity College, Dublin, in 1592.[34] However, the ban on studying abroad, which the Dublin government issued repeatedly, was ignored and did not stop Catholics from leaving Ireland for Continental universities. When more and more students from Ireland gathered at Catholic universities on the Continent, Irish colleges were founded there in order to prepare the students for their return to Ireland as priests and missionaries.[35]

Besides the lawyers and teachers, women played an important role for the cohesiveness of the Catholic community: they had Mass said in their homes, and they protected priests from persecution by the state authorities. They also taught and catechised children and servants in the Catholic faith. In his history of Ireland, the exiled Gaelic Irish nobleman Philip O'Sullivan Beare reported

THE CATHOLIC COMMUNITY IN IRELAND 175

that when, due to the wars with England, there were no teachers and no schools left in Gaelic Ireland, the children still knew about the faith from their mothers and nurses.[36] In the Old English community, the women were in many ways the pioneers of the development from the pre-confessional 'Old Religion' to Tridentine Catholicism; they were the first who stayed away from the services of the Church of Ireland in the 1570s, their menfolk following suit only in the 1580s.[37] This was also noted in a government report of 1606: 'The priests prevail mightily throughout all Ireland with the women, and they with their husbands.'[38]

Both the Gaelic Irish and the Old English communities constituted closely knit social networks: there were close family connections, constantly strengthened by intermarriage.[39] These Catholic communities exercised different forms of self-control within families and within the local community. When the reasons for the survival of Catholicism in Ireland are investigated, these close social networks cannot be overestimated. Here the individual was influenced and disciplined in favour of the Catholic religion. For example, Catholic elites influenced, and even put pressure on, their servants or tenants. In 1606 the Jesuits reported that after the president of Munster had forced peasants in Dungarvan to attend the services of the state church, their Catholic landlord refused to let them work on his land until they were reconciled to the Catholic Church.[40]

The Catholic priests obviously remained dependent on support from Catholic laypeople, so that the laity had considerable influence on the Catholic underground church, for example with regard to the spaces for saying Mass and the financial support of the clergy. In fact, the revenues from secularised church lands, which had fallen into Old English hands in the early sixteenth century, were a hundred years later used to provide for the Catholic clergy. Thus, the closely knit social networks of the Catholic communities enabled the Catholic clergy to minister quite freely in Ireland and offered protection in times of persecution.[41]

The Catholic community in Ireland was even able to break the Protestant monopoly over poor relief and establish its own – based on social networks and social consensus. For example, the Marian congregations founded by the Jesuits in the towns saw the relief of the poor as a major part of their activities.[42] Due to the fact that the Catholic urban elites also staffed the town councils, there even existed Catholic poor relief initiatives which were implemented by local governments: in Limerick, a Jesuit prevailed upon the urban magistrates and the citizens to build a hospital for the poor and other destitute persons; and when the initiative was interfered with by persecution initiated by the state authorities, the Catholic citizens voluntarily provided alms for the poor at intervals recommended by the Jesuit father.[43]

Conflict and coexistence in different spheres and spaces of everyday life

Everyday life in the confessionally split society of Ireland was determined by conflict or discrimination as well as by coexistence and even harmony. There were several spheres and spaces of everyday life where conflicts were less frequent or even entirely absent. In some town councils Catholics and Protestants worked peacefully together. During the late sixteenth century, the social networks of the urban elites became confessionally determined. This led to the separation of some families into Protestant and Catholic branches.[44] However, except among these urban elites, confessionally mixed marriages were quite common – and not only among the laity.[45] While the clerical elite on both sides of the confessional divide sharply condemned mixed marriages, the complaints of Protestant bishops about clergymen married to Catholic women clearly show that their own personnel did not heed them.[46] Even between theologians, relationships could be rather mixed: on the one hand, they fought over every soul, especially by publishing confessional propaganda. On the other hand, they often overcame confessional differences in favour of scholarly cooperation – for example, in order to exchange medieval manuscripts.[47]

However, there were also areas of life where conflicts, even violent clashes, were more frequent. These clashes occurred most often when the Catholic Church ventured into the public space. As visible (that is, public) Catholic church buildings were not allowed to exist in Ireland, there were – as enthusiastic Jesuits and appalled Protestants agreed – numerous Mass houses in backyards and rooms for saying Mass in private homes.[48] However, Catholics sometimes went public and thus became visible, that is, they entered officially Protestant spaces, which was made possible – or even necessary – by their sheer numbers. They used church buildings that were now officially in the hands of the Church of Ireland, and they buried their dead in old monastic cemeteries. For example, Sir John Davies reported from the town of New Ross in 1606: 'We found that albeit the greatest part of the townsmen be obstinate recusants, yet twice or thrice a year they all come into the church to make a superstitious offering at the place where the high altar stood. Last Christmas day the sovereign and inhabitants, to the number of 300, came into the church with extraordinary noise and tumult, and making their popish offering, then disturbed the poor minister from making a sermon which he had prepared for his small auditory. The same they did upon Easter day.'[49] And James Ussher was appalled by the experience of one of his clergymen, John Ankers, 'That going to read prayers at Kilkenny, in Westmeath, he found an old priest, and about forty with him, in the church; who was so bold as to require him (the said Ankers) to depart, until he had done his business.'[50]

It is striking that in such situations the Protestant New English often felt threatened by the Catholics rather than vice versa. For example, in the Old English towns, people sometimes 'mobbed' Protestant teachers, while urban officials refused to pay their income until they gave up and left.[51] When soldiers were billeted on urban households, Catholic office holders allegedly cheated on Protestants by billeting more soldiers on them than on Catholics.[52] And in 1622, when the Protestant mayor and the archbishop of Dublin had a Franciscan chapel in Dublin destroyed, a popular riot ensued.[53]

That such forms of discrimination and resistance by Catholics against Protestants in everyday life were possible clearly shows us the limits of the early modern state in Ireland and reminds us of the fact that a numerical majority, even if it was partly (and increasingly) disenfranchised, could – and did – find effective ways of resistance and retaliation.

Conclusion

As this cursory examination of the Catholic communities in sixteenth- and early seventeenth-century Ireland has made clear, two basic factors have to be considered. On the one hand is the political and social framework that was decisively influenced by the Protestant state and its state church. In both Ireland and the Generality Lands[54] a gap developed between the claim of the state to a confessional monopoly – at least in the public realm – and its inability to enforce the *cuius regio, eius religio* principle. This led to a situation in which phases of a *modus vivendi* with and practical toleration of the Catholic communities[55] alternated with phases of conflict and persecution. However, in Ireland this precarious situation resulted from a preceding long phase of instability in the sixteenth century, whereas in the Generality Lands it resulted from the fact that the *cuius regio, eius religio* principle had been successfully established in favour of Catholicism under Habsburg rule before the conquest by the Dutch Republic.[56]

On the other hand, the Catholic communities had to react to the demands of the state and state church, they had to develop survival strategies and – if possible – to negotiate compromises. In both Ireland and the Generality Lands this was an ongoing and precarious process. Although the state was too weak to enforce its will, it was still strong enough to define severe limits to the activities of the Catholic communities. As Keith Luria has written, 'Local people might cooperate with or obstruct government policies, but they could never escape them.'[57] Consequently, the Catholic communities had to rely heavily on individual agency and on strong social networks to establish spaces and infrastructure for the practice of their faith. In addition, social networks, spaces for worship and other infrastructure, such as educational institutions, provided beyond the borders of Ireland and the Generality Lands proved vital for the survival of the Catholic communities in these countries.

In the Irish case, two forms of survival strategy connected to the international dimension of Catholicism are difficult to gauge with respect to their effects on the Catholic communities. First, the path of military resistance chosen by many Anglo-Irish and Gaelic Irish lords: this 'military Counter-Reformation', which was at times supported by Spain, France and the papacy, was unsuccessful as an external survival strategy. As already hinted at above, it probably made it more difficult for the Catholics in Ireland to survive, because it put the English state and the New English on the alert.

Second, the question of Catholic identity construction: as Willem Frijhoff suggests, a 'social, political and cultural image' was an important survival strategy.[58] In the case of the Irish Catholic communities, the construction of a confessional identity through martyrs, saints and historical narratives was a complicated process. On the one hand, this kind of activity took place mostly in the Irish colleges on the Continent, so that it is difficult to gauge its effects in Ireland. On the other hand, the split between the Gaelic Irish and the Old English largely prevented the development of a 'coherent narrative' (Frijhoff) in the sixteenth and early seventeenth centuries. Rather, there were two narratives, one for each of the Catholic communities in Ireland.[59] In fact, it took a long time before Catholics in Ireland adopted an identity as Irish Catholics.

All in all, everyday life in both Ireland and the Generality Lands was, as the two chapters in this volume make clear, characterised by conflict and coexistence. When we discuss conflict and coexistence in a situation where a legal minority church confronts an illegal majority church, we have to look very carefully in which spaces (which have to be described not as a dichotomy, but as a spectrum between private and public) and in which spheres (such as everyday life or the political sphere on a local or national level) conflict and coexistence actually occurred and how this changed over time. We also have to think of conflict and coexistence themselves not as alternatives, but as opposite ends of a broad spectrum. As Keith Luria has put it: 'The answer lies in shifting our interpretative focus away from opposed religious cultures toward an examination of how group identities were constructed and reconstructed, a process that led at *specific* times in *specific* places to greater peace or conflict.'[60] Nevertheless, I think that we also have to ask 'where were the boundaries, where were the lines drawn?'. When everyday conflicts occurred, when state persecution was set in motion, when Catholic rebellions were organised, a line or lines had always been crossed beforehand: in each context, there was a conglomerate of factors that constituted such a line or boundary. In future, we will have to continue to examine our sources very closely to identify these factors.

THE CATHOLIC COMMUNITY IN IRELAND

Notes

1 For a more detailed description of late medieval Ireland see Ute Lotz-Heumann, *Die doppelte Konfessionalisierung in Irland. Konflikt und Koexistenz im 16. und in der ersten Hälfte des 17. Jahrhunderts* (Tübingen: Mohr Siebeck, 2000), pp. 44–63.
2 The term is Geoffrey Elton's. See Geoffrey R. Elton, *The Tudor revolution in government* (Cambridge: Cambridge University Press, 1953). For its application to Ireland see Brendan Bradshaw, *The Irish constitutional revolution of the sixteenth century* (Cambridge: Cambridge University Press, 1979).
3 See, e.g. Ciaran Brady, *The Chief Governors: the rise and fall of reform government in Tudor Ireland, 1536–1588* (Cambridge: Cambridge University Press, 1994).
4 The best-known of all plantations is the plantation of Ulster from 1607 onwards. See Raymond Gillespie, *Colonial Ulster: The settlement of East-Ulster, 1600–1641* (Cork: Cork University Press, 1985).
5 See the Acts of Supremacy and Uniformity, in Edmund Curtis and R.B. McDowell (eds), *Irish Historical Documents, 1172–1922* (New York, London: Barnes & Noble, reprint, 1968), pp. 121–5; see also Steven G. Ellis, *Ireland in the age of the Tudors, 1447–1603: English expansion and the end of Gaelic rule* (London, New York: Longman, 1998), pp. 225–6.
6 The standard treatments of the development of the Protestant state church is Alan Ford, *The Protestant Reformation in Ireland, 1590–1641* (Dublin: Four Courts Press, 2nd edn, 1997).
7 There is so far no standard monograph of the Catholic mission and church in sixteenth- and early seventeenth-century Ireland, but see Colm Lennon, *Sixteenth-century Ireland. The incomplete conquest* (Dublin: Gill & Macmillan, 1994); Colm Lennon, *The Lords of Dublin in the age of Reformation* (Dublin: Irish Academic Press, 1989); Colm Lennon, 'The counter-reformation in Ireland, 1542–1641', in Ciaran Brady and Raymond Gillespie (eds), *Natives and newcomers: essays on the making of Irish colonial society, 1534–1641* (Dublin: Irish Academic Press, 1986), pp. 75–92.
8 On terminology: the terms 'confessional church' and 'confession building' are derived from the German terms *Konfessionskirche* and *Konfessionsbildung*. 'Confession-building' refers to the development in the late sixteenth century of state and territorial churches which were clearly defined with regard to rites and theology. See, e.g. Ernst W. Zeeden, 'Grundlagen und Wege der Konfessionsbildung im Zeitalter der Glaubenskämpfe', *Historische Zeitschrift* 185 (1958), 249–99.
9 See Lotz-Heumann, *Die doppelte Konfessionalisierung in Irland*.
10 Insofar as this Protestant Reformation had been initiated by the prince, i.e. the English monarchs, and was embraced only by a ruling elite in state and church, i.e. the New English, it had many characteristics of the so-called 'Second Reformations' (or 'Calvinist confessionalisations') in the Holy Roman Empire. The Irish state church also developed a markedly Calvinist character, especially through its 104 Articles of Religion of 1615. For a comparative analysis of the failed Reformation in Ireland with the Second Reformations in the Empire see Karl S. Bottigheimer and Ute Lotz-Heumann, 'The Irish reformation in European perspective', *Archiv für Reformationsgeschichte* 89 (1998), 268–309.
11 See the chapter by Willem Frijhoff in this volume, pp. 1–17. In contrast to Frijhoff I would, however, argue that these survival strategies can be identified and adequately described by employing the concept of 'confessionalisation'. See in more detail my *Die doppelte Konfessionalisierung in Irland*, where I discuss political alliances, identity construction through language, propaganda and historiography, social networks and marriage, education, spaces for church buildings and monasteries, poor relief and other factors as internal and external survival strategies of the Catholic church in Ireland.
12 On the Catholic Old English see Nicholas P. Canny, *The formation of the Old English elite in Ireland*, O'Donnell Lecture (Dublin: National University of Ireland, 1975); Aidan Clarke, *The Old English in Ireland, 1625–42* (Ithaca, NY: Cornell University Press, 1966); Lennon, *Lords of Dublin*; Ciaran Brady, 'Conservative subversives: the community of the Pale and the Dublin administration, 1556–86', in Patrick J. Corish (ed.), *Radicals, rebels and establishments: Historical Studies XV* (Belfast: Appletree Press, 1985), pp. 11–32.

13 See Karl S. Bottigheimer, 'The failure of the reformation in Ireland: une question bien posée', *Journal of Ecclesiastical History* 36 (1985), 196–207.
14 See above note 12.
15 See Aidan Clark, *The Graces, 1625–41* (Dublin: Dundalgan Press, 1968).
16 See Clarke, *The Old English in Ireland*.
17 See in more detail Ute Lotz-Heumann, 'Aus "Anglo-Iren" werden "Altengländer": Die Hinwendung des anglo-irischen Stadtbürgertums zum Katholizismus als Wechselwirkungsprozess von Repräsentationen und Praktiken', in Vera Isaiasz, Ute Lotz-Heumann, Monika Mommertz and Matthias Pohlig (eds), *Stadt und Religion in der Frühen Neuzeit: Soziale Ordnungen und ihre Repräsentationen* (Frankfurt a.M.: Campus, 2007), pp. 275–305.
18 This had severe long-term consequences: first, between 1633 and 1640, under Lord Deputy Wentworth, the Old English faced dispossession and later, under Cromwell, they also faced expulsion from Ireland. See Nicholas P. Canny, 'The attempted anglicization of Ireland in the seventeenth century: an exemplar of "British history"', in Ronald G. Asch (ed.), *Three nations – a common history? England, Scotland, Ireland and British History c. 1600–1920* (Bochum: Brockmeyer, 1993), pp. 49–82; see also Clarke, *The Old English in Ireland* on the gradual loss of political power, land and economic privileges of the Old English.
19 See, e.g. Captain W. Piers to Lord Burghley in 1583, in *Calendar of the State Papers Relating to Ireland, 1574–1585* (London: Her Majesty's Stationary Office, 1867), p. 469.
20 See Alan Ford, 'The Protestant reformation in Ireland', in Brady and Gillespie (eds), *Natives and newcomers*, pp. 50–74, at pp. 59–61.
21 On this problem see in more detail: Ute Lotz-Heumann, 'Church discipline in a biconfessional country: Ireland in a European context', in Herman Roodenburg and Pieter Spierenburg (eds), *Social control in Europe*, vol. 1: *1500–1800* (Columbus, Ohio: Ohio State University Press, 2004), pp. 99–112. On the central institutions of Protestant discipline see also Helga Robinson-Hammerstein, 'Erzbischof Adam Loftus und die elisabethanische Reformationspolitik in Irland' (Ph.D. dissertation, University of Marburg, 1976), pp. 93–148.
22 Letter CLX: Bedell to Ussher in 1629, in C.R. Elrington and J.H. Todd (eds), *The Whole Works of … James Ussher*, 17 vols (Dublin: Hoidges and Smith, 1847–64), here vol. XV: *Letters*, p. 471.
23 Trinity College, Dublin, MS 4756, Entry Book of Reports of the Commissioners for Ireland, Appointed by James I in 1622, fol. 62v.
24 See Curtis and McDowell (eds), *Irish historical documents*, p. 123.
25 On the condemnation of *reservatio mentalis* by the Catholic clergy see provincial synod of Armagh, 1614, in Daniel McCarthy (ed.), *Collections on Irish Church History, from the Manuscripts of the Late Laurence F. Renehan*, vol. 1 (Dublin: Warren and Richardson, 1861), pp. 119–20. On the increasing pressure on the Old English Catholics to swear the oath see Colum Kenny, 'The exclusion of catholics from the legal profession in Ireland, 1537–1829', *Irish Historical Studies* XXV (1987), 349–55, at p. 339; Hans S. Pawlisch, *Sir John Davies and the conquest of Ireland: a study in legal imperialism* (Cambridge: Cambridge University Press, 1985), pp. 40–2.
26 See Kenny, 'Exclusion of Catholics', p. 343. On the problems resulting from local office holders', especially mayors', refusal to swear the oath of supremacy, see, e.g., Lennon, *Lords of Dublin*, pp. 175–84; Julian C. Walton, 'Church, crown and corporation in Waterford city, 1520–1620', in W. Nolan and T.P. Power (eds), *Waterford: history and society, interdisciplinary essays on the history of an Irish county* (Dublin: Geography Publication, 1992), pp. 177–97, esp. pp. 193–5.
27 The oath of allegiance was suggested by James I only for Catholics in England, not in Ireland. The oath is discussed in John J. LaRocca, "Who can't pray with me, can't love me": toleration and early Jacobean recusancy policy', *Journal of British Studies* 23 (1984), 22–36; Kenneth Fincham and Peter Lake, 'The ecclesiastical policy of King James I', *Journal of British Studies* 24 (1985), 169–207; Michael C. Questier, 'Loyalty, religion and state power in early modern England: English Romanism and the Jacobean oath of allegiance', *Historical Journal* 40 (1997), 311–29. However, this oath of allegiance also raised interest among the Old English in Ireland, who were later granted a similar oath in the graces.
28 William Lyon, Bishop of Cork and Ross, to Lord Hunsdon in 1596, in *Calendar of the State*

Papers Relating to Ireland, 1596–1597 (London: Her Majesty's Stationary Office, 1893), pp. 15–16, see also p. 13.

29 See Graham Kew (ed.), *The Irish Sections of Fynes Moryson's Unpublished Itinerary* (Dublin: Irish Manuscripts Commission, 1998), p. 63; Aidan Clarke (ed.), 'A discourse between two councillors of state, the one of England and the other of Ireland (1642)', *Analecta Hibernica* 26 (1970), 159–75, at p. 163.

30 See Helga Hammerstein, 'Aspects of the continental education of Irish students in the reign of Queen Elizabeth I', in T.D. Williams (ed.), *Historical Studies VIII* (Dublin: Gill and Macmillan, 1971), pp. 137–53, here p. 139; Lennon, *Sixteenth-century Ireland*, p. 314; Colm Lennon, 'The rise of recusancy among the Dublin patricians, 1580–1613', in William J. Sheils and Diana Wood (eds), *The churches, Ireland and the Irish* (Oxford, New York: Blackwell, 1989), pp. 123–32, at p. 124. Some of these private tutors are mentioned in the oaths of the students of the Irish college at Salamanca. See D.J. O'Doherty (ed.), 'Students of the Irish college Salamanca, 1595–1619', *Archivium Hibernicum* 2 (1913), 1–36.

31 'Ex illius enim schola, tanquam ex equo Troico, homines literatissimi in reipublica lucem prodierunt.' Richard Stanyhurst, 'De rebus in Hibernia gestis', in Timothy Corcoran (ed.), *State policy in Irish education, A.D. 1536 to 1816* (Dublin: Fallon, 1916), p. 45.

32 See Hammerstein, 'Aspects of the continental education', p. 140.

33 Constantia Maxwell (ed.), *Irish history from contemporary sources (1509–1610)* (London: Allen & Unwin, 1923), pp. 146–7.

34 The standard monograph on Trinity College, Dublin, is still John Pentland Mahaffy, *An epoch in Irish history: Trinity College, Dublin, its foundation and early fortunes, 1591–1660* (London: Fisher Unwin, 1903).

35 For an overview see Hammerstein, 'Aspects of the continental education'. With regard to book printing, Catholics were in a similar position as with regard to university education. They could not print books in Ireland because the state controlled the printing presses. During the intensive 'pamphlet war' between Catholic clergy (mostly Jesuits) and Protestant preachers (in particular the professors of theological controversy at Trinity College) in the early seventeenth century the Catholic pamphlets were printed on the Continent and then smuggled into Ireland. On the early seventeenth century 'pamphlet war' see Declan Gaffney, 'The practice of religious controversy in Dublin, 1600–1641', in Sheils and Wood (eds), *The churches, Ireland and the Irish*, pp. 145–58.

36 '... in locis compluribus juniores id tantum fidei callebant, quod a matribus nutricibusque didicerant ...'. Philip O'Sullivan Beare, *Historiae Catholicae Iberniae Compendium*, ed. Matthew Kelly (Dublin: O'Daly, 1850), p. 133.

37 Already in 1580 the Protestant Bishop of Waterford and Lismore, Marmaduke Middleton, complained: 'None of the women do come either to service or sermons.' Marmaduke Middleton to Walsingham in 1580, in William Maziere Brady (ed.), *State Papers Concerning the Irish Church in the Time of Queen Elizabeth* (London: Longmans, 1868), p. 40; see also Raymond Gillespie, *Devoted people: belief and religion in early modern Ireland* (Manchester, New York: Manchester University Press, 1997), p. 13. On the role of women see in more detail: Lotz-Heumann, *Die doppelte Konfessionalisierung in Irland*, pp. 298–300. See also on the situation in the English Catholic community: John Bossy, *The English Catholic community, 1570–1850* (London: Darton, Longman & Todd, 1975), pp. 155–7.

38 Concerning Reformation of Religion in Ireland (probably by Sir Henry Brouncker), 1606, in *Calendar of the State Papers Relating to Ireland, 1603–1606* (London: Her Majesty's Stationary Office, 1872), p. 544.

39 See Lennon, *Sixteenth-century Ireland*, p. 25.

40 See Edmund Hogan (ed.), *Words of Comfort to Persecuted Catholics Written in Exile in 1607, Letters from a Cell in Dublin Castle and Diary of the Bohemian War of 1620 by Father Fitzsimon* (Dublin: Gill & Son, 1881), p. 156. In 1612 the Protestant Bishop Ram of Ferns and Leighlin reported that 'the poorer sort' did not attend the services of the state church and told him 'that if they shuld be of our religion, no popish marchant wold employ them being sailors; – no popish landlord

wold lett them any lands being husbandmen, nor sett them houses in tenantry being artificers, and therefore they must either starve or doe as they doe'. Quoted in William Maziere Brady, *Essays on the English state church in Ireland* (London: Strahan & Co, 1869), p. 15; see also Maxwell (ed.), *Irish history*, p. 135.

41 See Lotz-Heumann, *Die doppelte Konfessionalisierung in Irland*, p. 300.
42 See John MacErlean, *The Sodality of the BlessedVirgin Mary in Ireland: a short history* (Dublin: Irish Messenger, 1928), pp. 14, 16.
43 See the letter from Christopher Holywood to General Aquaviva, 1605, in Edmund Hogan (ed.), *Ibernia Ignatiana Seu Ibernorum Societas Jesu Patrum Monumenta* (Dublin 1880), p. 157, see also p. 150.
44 For a detailed analysis of the development in Dublin see Lennon, *Lords of Dublin*.
45 It is impossible to give numbers here, but mixed marriages appear in the sources again and again. It is, for example, striking that the (Catholic) Confederation of Kilkenny included an article about the rights of Catholic women married to Protestant men in its government programme of 1642, thus indicating that mixed marriages were a common phenomenon. See the Actes of the Generall Assemblie of the Confederates, in Patrick Francis Moran (ed.), *Spicilegium Ossoriense: Being a Collection of Original Letters and Papers Illustrative of the History of the Irish Church from the Reformation to theYear 1800*, 3 vols (Dublin: Gill & Son, 1874–84), here vol. 2, p. 14.
46 See, e.g., Ford,'The Protestant reformation in Ireland', p. 70; Phil Kilroy,'Sermon and pamphlet literature in the Irish reformed church, 1613–1634', *Archivium Hibernicum* 33 (1975), 110–21, at p. 116; Hogan (ed.), *Words of Comfort*, p. 56; E.S. Shuckburgh (ed.), *Two biographies ofWilliam Bedell, Bishop of Kilmore* (Cambridge: Cambridge University Press, 1902), p. 101.
47 See, e.g., Aubrey Gwynn,'Archbishop Ussher and Father Brendan O Conor', in The Franciscan Fathers (eds), *Father LukeWadding: commemorative volume* (Dublin: Clonmore & Reynolds, 1957), pp. 263–83; William O'Sullivan (ed.), 'Correspondence of David Rothe and James Ussher, 1619–23', *Collectanea Hibernica* 36–7 (1994–95), 7–49.
48 See, e.g., British Library, Additional MS 4756, fols 22r–v; Edmund Hogan, *Distinguished Irishmen of the sixteenth century* (London: Burns and Oates, 1894), pp. 208–9.
49 Hogan (ed.), *Words of Comfort*, p. 147. See also Barnaby Rich's report on public Catholic funerals in Wexford, Waterford and Dublin. E.M. Hinton (ed.), 'Rych's anothomy of Ireland, with an account of the author', *Publications of the Modern Language Association of America* 55 (1949), 73–101, at p. 85.
50 Ussher to Lord Grandison in 1622, in Elrington and Todd (eds), *TheWhole Works of Ussher*, vol. XV, p. 181.
51 See, e.g. the case of John Shearman in Waterford, in Corcoran (ed.), *State policy in Irish education*, pp. 51–2; see also Robinson-Hammerstein,'Erzbischof Adam Loftus', p. 170.
52 See Barnaby Rich, *A New Description of Ireland* (London: T. Adams, 1610), pp. 62–9.
53 Sir Thomas Dutton to Lord Dorchester in 1629, in *Calendar of the State Papers Relating to Ireland, 1625–1632* (London: Her Majesty's Stationery Office, 1900), p. 500. Report of a Catholic Layman, in Brendan Jennings (ed.), *Wadding papers, 1614–38* (Dublin: Irish Manuscripts Commission, 1953), p. 330.
54 On the Generality Lands see the chapter by Charles de Mooij in this volume, pp. 156–67. The only other article in English accessible to me was J.S.A.M. van Koningsbrugge, 'The "Generaliteitslanden" as a periphery of the Republic of the Seven United Provinces', in Hans-Heinrich Nolte (ed.), *Internal peripheries in European history* (Göttingen, Zürich 1991), pp. 119–31.
55 It is difficult to find a fitting nomenclature for such situations in early modern Europe. Willem Frijhoff has suggested the term 'ecumenicity of everyday life'. See above p. 7 and his *Embodied belief: ten essays on religious culture in Dutch history* (Hilversum: Uitgeverij Verloren, 2002).
56 I should like to thank Raymond Gillespie for pointing this out in his comment.
57 Keith P. Luria, *Sacred boundaries: religious coexistence and conflict in early-modern France* (Washington: The Catholic University of America Press, 2005), p. xxii.
58 See the chapter by Willem Frijhoff above, p. 14.
59 See in more detail Lotz-Heumann, *Die doppelte Konfessionalisierung in Irland*, pp. 236–55.
60 Luria, *Sacred boundaries*, p. xxiii.

12

Orphans and students: recruiting boys and girls for the Holland Mission

JOKE SPAANS

Minority status in early modern Europe held both challenges and opportunities. The fate of religious minorities, 'Churches under the cross', has long been portrayed only in terms of the former. Thus, in his *The World of Catholic Renewal*, Ronnie Hsia describes the situation of Catholics in England, The Netherlands, and Ireland in a short chapter poignantly titled 'The martyred Church'.[1] Christine Kooi, in her work on minority Catholicism, emphasises the various disadvantages of minority status also, although she also points to the various ways in which Catholics could play the system and create opportunities for worship and community life.[2] Here I would like to elaborate on this latter aspect, the agency of minority communities, *in casu* the Dutch Catholics.

Their minority position forced Catholics to reinvent their ecclesiastical identities in a period when their Church as a whole was introducing reforms following the Council of Trent. These reforms were slowed down almost everywhere as a result of active resistance from groups who saw their interests threatened, or simply by institutional drag. Moreover, in countries turned Protestant, minority status forced them to improvise, to 'translate Trent' for their particular circumstances, to use Alexandra Walsham's phrase.[3] In England this reinvention was more drastic than in the Dutch Republic, as the penal laws against Catholics were much harsher and the percentage of recusants in the population was dramatically lower – while Dutch Catholics, especially in the north-western half of the country, made up a sizeable minority which came to enjoy considerable freedom over time.

Both English and Dutch historiographies tend to avoid the name 'Catholic Church' for minority Catholicism in the two countries.[4] In this way the perimeter of the subject is drawn around clergy and laity alike, allowing for a study of the interaction between the two, although for the Dutch Republic the viewpoint of formal ecclesiastical history still largely predominates. Here we find the image of a church, directed by the Propaganda through the nunciatures of Cologne and Leuven, with a problematic position, but ultimately circumscribed in the formal–juridical terms of canon law. Interest focuses first of all on the clergy. This is of course typical of much church history, and has a striking parallel with Dutch Protestant historiography. From the 1980s, our view on the Dutch religious landscape is gradually beginning to change, with a budding interest in the believers in the pews, in their houses, on the streets and in their contacts with those of other faiths. Building on these new beginnings, Charles Parker's book on the Dutch Catholics convincingly demonstrates the collaboration between clergy and laity in the Holland Mission.[5]

Women's history has added the gender perspective. The interest here tends to focus on women and their uphill battle against male prerogatives. Here the spiritual virgins, or *kloppen*, have been particularly highlighted as examples of non-ordained religious agency.[6] This, however, just adds another one-sidedness. We need a broader, comparative approach, encompassing the religiosity of both men and women. In the case of early modern Dutch Catholics this is quite a challenge. Sources are not particularly abundant, to start with, and are mostly institutional and thus centred on (ordained) males.

Worst of all, we are dramatically uninformed about the religious life in the mission stations that were established after the collapse of the regular parishes. These stations were initially dominated by locally influential families, which arranged space for worship in their houses or contributed to the building of 'hidden churches'.[7] In cities especially, the priests in these stations often belonged to, or were closely related to, these hosting families who could protect them through their local standing and connections. Catholic services in these churches must have had some manner of family worship, with trusted friends and neighbours as guests. Husbands, wives or widows could host such a 'hidden' church. During the course of the seventeenth century the house churches came into the hands of the priests during their time in office. By that time, however, another form of 'family' had emerged around the priests. Most station priests had spiritual direction over a group of spiritual virgins. These virgins, in their turn, often held much of the material direction over the day-to-day management of the station. Like the initial 'host families', they donated money, objects and time to the church, did the housekeeping for the priest and took a firm hand in the liturgy, in catechising and other forms of education, and in an active apostolate.[8]

How other lay members of a mission station participated in its religious life remains something of a guess, and gender differences even more so. In practically all Protestant churches, and in Jewish synagogues, women and men were seated separately. Although we know quite a lot about the furnishing and decoration of the Catholic hidden churches with works of art, we do not know how the congregation was seated. With Protestants, the women usually sat on chairs at the foot of the pulpit. The pews for the men were ranged around this area. Both women and men were seated according to social rank, and correct ranking was jealously guarded. Overall, the seats for males appear to have been fewer than those for women. Perhaps 'real men' preferred to stand. The poor often stood out of necessity, since most seats had to be rented. With the Jews, the men had the central floor, the women were hidden from (male) view on balconies. This pattern strongly suggests that Christian women were perceived as the more devout attendants at public worship, whereas men were somewhat more detached, with the opposite perception holding for the Jews. It is probable that Catholic congregations followed the Christian pattern, which had medieval roots, but we do not really know.[9]

Catholics, unlike Protestants, could enter fraternities or congregations devoted to various saints or devotional exercises. As far as we know, however, most of these fraternities and congregations catered for men and women, and there is no indication of specifically gendered communal devotions. Even the devotional routines available for the more devout individual Catholic laypeople may have been non-gender specific. The spiritual virgin Magdalena van Dam, orphaned when young and who lived with her grandmother, shared her devotions with one of her uncles. They urged each other on, rose early in the morning, attended an early service whenever one was to be had, or else prayed together at home – there is no hint of differing expectations for men and women. When later, as a spiritual virgin, she took to an elaborate life of prayer, centred on the life and passion of Christ, she called upon the intercession of a host of saints to aid her devotions. Again, there is no specifically feminine pattern. Mary and Joseph, virgin martyrs and Fathers of the Church, female mystics and the male founders of the major orders were invoked, apparently for their spiritual capabilities rather than their gendered identities. But then, Magdalena may or may not be representative.[10]

What we do know about lay religiosity is deduced more or less from the devotional literature and prints available at the time. As research into markets and reading audiences is still in its infancy, the impact of this material is hard to ascertain. It is commonly assumed that literature tends to appeal more to the intellect, pictures to the emotions. The suggestion, however, that pictures were aimed at a predominantly female audience, for whom the printed word was less accessible, does not make overly much sense in the Netherlands, with its high rates of literacy. There is no hard evidence that women had a predilection for mystical authors and female saints, and we know that the Dutch clergy did their best to discourage these and to promote a more austere, Christ-centred piety.[11]

To save this discussion from being stillborn, I will focus on the very first stages of the Holland Mission, and look at what the central authorities considered essential in their 'translation of Trent' for Dutch circumstances. When Catholic organisation and communal worship were formally outlawed in the United Provinces in 1581, this cannot have been totally unexpected, but even though the same had happened earlier elsewhere, the Catholic Church did not have a cut-and-dried contingency plan. This gave local Catholics, clergy and lay, men and women, the opportunity to experiment with new forms of community. In this chapter I will address these initiatives, with special attention to their consequences for local communities.

Boys

The clergy of the Holland Mission were concerned first and foremost with reorganising the clerical estate. Sasbout Vosmeer, apostolic vicar for the Holland Mission from 1692, estimated that in 1602, two decades after the first edicts against the exercise of the Catholic religion, only seventy priests had remained active in the rebellious provinces. It is impossible to determine whether the situation really was as dramatic as this. There must have been many footloose priests and monks, ejected from their former livings and bereft of other sources of income, who were willing to say Mass, dispense the sacraments, and do a bit of healing, blessing or outright magic on the side, as the opportunity presented itself.[12] Such men did not bother with supervision by apostolic vicars, and Vosmeer probably ignored them in his count. Even so, it is undeniable that priests were few and far between in these first decades. Many of Vosmeer's clergy lived in towns, where it was easier to remain *incognito*. They undertook regular forays into the countryside to lend their services to communities deprived of spiritual care. Even high-placed clerics lent a hand at this type of missionary work: in 1599 the vicar-general of the Haarlem chapter, Willem Coopal, drowned as he crossed Beemster lake on such an expedition.[13]

Training a new generation of missionary priests was not easy. The Council of Trent had just raised the standards for all ranks of clerics. For priests with the cure of souls it prescribed academic degrees in theology, and a communal life in a college or seminary under clerical supervision during the years of study. This meant that the Dutch Catholics, like their English co-religionists, had to resort to foreign universities or seminaries. Moreover, they had to recruit boys with the financial resources for an extended period of study abroad, and who would also be prepared to return to their native country afterwards to dedicate themselves to the rigours of a clandestine mission. Even though the dangers in the Dutch Republic were considerably less acute than in England, graduates often must have had far brighter prospects elsewhere.

In the last quarter of the sixteenth century several experiments were undertaken to find a working solution for this problem. The Haarlem priest Nicolaas Wiggerts Cousebant reputedly started a seminary in Cologne as early as 1579. Although evidence from this period is very sparse, it seems more likely that Cousebant, with two other Dutch clerics, Martinus Regius and Cornelis Arentz, merely ran a boarding house for students. They housed and perhaps tutored boys who took the arts courses at the University of Cologne and intended to take theology at a later stage, all in the hope that they could persuade them to enter the Dutch mission field after graduation. The students living with them did so at their own expense, and it is unclear whether Cousebant and his assistants actually taught them.

Apparently this did not work. Cousebant and Arentz returned to Haarlem in 1584, Regius left the next year. Cousebant and others then seem to have started collecting donations and bequests from pious Catholics in order to provide aspiring boys with scholarships. Individual priests also took boys into their homes and taught them, presumably in preparation for the required academic studies or to shorten the necessary stay at a foreign university in order to save expenses. Even the king of Spain was (unsuccessfully) solicited for money towards this end. The pope was more forthcoming; in 1592 he provided Sasbout Vosmeer, freshly appointed vicar apostolic, with twelve scholarships destined for candidates for the priesthood in the Holland Mission. But it took another ten years before an effective college was founded, again in Cologne. Several prominent Dutch priests served as its president, often for short periods, as most lacked the qualities needed for such an undertaking.

Gradually, however, these efforts gained momentum. In 1612 the college was reorganised and Vosmeer finally found a more permanent president. In 1616, a second college opened in Leuven, and over the years the Holland Mission also explored other venues for the training of both wealthy and poor boys. In the early decades of the seventeenth century, the apparently generous availability of scholarships made preparation for the priesthood so attractive that Vosmeer actually complained about a flood of applicants. His successors could afford to be fastidious over the help they accepted from regular clergy. By a rough estimate, at the end of the seventeenth century the Holland Mission numbered around three hundred thousand faithful, in about 250 mission stations manned by just over 450 priests. Distribution of Catholics, stations and priests was uneven, but the initial pressing shortages had by then been successfully overcome.[14]

It has been argued that the necessity to start training facilities from scratch enabled the Dutch apostolic vicars to create a modern, professional clerical apparatus, fully compliant with the norms set by the Council of Trent, long before the clergy of the surrounding Catholic countries got their acts together.[15] The new public Reformed Church followed essentially the same lines in the recruitment of candidates for the ministry. It also had to welcome assistance from ministers trained abroad, to obtain training facilities in the new Dutch universities, and to solicit endowments for scholarships to create a clergy that was up to newly adjusted standards.

Women

Although the earliest initiatives in this recruitment programme are often ascribed to individual priests like Cousebant or the apostolic vicars, it is clear that a network of closely cooperating individuals and residual institutions supported them. There was a considerable amount of improvisation, given the situation in which the traditional ecclesiastical organisation had crumbled; priests were scarce and canon law could not provide adequate guidance to determine valid chains of command and allow for coherent strategies. Inevitably there were differences of opinion and jurisdictional squabbles. Yet there appears to have been a general unanimity on the main thrust of reconstruction of viable Catholic life in the new Dutch Republic, and close cooperation on the ground – not only in the recruitment of new priests, but also in another experiment, which has no Protestant parallel.

Even before Cousebant and Arentz had given up their first apparently fruitless efforts in the recruitment of boys for the priesthood in Cologne in 1584, the two men periodically returned to Haarlem, and there created organisations for recruiting the laity, more specifically Catholic women, into the work of the Mission.[16] In 1583, Cousebant invited two young women to start a communal semireligious life in a converted peat shed behind his father's house. Subsequently, many followed their example and before the first decade of the seventeenth century was out, the community already reputedly had some two hundred members. These women called themselves *kloppen*, to distinguish themselves from the older Beguine communities, with which they had otherwise much in common. Unlike Beguines, *kloppen* were not bound to a specific rule and were free for a life of active ministry. As such, they seem to have been a typical Counter-Reformation invention, somewhat comparable to the Ursulines in the earlier stages of their development, before they took to the cloistered life.[17]

Cousebant led his virgins in an ascetic life of contemplation, inspired by the Poor Clares. Their daily lives were organised around the canonical hours, as much as was possible outside the protective walls of an endowed convent, and to be a continuous office of prayer for the restoration of the Catholic Church in the rebellious provinces. He also encouraged in his virgins a quest for mysticism. This combination of monastic discipline and mysticism proved too harsh for most of his spiritual daughters. Many died prematurely, whereas a few were considered by the church authorities to have developed heretical notions about the mysteries of the faith.

Cornelis Arentz appears to have been Cousebant's associate in this, as he had been in the Cologne venture. In Cousebant's frequent absences, he not only supervised the virgins but also admitted new members to the nascent community, which looked to him as their primary spiritual director. Quite unlike Cousebant, Arentz led his virgins in an unspectacular, but no less exacting, life of strict obedience to a rule of prayer, mortification and work. Much of this work consisted of teaching and charity in the world. His direction was focused on breaking their spirits into submission to a disciplined life of devotion, rather than on allowing them to soar towards mystical union. The differing approaches of the two priests towards their spiritual daughters reflected conflicting views of the Mission. Cousebant stuck more closely to Tridentine norms, with their penchant for clerical supervision; Arentz tended more towards experiments in lay ministry.

In the 1580s and 1590s both Cousebant and Arentz travelled as circuit priests. Cousebant, born to a wealthy Haarlem family of brewers and very much a man of the world, flamboyant and an exceptionally eloquent preacher, frequented the mansions of the Frisian landed 'nobility', quite a number of whom remained faithful to Catholicism and, like the English gentry, had the means to harbour priests and have Masses said in their houses. Arentz seems to have been of more ordinary burgher stock – he had a family name, Lichthert, but was always called by his patronym. He mainly toured the Noorderkwartier of Holland, preaching in the houses of dedicated Catholics. Both recruited girls into a life of celibacy and service to the Mission.[18]

This marshalling of lay Catholics for an active apostolate was very much in line with the policies of apostolic vicar Sasbout Vosmeer. Vosmeer was deeply concerned with the education of a new generation of missionary priests for the abandoned Dutch dioceses, but, realistically assessing the contribution his promising but still insufficient crop of new recruits could make in this daunting task, he also obtained authorisation from Rome to use laypersons to organise religious services without priests. These lay workers read sermons and led the audience in prayer and song. Others discreetly invited worshipers and guarded the place of assembly against raids by the Protestant authorities.[19] Arentz groomed his virgins to perform all these tasks. Quite a number of them did not come to Haarlem to live in the new community, but used their family homes as bases for missionary work. From time to time circuit priests would visit their stations from Haarlem.[20] Needless to say, the more monastically inclined spiritual daughters of Cousebant, with their focus upon liturgical prayer and mystical union, were unfit for these tasks.

These differences of approach caused a rift between Cousebant and Arentz. Increasingly they became rivals in their recruitment of spiritual daughters, who could choose between the two of them as confessors and spiritual directors.

The relationship between the two men, who had been close collaborators both in Cologne and in Holland, now turned acrimonious, scandalising the Catholic community. Cousebant was a forceful man and he had offered signal service to the Mission. Nonetheless, in 1598 the vicar apostolic and the Haarlem chapter intervened and removed him as director of the community, placing it entirely in the hands of Arentz. Cousebant returned to Cologne, taking a number of his virgins with him and setting them up as a Dutch convent of Poor Clares. He himself entered a Franciscan monastery and died in 1628 as its prior and superior of the Franciscan province of the Rhineland.[21]

Once the community of virgins had become settled under Cornelis Arentz, they were involved in an imposing array of tasks. Virgins acted as housekeepers who took care of their spiritual director and of his clerical guests. This was an exacting task. The priests would come in at all hours and had to be kept out of sight of unsympathetic heretics, as the performance of their priestly duties was formally prohibited and carried hefty fines. Others acted as sextons in their own *schuilkerk*. The church was in constant use, for the celebration of Mass every morning, for daily sermons and as a place of meditation and silent prayer for the sisters. Especially during the first period, the sisters would have to take turns coming to Mass and communion, so as to avoid notice by hostile neighbours, and the sextons also had to do the invitations – very discreetly. Moreover, the sisters-sextons were responsible for the safekeeping and maintenance of valuables, had to oversee repairs, and of course cleaned and appropriately decorated the church – work that under normal circumstances was a male preserve. In the Reformed Church, the office of sexton was not only perceived as unfit for women because it was a public office and entailed responsibility for buildings and funds, but apparently also for more ritual reasons. The Amsterdam Reformed sextons were expressly forbidden to let women enter the pulpits, even for the purpose of cleaning them – which rather overturns common assumptions about which church feared female sexuality the most.[22]

Equally important was the work of the Haarlem virgins outside their own community. They 'manned' mission bases in the rural hinterland of Haarlem, where priests were reluctant to settle. They ran a Girls' Home, recruited new novices for the community, and trained them in both the spiritual and the active religious life. The wealthier among them supported the recruitment and training of boys for the ministry by donating money for scholarships, the poorer collected alms for this purpose and all stimulated vocations in the circle of their relatives.[23] They cared for the older sisters and for the sick among them, and performed an active ministry of admonition, teaching and consolation in the lay community, in Haarlem itself and beyond.

The Haarlem virgins may also have taken a lead in liturgical experiments adapted to the new situation, and which ignored traditional gender divides. The sisters officiated as acolytes in their own house churches and provided vocal and instrumental music during the services. They also provided objects of devotion. They copied devotional books for use in the community (the collection preserved in the library of the Catharijneconvent Museum in Utrecht still bears witness to this), and several virgins are described as having spent long hours at this work, producing literally cartloads of books during their lives, which suggests that these books may have found a much wider audience. They also copied out musical scores, which were hard to obtain, again, undoubtedly for the community, but probably also for others.[24] They produced devotional pictures, both for their own use and for wider distribution. Some restored and perhaps produced statues of the saints, others sewed and embroidered liturgical vestments and altar cloths destined for house churches, so that laypeople could have Masses said there. Some sold their products, for which there must indeed have been a market, especially in larger cities like Amsterdam and Haarlem.[25]

The Haarlem community was not the only community of lay religious women, but it was the largest. It was closely connected to the Haarlem chapter, and some of the sisters were related to Sasbout Vosmeer. More generally, multiple ties of family and friendship connected priests, devout widows and spiritual virgins into a network that centred on the larger communities in Haarlem, Delft and Utrecht, but practically spanned the entire Republic and reached across its borders into the Southern Netherlands and even to Spain. The Haarlem community may have been meant as something like a headquarters and service centre for lay ministry in the Mission. Whenever the safety of the community allowed, the Haarlem sisters generously invited guests into their homes and their church, and it was not unusual for *kloppen* to change residence from time to time. In this way they could spread their example of religious activism, spirituality and liturgical innovations, not only to other communities, but also into the routines of the mission stations, the majority of which had one or more *kloppen* to care for the priest and assist in his ministry. In the middle of the seventeenth century an estimated 3,500 *kloppen* were active in the Dutch Republic, and by the end of that century they numbered as many as 4,800 – or ten times the number of active priests.[26]

Official Roman policy limited the presence of women in ecclesiastical life far more strictly. These Dutch experiments invited very critical scrutiny from the central authorities of the Church. As early as 1609–10 a smear campaign, inspired by the Jesuits, aimed at discrediting the work of the Dutch *kloppen*. Accusations of too close a familiarity between priests and their spiritual daughters were made, resulting in everything from unseemly rivalry between priests to gain exclusive spiritual directorship over wealthy *kloppen* in order to get hold of their estates, to sexual impropriety. The case was brought before the Roman curia and the pope himself. Vosmeer and the Haarlem chapter staunchly defended the use of *kloppen* in the Mission and carried the day, even though some of the allegations may not have been groundless. The women had simply become indispensable.[27]

The ambiguity of the Tridentine Church over the desirability of non-cloistered female religious involved in active lay ministry largely explains the very divergent destinies of the Dutch *kloppen* and the initiatives of English women such as the Institute of Mary Ward. Founded in the Southern Netherlands, where active lay religious were common, the Institute was able to flourish for some time, even without official papal approval of its rule. Daughter houses could, to some extent, even spread on the Continent, wherever Catholic princes and local bishops welcomed religious women's contributions to active ministry. During the seventeenth century, however, the Institute suffered severe setbacks, and, most frustratingly perhaps, was never allowed into England, where it might have done much good.[28] The same ambiguities lay behind the rift between Cousebant and Arentz and the troubles with the Jesuits in 1609–10, but the leading Dutch Catholic clergy valued the contribution of the *kloppen* as much as they did that of their priests.

Girls

It was mentioned above that the Haarlem community of virgins ran a Girls' Home or *maagdenhuis*, dedicated to giving girls an otherwise normal education, reading, writing and learning a (textile related) trade, but in a Catholic spirit. Initially it was neither an orphanage nor a charitable institution in the strict sense, although it did accept (half) orphans and occasionally children for whom no tuition fees could be paid. The institution was explicitly intended for girls who were in danger of falling away from the Catholic faith through the conversion or loss of parents, or through pressure from 'heretical' relatives or legal custodians.

The first such Girls' Home was founded in Amsterdam by pious Catholic laywomen in the early 1570s. It survived the Alteration of 1578, which ousted the Catholic magistrate and put the new Reformed regime in place. In 1590 the trusteeship of the home was wrested from the hands of the female founders by their male relatives, wealthy men with good connections both with the Haarlem chapter and with the magistracy of Amsterdam. Henceforth, the vicar-general of the Haarlem chapter appointed the lay trustees. The Amsterdam pastor and Canon of the chapter, Albert Eggius, was appointed its confessor and schoolmaster. An endowed institution with such a distinctively Catholic character was an anomaly in a Protestant city. Also, legislation strongly supported the rights of relatives and guardians belonging to the public church, in order to save children from 'popish superstition'. Occasionally the Amsterdam magistrate urged its dissolution or transformation into a charitable institution, accessible for boys and girls of all religions.[29] However, the excellent connections of the trustees with the Amsterdam elite ultimately protected the foundation, as the stately building on the Spui, now home to the Board of the University of Amsterdam, testifies to this day.[30]

This is not to say that the Girls' Home had an unbroken history or prospered from the start. Again, as with the early history of the colleges for candidates for the priesthood, sources are sparse and sometimes contradictory. Similar girls' homes are known to have existed in several Dutch towns in the seventeenth century. Some catered only for the poor, others exclusively for the wealthy; most were boarding schools attracting girls from a wider region, but they sometimes also had (local) day pupils. Usually the *maagdenhuis* run by the Haarlem community of virgins has been perceived as located in Haarlem itself.[31] There is, however, a certain logic to the assumption that the Haarlem virgins were set to work in the Amsterdam Girls' Home after the chapter took control.

The presumed Haarlem institution is always called '*het maechdenhuis*', a name that is otherwise rather specific for the Amsterdam Girls' Home. It is said to have been an initiative of the very same Cornelis Arentz whom we met earlier as the co-worker of Cousebant in the college in Cologne and as his rival and successor in the directorship of the Haarlem community of virgins. He was also its father confessor. As such, he may have succeeded Albertus Eggius, who, at about the same time as he was appointed to the Amsterdam *maagdenhuis*, started to take in students to prepare them for their academic studies. Soon afterwards Eggius rose to responsible positions in the chapter, which probably left him little time to teach young girls their letters. Later he moved to Haarlem, where he was captured in a raid by the authorities in 1602. Eventually he had to leave the country and went to Cologne as president of the fledgling college. Arentz, himself born in Amsterdam, closely connected to the chapter, and as a spiritual director of a community of women dedicated to teaching and service to the church, was eminently suited to take over. Many of the *kloppen* came from Amsterdam, and it was not unusual for them to live with relatives outside Haarlem for extended periods, commuting back and forth for religious holidays. Probably there was no separate 'Haarlem *maagdenhuis*', but the Haarlem virgins ran the Amsterdam Girls' Home. Of one of the teachers of the *maagdenhuis* it is said she left the place in the care of one of the older pupils from time to time when she herself went to Haarlem to attend Mass at the church of the community and was therefore absent for a few days – which would be unnecessary if the Girls' Home was located in Haarlem itself.[32]

The Girls' Home suffered at least two bouts of real persecution: in 1592, when Vosmeer was appointed as vicar apostolic, and again in 1602 when he received his episcopal ordination. Both occasions caused offence to the Protestant Dutch authorities as infringements of the anti-Catholic edicts. Prominent priests were arrested, fined and banished, their houses searched, correspondence and sacred objects confiscated. The community of virgins and the *maagdenhuis* had their share of these troubles, which, incidentally, indicates that the Protestant authorities considered them part of the new Catholic ecclesiastical establishment they were trying to suppress. They broke up the *maagdenhuis*: the girls could still take lessons together, but the house could no longer be kept as a boarding school. They were housed in smaller groups, presumably with *kloppen*, some perhaps even in Haarlem. Each time, these measures were only temporary.

Kloppen were valued as managers for such a Girls' Home. They did the general housekeeping, sewed and mended the girls' clothing, oversaw cleanliness and health and, of course, taught them. As many of the Haarlem virgins were of burgher or even noble families and had themselves been well educated (often being literate in Latin and schooled in instrumental and vocal music and the figurative arts, notably fine needlework) the *maagdenhuis* could provide a substantial education. As could be expected, the school produced a number of spiritual virgins. More importantly, perhaps, *alumnae* from burgher families also married into the confessionally mixed urban elite and became the mothers of the next generation of Catholics. They also may have predisposed their relatives among the town magistrates to toleration and even protection of the nascent Catholic establishment.[33] Like the seminary and the communities of virgins, the Girls' Homes were actively fostered by the top echelon of the Holland Mission, as part of its recruitment policy.

Priests of God and Brides of Christ in the Holland Mission

The efforts made to recruit women alongside men and to entrust them with a range of tasks in the Mission are undoubtedly remarkable. It often seems that the contributions of both sexes were valued equally. Women played an important role in Counter-Reformation piety and charity, but usually in much more 'controlled' situations: in claustration,[34] in active but still strictly regulated orders and congregations or, at the very least, under close clerical supervision.[35] The *kloppen*, though acknowledging the authority of their father confessors, nonetheless appear to have had a free hand in their outreach to their families and neighbours. The girls trained in the *maagdenhuis* to uphold the faith as Catholic wives, matrons and employers were under even less restraint. Not only the clergy valued the work of these women: families considered having a religious among them to be a divine blessing, in whatever calling, whether as ordained priests, monks or professed nuns, or as spiritual virgins.[36]

Some of their activities may well have made their superiors flinch, as when Maritgen Wouters practically abducted a niece and placed her in the Girls' Home against the will of her mother. Such actions caused unrest, attracted the attention of the Reformed consistory and could well provoke the magistrate into action against priests and mission stations.[37] On the whole, however, evangelising and even proselytising by laypeople, within the circle of their relatives, friends and neighbours, was not forbidden. From the very beginning Vosmeer stimulated lay apostolate, and his successors continued this policy. Moreover, they organised men and women in fraternities and third orders, which not only catered to their personal devotion but also tried to involve them in support for the Mission. Apparently, however, these mainly focused on prayer and fundraising, whereas the *kloppen* used more aggressive tactics in their ministry.[38]

How should we evaluate the gender roles of these priests and laywomen? Women may not have had much control over formal religious ritual, the exclusive preserve of the male, ordained priesthood, but their easy access to the 'lived religion' in the intimate sphere of homes and informal gatherings amply made up for that. As Catholics were excluded from the public sphere in the Protestant Republic, this may well have been the most promising mission field. *Kloppen*, especially, had a reputation for insinuating themselves into homes, fostering Catholic devotion and even conversion of Protestants, notably in education and at sickbeds and deathbeds, even in public hospitals.[39] The vociferous protests of Protestant consistories testify to their rate of success. Lay*men* are hardly mentioned in this role: complaints about 'seductions to popery' always involve either priests or *kloppen*.

Also, the prominent role of women may have screened the priests and Catholic menfolk generally from attention, blame and the risk of harsh punishment under the penal laws. This allowed priests to keep their activities discreetly hidden and protected the Mission as a whole. It relieved male Catholics from the responsibility to act openly as pillars of a forbidden faith, and enabled them to conform to the Protestant regime in order to qualify for public office. Meanwhile, the women sustained the lived religion of their families. For the men, the option of deathbed reconciliation always remained, and the vicars apostolic actively supported this practice.

Apart from this separation between female Catholic piety and male conformity to the Protestant environment, the cooperation of priests and laywomen in the Holland Mission does not seem to have been conducive to gendered patterns of piety. It appears to have supported a uniform, or rather unisex, devotion centred on Christ and the central mysteries of the faith. Moreover, the close cooperation of priests and laywomen urged on the former an exemplary pious lifestyle, informed not only by priestly but also by monastic ideals — and the latter were not gender specific.[40] Both tendencies may have been at the root of the austere Catholicism that set the Dutch Catholics apart from those of the rest of the Continent, or rather, the type of piety on which Catholic and Protestant spirituality converged in the sixteenth century.[41]

The presence of a household of religious women may also have helped the Catholic priest to relate to his parishioners in a personal, familiar way.[42] Early on, the priests of the Mission thus developed a 'modern', 'feminised' style of ministry, which would become the norm for Dutch Reformed ministers around 1800, as religion became localised in the heart of the believer, rather than in public order.[43] Minority Catholics made the private, feminine religious sphere of the home coincide with the more public and formal, 'masculine' rituals in churches and places of pilgrimage.

By contrast, the Protestant churches insisted on a piety centred on public worship. As much as they stimulated private Bible study, meditation and prayer, and regular family worship in the homes of the godly, these always took second place, after the preaching, teaching and administration of the sacraments in the male-dominated public services. The more private forms of Catholic worship in the 'hidden churches' may have provoked the development in these communities of a precociously modern, individual religiosity, for both men and women.[44] This was reinforced by the redefinition of the position of the priests in a minority religion. They lacked public authority, which was by definition masculine. The gender identity of clergy who had to restrict their activities to the private sphere may have been intrinsically ambiguous.

These characteristics of Catholic minority religion may even have inspired developments in the Dutch Reformed Church. The seventeenth century witnessed several challenges to its emphasis on (by definition male dominated) public ministry and communal worship. The deaconesses that appear again and again in local Reformed congregations, despite the reluctance of synods to recognise them as occupying a proper ecclesiastical office, may well have been inspired by the activities of Catholic laywomen, notably the *kloppen*, who were so notorious for their pastoral success in counselling the sick and the dying. The Reformed churches accepted women as teachers of the catechism – again, a parallel to the activities of the *kloppen*. The conventicles of the godly, valued as supporters of true piety despite the constant anxiety over their potential for separatism, provided the Reformed with a format for convivial private religious exercise which mirrored Catholic practice.

The evidence for a close and to some extent egalitarian cooperation of men and women in the Holland Mission overwhelmingly stems from the first half of the seventeenth century, the period during which the shortage of priests was most pressing and the acceptance of experiments was at its maximum. There is a marked tendency, observable after Rovenius' succession to Vosmeer, towards the normalisation of the ecclesiastical situation. The apostolic vicars partly restored parish structures, and set up lay boards for the administration of the stations and the relief of the Catholic poor. These lay boards were exclusively male — almost emphatically so, as in many places they went under the name of 'the Catholic Men'.[45] Still, the gender characteristics of Dutch Catholicism, as suggested above, may not have been limited to the first decades of the Mission. Spiritual virgins were never entirely removed from the more managerial roles in the Mission. They remained active in religious education, in the liturgy and as examples of piety until well into the nineteenth century — in fact until a public Catholic Church came into existence in the Netherlands.[46]

Notes

1. R. Po-chia Hsia, *The world of Catholic renewal 1540–1770* (Cambridge/New York/Melbourne: Cambridge University Press, 1998), pp. 80–91.
2. Christine Kooi, '*Sub iugo hereticorum*: minority Catholicism in early modern Europe', in Kathleen M. Comerford and Hilmar M. Pabel (eds), *Early modern Catholicism. Essays in honour of John W. O'Malley, S.J.*, Toronto (Buffalo/London: University of Toronto Press, 2001), pp. 147–62; 'Paying off the sheriff; strategies of Catholic toleration in Golden Age Holland', in R. Po-chia Hsia and Henk van Nierop, *Calvinism and religious toleration in the Dutch Golden Age* (Cambridge: Cambridge University Press, 2002), pp. 87–101.
3. Alexandra Walsham, 'Translating Trent? English Catholicism and the Counter Reformation', *Historical Research* 78 (2005), 288–310.
4. Notably John Bossy, *The English Catholic community 1570–1850* (London, Darton, Longman and Todd, 1975); L.J. Rogier, *Geschiedenis van het Katholicisme in Noord-Nederland in de 16e en 17e eeuw*, 3 vols (Amsterdam: Urbi et Orbi, 1945–1947); P. Polman, *Katholiek Nederland in de achttiende eeuw*, 3 vols (Hilversum: Brand, 1968).
5. Joris van Eijnatten and Fred van Lieburg, *Nederlandse religiegeschiedenis* (Hilversum: Verloren, 2005); Charles H. Parker, *Faith on the margins: Catholic identity in the Dutch Golden Age* (Cambridge, MA: Harvard University Press, 2007).
6. E.E.A.J.M. Theissing, *Over klopjes en kwezels* (Utrecht / Nijmegen: Dekker en Van de Vegt N.V., 1935); Elisja Schulte van Kessel, *Geest en vlees in godsdienst en wetenschap, Vijf opstellen over gezagsconflicten in de zeventiende eeuw* ('s-Gravenhage: Staatsuitgeverij, 1980), pp. 51–115; Marit Monteiro, *Geestelijke maagden. Leven tussen klooster en wereld in Noord-Nederland gedurende de zeventiende eeuw* (Hilversum: Verloren, 1996).
7. Cf. for terminology S.A.C. Dudok van Heel, 'Amsterdamse schuil- of huiskerken?' *Holland* 25 (1993), 1–10.
8. Examples in Xander van Eck, *Kunst, twist en devotie. Goudse katholieke schuilkerken 1572–1795* (Delft: Eburon, 1994).
9. Joke Spaans, 'Stad van vele geloven 1578–1795', in Willem Frijhoff and Maarten Prak, *Geschiedenis van Amsterdam. Centrum van de wereld 1578–1650* [Geschiedenis van Amsterdam II-1] (Amsterdam: Sun, 2004), pp. 429–32; Christine Peters, *Patterns of piety. Women, gender and religion in late medieval and Reformation England* (Cambridge: Cambridge University Press, 2003), pp. 22–4, 171–8.
10. Catharina Jans Oly, 'Levens der maechden', 3 vols MS, Library Museum Catharijneconvent, Utrecht, vol. II, fols 182r–217v.
11. F.M.J. Hoppenbrouwers, *Oefening in volmaaktheid. De zeventiende-eeuwse rooms-katholieke spiritualiteit in de Republiek* [IJkpunt 1650] ('s-Gravenhage: Sdu, 1996); Charles van Leeuwen, *Hemelse voorbeelden. De heiligenliederen van Joannes Stalpart van der Wiele, 1579–1630* (Nijmegen: Sun, 200); Evelyne M.F. Verheggen, *Beelden voor passie en hartstocht. Bid- en devotieprenten in de Noordelijke Nederlanden, 17e en 18e eeuw* (Zutphen: Walburg Pers, 2006).
12. Spaans, 'Stad van vele geloven', pp. 416–17; P.H.A.M. Abels, *Ovittius' metamorphosen. De onnavolgbare gedaantewisselingen van een (zielen)dokter in de Reformatietijd* (Delft: Eburon, 2003).

13 Monteiro, *Geestelijke maagden*, p. 50; Rogier, *Geschiedenis*, II, p. 359.
14 Monteiro, *Geestelijke maagden*, p. 54.
15 Fred Smit and Jan Jacobs, *Van den Hogenheuvel gekomen. Bijdrage tot de geschiedenis van de priesteropleiding in de kerk van Utrecht 1683–1723* (Nijmegen: Valkhof Pers, 1994), pp. 31–7; B.A. Vermaseren, 'Het z.g.n. seminarie van Nicolaas Wiggers Cousebant te Keulen', *Archief voor de geschiedenis van het aartsbisdom Utrecht (AAU)* 65 (1945), 253–69; Gian Ackermans, *Herders en huurlingen. Bisschoppen en priesters in de Republiek (1663–1705)* (Amsterdam: Prometheus/Bakker, 2003), p. 77; cf. also Parker, *Faith on the margins*, chapter 4.
16 W.L.S. Knuif and R.G.R. Smeets, 'Sasbout Vosmeer', *AAU* 41 (1915), 389–90.
17 Verheggen, *Beelden*, pp. 100–1; Joke Spaans, 'Time for prayer and time for work. Rule and practice among Catholic lay sisters in the Dutch Republic', in R.N. Swanson (ed.), *The use and abuse of time in Christian history*, Studies in Church History 37 (Woodbridge: The Boydell Press, 2002), pp. 161–72.
18 H. Oldenhof, 'De eerste Friese contacten van Sasbout Vosmeer', *Archief voor de geschiedenis van de katholieke kerk in Nederland* 6 (1964), 241–55; Dalmatius van Heel, 'Nicolaas Wiggers Cousebant', *Bijdragen voor de geschiedenis van het bisdom Haarlem (BBH)* 27 (1903), 70–103; 30 (1906), 1–20; Joke Spaans, 'Paragons of piety: representations of priesthood in the lives of the Haarlem virgins', in *The Pastor Bonus*, papers read at the British–Dutch Colloquium at Utrecht, 18–21 September 2002, *Dutch Review of Church History* 83 (2003), 235–46.
19 Knuif and Smeets, 'Sasbout Vosmeer', pp. 344, 350.
20 Prime example Life of Giert Hendriks, in Oly, *Levens*, II, fols 249r–259r.
21 Spaans, 'Paragons'.
22 Instructions for the sextons, Municipal Archive Amsterdam (GAA), Archive Churchwardens Noorderkerk, inv. nr. 92, doc. nr. 10 (30 January 1655). The prestigious New Church hired a carpenter for the spring-cleaning of its pulpit, GAA, Archive Churchwardens New Church, inv. nr. 1, p. 87 (Nov. 7, 1664), inv. nr. 251 (1711).
23 Cf. Life of Machtelt Pieters Bicker, Oly, *Levens*, I, fol. 161v.
24 Cf. Anne Winston-Allen, *Convent chronicles. Women writing about women and reform in the late Middle Ages* (University Park, PA: Pennsylvania State University Press, 2004), pp. 169–204.
25 Verheggen, *Beelden*, pp. 90–2; Monteiro, *Geestelijke maagden*, pp. 84–6.
26 Monteiro, *Geestelijke maagden*, pp. 51–5.
27 Gerrit vanden Bosch, 'Pionnen op een schaakbord? De rol van klopjes in de belangenstrijd tussen jezuieten en seculiere priesters in de Republiek omstreeks 1609–1610', *Trajecta* 9 (2000), 252–83.
28 Hsia, *World of Catholic renewal*, pp. 37–8; Bossy, *English Catholic community*, p. 282.
29 GAA, Archive Burgomasters, inv. nr. 1, f. 32v (Aug. 12, 1615); inv. nr. 2, p. 30 (Sept. 8, 1651), cf. GAA, Archive Consistory Dutch Reformed Church, inv. nr. 15, p. 5 (April 8, 1683).
30 H.C. de Wolf, *De kerk en het maagdenhuis* (Utrecht/Antwerpen: Het Spectrum, 1970), pp. 263–85, cf. W.P.C. Knuttel, *De toestand der Nederlandsche katholieken ten tijde der Republiek*, 2 vols ('s-Gravenhage: Martinus Nijhoff, 1892), I, pp. 145–9; Spaans, 'Stad van vele geloven', p. 463; cf. for a similar situation Keith P. Luria, *Sacred boundaries. Religious coexistence and conflict in early modern France* (Washington DC: The Catholic University of America Press, 2005), pp. 180–9.
31 Theissing, *Over klopjes en kwezels*, pp. 150–4; Monteiro, *Geestelijke maagden*, pp. 95–9.
32 Life of Maritgen Isbrantsdr., Oly, *Levens*, III, f. 254r, cf. *ibid*. I, f. 195r.
33 J.J. Graaf, 'De "vergaderinghe der Maechden van den Hoeck" te Haarlem', *BBH* 35 (1913), p. 289.
34 Claustration is the technical term for living behind locked (convent) doors, as professed nuns were supposed to do.
35 Hsia, *World of Catholic renewal*, pp. 33–41.
36 Passim in Oly, *Levens*; cf. Monteiro, *Geestelijke maagden*, pp. 99–103 and chapter 3.
37 Graaf, 'Vergaderinghe', pp. 309–11, cf. Municipal Archive Haarlem, Archive Consistory Dutch Reformed Church, inv. nr. 3 (Nov. 5, 1619).
38 Monteiro, *Geestelijke maagden*, pp. 65–75.

39 Monteiro, *Geestelijke maagden*, pp. 86–7; cf. A.Th. van Deursen, *Mensen van klein vermogen. Het 'kopergeld' van de Gouden Eeuw* (Amsterdam: Bert Bakker, 1991), pp. 321–3.
40 Spaans, 'Paragons'.
41 Peters, *Patterns of piety*, passim.
42 Monteiro, *Geestelijke maagden*, pp. 95–109. Cf. the claims made for the role of wives and daughters of the married Anglican clergy by Jeremy Gregory, 'Gender and the clerical profession', in R.N. Swanson, *Gender and Christian religion*, Studies in Church History 34 (Woodbridge: The Boydell Press, 1998), pp. 259–70.
43 Peter van Rooden, 'Ministerial authority and gender in Dutch Protestantism around 1800', in Swanson, *Gender and Christian religion*, pp. 287–94.
44 Sara T. Nalle, 'Self-correction and social change in the Spanish Counter Reformation', in James D. Tracy and Marguerite Ragnow (eds), *Religion and the early modern state. Views from China, Russia and the West*, Cambridge: Cambridge University Press, 2004), p. 323.
45 M.G. Spiertz, 'Priest and layman in a minority church: the Roman Catholic Church in the Northern Netherlands 1592–1686', in W.J. Sheils and Diana Wood (eds), *The ministry clerical and lay* (Oxford: Basil Blackwell, 1989), p. 297.
46 Theissing, *Klopjes en kwezels*, pp. 207–14.

13

Harbourers and housekeepers: Catholic women in England 1570–1720

MARIE B. ROWLANDS

Alexandra Walsham, in placing English Catholicism in the context of the Catholic Reformation as a whole, has both illuminated our present knowledge and pointed the way for further study. She is one of several scholars who have taught us to go beyond the insularity and confessional divisions of earlier scholarship.[1]

Since the late 1980s there have been many studies of particular Catholic women and of issues relating to them, many of which make use of literary sources. At the same time, local and prosopographical studies have deepened our understanding of local communities and of networks of relationships. This article surveys the period 1560–1720, to place the specialist studies in context. Continuity and stability are often said to be more evident than change in women's history but, as Patricia Crawford says, 'stability does not denote *stasis*, the state of nothing happening, but rather the dynamic ability to compensate for change, to adapt the gender order to a new position'.[2] This chapter shows Catholic women being influenced by change, but also influencing change in the Catholic Church over the period under review and adapting to times of confrontation and of coexistence.

English Catholic women and the Continent

Catholic women who were English, although in a minority in England, saw themselves as part of the wider church, which claimed a universal mission. In reality, this mission had been confined to the Continent in the Middle Ages, but during the sixteenth century it was expanding to the New World and to the East. At the same time, the church was vigorously strengthening its discipline and central authority as it confronted the Protestant Reformation. In the face of the Protestant revolt, the Roman Church forbade *communicatio in sacris* with pagans, heretics and schismatics, and ordered the faithful to avoid associating with them. The problems this caused for Catholics in Protestant states, such as England and Holland, did not affect this imperative. Attempts to modify it for Catholics in England only stirred up bitter dissension without achieving any change. Catholics in countries where they were in a minority were caught up in a conflict which was being fought out on a much larger stage. Women were both active agents and passive subordinates in this drama.

For English Catholics, the Channel was not so much a barrier as a link with the wider world. There were many close links, especially with France and the Spanish Netherlands. On good days, the crossing took about four hours. The English coast was dotted with small seaports and although the English state tried to control movement, it was impossible to prevent priests from entering the country, or individuals from going abroad. English Catholic families moved temporarily or permanently to the Low Countries, just as many Protestants moved to England. English convents were founded on the Continent and English women supported them financially and by their patronage, prayers and family connections.[3]

Despite the customs searchers, English Catholics were constantly supplied from the Continent with the new books that were a central element of the Catholic Reformation. The New Testament in English was published at Douai in 1582 and the Old Testament in 1609; and the Latin Lectionary, Missal, Manual and Primer were essential to Catholic liturgy and every priest was required to have the Latin Catechism of the Council of Trent. They used the English Vaux' *Catechism* (1566) for the instruction of the faithful. The corpus of works of spirituality included medieval writers such as Julian of Norwich and the *Cloud of unknowing* in English and Latin. There were forty-five English editions of Thomas à Kempis' *Imitation of Christ* in English by 1700, over a dozen in Protestant versions. However, the majority of Catholic books coming into England were works by Catholic Reformation authors such as St Teresa, St John of the Cross, the layman John Heigham and Charles Borromeo. One of the most frequently republished and influential authors was Francis de Sales, drawing upon his pastoral experience in the missions of the Savoy and as a spiritual director to women.[4] As Joke Spaans emphasises in her chapter, such books were as much part of the spiritual reading of Catholic men as of women.

The same applies to the production and distribution of Catholic books. Men and women in England were active in both the distribution and safekeeping of proscribed Catholic books. In 1584, the house of Mrs Hampden of Stoke Bucks revealed a typical collection: Vaux' *Catechism*, three Jesus Psalters, manuals, Mass books, masses for particular saints' days, the Office of the Blessed Virgin

Mary, a Rheims (Douai) testament and a papal indulgence. In 1589, popish books were seized 'upon the person of a maid', Eleanor Morgan, servant to Mrs Seaborn of Sutton. John Heigham of St Omer was said by a spy to have sent his wife to England 'under the habit of a Dutchwoman, who hath dispersed numbers of books since her coming'. He added that she was caught and kept for sixteen days before being released.[5] It is evident that Catholics in England were not isolated or backward looking, but very actively part of the post-Reformation Church and in close touch with its leaders, debates and spirituality.

Confronting the authorities

England in the sixteenth and seventeenth centuries was building a nation united in belief and in worship, symbolically identified in the monarch as head of both the church and the state. Adherence to Roman Catholic belief was thus a failure in loyalty to the monarch and to the consensus of society. The authority and order in the nation depended on cohesion in belief. This was in contrast to the Dutch Republic, where, although Calvinism was the official religion, diversity of belief was recognised and Roman Catholic worship in private churches was tolerated in practice if not in theory. The Dutch Reformed Church was privileged but never given the status of a state church. In England, weekly church attendance in the parish church where the person resided was the public act of personal obedience and orderly conduct. It was required of every man and woman over sixteen. Loyalty was fostered by the Book of Common Prayer and the King James Bible, and by monthly anti-Catholic sermons. Regular attendance at the parish church was rewarded by social inclusion, by standing and respectability. The proportion of Catholics in Holland was substantial, but they were excluded from positions of influence. In contrast, in England by 1600 the numbers were as few as 1 or 2 per cent, but throughout the seventeenth century there were influential Catholics at court, including each of the queens from 1603 to 1689. The distribution of Catholics varied greatly in different parts of England, being most numerous in London, parts of Lancashire, North Yorkshire, the West Midlands and Monmouthshire, and although secular priests, Jesuits and the regulars all had structures of organisation there was no overall leadership. This contrasts with Holland, where, as Joke Spaans demonstrates, the vicars apostolic were of great significance. Although there were periods of relative calm in England, until 1688 the situation was one of crisis; priests and those who helped them were in real danger and Catholics, including women, were often forced to act on their own initiative. Such action, however, is not evidence of an attempt to change the relationships of church and women, but more of a desire to protect their continuance.

Scholarship and hagiography have both concentrated on recusants, martyrs and confessors, but English Catholics were very far from being a homogenous group. Some women and many men were Catholics at home, but conformed in public, becoming known as church papists. While it is true that some risked death, and many forfeited wealth, many more were careful to risk nothing. Clerical casuists and English lawyers alike offered Catholics advice on how far a person might go in deceiving the authorities without putting soul or body at risk. Catholics developed recognised techniques of avoidance, coded phrases and formulaic answers to be used under questioning.[6]

It would be simplistic to see the conflict of loyalties for Catholic women as being only a choice between church and state. Women had to choose between religious and domestic duties, between family ties and public duty, between keeping children at home and sending them away, between furtive piety and active mission. There was the duty to protect her family and the duty to risk their safety for a higher call. A woman had to manage her duty of obedience to the authority of her husband and her duty to the authority of the priest, as well as her own perception of her duty to God. They had to work out their actions on a day-to-day basis, constantly adjusting and negotiating circumstances. In this, they differed radically from priests, who were automatically subject to the death penalty if they were found in England and whose choices had already been determined for life by the fact of their ordination. Catholic men, too, had to negotiate choices from day to day and as heads of household with community responsibilities. It is certainly true that more men than women were executed, but heavy fines affected the family as a whole. Men were more exposed to the penalties of the law, but they also had more opportunities to evade those penalties through influence or manipulation of the law. There were many individual Catholic men in prominent positions at court, in the county or in the parish who used their connections to evade the penalties of the law. Artists, poets and musicians could find both Catholic and Protestant patrons. Money and contacts had a big part to play in resistance to the religious settlement and in escaping fines, imprisonments and confiscations. Harbouring priests, however, was a matter for the whole family, including the children and servants.

The narratives of women's resistance were themselves part of the international struggle and the propaganda war. Michael Questier has demonstrated the complex web of motives and influences informing John Mush's narrative of Margaret Clitherow.[7] The life of Lady Montague is another much-quoted example of Catholic womanhood and the devout household. The author Richard Smith was theological adviser to Richelieu and involved in the negotiations of the French marriage of Charles I. He was an important proponent in the Archpriest controversy, which divided the Catholic clergy. His appointment as bishop in England in 1624 was an attempt to control faction among English Catholic clergy and was part of an international political negotiation.[8]

There were only three women martyrs in England, all between 1588 and 1601. This is in comparison to 123 priests in the same period. The women died at a time of exceptional public anxiety in politics, social upheaval and economic distress. Margaret Clitherow was prosecuted in 1586, when the Council of the North was conducting a vigorous campaign against Catholics. Strictly speaking, she was not executed, but died in the process of *peine fort et dure*, the standard means of forcing plaintiffs to give evidence on oath before the court. Margaret Ward was executed on 30 September 1588, a day on which twelve priests were also executed in London, an *auto da fé* one month after the defeat of the Spanish Armada. Ann Line, who had run safe houses for priests in London, was executed on 27 February 1601, at the height of the campaign against recusant wives and two days after the execution of the Earl of Essex. Six other women were condemned to death between 1588 and 1601, though none of them was executed. They were Dorothy White, Margaret Norton, Eleanor Hunt, Anne Tesse (condemned to be burned for persuading a minister to become a Catholic), Jane Wiseman and Mrs Swithin Wells.[9] The last mentioned died in prison under sentence of death. However, numbers of women, uncounted but certainly running into thousands, were imprisoned in royal and county gaols. Robert Cecil and Chief Justice Popham were determined to deal with the problem of recusant wives by legislation, by fines, by exemplary imprisonments and by house arrests. Nevertheless, the campaign failed, partly because of the reluctance of some members of Parliament to legislate on a matter that intruded upon the family, and also because of the networks of ties between Catholics and their Protestant kindred and neighbours.[10]

The gentry had had private chapels and chaplains in their houses since the late Middle Ages, and still had control over what was done there. Mass was said in their chapels, in upper rooms and in outhouses, but all of this was in domestic spaces managed and controlled by women. Women faced with extreme situations demonstrated their ability to cope. They harboured priests, argued with the authorities, and a few resorted to small protest riots. Women were adept at providing and hiding altars, vestments and chalices, keeping the children and servants quiet and distracting the searchers by offering food or feigning sickness. They even answered Mass if there were no men present – although at first some authorities had questioned whether Mass could be said at all in the absence of men.

After 1610, the pressure on Catholics became more intermittent. Catholic priests and laymen were imprisoned during the period of the civil war (1640–58) and also during the Oates Plot (1678–81), and in each of these times of crisis women were conspicuously active. During the Civil War some organised the military defence of their manor houses. During the crisis of the Oates Plot, the widow Elizabeth Cellier defended herself in court against a charge of treason, and then took on the government by writing, publishing and selling a pamphlet, *Malice Defeated*.[11]

Sustaining the faith

The pressure on Catholics fluctuated in accordance with politics and the personalities in power. Increasingly both central and local government contained Catholics by listing, fines and compounding, and by the constant activities of informers. Catholic women nevertheless contributed significantly to the maintenance of their church, in England and abroad. Women were expected by the church to be either married or nuns. As brides of Christ, nuns committed themselves to their divine Spouse until death. They had their bridal day with bridal clothes, jewels and wreath. Their families negotiated a dowry, and wedding presents were given. Thus, they preserved their chastity behind the grille and devoted themselves for most of every day to the *opus dei*, the service of God in prayer. Much of the language of nuns' prayers and spirituality reflected the language of married love and, in some cases, has an erotic element. Nevertheless, Claire Walker has shown that their contacts and influence extended beyond the convent. Nuns made important contributions to Catholic book culture. All nuns spent time in spiritual reading; convents and individual nuns had libraries and, despite their poverty, they bought and commissioned books. Women such as Catherine Greenbury, Agnes More, Lady Mary Percy and Anne Dormer published translations, as did Anne Percy from works in French. Barbara Constable was a copyist. A translation of Francis de Sales's *Delicious entertainments of the soul* was made by the Cambrai Benedictine nuns – probably by Agnes More. The spiritual writings of abbess Gertrude More were edited and published by her confessor, Augustine Baker, in 1658 under the title *Confessiones Amantis, a lover's confessions*.[12]

Clausura (enclosure) was insisted upon, even for the schools on which the nuns often depended for income. The church was deeply disturbed by women who wanted to take on a role similar to that of the Jesuits, independently of the bishops and outside the enclosure. All those orders that had originally undertaken work outside the convent were required to accept enclosure in the early seventeenth century. The Mary Ward Sisters were abolished in 1631 and Luisa de Carajaval's missionary group of women in London only lasted two years, despite her influential connections. Similarly, on the Continent, the community of Isabella Roser of Barcelona was put down in 1630.[13]

Marriage was a lesser vocation in comparison to celibacy, but was necessarily that of the majority. Catholic gentlewomen were linked by marriage with a supportive network of Catholic families, which included families in England

and the expatriates and nuns abroad. They were in correspondence, and there was much visiting and news of family, priests and experiences. Catholic women educated children and servants, arranged the meals for the many fasts and abstinence days, and looked after their husbands and the priests. They distributed food, assisted poor and vagrant women in childbirth, nursing and giving food and medicine. They visited prisons in London and the county towns, taking in food, letters and necessities for Mass, and caring for sick and tortured prisoners. Their services were voluntary but also well organised and regular. However, there is not as yet evidence of anything in England comparable to the *kloppen* in Holland.

Widows had greater independence and greater control over their money and their time, and they are prominent in the narratives. Some became nuns. Widows were often prominent in helping priests. Aveling, Sheils and others have noted a predominance of widows in some listings,[14] but it is difficult to interpret the significance of this evidence. So much depends on the purpose of particular listings; more needs to be done to relate these indications to local circumstances and to national demographics.

Catholic women made use of both medieval pieties and the newer fashions of prayer. They met to say the rosary and gathered at ancient crosses. Women were prominent in pilgrimages to Ladywell in Lancashire, St Robert's Well at Knaresborough and Holywell in North Wales. The cult of St Winifred had no authority, but there is a hymn to St Winifred in Peter Mowle's commonplace book, two more are found in another Catholic commonplace book circulated among yeomen and lesser gentry in Warwickshire. There is also a hymn of uncertain date relating to Ladywell, a place of continued pilgrimage near Preston. They also practised the newer forms of devotion, such as that to the Infant Jesus, the Sacred Heart, Mary Magdalene and the Immaculate Conception of Mary. Elizabeth Bishop of Brailes, Warwickshire, owned a copy of the *Apologia for the Roman church* by John Brerely 1608; Lady Mary Packington of Harvington owned an Office of the Blessed Virgin Mary, published in Douai in 1652. Mary Tichbourne owned a copy of *Les Tableaux de la penitence* by A. Godeau, published in 1684 in Paris. This last was a series of pictures of repentance from the Old and New Testaments, with an appropriate sermon on each. Jane Owen of Godstow, Oxfordshire, spinster and laywoman, wrote *An antidote against purgatory*. It was published immediately after her death at St Omer in 1634 and is, in part, a translation of a work by Robert Bellarmine, SJ.[15] The most committed Catholic women accepted spiritual direction by a 'ghostly father'. There was in England, as on the Continent, an increasing emphasis on the personal relationship of the individual soul with God in the person of Jesus Christ. However, as yet no '*beata*' have been identified in England such as those in France, Italy and Spain.[16]

Opportunities for hearing Mass in England varied greatly from place to place. Priests usually returned to their home district after ordination, so that there was little correlation between numbers of souls and numbers of priests. The narratives show that some women had daily access to the sacraments and the services of two or three priests, while other families might see a priest only occasionally. Nevertheless, the proportion of priests to people in England was probably higher than in Holland. Until the end of the sixteenth century, there were considerable numbers of Marian priests, who had been ordained before 1558. As they died during the 1580s and 1590s, they were replaced by increasing numbers from the seminaries, as well as by some Benedictines and Franciscans. The number of priests was at its highest in 1634, when it was about 750, and steadied at around 500 in the second half of the century. Bellenger lists over 3,000 priests ordained for the English Mission in the seventeenth century. Of these, sixty-eight were executed and more died in prison, but even these had mostly laboured on the Mission for many years. The average length of time between ordination and death was thirty-two years.[17] English circumstances probably enhanced the status of the clergy in the eyes of English Catholic women. Seventeenth-century English priests had a prolonged intellectual education and were celibate, separated from women from the age of twelve or so. Their ordination set an irremovable seal upon their souls, and they remained priests in the eyes of the Catholic Church even if they conformed. They ruled with confident authority over behaviour and belief. They continued to be in real danger of imprisonment and death. All of this may well have encouraged women to put priests on the pedestal that the Catholic Reformation encouraged them to occupy.

Catholic working women

Details about the lives of Catholic working women are still difficult to recover from existing records. The many listings show that they were numerous, and not only as servants in Catholic gentry households. Some working women harboured priests: William Southerne lived in the house of a widow who sold ropes, red herrings and salt fish in her shop in Newcastle on Tyne. The chapel in her house had an altar with a picture of Christ at the top and a picture of Christ preaching at the bottom. Alice Tully of Stafford harboured Perton and Barclay, both Marian priests.[18]

Alehouses provided a convenient place for Mass, since comings and goings could be disguised; many were kept by women. Mrs Williams, of the Star in Oxford, was a recusant and sheltered priests even though her husband was a magistrate and an alderman. Her son and her daughter were also recusants. Another son, Thomas, was one of the first Englishmen to join the Society of Jesus. Agnes Rawson, innkeeper, harboured Marian priests at Sherburne, Yorkshire. At Holywell, North Wales the Jesuits lived at the Star and the secular priests at the

Cross Keys and ministered to the large numbers of Catholic pilgrims who came to the shrine of St Winifred, as well as to local Catholics.[19]

Those women who earned their living as servants, although paid, had no defined hours or conditions of work. Their work was essentially service to others, whether in gentry households, farmhouses or alehouses. In independent working families success depended on the cooperation of all members, husband, wife and children. It was characteristic of almost all women's work, whether in service or in their own family, that it supported, supplemented and served the work of others, mainly in the immediate vicinity of the home. The work itself was often laborious, tedious and without status. Women's work therefore fitted well with the religious concept of service – as the prayer of St Ignatius put it, to serve, as you (God) deserve, to give and not to count the cost, to toil and not to seek for rest, to labour and to ask for no reward.

Separation from the Protestant parish church had social as well as religious implications for working women, since it cut them off from many community activities. Given the violence of anti-Catholic prejudice, being a Catholic may well have limited the range of clients and it certainly increased divisions in families. The position of a Catholic midwife raised special problems, as midwives were sworn in the ecclesiastical courts and subject to visitation. In many parishes, the midwife was expected to go to the parish church with mothers and their friends for the churching ceremony. Opportunities for apprenticeship for sons may also have been limited, since indentures of apprenticeship were sworn in the parish church.[20]

Baptisms could take place in the home, and marriages clandestinely, before a Catholic priest. Burials could not so easily be concealed, and burial of excommunicated Catholics in the churchyard required a bishop's licence. In the early seventeenth century, burials of Catholics sometimes took place outside the churchyard. Catholic women are reported as carrying out Catholic burials at Solihull, though it is not yet known how common this practice was.[21]

Catholic women of all degrees and circumstances in England and on the Continent played a large part in promoting the cult of the English martyrs, who, it should not be forgotten, were often related to them. They were zealous in recovering body parts after execution, and while the priests took charge of the main relics, many women passed down small relics in their families. The cult of the martyrs was part of a broader ethos relating suffering to salvation. All sufferings, all labours, all pains, from the pains of childbirth to those of martyrdom, were explicitly identified with the sufferings of Christ. Submission to the will of God, the instruction to 'take up your Cross and Follow Me', was at the heart of their piety, and through suffering came redemption and new life.

Women in the period of reconstruction and coexistence

In some ways, the situation of English Catholics after 1688 was similar to that of their co-religionists in Holland in the early seventeenth century. The accession of William III, the limited toleration of Protestant dissent and the appointment of the Catholic vicars apostolic (1686–88) substantially altered the political and ecclesiastical context. The secular clergy became predominant and missions became continuous and financially secure. More Catholics worshipped in small, purpose-built chapels, officially illegal but in practice resorted to openly.

Catholics continued to be identified with political opposition but it was now because of their loyalty to James II rather than owing to their religion. Stables were searched for horses, rather than houses for priests. Legislation controlling Catholic landholding was strengthened and Catholics were excluded from positions of influence in state and county. Women as well as men who held land or houses had to register their property with the county court. Women, like men, were subject to double land tax, special levies, and limitations on patronage and inheritance. Money could not legally be left to priests or for 'superstitious uses', though in practice there were recognised ways of circumventing the law.

The appointment of the four vicars apostolic in 1686–88, each with his own district, though technically an abnormal kind of church government appropriate for Mission countries, was deliberately adapted in England to provide a structure of authority and organisation which approximated as far as possible to that in Catholic countries. In 1698, Bishop Leyburne reported to Rome 'the Catholic religion is fully exercised, albeit in private. There are sacraments, catechism and preaching twice on Sundays and feast days'.[22] After some difficulties, the clergy of the religious orders working on the Mission eventually accepted episcopal oversight. Technically, English Catholic parishes were not officially restored until 1918, but were known as 'missions'. However, by the eighteenth century they were known as '*quasi parochiae*', with permanent endowments and a regular succession of clergy, appointed and supervised by the bishops. If a priest had to be absent, even if only for a week or two, a replacement was sent. The chapels were well furnished to meet the demands of the full liturgy and liturgical cycle.[23]

Both central and local government after 1688 were more secure and the management of minorities became less confrontational. The gentry retired into their parks, clearing away villages, distancing themselves from their tenants and employing fewer household servants. There was a marked reduction in the number of Catholic gentry families and, correspondingly, of active Catholic gentlewomen. Priests lived independently of the gentry and separate and more accessible chapels were built on the estate or in the village. Chapels with resident priests were opened in towns. Women, in their weakness and frailty, continued to serve, but they were no longer called upon to face physical danger or to take the initiative.

The role of women as instructors of the faith became supportive and ancillary. Religious instruction was usually given to the congregation as a group, often at a Sunday afternoon service, and children and servants were catechised in the chapel by the priest. Both Jesuit and secular priests distributed large numbers of catechisms, prayer books and books of spirituality in colloquial English to women and children. It was priests, rather than women, who visited the sick, the dying and the imprisoned.

Religious orders of women were gradually allowed by the church to work outside the cloister, especially among the poor, and to go to the New World. Some French nuns seized these new opportunities, but no English nuns did so and their overall numbers dwindled.[24] The Mary Ward Sisters were given permission to govern themselves, though not to recognise Mary Ward as their founder or to consider themselves a religious order. However, the Hammersmith sisters accepted episcopal control, to the great distress of their York sisters.[25] Upper-class girls continued to be sent to the convents abroad for education. The rules for the life and work of 'the young gentlewomen pensioners' at the convent of the English Augustinian Canonesses at Windesheim in 1697 were closely modelled on the religious life. They emphasised obedience, quietness, humility and simplicity, yet the girls were constantly reminded to live up to their good birth and were taught the customs of civility and deportment. Every hour of the day was regulated; the girls learned reading, writing, arithmetic, casting accounts, French and Latin. In the afternoons they learned needlework and music. They attended daily Mass, vespers and evening prayers. In the chapel they were directed to pray kneeling up straight, and to make a low curtsey to the Blessed Sacrament when leaving. They were encouraged to sleep with a rosary about their wrists. Great emphasis was placed on devotion to the Blessed Sacrament and the girls were allowed to receive communion even though they were below the usual age.[26]

Working Catholic women in the early eighteenth century continued to be listed alongside their husbands and fathers in visitation and other returns. Their work and social status reflected that of their local community. Thus, in the industrial village of Sedgley, Staffordshire, the Catholic women comprised the wives of a shoemaker, a tailor, five nailers, two lockmakers, a leatherworker and a collier. There were several spinsters and two widows, one the mother of a quack doctor. They belonged to families whose names had been appearing in the lists of papists for many generations, for this was a parish with a rapidly growing population and little outward migration. They were visited regularly by a priest on circuit, and a permanent Mass centre with two resident priests was only four miles away. In the arable parish of Longford in Derbyshire, with a very small and probably declining population, the Catholic women comprised a gentleman's wife, a widow, three wives of paupers and a spinster. The squire was not a Catholic and the nearest mass centre was six miles away. Pauper women appear in returns from parishes all over the country, implying that they were not barred from poor relief.[27]

The listings allow brief glimpses of Catholic women who earned their living by keeping little schools. By 1710, however, such a school could be long term, influential and provide an independent income for a single woman. Alice Harrison became a Catholic through reading books. She experienced great hostility from her parents, who finally 'shut the door on her'. The local priest at Fernyhalgh, Lancashire suggested that she start a little school to teach poor children to read and to say their prayers and their catechism. The school attracted children from all over the north-west, non-Catholics as well as Catholics, who boarded with the local cottagers and farmers. They paid 1s 6d per quarter for schooling and £5 a year for board and lodging. At its largest, the school was said to have over a hundred pupils, some of whom eventually became priests. Alice took all her scholars to Mass in the chapel every day, and they stopped on their return at the local holy shrine, the well of Our Lady, to say the Pater, Ave Maria and Creed. The endowed house next to the well dates from about 1687. The priest lived on the ground floor and the upper floor was used for the chapel.[28]

Priests who lived in their own houses or lodgings needed cleaning women and housekeepers. Some housekeepers also acted as trustees for clandestine trusts and endowments. Priests' housekeepers came from lesser gentry families and were, as canon law required, women of mature years, plain appearance and good behaviour. Oscott (Staffordshire) was a former farmhouse that from 1686 was home to the priest Andrew Bromwich. His housekeeper for many years was Juliana Dorrington. She was also financial trustee and responsible to the bishop for the accounts, to the government for payment of taxes, and for dealing with the local authorities. She successfully fended off a Protestant relative who tried to claim the estate. After Bromwich's death she continued as housekeeper to the next two priests and remained at Oscott until she was over eighty. Juliana's books included *Instructions for the care of the sick and afflicted* by John Gother, left to her by Andrew Bromwich in recognition of the care with which she had nursed him and his mother though their long, tedious sicknesses. She also treasured a relic of the martyr Nicholas Postgate, 'a piece of linen stuff lined with canvas with a button hole in one corner and the inscription "Mr Posket's [that is, Nicholas Postgate, martyr] cape he wore thirty year".[29]

In those missions where the priest was a member of a religious order, sodalities and other religious societies were established, as on the Continent. In Europe, sodalities played a part in the reclamation of the countryside to the church, but in England they had no role other than strengthening the faith of the individual and attaching the laity to the regular clergy. They were set up by papal appointment and encouraged personal devotion and a monastic type of spirituality. The Bona Mors societies in Jesuit missions often included most of the congregation, but the membership of the Franciscan sodality at Edgbaston, Warwickshire, was predominantly of women; and of the seven Third Order members, six were women. The secular clergy did not establish confraternities, but continued to encourage the Salesian tradition of piety emphasising the sanctification of every day life, and participation in the collective liturgy. They also placed less emphasis on frequent communion.[30]

By 1720, the pastoral pattern had already emerged which was to be the basic building block of English Catholicism until well into the second half of the twentieth century. The Catholic registers show regular routines of baptisms, Easter communions and marriages. The bishop visited regularly for confirmation.[31] The priest's house, the school and the chapel were the focus for a particular community of the faithful, which included many women, widows, wives and women wage earners, including some in very poorly paid occupations. There was a developing body of catechisms and short devotional publications and prayer books explicitly addressed to working Catholics, though their titles suggest the publishers had men rather than women in mind.[32] For the most part, 'men includes women' in these little books written and authorised by priests. Except in the prayers for widows, and for women child bearing and giving birth, here is no suggestion of a distinctive feminine spirituality. English translations of the liturgy and English versions of the Bible were increasingly available, but the serious study of scripture and theology were confined exclusively to priests. Mass, vespers, benediction, the rosary, the feasts, fasts and abstinence, separated these Catholic women from other Englishwomen, but not from their Catholic menfolk. The same practices linked them culturally with devout Catholic women and men abroad.

In comparison to Catholic women of the seventeenth century, those of the eighteenth century have received little attention. There is a need for a survey of their writing, both public and private.[33] There is also a need to bring together the scattered evidence about individuals and their families, their occupations and social statuses. This will then allow consideration of issues such as the feminisation of religion, and the effects on women's religious practice of demographic change and of industrialisation. These wider issues can then be addressed by regional studies of Catholic women's life that compare not only in different parts of England, but also English and Continental experience. The two studies here presented have already begun to suggest how Catholic women could be affected by the differences in numbers of Catholics, the availability of priests, the structures of Catholic clerical organisation, and the nature and security of political authority. Much remains to be done.

Notes

1. A. Walsham, 'Translating Trent? English Catholicism and the Counter Reformation', *Historical Research* 78, no. 201 (2005), 228–310; R. Po-Chia Hsia, *The world of Catholic renewal* (Cambridge: Cambridge University 1998); J. Birely, *The re-fashioning of Catholicism in Europe 1450–1700* (Basingstoke: Macmillan, 1999), pp. 83–6; O. Hufton, *The prospect before her* (London: Harper Collins, 1995), p. 366.
2. S. Mendelson and P. Crawford, *Women in early modern England* (Oxford: Clarendon Press, 2003), p. 432.
3. P. Guilday, *The English Catholic refugees on the Continent 1558–1795* (London: Longmans, 1914), pp. 5–32; C. Durrant, *A link between Flemish mystics and English martyrs* (London: Burns Oates, 1925), pp. 271–307; R. Clark, *Strangers and sojourners at Port Royale* (Cambridge: Cambridge University Press, 1932.), p. 73; C. Bowden, 'The Abbess and Mrs Brown', *Recusant History* 24: 3 (1999), p. 288; C. Walker, *Gender, religion and politics in early modern Europe. English convents in France and the Low Countries* (Basingstoke: Palgrave Macmillan, 2003.), pp. 13–48.
4. A. Allison and D. Rogers, *The contemporary printed literature of the English Counter Reformation between 1558 and 1640* (London: Scolar Press 1989 and 1994); J. Blom, *The post-Tridentine English primer* (Catholic Record Society, Monograph series, 3 1982); T. Birrell. 'The English Counter Reformation book culture', *Recusant History* 22: 2, 1994, pp. 113–23; T. Clancy, *English Catholic books 1641–1700; a bibliography* (London: Scolar Press, 1996), pp. 208–10; A. Allison 'John Heigham at St Omer', *Recusant History* 4:6 (1957), p. 231. S. Mendelson 'Stuart women's diaries and occasional memoirs 1500–1800', in M. Prior (ed.), *Women in English society 1500–1800* (London: Methuen, 1985), pp. 181–211. P. Crawford, 'Women's published writings 1600–1700', in Prior, *ibid.*, pp. 211–83.
5. PRO Calendar of State Papers Domestic, Elizabeth. 1584; CCXVII, 17; S.P. Dom. Eliz.; 1589, CCXXVII; Allison, 'John Heigham at St Omer', p. 231.
6. A. Walsham, *Church papists*, Royal Historical Society, Studies in History 68 (Boydell Press, 1993), p. 81; E. Rose, *Cases of conscience: alternatives open to Catholics and Puritans under Elizabeth and James I* (Cambridge: Cambridge University Press, 1975); P.J. Holmes, *Resistance and compromise* (Cambridge: Cambridge University Press, 1982); P.J. Holmes, *Elizabethan casuistry* (London: Catholic Records Society [CRS] 67, 1981); J. Mathews, 'Papers from the Courtfield muniments,' *Miscellanea* VIII (London: CRS 13, 1913), pp. 150–9.
7. P. Lake and M. Questier 'Margaret Clitherow; Catholic nonconformity, martyrology and the politics of religious change in Elizabethan England', *Past and Present* 185:1 (2004), 43–90; A. Dillon, *The construction of martyrdom in the English Catholic community 1535–1603* (Aldershot: Ashgate, 2003).
8. A. Allison, 'Richard Smith, Richelieu and the French marriage, the political context of Smith's appointment as Bishop for England in 1624', *Recusant History* 7:4 (1964), p. 148; A.F. Allison, 'Richard Smith's Gallican backers and opponents', *Recusant History* 18:4 (1987), 329–402, 19:3 (1989), 23–85, 20:2 (1990), 164–207.
9. J. Pollen (ed.), *Memoirs of Missionary Priests and other Catholics of both Sexes who suffered Death or Imprisonment in England on account of their Religion, from the year 1577 till the end of the reign of Charles II, by Richard Challoner* (London: Burns, Oates and Washbourne, 1924), pp. xxvii, 119, 141, 257. Originally published 1741.
10. J. Bossy, *The English Catholic community, 1570–1850* (London: Darton, Longman and Todd, 1975), pp. 152–3; J. Neale, *Elizabeth I and her Parliaments*, vol. 2 (London: Cape, 1958), pp. 260–94, 396–405. M. Rowlands 'Recusant women', in M. Prior (ed.), *Women in English society 1500–1800* (London: Methuen, 1985), pp. 149–89; Walsham, *Church papists*, p. 81.
11. P. Crawford, *Women and religion in England* (London: Routledge, 1993), pp. 58–69. Frances Dolan, *Whores of Babylon, Catholicism and seventeenth century print culture* (London: Cornell University Press 1999), pp. 157–211.
12. Walker, *Gender, religion and politics*, *passim*; A.F. Allison and D. Rogers, *The contemporary printed literature of the English Counter Reformation between 1558 and 1640* (London: Scolar Press 1989 and 1994); T. Clancy, *English Catholic books*.

13 M. Chambers, *The Life of Mary Ward* (London: Burns Oates, 1882), pp. 93–100, 196; G[eorgina] F[ullerton], *Life of Luisa Carajaval* (London: Burns Oates, 1873), p. 196; Merry Wiesner, *Women and gender in early modern Europe* (Cambridge: Cambridge University Press, 1983), p. 196; H. Daniel Rops, *The Catholic Reformation* (London: Dent 1962), p. 53.

14 J.C.H. Aveling, 'The marriages of recusants 1559–1642', *Journal of Ecclesiastical History* 14 (1968), 68–83; J.C.H. Aveling 'Catholic households in Yorkshire 1580–1603', *Northern History* 16 (1980), 85–101; W. Sheils, 'Household age and gender among Jacobean Yorkshire recusants', in *Catholics of parish and town* (London: Catholic Record Society, 1999), pp. 137–41; B. Hill, *Women, work and sexual politics in 18th century England* (London: University College, 1994), pp. 223, 240, 241.

15 Oscott Recusant Library (ORL) 1/878, 1/341, 1/342, b291. I am grateful to the Librarian, Mr Gerard Boylan, for drawing these and other books in the collection to my attention. B.S. Benedikz, 'A Catalogue of the Little Malvern Devotional Collection', ts., University of Birmingham Library.

16 ORL 18; C. Brown, 'Recusant community and Jesuit mission', *Yearbook of English Studies* 33:1 (Modern Humanities Research Association 2003), 290–315; J. Foley, *Records of the English Province of the Society of Jesus*, IV (London: 1878), pp. 528–30; G. Corr, *Devotion to Our Lady among English Catholics in the seventeenth and eighteenth centuries* (London 1992); L. McClain 'Using what's at hand. Catholic reinterpretations of the rosary', *Journal of Religious History* 27.2 (2003), p. 161; L.F. Lebrun, 'The two reformations, communal devotion and personal piety', in R. Chartier, *A history of private life. III. Passions of the Renaissance* (Cambridge, MA: Harvard University Press, 1989), pp. 69–109.

17 A. Bellenger, *English and Welsh priests* (Bath: Downside Abbey, 1984), p. 246; P. McGrath and J. Rowe, 'Anstruther analysed; the Elizabethan seminary priests', *Recusant History* 18:1 (1986), 1–14; P. McGrath and J. Rowe, 'Elizabethan priests their harbourers and helpers', *Recusant History* 19:3 (1989), p. 209, G. Anstruther, *The seminary priests: a dictionary of the secular clergy in England and Wales, 1558–1850*, vol. 2 (Essex: Mayhew McCrimmon 1969–77), p. 55.

18 A. Forster, 'A Tyneside martyr', *Recusant History* 4 (1957), 206–7; H.S. Burne (ed.), 'Staffordshire Quarter Sessions Rolls, 1590–93', *Staffordshire Historical Collections for 1930* (Kendal: Titus Wilson, 1932), p. 255.

19 A. Davidson, 'Edward Williams of Oxford', *Worcestershire Recusant* 25 (1975), p. 1; A. Petti, 'Roman Catholicism in Elizabethan and Jacobean Staffordshire', *Staffordshire Historical Collections* 4th series, 9 (1979), pp. 56, 57; J. Morris, *The troubles of our Catholic forefathers*, third series (London: Burns Oates, 1877), p. 92

20 Westminster Archdiocesan Archives (WAA), XV111, D6, letter from a secular priest to the president of the Chapter; E. Rose, *Cases of conscience*, pp. 242–50.

21 Lichfield Joint Record Office B/C/5/1626, Acta; P. Bailey, 'Painsley', *Midland Catholic History Society* (2006), p. 16; Warwick Solihull Local Studies Library, Solihull, St Alphege Church Parish Register, baptisms and burials 1538–1769, Warwickshire Record Office, microfilm PR21; G. Anstruther, 'Recusant burials', *London Recusant* 1:3 (1972), 103–7.

22 WAA, XXXVII, 1, Report of Bishop Leyburne to Propaganda 1692.

23 M. Rowlands, 'The things that are not Caesar's', *Midland History* 25 (2000), 78–98. WAA, XXXIX, 28–9, Chapel inventory; J. Delameau, *Catholicism between Luther and Voltaire* (London: Burns and Oates, 1977), pp. 194–9; L. Chatellier *The Europe of the devout* (Cambridge: Cambridge University Press, 1989), pp. 44–78.

24 C. Walker, *Gender, religion and politics*, pp. 20, 21; O. Hufton, *The prospect before her*, pp. 375–84.

25 Sister Gregory Kirkus, 'Biographical dictionary of the English members and benefactors of the I.B.V.M.' (London, Catholic Record Society, 78, 2001), p. 5.

26 C. Durrant, *Flemish martyrs and English mystics*, pp. 417–39.

27 Staffordshire Record Office. B/A/12/1 Sedgley 1706 return; R. Clark, 'The Derbyshire Papist returns 1705–6', *Derbyshire Record Society Occasional Paper* 5 (Chesterfield: Derbyshire Record Society, 1983), p. 16.

28 B.C. Foley, *Some people of the penal times* (Lancaster: The Cathedral Bookshop, 1991), pp. 51–9.
29 Birmingham Archdiocesan Archives, A 158a, A 592b, C 110 letters and papers referring to the common funds of the clergy; B. Camm; *Forgotten shrines* (London: Macdonald and Evans, 1910), p. 373.
30 *Registers of Brindle and Salmesbury* (London: CRS 23, 1922); 'Rosary confraternity lists,' *Miscellanea* (London: CRS 14, 1914), pp. 205–36; W. Phillimore, *Warwickshire Parish Registers*, 1 and 3 (London: Phillimore, 1901–1906).
31 About forty Catholic registers are extant from before 1750. For a full list see M. Gandy, *Catholic missions and registers 1700–1880*, 4 vols (London: Michael Gandy, privately published 1993). M. Rowlands *Parish and town*, pp. 266–83; G. Every, 'The laity and the liturgy 1600–1800', *Worcestershire Recusant* 43 (1984), 3–15; J. Birely *The refashioning of Catholicism*, pp. 96–120.
32 ORL, 2612/ R.L 4 Anon, Pastoral Instructions ... designed especially for the poor and such as want money to buy or will and leisure to read more ample treatises (London: 1713); M. Norman, 'John Gother and the English way of spirituality', *Recusant History* 11:6 (1972), 306–17; E. Duffy, 'Richard Challoner and the English Salesian Tradition', *Clergy Review* LXVI (December 1981), 445–9.
33 J. Blom et al., *English Catholic books 1701–1800* (Brookfield VT: Scolar Press 1996); M. Mullett (ed.), *English Catholicism 1680–1830* (London: Pickering and Chatto, 2006); both refer only to Lady Lucy Herbert (1669–1744), OSA, author of several devotional works.

14

Paintings for clandestine Catholic churches in the Republic: typically Dutch?

XANDER VAN ECK

Dutch painting in the seventeenth and eighteenth centuries has long been defined as a Protestant art. The French art critic Théophile Thoré (1807–69), whose ideas have remained influential to the present day, identified realist landscapes, still lives, portraits and genre pieces as a democratic art made for freedom-loving Protestant citizens, in contrast to the large figure paintings Rubens produced in the Spanish Netherlands through commissions from the Catholic oppressors.[1]

More or less watered-down versions of this view persist to this day, although more recent historical research has demonstrated that, while Johannes Vermeer and Jan Steen were Catholics, Rembrandt did not belong to any church and the religious landscape of the Republic as a whole was very varied indeed. One of the effects of the persistence of Thoré's ideas has been that the large history subjects undertaken by Northern Netherlandish painters have long been neglected because they were considered to be 'un-Dutch'. Moreover, if they had been painted for Catholic patrons, they were twice damned.

This line of thought was seriously challenged in 1978, when Albert Blankert drew attention to the importance of Catholic painting in the Republic in a booklet devoted to the art treasures of a former clandestine Catholic church in The Hague.[2] Describing pictures by Abraham Bloemaert, Pieter de Grebber and others, Blankert even ventured the idea that a typically Dutch variant of Catholic painting had emerged. Since then, a steady flow of publications has documented the provenance of many paintings from clandestine Catholic churches. Their iconography was discussed, and the identity of patrons and the goals they pursued were also taken into consideration.[3] However, the question of whether they represented a typically Dutch branch of Counter-Reformation art remains to be answered. Put another way, did the position of Catholics, as

PAINTINGS FOR CLANDESTINE CATHOLIC CHURCHES   217

an oppressed minority, affect the iconography and/or the style of the art that adorned their churches?

A tentative new beginning

After Catholic worship was forbidden in the 1570s, it took Catholics in the Republic about half a century before they started to commission large-scale monumental altarpieces and other devotional paintings for their chapels. The fact that this took so long had, it seems, more to do with the nature of the spaces of worship than with any reluctance to spend money on artefacts that ran the risk of being confiscated. Until the third decade of the seventeenth century, most Masses were still said in private houses and communities usually lacked a fixed place of worship. They generally used a number of privately owned Catholic homes, where a suitable room would be converted into a chapel for the occasion. Between 1600 and 1650 a gradual shift took place from makeshift, temporary religious spaces to a situation where Catholic communities started to use fixed mission stations with a separate priest's dwelling and a church. Such a complex usually resulted from structural alterations within a large house, leaving the outer façade intact. City governments and the police would know where these buildings were and for what purpose they were used, but closing them all down was considered likely to be too disruptive. In this way the secular authorities, in collusion with the Catholic community, kept alive the fiction that these locations were private spaces where they had no jurisdiction.[4]

The first custom-made paintings for this new environment were transitional in character. In style, and in the materials used, they were reminiscent of the times when the Catholic faith still reigned supreme. At the Roman Catholic parish of Kethel, near Rotterdam there were two altar shutters portraying the saints Cornelius and Cyprian, painted around 1600 on parts of a dismantled altarpiece from a century earlier. On the reverse sides, some damaged inscriptions, along with parts of a scene portraying Adam and Eve and a *Crucifixion* are still visible.[5] The position of the Catholic community in the Republic, trying to build a new organisation on the rubble of the once-mighty Catholic Church, could hardly have been symbolised any better.

A small but interesting group of triptychs remains from the same period, all with a provenance from clandestine churches that were at the time in transition from private to institutional settings. Some were made for the private chapels of genteel houses, which were accustomed to host nearby communities robbed of their old churches; some for the homes of rich patricians in the cities; and one for a house belonging to a cluster of buildings occupied by a congregation of religious women. A typical example is a triptych from Kasteel Den Ham

Figure 14.1 Anonymous, *Laudes Marianae* triptych.

at Vleuten, near Utrecht. At the beginning of the seventeenth century it was the residence of Johan van Wanroy Utenham and his wife, Margaretha de Brouxelles. They were portrayed, kneeling with their patron saints and their five children, on the inside of the left wing (Figure 14.1).

Until 1631, when a permanent clandestine church was founded in the village, the Catholic community of Vleuten regularly convened in the chapel where the triptych adorned the altar. The central panel represents the so-called *Laudes Marianae* (Mary, accompanied by Old Testament symbols of chastity); the kneeling clergyman on the opposite wing has been identified as the Jesuit missionary Johannes Ludolphi van Rhenen, with the patron saints John the Evangelist and Cunera. She is there because the Jesuit himself played an important role in bringing her relics into safety in his home town of Rhenen.

The iconography of the *Laudes Marianae* was based on a print made on a Jesuit commission and as such was completely in tune with later developments in the Counter-Reformation. The style of the altarpiece as a whole, however, seems to belong to a completely different era. The way the donors are portrayed reflects the Southern Netherlandish art of the sixteenth century, and the golden background of the central scene takes us back even further, even as we realise that it is fake gold, suggested by yellowish paint.[6]

A similar triptych was made in 1626 by the still-life painter Willem Claesz Heda, a devout Catholic himself and also involved in the production of prints with saints and portraits of missionaries. On the wings he did not include portraits of the donors, but just the figures of St Francis and St Clare. The triptych comes from the community of the so-called 'Maechden in Den Hoek', a congregation of spiritual daughters living in a collection of houses in Haarlem. Just over one metre high, it most probably adorned one of the larger rooms in one of the houses, where Mass would be said occasionally.[7]

When comparing these works to what Rubens and Van Dijck were painting in Antwerp in the same period, or Reni and Guercino in Rome, for that matter, it becomes clear how old-fashioned they were. A kind of nostalgia for the good old days, when Catholic churches in the Netherlands abounded with altarpieces like these, may have played a role. The experiences of the artists may also have been a factor. For them, commissions like these were few and far between, and one could hardly expect them to be completely up to date on the latest international trends in monumental religious painting. The kind of religious art they encountered most often was what the Dutch Catholics had been able to salvage from the old churches.

The first monumental altarpieces in Utrecht and Haarlem

These precedents give few clues as to what was to happen in the 1620s in Utrecht. There, it was mainly Abraham Bloemaert who suddenly raised the standard of ecclesiastical painting in the Republic to an international level, using his up-to-date knowledge of Italian and Flemish religious art and his experiences of completing commissions from churches in the Catholic parts of the Netherlands. It was one of the three instances in the history of Catholicism in the Republic when an original contribution to Counter-Reformation painting was made; the second came in the 1630s in Haarlem, with Pieter de Grebber as the leading figure, and the third when Jacob de Wit arrived on the scene in Amsterdam.

Although living in the Northern Netherlands, Bloemaert was able to build a reputation for himself as a painter of monumental altarpieces. In 1610 he received a commission for an altarpiece for the convent of the Poor Clares in Den Bosch, where his sister lived; five years later he produced a painting, more than four metres high, for the high altar of St John's church in Den Bosch. In 1623 he provided the main altarpiece for the church of the Brussels' Jesuits, flanked by two Rubens paintings of saints Ignatius and Francis Xaverius.[8]

In the same years, Bloemaert introduced the international fashion for monumental altar paintings of a standing format to the Northern Netherlands. With its well-digested influences from sixteenth-century Northern Italian art and a whiff of Rubens, the *Adoration of the Shepherds*, really marks the beginning of a new phase in the interior decoration of clandestine Catholic churches.[9] The life-size figures and the possibilities for emotional involvement answered the renewed need for monumental decoration in the newly established permanent, clandestine churches, and the devotional politics of the new generation of clergy, steeply educated in Counter-Reformation ideals. By this stage, Bloemaert was a man in his fifties and a well-established master from the last decade of the sixteenth century but when he made his best-known work in a fiercely mannerist style his career reached a new peak during the 1620s. This certainly owed a great deal to the exciting developments in figure painting in Flanders and Italy and, although he never travelled to the latter country, the nearness of Rubens and the return of several of his former pupils from Rome around 1621 were important stimuli for his own work.

The use of candlelight in *The supper at Emmaus* (Figure 14.2), from 1622, is immediately resonant of Bloemaert's pupil Honthorst, who brought his own

Figure 14.2 Abraham Bloemaert, *The supper at Emmaus* (1622).

PAINTINGS FOR CLANDESTINE CATHOLIC CHURCHES 221

version of Caravaggio's style back from Rome to Utrecht. At the same time, it should not be forgotten that Bloemaert, like his contemporary Goltzius, had devised very sophisticated scenes with artificial light sources much earlier in his career, and in this painting he easily outdoes Honthorst in the subtlety of his chiaroscuro effects. The composition of *The supper at Emmaus* owes much to a Rubens print of the same subject, but in this case, too, Bloemaert emulates the great master in a very sophisticated way, posing models anew to study the form and the light effects.[10]

Bloemaert was not the only painter in Utrecht at that time who worked for the church, but he was certainly the market leader; we know of about ten altarpieces and other large compositions with a church provenance, whereas Jan van Bijlert and Gerard van Honthorst are credited with only two apiece. The fact that Bloemaert was a staunch defender of the faith certainly helped his cause. The inscriptions on several of his prints show his support for the clergy and the Church of Rome, and there are well-documented anecdotes that he even proselytised on the Utrecht streets.[11] The importance of Bloemaert's individual contribution can be seen in the further development of painting for clandestine churches in Utrecht. After Hendrick Bloemaert took over his father's workshop, and his position as the most important provider of monumental religious painting, the city lost contact with the latest trends in Counter-Reformation art. Instead of following the latest trends in Roman art, as his father had done, Hendrick merely kept on milking the formulas his father had developed in the 1620s.[12]

In Haarlem, too, one painter was able to fulfil practically all the needs of the local clergy. His name was Pieter de Grebber, a man who was closely associated with the clergy of the Haarlem chapter, the most prestigious Catholic institution in the Republic that had survived the Reformation. Although the Haarlem see remained vacant, the chapter continued to govern the bishopric as if a new incumbent would soon be installed. One of its canons, Jan Albert Ban, priest of the Haarlem *beguinage* and a highly cultured man, was well acquainted with the painter who lived next door. The records of the *beguinage* show that De Grebber regularly appeared as a witness to marriages and baptisms, and priest and painter are reported to have made music together in Ban's house, often in the company of other music lovers, like Constantijn Huyghens and Rene Descartes.[13]

Aside from several altarpieces, De Grebber painted large religious pictures of a horizontal format that must have served another purpose. His rendering of the conversion of Haarlem's patron saint, Saint Bavo (Figure 14.3), was very much in tune with the chapter's politics. The picture, now in a modern church in a Haarlem suburb, shows how the repentant knight Bavo met the bishop Amandus, knelt before him, gave up all his earthly belongings and entered a monastery. Stylistically, the painting has little in common with Bloemaert's works: the clear,

Figure 14.3 Pieter de Grebber, *St Bavo blessed by St Amand*.

relief-like composition that De Grebber chose is combined with a subdued, silvery colour scheme that makes it typical of Haarlem classicist painting.

Jan Albert Ban worked hard for the renewal of the cult of St Bavo in the 1630s, the period when this painting was made. Ban had even composed a Mass for St Bavo's day, which he had offered to the Ghent chapter of St Bavo in hopes of strengthening the ties with this well-established institution and relieving the isolation of the leaderless Haarlem clergy. At the same time, the common Haarlem Catholics were educated on the life of their city's patron saint, as appears from the sermons of Judocus Cats, another prominent Haarlem canon. On St Bavo's day he admonished his audience that, as humble human beings, they could hardly hope to be as pious as the Saint, but that, 'like the little grasshoppers we are', they should try to imitate him to the best of their ability. And of course, just as Bavo had donated all his belongings to the church, so the congregation was encouraged to hand over all the money it could spare. The exemplary role of the Saint, in the sermon as well as in the painting, is typical of Counter-Reformation ideology.[14]

Large paintings like this one, meant not as altarpieces but as wall decoration, were often made in the first half of the seventeenth century, whereas they

PAINTINGS FOR CLANDESTINE CATHOLIC CHURCHES 223

Figure 14.4 Interior of the former clandestine church 't Hert (now Museum Amstelkring), Amsterdam.

almost completely disappeared thereafter. This seems to have something to do with the architecture of the churches themselves. It was about 1650 before most clandestine churches were equipped with galleries, and whereas these galleries augmented the seating capacity, they considerably limited the wall space for large paintings (Figure 14.4).

After De Grebber and his imaginative religious patrons made way for the next generation, things would never be the same in Haarlem. Although a young history painter by the name of Jan de Bray emerged, in the 1640s, who could fulfil similar commissions and who portrayed many priests and sometimes contributed to the decoration of clandestine churches, this did not lead to Catholic history painting blossoming as it had done in De Grebber's days.

Amsterdam: interchangeable altarpieces 1650–1750

Utrecht, Haarlem and Amsterdam housed not only the most important schools of history painting, but also the largest populations of priests and the liveliest and largest Catholic communities. Utrecht, as the former see of the archbishops,

Figure 14.5 N. Roosendael, *Christ after the Flagellation* (1677).

PAINTINGS FOR CLANDESTINE CATHOLIC CHURCHES 225

remained what the leaders among the clergy saw as the administrative centre; Haarlem, as we saw, still had its chapter and Amsterdam, as the richest and largest city, attracted some of the most ambitious and highly educated priests, among them many Jesuits and Franciscans.

Strangely, we know of only very few paintings before 1650 from clandestine churches in Amsterdam. Amsterdam communities convened in private houses for a longer time than in Haarlem and Utrecht, not, I believe, because of stricter regulations or persecution, as is usually thought, but because they had so many suitable large rooms at their disposal in their canalside houses. Most clandestine churches only became permanent in the second half of the century. Once that process had crystallised, they totalled about twenty-five, thus outnumbering all those in Haarlem and Utrecht combined.[15] In that 'golden age of clandestine churches' between 1650 and 1700, many altarpieces were executed by now-forgotten painters like Johannes Voorhout, Nicoales Roosendael (Figure 14.5) and Carel van Savoy, but virtually none of them still make a memorable impression. That may have something to do with the fact that most successful history painters in Amsterdam (Rembrandt, Flinck, Bol) were Protestants, or at least non-Catholics, and patrons usually employed Catholic artists for church decoration.

The best altarpieces in the Amsterdam chapels were those that were imported from Antwerp by priests from the Jesuit or Franciscan orders. The Krijtberg church on the Koningsgracht was founded by the Jesuits in 1654, and it was adorned by a series of altarpieces by Jan Cossiers, Erasmus Quellinus and a certain P.N. Bosch in the year 1656. They respectively showed the *Adoration of the Shepherds*, the *Apparition of the Madonna to St Francis Xavier* and *The Vision of S. Ignatius at La Storta*. All these altarpieces were exactly the same size. They were about two and a half metres high and, like theatrical set pieces, they would be used according to the requirements of liturgy.[16]

We often speak of the church of the Counter-Reformation as a *theatrum sacrum*, and this phenomenon is one of the most explicitly theatrical elements. It was introduced by Rubens in 1617 in the church of St Ignatius in Antwerp, later called the church of St Carolus Borromeus. It recurred in several other churches and, especially in Germany, changing decors above the altars, involving polychrome sculpture as well as paintings, can still be found. But nowhere were interchangeable altarpieces as common as in the clandestine churches in the Republic. In Amsterdam alone, there were at least ten clandestine churches with two or more altarpieces destined for the high altar, and probably some of the others had them, too; further, we know of similar series in Gouda, Amersfoort, Utrecht and Haarlem.[17]

As the side walls of clandestine churches left little room for striking pictures, anyone wanting to donate an important painting would want it to be an

Figure 14.6 Jacob de Wit, oil study for *The Resurrection*.

altarpiece, and any priest wanting to stimulate special devotions through paintings had little choice as to where to do that. So, indirectly, government policy had an impact on the way art was used in clandestine churches, not because it actively campaigned against religious images, but because it restricted the available space.

Traditionally, the period between 1716 and 1752, when Jacob de Wit was active in Amsterdam, has been portrayed as a period when the Amsterdam Catholics finally felt free to decorate their clandestine churches with as many paintings as they wished.[18] However, if we look at the numbers, this view is unsustainable. For the first half of the eighteenth century we know of about a dozen altarpieces made by Jacob de Wit and two or three by other painters, whereas in the preceding half century more than thirty are recorded, made by a dozen different painters.[19] So, in fact, the numbers of commissioned altarpieces rapidly declined after 1700, but the decline was masked by the quality and splendour of De Wit's paintings.

Jacob de Wit had spent several years in Antwerp. There he thoroughly studied the works of Rubens, Van Dijck and their followers, and interpreted these examples with a lightness and facility that is typical of the best of eighteenth-century art. He was a member of the parish of Mozes and Aaron, ministered by Franciscan missionaries. Soon after his return from Antwerp in 1716, he decorated their library and the representative rooms of their living quarters, before he was asked to make two ceiling paintings in the choir and two altarpieces: a *Christ on the Cross* and an *Annunciation* that could be alternated with an already existing seventeenth-century painting showing the *Resurrection*.[20] Another large commission also came from regular priests, the Carmelites who ministered the so-called Roman Catholic French church. They augmented and completely redecorated their church in the 1730s, and De Wit's paintings fitted into a decoration programme that included stucco decorations, woodcarvings and statues. The altarpiece depicted the *Resurrection* (Figure 14.6), above that was another painting with angels and, on the side walls underneath the galleries, De Wit made monochrome works depicting the evangelists and church fathers.[21] These brownish paintings seem at first to open up new possibilities for clandestine church interiors, but the fact that they suggested wooden reliefs points forward to the biggest 'threat' to painting for clandestine churches; after De Wit died, many churches were (re)built and (re)decorated, but painters were scarcely called upon to help any more.[22] Stucco and sculpture were *en vogue*, in domestic interiors as well as in churches, and in any case, there were few good painters left.

Is it therefore possible to give a general characteristic of Northern Netherlandish painting for clandestine churches? The more or less random results of Catholic patronage during the seventeenth and eighteenth centuries seem to preclude a positive answer, other than to say that there was less space for paintings than in churches in Flanders or Italy, and in the Republic they were, on average, smaller, and fewer in number. Many works were mediocre, but some were as good as the best that Northern Netherlandish history painting as a whole had to offer. The latter occurred in the three cases described above, where prominent history painters who happened to be devout Catholics became engaged with a group of inspired clergy in the city where they lived. Iconographically, their works were in complete conformity with international Counter-Reformation art; stylistically, they fit seamlessly into their own oeuvres. A Catholic painting by De Grebber is a typical De Grebber, a Catholic painting by Bloemaert a typical Bloemaert, a Catholic painting by De Wit a typical De Wit. In other words, clandestine churches were able to profit by the blossoming of painting in the Republic, but their patronage lacked the critical mass to generate distinctive developments in painting.

Notes
1 P. Hecht, 'Rembrandt and Raphael back to back: the contribution of Thoré', *Simiolus* 26 (1998), 162–78, at pp. 164–73.
2 A. Blankert, *Kunstbezit Parkstraatkerk* (Den Haag, 1978).
3 Cf. P. Dirkse, *Kunst uit Oud-Katholieke kerken* (Utrecht, 1989); P. Dirkse, *Begijnen, pastoors en predikanten* (Leiden, 2001); P.J.J. van Thiel, 'Catholic elements in seventeenth-century Dutch painting, apropos of a children's portrait by Thomas de Keyser', *Simiolus* 20 (1990/91), 39–62; R. Schillemans, 'Schilderijen in Noordnederlandse katholieke kerken uit de eerste helft van de zeventiende eeuw', *De Zeventiende Eeuw* 8 (1992), 41–52; R. Schillemans, 'Zeventiende- en vroeg achttiende-eeuwse wisselaltaarstukken in de Amsterdamse begijnhofkerk', *De Zeventiende Eeuw* 15 (1999), 204–21; X. van Eck, *Kunst, twist en devotie. Goudse katholieke schuilkerken 1572–1795* (Delft, 1994); X. van Eck, 'The artist's religion: paintings commissioned for clandestine Catholic churches in the northern Netherlands, 1600–1800', *Simiolus* 27 (1999), 70–94; X. van Eck, 'Resuscitating a languishing bishopric: Pieter de Grebber and the Haarlem chapter', *Bulletin van het Rijksmuseum* 52 (2004), 254–69 (Dutch text), 371–8 (English text); R. Nachbahr, 'Het altaarschilderij door Jacob de Wit voor de kerk van de Cleresie in Delft,' *Bulletin van het Rijksmuseum* 45 (1997), 99–134; G. Seelig, *Abraham Bloemaert 1566–1651. Studiens zur Utrechter Malerei um 1620* (Berlin, 1997).
4 B.J. Kaplan, 'Fictions of privacy: house chapels and the spatial accommodation of religious dissent in early modern Europe', *The American Historical Review* 107 (2002), 1030–64, at pp. 1030–36.
5 J. Dijkstra, P.P.W.M. Dirkse(+) and A.E.A.M. Smits, *De schilderijen van Museum Catharijneconvent* (Zwolle, 2002), pp. 132–3.
6 C.J. Staal, 'Johan Ludolph van Rhenen, vicaris te Vleuten, paap op Den Ham en redder van de Cunerarelieken', *Jaarboek Oud-Utrecht* (1996), pp. 70–86.
7 Van Eck, *Kunst, twist en devotie*, pp. 77–8.
8 M.G. Roethlisberger and M.J. Bok, *Abraham Bloemaert and his sons*, 2 vols (Doornspijk, 1993), pp. 252–4.
9 Seelig, *Abraham Bloemaert*, pp. 97–100.
10 *Ibid.*, pp. 87–93.
11 Roethlisberger and Bok, *Abraham Bloemaert and his sons*, vol. I, pp. 551–87, 618–44.
12 Seelig, *Abraham Bloemaert*, pp. 270–4.
13 Dirkse, *Begijnen, pastoors en predikanten*, pp. 137–42.
14 Van Eck, 'Resuscitating a languishing bishopric', pp. 266–8, 377–8.
15 A.P.J.H. van den Hout en R. Schillemans (red.), *Putti en cherubijntjes* (Amsterdam 1995), pp. 53–74.

16 Schillemans, 'Zeventiende- en vroeg achttiende-eeuwse wisselaltaarstukken', pp. 204–21.
17 Van Eck, 'The artist's religion', pp. 85–94.
18 L.J. Rogier, *Geschiedenis van het katholicisme in Noord-Nederland in de zestiende en zeventiende eeuw* (Amsterdam, 1946, 2nd edn 1964), pp. 676–7; A.P.J.H. van den Hout, "Een schoon gebouw, welks wederga zeker zelden op het platteland gevonden wordt." De bouw en decoratie van het kerkhuis De Hoop in Diemen', in J.P.P. Hinssen and J. Haag (eds), *Het Rooms Kerkhuys te Diemen* (Amsterdam, 1993), p. 60.
19 Van Eck, 'The artist's religion', pp. 85–94.
20 Van den Hout and Schillemans, *Putti en cherubijntjes*, pp. 123–8.
21 Van den Hout and Schillemans, *Putti en cherubijntjes*, p. 65.
22 Van den Hout, "Een schoon gebouw", p. 60.

15

Cultures of dissent: English Catholics and the visual arts

RICHARD WILLIAMS

Many of the differences and similarities in the religious, cultural and social experience of the Catholic minorities of England and the Dutch Republic are revealed through their patronage of the visual arts. This chapter will seek to address some of these issues by focusing in particular on England in the late sixteenth and the early seventeenth centuries. It will also consider the extent to which the visual culture of Catholicism in England at this time was distinct from that country's dominant Protestant culture.

One of the most provocative sites of contention in the religious struggles in the Northern Netherlands and England was the Catholic chapel and its ornamentation. That Catholic house chapels in the Dutch Republic, such as the Amstelkring chapel in Amsterdam, could be expected to remain unmolested by the authorities so long as they were discreet, is representative of the more general degree of tolerance enjoyed by Dutch Catholics as compared to their English counterparts. There were, however, one or two rare exceptions in England. In the late sixteenth century Lady Magdalen, Viscountess Montague built a highly elaborate chapel at Battle Abbey, her country seat in Sussex. It was reportedly large enough to hold 120 faithful Catholics at a time. A series of steps ascended to a stone altar enclosed with rails, and not only was there a pulpit but also a full choir for sung Masses. So notorious was her house as a Catholic refuge that it was known locally as 'Little Rome'. Although during the reign of Elizabeth her house was searched twice for priests, one being taken and imprisoned, no further action was brought against the Viscountess.[1] In fact, in 1607, James I's Privy Council reported to the attorney general that 'in regard that she is a nobleman, aged, and by reason of her fidelity in the time of Queen Elizabeth was never in question, it pleaseth the King's Majesty that in her old years she be free from molestation'.[2]

Clearly this was exceptional treatment for an exceptional noblewoman; as her contemporary biographer admitted, such a chapel was 'perhaps not to be seen in all England besides'.

The more usual practice in England was to enforce the harshest measures against those suspected of hosting or celebrating illegal Masses. With regard to this it seems relevant that Catholic survivalism in England was far more dependent on the gentry than it was in the Dutch Republic. The English government recognised that the Catholic gentry, in some counties at least, retained much of the power and influence due to that class. Consequently, the maintenance of a fully furnished Catholic chapel, in direct contravention of the stipulations of the Elizabethan Settlement, may have constituted an act of defiance too conspicuous to be tolerated. However, as the political situation rapidly worsened for Catholics in England, what had previously been treated as a matter of religious nonconformity was redefined as a potentially threatening act of sedition. The Northern Rebellion of 1569 was presented as an attempted coup against the Protestant government, involving the assassination of Queen Elizabeth to enable the succession of Mary Queen of Scots. Failing to realise its minimal chances of success, the pope attempted to support the rebellion by issuing the notorious bull of excommunication against Elizabeth. This, however, only served to blight Catholics in England with the stigma of treason. Subsequent Catholic plots and numerous public scares, including the threat of the Spanish Armada, provoked the language and frames of reference particular to English anti-Catholicism that was to endure for centuries to come.[3]

In such a heightened state of suspicion, a gentleman who set up 'popish' images in his private chapel might not merely face the sanctions of an ecclesiastical court, he could merit investigation by the secular authorities, even to the level of the Privy Council. This was the case in 1571, when Sir Thomas Stanley, the second son of the Earl of Derby, was discovered to be involved in a hopelessly naive plot to liberate Mary Queen of Scots from Chatsworth. Among the Hatfield papers are some last-minute instructions sent by Lord Burghley to Sir Thomas Smith regarding the interrogation of Stanley, comprising three questions. The first related to weapons and armour, the second concerned the Earl of Derby's servants, but the third asked, 'What images were set up of late in the chapel of Lathom, by whose commandment?'[4] The chapel at Lathom House had been consecrated in 1500 and still exists.[5] The reported reply to the latter question claimed, 'There are no images newly set up in any chapel the Earl has, that he knows of, that ever he saw, since the Queen's Majesty's reign.' Whatever the truth in this matter, the 'newly setting up' of images in the Stanley chapel was potentially useful corroborative evidence in proving treasonous allegiances and seditious intent.

Not all chapels set aside for clandestine Masses were private chapels in

Figure 15.1 Unknown sculptor, plaster relief of the Crucifixion (1577). Rushton Hall, Northamptonshire.

country houses. Many of the 'chapels' referred to were simply unconsecrated rooms in houses or elsewhere that were to be used for liturgical celebration. Many of these employed the visual arts as a means to help transform such interiors into 'sacred spaces'.[6] An attic room at Harvington Hall in Worcestershire, thought to have been used as a recusant chapel, still bears what appear to be symbolic drops of blood and water painted in distemper on the walls. Croft-Murray has made the convincing suggestion that the blood shed by Christ and the water that issued from the wound in his side are being represented in a symbolic allusion to the Passion.[7] A similar attic room at Quendon Hall in Essex retains barely visible remnants of a scheme of saints' and cherubs' heads painted onto the sloping roof.[8] There are even documented examples of barns in Lancashire having some sort of painted work to help transform them into sites suitable for the Mass.[9]

Some of these chapels could employ altarpieces and other images that had been rescued from churches before the official programme of iconoclasm had been enforced. Court reports of ecclesiastical commissions, church courts and courts of assize contain many examples of individuals prosecuted for concealing such pre-Reformation imagery.[10] However, Catholic religious images continued to be made in England in the late sixteenth and seventeenth centuries, if only on a very limited scale. One of the most elaborate surviving examples is the large, painted plaster relief of the Crucifixion set high into the wall of a small closet in Rushton Hall in Northamptonshire (Figure 15.1). This was the country house of Sir Thomas Tresham, well known as one of the most notorious recusant gentlemen of the late sixteenth century. Sir Thomas's coat of arms is incorporated at the bottom and the work is dated 1577.[11] The original setting and function of the relief is by no means certain, and one speculation is that it may have been a decorative scheme set above rows of bookshelves.[12] This would suggest that the room was principally a private retreat or oratory for Sir Thomas. Indeed, its Latin verses seek to stimulate a private devotional response from the viewer. However, it also seems likely that the sculpture could have served as a reredos for the celebration of Mass. Its position in the east wall of the room would, of course, have been the correct liturgical orientation for such a role.

Few Catholics would have had either the opportunity or the resources for patronage of the visual arts on the same scale as Sir Thomas Tresham. However, more modest forms of imagery were in circulation among the English Catholic community, many of them having been smuggled into the country from Catholic centres abroad. This imagery, produced in a wide range of media, effectively constituted a visual subculture that has remained largely excluded from art-historical accounts of early modern England. Yet this traffic in illegal Catholic imagery was on such a scale and deemed sufficiently troubling that the government enacted legislation in response to it. A bill was enacted in 1571, entitled 'An Acte agaynste the bringing in and putting in Execution of Bulls and other Instruments from the Sea of Rome.' Although it was primarily a measure against the pope's bull of excommunication against Elizabeth, section four concerned the importation of

> Any Token or Tokens Thing or Thynges called or named by the Name of an Agnus Dei, or any Crosses Pyctures Beades or such lyke vayne and superstitious Thynges from the Bysshop or Sea of Rome, or from any person or persons aucthorized or clayming aucthorytie by or from the sayd Bysshop or Sea of Rome to consecrate or halowe the same ...[13]

Should any person deliver or cause to be delivered these 'Pyctures' or other objects to any subject of the realm that person and the individual receiving them would be liable to the penalties defined by the Statute of Praemunire. The latter would result in the forfeiture of 'lands, tenements, goods and chattels' belonging to the persons convicted.[14]

Border guards and port officials were charged to discover these items in the course of their duties. In order to help identify subversive Catholic goods an illustrated broadsheet print was issued in 1579, entitled 'Certaine of the Popes Merchandize lately sent ouer into Englande' (see Figure 7.1). This print was folded into a book published under the title, *A new years gifte, dedicated to the popes holiness* (London, 1579). Liturgical objects such as a super-altar and cross are illustrated, together with rosary beads and other items used for private devotion. At the centre of the broadsheet is a single-leaf devotional print, copied from examples produced in the Netherlands. It depicts St Nicholas in prayer between Christ and the Virgin Mary, following a wholly orthodox iconography that Rubens was later to paint.[15]

Single-leaf prints such as this could serve a series of different functions within the English Catholic community. The Jesuit priest William Weston was possibly referring to prints when he described how 'pictures of saints' were attached to the wall of his cell in the Clink gaol. By displaying them behind a table 'which served as an altar' they acted as a reredos.[16] Similarly, England's most famous Catholic prisoner, Mary Queen of Scots, had 'eight or ten pictures in paper of the Passion of Christ, and of other like stuff fastened upon the hangings over the chimney' in her quarters, according to her keeper, Sir Amias Paulet, in 1586.[17] Nevertheless, it is improbable that Mary would have had the opportunity to celebrate the Mass under such close confinement and so it is more likely that the paper images were an aid to her private devotions.

As for illegal Catholic pictures created in media other than print, examples can be found listed in inventories of objects seized from the houses of Catholics suspected of harbouring priests. Whether or not a priest was apprehended, objects were confiscated as incriminating, corroborative evidence of seditious Catholic activity. A typical example survives in The National Archives, headed 'A particuler noet of such things as were founde in the howse of M^{ris} hampden of Stoke in the County of Buck the xxvth daie of January 1583, And caryed away from there by m^r pawle Wentworth etc.' Its room-by-room inventory of items seized includes 'v picktures payntd upon past bords' taken from the 'maides chamber'.[18] These continued to be imported into England in the reign of James I, '3 little pictures made upon pastbords' and '2 tables of pictures, made on pastbord' being among the cargo impounded in 1623 from a ship docked at Dover.[19] The firm foundation of pasteboard made it ideal for hanging from the wall or standing upon a table, either for private prayers or as an altarpiece.

In the 'Litel gallery' of the same Buckinghamshire house, the searchers discovered 'In a chest of Richard Brudd ii pictures of nedleworke sett into Frames of bordes.'[20] Again, these pictures are likely to have been set into these supports in order to hang on a wall or to stand upon an altar. Free-standing needlework had, for example, been on display in Hampton Court during the reign of Henry VIII, whose 1547 inventory recorded 'A cupboard of printed leather standing upon the same o'r ladiee saluted by Gabriell w^t diverse goodlye flowers and consists of nedlework within a glasse.'[21]

Another common medium for Catholic pictures was silk. Specimens of these were also found at Mistress Hampden's house. In the room assigned to Mr

Fitton were 'ii pictures one upon yellowe sarcnet, thother upon parchment wch are wrapped togeither in a paper', and in Mistress Hampden's own bedchamber was 'a pickture made upon yewloe sarssarnet'. Sarsanet was a kind of silk and thus a costly material. Whereas it is possible that the pictures had been created in fabric and stitched onto the silk, they may, alternatively, have been painted; which was certainly the case with several such pictures in Henry VIII's collection. These were described as 'stayned', such as the 'table with the name of Jhesus and the fowre Evangelists stayned upon single sarconet', kept at the Palace of Westminster.[22] That this may have been the technique employed for the pictures belonging to Elizabethan Catholics, is suggested by one example at least, removed from the Hoxton house of Sir Thomas Tresham in 1584, which was listed as 'a painted crucifix upon orenge colo^d satten'.[23]

The widespread dissemination of these silk pictures can be inferred by the large numbers intercepted by the constables of Lewes in 1584. Upon opening a fardel containing numerous Catholic books, rosary beads and relics, the constables noted 'Pictures in sylks: of the greater sorte, xix Pictures in silke of the lesser sorte xxvii.'[24] Presumably these objects were destined for distribution among the Catholic households in the area or even further afield. Some examples were undoubtedly intended for use in private devotion, such as 'a pickture made upon yewloe sarsanet called by Mr Fytton veronyca'.[25] What was presumably the Sudarium of St Veronica, with its indulgenced image of the Holy Face of Christ, had been kept by Mistress Hampden in her own bedchamber. By contrast, it seems quite possible that the 'greater sorte' of silk pictures may have made suitable dressings for the liturgy, perhaps adorning the altar as an overfront, a netherfront or even a reredos.

When the medium of Catholic pictures was not noted by the Protestant authorities this may indicate that the materials were of low value. The 'xii sevrall pictures rolled togeither' at Mistress Hampden's house may have been inexpensive prints, such as the 'xii printed supercycyous pyctuers' seized from Roger Smythes's house in Holborn in 1584.[26] By contrast, costly materials could be of greater significance than the subject matter, as was the case with 'A tablet of gold wth a picture upon thone syd and a superscripcion one thother', belonging to Mistress Hampden. The latter may have been one of the 'blessed medals' illustrated in the woodcut of the *Pope's merchandize* (see Figure 15.2), which were evidently a popular gift for Catholics abroad to send back to family and friends in England. This is apparent from letters that frequently mention various presents enclosed. In 1584, R. Debdall sent an assortment of 'tokens' for his parents and siblings, including 'a gilted crucifyxe & medals unto my Father',[27] and an unnamed fellow of the English College in Rome sent 'iiii medals' to his cousin in England as 'a small remembrance from me'.[28]

From the examples discussed above, the nature of the images commissioned or imported by English Catholics, particularly those to adorn their chapels, appears to make a stark contrast with patronage of the visual arts by the Catholic minority of the Dutch Republic. Clandestine chapels in the Northern Netherlands were far more likely to have painted altarpieces as a focal point; some, as Xander van Eck demonstrates in this volume, so elaborate that a series of large-scale canvases might be kept for insertion into a frame in accordance with the changing liturgical seasons. Such paintings did not even necessarily have to be entrusted to known Catholics, as there are instances of Protestant painters being so commissioned.[29]

In late sixteenth- and early seventeenth-century England, wealthy Catholics certainly had the opportunity to secure the services of painters, including Protestant ones. In the 1590s, the descendants of Sir Thomas More commissioned Roland Lockey to paint copies after Holbein's famous group portrait of Sir Thomas and family, but with the interpolation of the Elizabethan generation of the family.[30] Whatever part these pictures may have played for the More family in fashioning a Catholic identity for itself, they certainly did not flaunt overt Catholic iconography. Indeed, it is difficult to conceive that a Protestant painter in England would have had the inclination, let alone been willing to take the risk of creating imagery of an identifiably Catholic iconography for illegal use.

However, a more fundamental cultural difference in attitudes to the visual arts in England and the Northern Netherlands can be seen to be in operation, irrespective of religious affiliation. It would be a serious misunderstanding to make the assumption that English Catholics employed imagery in needlework, silk and the like as an inferior substitute for painting. The privileged position assumed by painting as a 'fine art' over the so-called 'decorative arts' belongs to a body of art theory that was not to take hold in England until after the period in question. It has already been noted that pictures on silk were of sufficient prestige to figure in Henry VIII's collection. The same was true of needlework pictures, even of a religious subject matter, which continued to be given positions of prominence by royalty and the aristocracy. For example, after expending vast sums on the building of Hardwick Hall in Derbyshire, the Protestant noblewoman the Countess of Shrewsbury erected in the chapel 'a Crucefixe of imbrodered worke.'[31] At one stage it was suggested that Queen Elizabeth replace the controversial silver crucifix on the communion table of the Chapel Royal with an embroidery of the Crucifixion.[32] This would have tempered the threat of idolatry posed by a 'graven image', but it is more important to note that the substitution would hardly have been suggested had embroidery been seen as anything to impugn the Queen's magnificence.

The theory of 'magnificence', from its initial formulation by Aristotle, had come to exert a governing influence on the patronage of the visual arts in medieval and early modern Europe.[33] An individual of high standing was expected to make an outward display commensurate with his or her social status. Elite members of society had traditionally achieved this by favouring objects fashioned from the most expensive materials. The corollary of this was that, in Tudor England, the visual arts were still largely valued according to their material cost, and thus a painting, which was nothing more than a piece of wood or canvas covered in oil, could not compete in magnificence with tapestry or goldsmiths' work. Thus the hierarchy in which 'fine art' enjoys a privileged status over the 'decorative arts' was effectively reversed in sixteenth- and early seventeenth-century England.[34] By contrast, the Northern Netherlands had acknowledged the cultural prestige of painting, influenced by Italian theory that sought to elevate it from a lowly 'mechanical art' to a 'liberal art'.[35]

It would, therefore, be wholly anachronistic to judge the imagery found in the houses and chapels of English Catholics according to aesthetic and cultural criteria that were either unknown or largely unacknowledged in England at this time. It is hardly appropriate to decry the absence or poor quality of painted altarpieces when English Catholics were far more likely to appreciate and esteem richly embroidered vestments, gold crosses set with precious gems, or costly hangings.

However, the value and importance attached to the cheap woodcut pictures, rosary beads and the like lay elsewhere than in the materials. The importance imputed to them is signified by the risks taken in their importation. As with the cases cited above, of students at the English colleges abroad sending tokens to family and friends in England, this clandestine activity appears to have occurred largely as a series of informal acts of gift-giving rather than as a fully coordinated smuggling operation.

Yet the English seminary colleges abroad did take a direct interest in the distribution and use of these objects. The novices, for example, were instructed by an authoritative casuist text that such items were 'not by themselves necessary to the practice of the Catholic faith'. Nevertheless, it was ruled legitimate for priests and laypeople to endanger their lives by smuggling or using objects for private devotion, owing to the 'spiritual benefits' that could 'contribute substantially to [their] salvation'. The decision to run such a risk was to be left entirely to the individual, who was to follow the personal prompting of the Holy Ghost.[36] Even so, the Catholic hierarchy was keen to stress the tremendous benefits of making these items available in England and, in a postscript to the casuist text, Fathers William Allen and Robert Persons jointly added that 'Pious things are not to be neglected because of danger.'[37]

What marked out these pictures and other Catholic objects for private devotion, in the eyes of the English state as well as of the Catholic community itself, was that they had been 'hallowed' or consecrated by the pope or senior clergy. For the English government, this rendered them instruments of the 'usurped authority' of the pope, aligning them with papal bulls.[38] Even a cheap woodcut print could thus appear threatening to England's Protestant regime, owing to the religious and political connotations of this consecration. Yet it was not illegal to import pictures per se into England. Indeed, large numbers of prints, often entire suites of engravings, were brought in from the Netherlands and elsewhere quite openly and legitimately, to be appreciated in their own right or to be used as models by English craftsmen in virtually all media.[39] However, suspicions were automatically raised if a known Catholic was involved. This applied even to a Catholic peer such as Lord Vaux, who, on his return from a trip abroad in 1583, was asked 'what things he hath brought over with him and whether they be not consecrated after the popes manner'.[40]

If an illegal Catholic image had not been consecrated it might still be easily distinguishable from legitimate pictures, on account of its iconography. Unfortunately, the survival rate of Catholic imagery is so poor and even the documentary evidence discussed earlier is so insufficiently detailed that the subject matter of these images is mostly irrecoverable. However, a significant body of illegal imagery used by Catholics in sixteenth- and seventeenth-century England survives in the form of book illustrations.

Books intended for the English Catholic community were published at major centres for printing on the Continent, such as Antwerp, Leuven, Rouen and elsewhere. The woodcut and engraved pictures in these volumes offer at least some idea of the sorts of imagery favoured by the English Catholic market, which appears to have been predominantly devotional or didactic in nature. For example, the title page created at Antwerp for Thomas Heskyns's *The Parliament of Christ* (1566) encapsulated the author's defence of the Catholic theology of the sacrament in subsidiary illustrations. These depicted scenes of the celebration of Mass, its Old Testament prefigurations, its inauguration at the Last Supper and, at the centre, the Host being venerated. The devotional needs of readers were supported with series of illustrations, often of the life and Passion of Christ, printed into books for private meditation.[41]

Yet the illiterate were also explicitly catered for in publications such as John Fowler's book of sixty-two woodcuts printed at Antwerp in 1575 under the title *Godly Contemplations for the Unlearned*. In Leuven, a similar attempt was made to render John Bucke's 1589 instructional book of rosary devotion more accessible by including a pull-out broadsheet with illustrations featuring the Joys and Sorrows of the Virgin, and a text in rhyming verses (see Figure 7.2). This, as Bucke freely admitted, was aimed at those 'here to fore delited with vain ballads and sonets',[42] suggesting that it was a direct Catholic answer to the popularity of Protestant godly ballads in England. At the higher end of the scale was Richard Verstegan's lavishly illustrated *Primer or Office of the Blessed Virgin Marie*, published in Antwerp in 1599 using high-quality engravings of the Assumption of the

Virgin and the other illustrations that had traditionally accompanied that text. The following year at Antwerp, Thomas Worthington published his *The rosarie of our Ladie* with expensive engravings designed by Maarten de Vos.

Catholic books were, of course, also produced illegally in England using clandestine presses, but the inclusion of illustrations clearly presented practical problems. Neither the talent nor the resources were available to generate original printed illustrations in England. The solution followed in *A methode, to meditate on the psalter, or the great rosarie of our blessed Ladie*, printed in England in 1598, was to leave gaps on its pages for engraved prints of the *Fifteen Mysteries of the Virgin* from Antwerp to be pasted into position. More commonly, very old wood blocks were used, clearly dating from before the Reformation.[43] In many instances no illustrations were included. Such piecemeal working practices hardly allowed English Catholics to develop a distinctive print culture of visual imagery. Yet, in this respect there was little difference from the book illustrations produced for the dominant, Protestant culture. The printing industry had never been as highly developed in England as it had been elsewhere. Relatively few Protestant books were illustrated, and even the most celebrated are often thought, as in the case of Foxe's *Book of Martyrs*, to have been cut by foreign workers.[44] To illustrate the *Bishops' Bible*, woodblocks had to be brought over under a temporary lease from a foreign printer.[45]

In spite of the difficulties and obstacles, English Catholic books appear to have been illustrated as and when resources allowed, perhaps making use of whatever imagery happened to be available. The iconography comprised mainly traditional subjects from the lives of Christ and the Virgin. In other instances, English Catholic iconography had to make concessions to the circumstances in which it was to be displayed.

The need for Catholic gentlemen to exercise a degree of self-censorship in devising an iconographic display is attested by Sir Thomas Tresham in a memorandum dated 1597, which he wrote while interned at the Bishop's Palace at Ely. Several of his fellow Catholic gentlemen detainees had painted the walls of their rooms with the crucifix, coats of arms and inscriptions. While they were absent the guards had washed out and defaced the crucifixes but typically left the coats of arms and inscriptions untouched. Sir Thomas resolved to paint his scheme on cloth so that he could easily take it down, should objections be raised, and that he would 'putt nothing wheratt offence ys to bee taken ...'. Instead of the crucifix he would use symbols such as sacred names, triangles, circles, the cross of Constantine, and symbolic creatures such as the lamb, serpent, dove and stork.[46] These, together with the inscriptions written in Latin, Greek and Hebrew, conformed to the Elizabethan fashion for the impresa, in which a visual representation combined with a learned motto to generate a symbolic meaning personal to its deviser.[47] Imprese, according to Tresham, were a form

Figure 15.2 Rushton Triangular Lodge 1594–97. Rushton, Northamptonshire.

of communication 'as differ from vulgar apprehension and yett wyll redely bee interpreted by men of skyll'.[48] He was thus deliberately aiming above the heads of his gaolers.

Sir Thomas Tresham famously employed the language of visual symbols, what the Elizabethans termed a 'device', in a series of buildings in or near his country estate in Northamptonshire. Perhaps the best known of these is Rushton Triangular Lodge (Figure 15.2), constructed between 1594 and 1597, that honoured the Trinity by using various forms of architectural and iconographic symbolism. Its three walls each measure thirty-three feet in length and are set in the form of a perfect equilateral triangle. Each façade comprises rows of three windows for each of its three floors, leading up to three gables surmounted by a three-sided chimney. The members of the Trinity are represented symbolically, such as relief carvings of the hen and the pelican, in allusion to Christ.[49]

More daringly, there are more abstruse references to the Mass in some of the inscriptions and in the symbols on the chimney. Whether the building's intended purpose was as a space for the celebration of clandestine Masses cannot be proved. The only contemporary documented reference to its function is its description in Tresham's accounts as 'The Warryners Lodge'. The architectural historian Mark Girouard has demonstrated that this description may not have been mere dissimulation, since Tresham bred rabbits for profit and one of his rabbit warrens was built around the Triangular Lodge. A building of two storeys was standard for a warren lodge: the lower floor for keeping equipment and drying the rabbit skins and the upper floor to accommodate the warrener when he needed to keep watch over the warren.[50] However, this does not preclude the building from having a secret dual purpose, even if only as a space for private reflection or meditation. The ephemeral Catholic imagery discussed above could have helped transform the lodge at a stroke into a sacred space.

In 1594 Tresham began building another lodge nearby called Lyveden New Bield (Figure 15.3) but, on learning of his death in 1605, the workmen downed their tools and the building remains unfinished to this day. This lodge was dedicated to the Passion of Christ through its plan, which forms the shape of a Greek cross, and in the emblems of the Passion carved into the frieze that runs around the entire building.[51] Prominent among these emblems were the same 'Instruments of the Passion' or *arma Christi* which had appeared on pre-Reformation printed indulgences.[52] Yet, Tresham's carved frieze ought not to be misinterpreted as a reckless and provocative projection of Catholic identity. Discretion ruled the choice as to which traditional Instruments of the Passion be included or excluded. For example, St Veronica's cloth had been a standard element in pre-Reformation representations of the *arma Christi*, but the distaste Protestant critics had for such unscriptural details may have persuaded Sir Thomas not to include this on his building. Moreover, the Instruments of the Passion were not

Figure 15.3 Lyveden New Bield (Northamptonshire), begun 1594 but left unfinished at the death of Sir Thomas Tresham in 1605.

of themselves controversial, since they were printed quite openly and under licence on the title page of an almost exactly contemporary English Protestant book entitled *The Betraying of Christ*, printed in London by John Islip in 1598 (Figure 15.4).

It is also important to examine the shapes of Tresham's buildings in the wider cultural context. Buildings constructed in symbolic shapes, even as an expression of religious faith, were nothing new in England.[53] It should not necessarily be assumed that Tresham felt forced to retreat into an arcane language of symbols out of fear of persecution, when such architectural 'devices' were the height of fashion at the time for members of his class, across the religious divide.

The general fascination for buildings of a witty or unusual shape is confirmed by the numbers of plans for such structures in various collections of architectural drawings from the period. From the collections of Lord Burghley and other Protestant courtiers to those of surveyors and masons, designs survive in significant numbers for buildings in such shapes as a circle, a cross, the letter 'y', and even the designer's own initials.[54] Although most of these were never built, Longford Castle in Wiltshire is an exception, being completed in 1580. The significance of this building is that it was built in the shape of an equilateral triangle and predates Sir Thomas's Triangular Lodge at Rushton by thirteen years. As with the Rushton lodge, Longford Castle appears to have been intended to honour the Trinity, since a contemporary copy of the plan makes a prominent

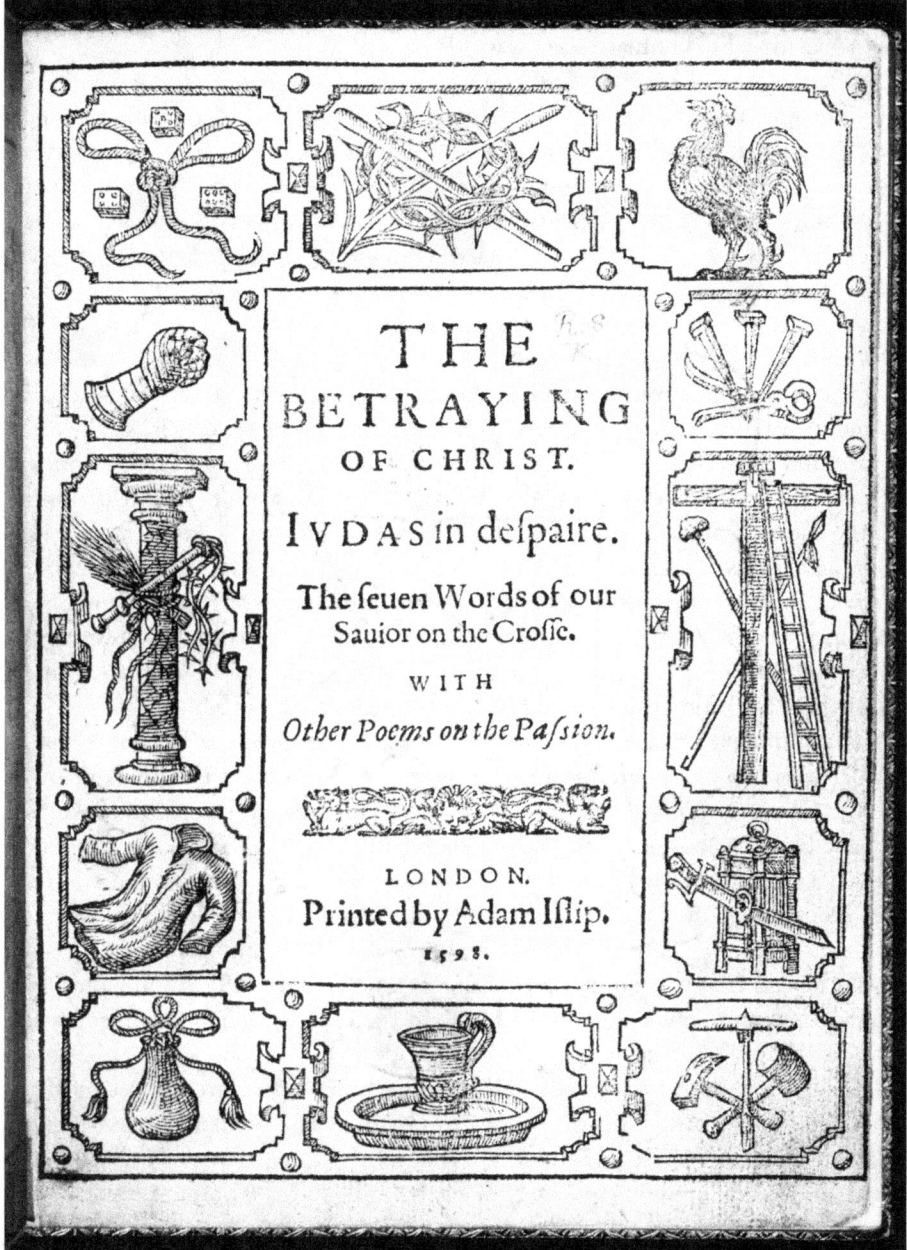

Figure 15.4 Book title page of *The Betraying of Christ* (London: Adam Islip, 1598).

display of the symbol of the Trinity drawn in the middle. Most significantly, the builder of this, Sir Thomas Gorges, was Protestant.[55]

The plan of Longford Castle was copied by the contemporary surveyor, John Thorpe, whose collection of architectural drawings includes other designs for triangular houses. There is also a copy of the design for Tresham's Lyveden New Bield.[56] There was nothing subversive in constructing a building in the shape of a Greek cross, and Thorpe had no qualms in copying the design. In fact, Lyveden was also predated by a Protestant building, in the form of Hardwick Hall. Mentioned earlier as having been built in the 1590s for the Protestant Countess of Shrewsbury, Hardwick followed an outline in the shape of two Greek crosses side by side.

Set within this context, Sir Thomas Tresham appears less unconventional as a builder than is sometimes supposed. His use of the device reflects his enthusiasm for architectural fashion. His buildings remind us that there was not one uniform culture of English Catholicism. Although most priests were recruited from the gentry, the lay Catholic gentry could often employ the visual arts in more traditional assertions of social status. It is highly characteristic that, running around the base of Lyveden New Bield, as a counterpart to the frieze of Passion symbolism, is a continuous row of armorial shields still awaiting to be painted with the coats of arms of Sir Thomas, his family and allies. These would have helped to position him within the older, established norms of the county hierarchy.

A similar motivation can be seen to have exercised Sir Thomas's fellow gentlemen inmates in detention at the Bishop's Palace at Ely. The description of their painted displays of religious scenes, coats of arms and inscriptions finds a remarkable parallel in a painted cloth dated 1596. It is preserved at Coughton Court in Warwickshire, home to the Throckmorton family. Although it was only first recorded in the house during the eighteenth century, it is possible that its original owner was Thomas Throckmorton, fellow recusant and brother-in-law of Sir Thomas Tresham. Painted in oil on cloth, it measures 9 ft 2¾ in wide and 7 ft 1½ in in height. The date appears at the top, and beneath it is a representation of Ely Cathedral (formerly the Benedictine Abbey). The abbots and abbesses of Ely, together with the monarchs under whom they served, are commemorated as a sequence of painted heads dating from before the Norman Conquest to the reign of Elizabeth I. The sequence is broken by the inclusion of forty knights who had been billeted on the Abbey of Ely by William the Conqueror and whose eventual departure caused great sorrow among the monks.[57]

The lower part of the painted cloth is partitioned into panels comprising the coats of arms of recusant gentlemen, according to five different occasions of incarceration. Numerous inscriptions meticulously record such details as the precise dates of imprisonment, the names of the prisoners' custodians, and even the itemised conditions of the recusants' release under bond.

The painting appears to have been inspired by a medieval wall painting at Ely called the *Tabula Eliensis*, which is no longer extant. It commemorated the episode of William the Conqueror's forty knights, each of whom was illustrated paired with one of the monks of the abbey. The painting at Coughton Court is thus an exercise in Catholic historiography. The viewer is invited to perceive a continuum between the knights sent to Ely by William the Conqueror and the modern-day knights sent there by Queen Elizabeth. This is effectively a secular counterpart to the history of the Catholic faith in England through its saints and martyrs, so often promoted by the clerical hierarchy.[58] It is a construction of identity focused more on lineage and class, these being particularly sensitive issues for gentlemen whose recusancy disqualified them from holding office and diminished their power by other humiliating means.

In public displays such as Tresham's buildings, expressions of Catholic identity were effectively marginalised, restricted to the smallest details on structures which otherwise might have been built by a Protestant. This apparent conformity to the dominant culture parallels the personal conduct of many recusant gentlemen, including Tresham, who felt unable to compromise in matters of faith but outwardly insisted on their loyalty to the queen. In many respects English Catholic visual culture is to be defined more in the interpretation and above all the function of its artefacts than in terms of a distinctive style or even iconography.

This is also true of pictures, including religious pictures, which were openly acquired and publicly displayed as part of the new fashion for collecting. The general low esteem in which the visual arts were held in England began to change in the late sixteenth century, at least for a small elite of courtiers who followed the lead of their counterparts abroad in collecting pictures on account of the name of the artist and the aesthetic qualities of the work.[59] Catholic gentlemen such as John, Lord Lumley were able to amass collections of paintings, including religious pictures, many by Netherlandish artists. Lumley's 1590 inventory includes a Crucifixion attributed to Jan van Scorel, a painting of the Virgin and Child with saints Catherine and John the Baptist, the temptation of St Anthony, and other examples.[60] That paintings, even former Catholic altarpieces, could now be disassociated from the stigma of 'popery' and appreciated as cultural artefacts is attested by their presence in the collections of staunch English Protestants. For example, the Earl of Leicester owned a painting of Christ's deposition from the Cross and 'the picture of Christe how he was borne in an ox stall, with 2 leaves to foulde and unfoulde', which was presumably an altarpiece.[61] Leicester's loyal Protestantism was never in doubt and his religious pictures were displayed in the secular spaces of his houses rather than in his private chapel, which greatly reduced the threat of their idolatrous misuse. However, in the hands of a militant Catholic, a presumption was made of illegal misuse. This was the case with Sir Thomas Tresham, whose house in Hoxton was found by the authorities to contain a picture with folding wings that was automatically assumed to be used as an altarpiece in clandestine Masses.[62]

For more discreet Catholic gentlemen, opportunities increased to acquire religious art. Owing to new directions in international relations and in cultural policy taken by the Stuart kings, paintings by celebrated Italian artists began to be collected in England. It has sometimes been assumed that Catholics in England were automatically more responsive to the concept of appreciating 'art', but the surviving evidence does not support this. Catholics may have been more responsive to images, given their commitment to the use of visual stimulus in religious practice, but, remembering the nature of many of the pictures described above which served such a utilitarian role, this was not the same as being responsive to 'works of art'. The theoretical framework necessary to appreciate 'art' was something that could be embraced by Catholics and Protestants alike.

This chapter has attempted to redress at least part of the often-caricatured view of English Catholics and their relationships with the visual arts by stressing the diversity in production and consumption of visual material by different groups of Catholics. The contrast drawn between Catholics in England and in the Dutch Republic highlights how a more extensive and developed patronage of the visual arts was able to flourish in the Northern Netherlands, not only on account of a greater level of toleration but also owing to broader cultural differences which extended beyond the concerns of religion. Catholic visual culture in England and in the Northern Netherlands is still under-researched; but it may be hoped that this work is not undertaken in provincial isolation, but, inspired by the sort of enterprise of which this book is a part, made as a parallel study, so that a richer understanding of both may be gained.

Notes
1 A.C. Southern (ed.), *An Elizabethan recusant house comprising the life of Lady Magdalen Viscountess Montague (1538–1608)* (London: Sands and Co., 1954), p. 43.
2 Southern (ed.), *An Elizabethan recusant house*, p. 54.
3 For a summary of the deteriorating position of Catholics in England see P. McGrath, *Papists and Puritans under Elizabeth I* (London: Blandford Press, 1967), pp. 161–204.
4 Hatfield Papers MS 157, fol. 136.
5 N. Pevsner, *The Buildings of England: Lancashire: 2 The Rural North* (London: Penguin, 1969), p. 165.
6 R.L. Williams, 'Forbidden sacred spaces in Reformation England', in A. Spicer and S. Hamilton (eds), *Defining the holy: sacred space in medieval and early modern Europe* (Aldershot: Ashgate, 2005), pp. 95–114.
7 E. Croft-Murray, *Decorative painting in England 1537–1837* (London: Country Life, 1962), 1, p. 188.
8 G.M. Benton, 'Wall paintings at Quendon Hall', *Essex Archaeological Society* 18 (1928), 188.
9 J. Tait (ed.), 'Lancashire Quarter Sessions Records, Volume I', *Cheetham Society New Series*, 77 (1917), 12; C. Haigh 'The continuity of Catholicism in the English Reformation', in C. Haigh (ed.), *The English Reformation revised* (Cambridge: Cambridge University Press, 1987), p. 184.

10 R.L. Williams, 'Religious pictures and sculpture in Elizabethan England: censure, appreciation and devotion' (Ph.D. dissertation, Courtauld Institute of Art, University of London, 2003), pp. 46–66.
11 R.L. Williams, 'A Catholic sculpture in Elizabethan England: Sir Thomas Tresham's reredos at Rushton Hall', *Architectural History* 44 (2001), 221–7; J. Heward and R. Taylor, *The country houses of Northamptonshire* (Swindon: Royal Commission on the Historic Monuments of England, 1996), pp. 298–306.
12 M. Girouard, *Rushton Triangular Lodge* (London: English Heritage, 2004), p. 23.
13 A. Lauders et al. (eds), *The Statutes of the Realm*, 12 vols (London: Record Commission, 1810–28), IV, pp. 528–31.
14 J.R. Tanner, *Tudor constitutional documents* (Cambridge: Cambridge University Press, 2nd edn, 1951), p. 17.
15 Williams, 'Religious pictures and sculpture in Elizabethan England', pp. 212–13 for a correction of T. Watt, *Cheap print and popular piety, 1550–1640* (Cambridge: Cambridge University Press, 1994), p. 179; J.B. Knipping, *Iconography of the Counter Reformation in the Netherlands*, 2 vols (Nieuwkoop: de Graaf, 1974), II, p. 275.
16 W. Weston, *William Weston: the autobiography of an Elizabethan*, trans. P. Caraman (London, 1955), p. 166.
17 J. Morris, *The letter-books of Sir Amias Poulet* (London: Burns and Oates, 1874), pp. 317–18, cited in P. Collinson, *The birthpangs of Protestant England* (Cambridge: Cambridge University Press, 1988), pp. 118.
18 Public Record Office, London (hereafter PRO), SP 12/167, fol.47.
19 PRO, SP 14/151, fol.24.
20 PRO, SP 12/167, fol. 47.
21 D. Starkey (ed.), *The inventory of Henry VIII* (London: Society of Antiquaries, 1998), p. 288.
22 S. Foister, 'Paintings and other works of art in sixteenth-century English inventories', *Burlington Magazine*, 123:938 (1981), 275.
23 PRO, SP 12/172, fol. 113.
24 PRO, SP 12/156, fol. 15.
25 PRO, SP 12/167, fol. 47.
26 PRO, SP 12/172, fol. 111.
27 PRO, SP 12/179, fol. 4.
28 PRO, SP 12/137, fol. 47.
29 V. Manuth, 'Denomination and iconography: the choice of subject matter in the biblical painting of the Rembrandt circle', *Simiolus* 22 (1993/4), 238.
30 Lockey executed a cabinet miniature and two full-scale versions in oils. K. Hearn (ed.), *Dynasties. Painting in Tudor and Jacobean England 1530–1630* (London: Tate Publishing, 1995), pp. 128–9; R. Strong, *Tudor and Jacobean portraits* (London: National Portrait Gallery, 1969), I, pp. 345–51.
31 L. Boynton and P. Thornton, 'The Hardwick Hall inventory of 1601', *Furniture History*, 7 (1971), 30.
32 W.P. Haugaard, *Elizabeth and the English Reformation* (Cambridge: Cambridge University Press, 1968), pp. 188–9.
33 R. Lightbown, 'Charles I and the tradition of European collecting', in A. MacGregor (ed.), *The late King's goods* (London and Oxford: Oxford University Press, 1989), pp. 53–65.
34 R.L. Williams, 'Collecting and religion in late sixteenth-century England', in E. Chaney (ed.), *The evolution of English collecting: receptions of Italian art in the Tudor and Stuart periods* (New Haven and London: Yale University Press, 2003), pp. 159–201; L. Gent, *Picture and poetry 1560–1620* (Leamington Spa: Hall, 1981), chapter 1.
35 See for example Karel van Mander's book of 1601: K. van Mander, *The Lives of the Illustrious Netherlandish and German Painters*, trans. H. Miedema (Doornspijk: Davaco, 1994).
36 P.J. Holmes (ed.), *Elizabethan casuistry* (London: Catholic Record Society, 1981), pp. 66–7.
37 Holmes (ed.), *Elizabethan casuistry*, p. 67.

38 Lauders et al. (eds), *The Statutes of the realm*, IV, pp. 528–31.
39 Williams, 'Collecting and religion', pp. 180–6.
40 PRO, SP 12/165, fol. 18.
41 A.C. Southern, *Elizabethan recusant prose 1559–1582* (London and Glasgow: Sands and Co., 1950); Williams, 'Religious pictures and sculpture in Elizabethan England', pp. 78–105, 214–33.
42 J. Bucke, *Instructions for the use of the beades, containing many matters of meditacion or mentall prayer* (Leuven, 1589), pp. 84–5.
43 Williams, 'Religious pictures and sculpture in Elizabethan England', p. 224.
44 T. Watt, *Cheap print and popular piety*, pp. 140–50; M. Aston, *The King's bedpost* (Cambridge: Cambridge University Press, 1993), p. 167.
45 M. Aston, 'The Bishops' bible illustrated', in D. Wood (ed.), *The church and the arts* (Oxford: Ecclesiastical History Society, 1992), pp. 267–85.
46 British Library, Additional MS 39832, fol. 5 printed in Historical Manuscripts Commission, *Report of the Manuscripts in Various Collections III*, 55 (1904), p. 91.
47 M. Girouard, *Robert Smythson and the Elizabethan country house* (New Haven and London: Yale University Press, 1983), pp. 7–10.
48 British Library, Additional MS 39832, fol. 5.
49 M. Girouard, *Rushton Triangular Lodge:* J.A. Gotch, *The buildings of Sir Thomas Tresham* (London: Barsford, 1883); G. Kilroy, *Edmund Campion. Memory and transcription* (Aldershot: Ashgate, 2005), pp. 137–40.
50 Girouard, *Rushton Triangular Lodge*, p. 8.
51 M. Girouard, *Lyveden New Bield* (London: National Trust, 2001).
52 E. Duffy, *The stripping of the altars* (New Haven and London: Yale University Press, 1992), pp. 239–42 and figure 85.
53 M. Airs, *The Tudor and Jacobean country house: a building history* (Stroud: Alan Sutton, 1995), pp. 7–14.
54 Airs, *The Tudor and Jacobean country house*, pp. 7–14; Girouard, *Robert Smythson and the Elizabethan country house*, pp. 11–14.
55 J. Summerson, 'The Book of Architecture of John Thorpe in Sir John Soane's Museum', *The Walpole Society* 40 (1966), 87; Airs, *The Tudor and Jacobean country house*, p. 7; C. Hussey, 'Longford Castle, Wiltshire', *Country Life* 70 (1931) 648–55.
56 Summerson, 'The Book of Architecture of John Thorpe', pp. 89, 101.
57 W.H. St John Hope, 'The Painted Cloth of 1596 with memorials of Ely etc. from Coughton Court', *Proceedings of the Society of Antiquaries of London* 2nd Series, 23 (1910) 255–62.
58 R.L. Williams, '"Libels and payntinges": Elizabethan Catholics and the international campaign of visual propaganda', in C. Highley and J. King (eds), *John Foxe and his world* (Aldershot: Ashgate, 2002); A. Dillon, *The construction of martyrdom in the English Catholic community, 1535–1604* (Aldershot: Ashgate, 2002).
59 Williams, 'Collecting and religion in late sixteenth-century England', pp. 159–79.
60 L. Cust, 'The Lumley inventories', *The Walpole Society* 6 (1917–18), 27.
61 J. Clarke, 'The buildings and art collections of Robert Dudley, Earl of Leicester' (MA dissertation, Courtauld Institute, University of London, 1981), pp. 37–8.
62 PRO, SP 12/172, fol. 113.

16

Conclusion: Catholic minorities in Protestant states, Britain and the Netherlands, c.1570–1720[1]

BENJAMIN KAPLAN AND JUDITH POLLMANN

The Catholic Church of the seventeenth century is usually thought of as a church militant and triumphant: a church of monumental buildings and baroque art, of spectacular processions and dramatic devotions, a church that was closely connected to the state and that sought to control hearts and minds through inquisition and censorship, discipline and ritual. The Catholics who lived in the British Isles and in the Dutch Republic, however, had a very different experience. As a result of the Protestant Reformation and political developments, the kingdoms of the British Isles and provinces of the Northern Netherlands became, in the latter half of the sixteenth century, officially Protestant lands. Reduced to the status of dissenters, Catholics lost control over the old parish churches and saw the closure of monasteries and convents. The Mass was outlawed, as were many other Catholic religious practices. Catholic priests had to be trained abroad, and those who returned to their homelands, a tiny number compared to the clerical contingents of pre-Reformation days, faced imprisonment or even death. Lay Catholics encountered difficulties over education, marriage, inheritance, burial, and other matters. Access to the sacraments, crucial for salvation, became problematic. Catholic elites were largely (though not always completely) excluded from political office, while the political loyalty of all Catholics was constantly under question.

The history of Catholics living in Protestant lands (as of Protestants living in Catholic ones) has always fallen outside the mainstream of early modern religious history. It does not fit neatly into the story of either the Protestant Reformation or the Counter-Reformation, while the elimination, rather than survival, of such groups figures in histories that trace the gradual 'confessionalisation' of European society in the wake of those two great upheavals. In fact, the history of religious minorities has generally been a subject of concern primarily to latter-day members of those minorities, who search it for keys to their own identity and place in the world. This lack of integration and of broader scholarly interest has had regrettable effects. Speaking of England, but in words that apply almost as well to the Netherlands, Christopher Haigh has bemoaned the fact that 'the study of Catholic history and literature is still an intellectual backwater, mainly worked at by Catholics who publish in house journals'.[2] The resulting historiography has typically had several characteristics. It has been unremittingly national, explaining the survival of Catholicism through the unique course of events and circumstances in a particular land. Thus, for example, L.G. Rogier sought to explain the religious map of the Netherlands, pinpointing the factors that explained why efforts to 'Protestantise' Dutch society succeeded or failed in different parts of the Netherlands.[3] The historiography has also had a clerical bias, constructing its story primarily through official, ecclesiastic documents and casting the Catholic missionary clergy as its heroes. Often unselfconsciously, it has incorporated clerical norms and definitions, as did John Bossy when he defined the English Catholic community, restricting its members to those persons who refused to conform in any way to the Protestant Church of England. By concentrating on heroes and stoical victims, the martyrs and recusants, historians lost sight of those who adopted other strategies for dealing with persecution.[4] Finally, traditional historiography has cast the Catholic minorities of these lands, especially the laity, not as shapers of their own history but as passive victims, emphasising and sometimes exaggerating the persecution to which they were subjected. There has prevailed what Willem Frijhoff calls a '*schuilkerk* mentality', referring to the semi-clandestine churches in which Dutch Catholics formerly worshiped, conceived by their descendants as cramped, inglorious, and wholly unsatisfactory.

If this is how past work on the history of Catholic minorities in Britain and the Netherlands has been framed, it is not the tenor of current research. This volume reaps a few fruits from a harvest of new work being completed. It effects a rupture with the old historiographic patterns, first by adopting a comparative perspective, examining side by side the experience of British (primarily English) and Dutch Catholics. In this way the volume probes and tests the idea that what Christine Kooi has called 'minority Catholicism' was a distinct type of early modern Catholicism, fundamentally the same in different lands.[5] Generalising a step further, this comparative approach offers insights into the effects of minority status, legal sanctions, and, in some cases, persecution not just on Catholics but on religious communities generally. What happens to religious culture when a community is forced to worship in semi-clandestine fashion? If persecution subjects a community to obvious dangers, what more subtle ones does toleration bring? How do minorities avoid assimilation and assure the continuance of their beliefs and practices down the generations? What political strategies do they deploy on local, regional, and national levels? In answering these questions, we see British and Dutch Catholics not just adapting reactively to circumstances beyond their control, but making deliberate choices and shaping, in part, their own destinies. At the same time, this volume places the experience of British and Dutch Catholics in a broader context. For in fact, neither community was isolated from developments in officially Catholic lands. On the contrary, both had intimate contacts abroad, especially with the Spanish Netherlands, which formed, as it were, the church militant's spearhead into northern Europe. Both communities were also touched by the international reform movements associated most particularly with the Jesuits and the Council of Trent.

Legally, the position of Catholics in Britain and the Netherlands was very different. In England, all subjects of the crown were deemed to be members of the Church of England, so that a refusal to attend that church automatically involved breaking the law. Labelled 'recusants', those who stayed away from services were subject to stiff fines and potentially, after 1593, to banishment. Catholics who satisfied the law by occasional attendance (known as 'occasional conformity') were targeted in 1606 when James I and parliament extended the requirement of church attendance to include annual Communion. Meanwhile, those who refused to repudiate the spiritual authority of the popes were deemed guilty of treason. In the Dutch Republic, by contrast, membership in the official Reformed Church remained always voluntary. Indeed, the Reformed Church itself put obstacles in the way of potential members, demanding of them (albeit with varying strictness) knowledge of doctrine, unimpeachable morals, and willingness to submit to the discipline administered by local consistories. No law required membership in the church, even of public office holders, who had only to be 'supporters' or 'adherents' of the Reformed religion, a standard that could be satisfied by attendance at sermons without a person taking Communion. For the rest of the population, such attendance was optional, as was recourse to Reformed ministers for the rites of baptism and marriage: except in Zeeland, Drenthe, and the Ommelanden of Groningen, dissenters had the option of being married in a civil ceremony. These facts begin to explain why, around the middle of the seventeenth century, there were fewer Catholics in England than in the Republic (although it should be noted that it difficult to establish Catholic numbers in both countries). Bossy estimated that English Catholics only numbered some 60,000, amounting to little over 1 per cent of the total population, yet since he restricted his estimate to recusant Catholics, the actual figure may have been considerably higher.[6] Even taking that into account, it is evident that English Catholics were a much smaller minority than were the Catholic population in the Netherlands: Dutch Catholics may have constituted a third of the Republic's population. Of course, these figures varied enormously by region, and the Dutch figures include the Generality Lands, which, as Charles de Mooij shows, formed a special case. Excluding them, a rough estimate would put the number of Catholics in the seven United Provinces around 1650 at about 300,000.[7]

In a way in which Dutch Catholics never did, English Catholics had to violate the law in order simply to be Catholics. They confronted this quandary from the earliest years of Elizabeth's reign and it only grew sharper in the decades immediately following. As a consequence, there arose among them an intense debate, some of it echoed in printed texts, concerning the limits of conformity and obedience. The notion that a sovereign could legitimately order some of the externals of religious worship, and that loyalty to ruler and realm required at least a degree of outward conformity, commanded the support of most Englishmen and women, including some Catholics. Nor were Catholic clergy as unrelenting on this point in private, as confessors, as their public stance suggested. Ironically, however, the resulting phenomenon of the 'church papist' only added fuel to the vehement anti-popery that developed among the English public during the reigns of Elizabeth I and James I.[8] It gave plausibility to the widespread fear that the greatest threat to England's Protestant establishment came from within, from a hidden 'fifth column' of church members who at heart were actually papists. Exacerbating this fear in the following decades was the suspicion that Charles I and subsequently Charles II (both married, as James I had been, to Catholic queens) were themselves closet papists. The threat posed by the openly Catholic James II was of course more blatant, and after the Glorious Revolution there was always, until 1766, a Catholic claimant to the throne from the house of Stuart. Throughout the seventeenth and into the eighteenth centuries, then, English Protestants continued to fear, and English Catholics to hope for, a restoration of Catholicism by its domestic champions. In the Netherlands, by contrast, the threat or promise of a restoration of Catholicism seemed to come from forces outside the polity: first the Spanish army, later the French. And while the fear among Protestants lingered long after their doomsday scenarios lost any likelihood, anti-popery was never the driving force in Dutch politics that it was in English. Not even in 1629 or 1672, when Catholic armies invaded the Republic, did Dutch rioters target Catholics, although there was an isolated outbreak of anti-Catholic rioting in Leeuwarden in 1687 in the wake of the Revocation of the Edict of Nantes, which stirred a wave of anti-Catholic sentiment among Dutch Protestants. The year 1734 saw the first 'panic fear' about Catholic plotting in the Republic since the early years of the Revolt, whereas seventeenth-century England was swept repeatedly by such.[9]

In terms of official persecution, Catholic laypeople had a harder time of it in England than in the Netherlands. In the former, some laypeople were imprisoned or even executed for their faith; rich recusants might have their property sequestrated, while many more paid crippling fines. By the 1610s, the

English Exchequer was treating recusants as a convenient source of revenue, to be squeezed – but not to the point that they would be so discomfited that their number, and hence their yield, might drop sharply. In the Netherlands Catholic laypeople seldom had to fear more than fines, though these were often substantial enough. In the decentralised polity of the Republic, it was local sheriffs and bailiffs who profited from a Catholic presence. Raids on illegal Catholic services provided them opportunities to slap heavy fines on those attending, and even heavier ones on the person in whose house (or barn or warehouse) services were held. Over time, such irregular strikes tended to be replaced by a system of annual 'recognition payments', in exchange for which Catholic congregations were usually left in peace. In both Britain and the Netherlands, however, persecution was targeted first and foremost at priests, who were branded professional agents of a foreign prince, namely the pope. Of the more than 260 Catholics executed in post-Reformation England, no fewer than 216 were priests.[10] Invariably, they were executed for treason, though in most cases their only real offence had been to practise and promote their faith. Given the monarch's position as Supreme Governor of the Church of England, it is perhaps not surprising that many more priests were executed in England than in the Netherlands, where even the head of the Holland mission, Apostolic Vicar Sasbout Vosmeer, was allowed discreetly to slip away when caught presiding over a Catholic service in Delft.[11] Only in the early, precarious years of the Revolt against Spain were any Dutch Catholics, lay or clerical, executed for religious or political offences. By the latter half of the seventeenth century, some Dutch magistrates routinely approved the appointment of Catholic pastors, having a large, if informal, say over their selection.

The fact remained that, in both England and the Republic, the Reformation stripped the Catholic Church of its privileges, powers, and wealth; destroyed (or in England appropriated) its institutional structure; and turned the country, from a Roman perspective, into mission territory.[12] Historians debate the degree to which the post-Reformation Catholic Church in England was a continuation of its Marian predecessor or was built *de novo* by missionary priests trained at seminaries on the Continent, chiefly at Douai and St Omer.[13] At any rate, it is clear that in both England and the Republic a large segment of the Catholic secular clergy longed, after the Reformation, for a restoration of the old episcopal hierarchy with its full traditional powers. This desire set secular clergy on a collision course with Jesuits and other regulars, who embraced the missionary character of their enterprise and took what advantage they could of the institutional vacuum to operate as effectively – seculars would say opportunistically – as possible. In England, especially the southern half of the country, seculars and regulars competed for the patronage of aristocratic and gentry families, whom they lived with and served as resident chaplains.[14] This clash escalated to dangerous proportions in the Netherlands, where it took on a doctrinal and spiritual dimension when most secular clergy embraced Jansenism, with its austere, predestinarian piety. Eventually it resulted in a formal schism, the Jansenist clergy electing in 1723 an archbishop of Utrecht who lacked papal mandate and was subsequently excommunicated by Rome.[15] How lay Catholics felt about and responded to this clash is a subject historians have little studied.

Surprisingly understudied also are the roles of the Jesuits and of Catholic nobles in the Netherlands in patronising and protecting the Catholic mission. Indeed, we need to know much more about the finances and patronage of the Catholic Church in the Republic generally. Clearly, in both England and the Republic, Catholic clergy were dependent on the laity in ways they were not in Catholic countries. According to Michael Mullett, that dependence made it impossible for clergy in England to fulfil the role laid out for them by the Council of Trent. An oversupply of priests may well have produced what Mullett calls a clerical proletariat in some parts of the country.[16] Yet a shortage was the rule in England, and this was even worse in the Netherlands. At their peak, around 1640, English priests numbered around 750, compared to between 400 and 500 serving a Catholic population possibly five times as large in the territory of the Holland mission. Charles Parker, by contrast, suggests that the very factors that made the clergy so dependent – the destruction, with the Reformation, of ecclesiastic institutions and the seizure of funds – also removed many obstacles to reform. Parker sees at work in the Netherlands a process which he calls 'cooperative confessionalization', in which clergy and laity cooperate to (re)build a Catholic Church that in some respects was, paradoxically, more Tridentine than in Catholic countries.[17] Judith Pollmann holds a similar view, as does Alexandra Walsham writing about England. These and other scholars now question the conventional image of a Catholic Church suffering in Protestant lands a sort of 'martyrdom' that left it incapacitated.[18]

Among the laity on whom Catholic clergy depended in Britain and the Netherlands were women, and in the latter country a special category of women known as 'spiritual maidens' (*geestelijke maagden*) came in the seventeenth century to play roles in Catholic life whose importance can scarcely be exaggerated.[19] *Kloppen* or *klopjes*, as the women were colloquially called, went from door to door alerting Catholics when Mass would be held; they catechised children, cared for the poor, visited the sick, made liturgical garments, sang at services, adorned and cleaned *schuilkerken*, and in fact also donated substantial sums of money and other gifts. Remaining celibate but forming no religious order, they lived either with their families or in groups. Numbering by 1700 over 5,000, they had no counterpart in England, where it was, rather, the wives who ran aristocratic and gentry households who seem to have been, at least through the 1620s, the most active patrons and supporters of the missionary priests. Many elite families in England were headed by a man who, to protect the family, conformed publicly to the

Church of England, while other members of the household, under the direction of a resident priest, practised privately the Catholic faith. Anecdotal evidence suggests a similar pattern may have prevailed in the Netherlands within some Catholic patrician families. Whether the role of *mater familias* ever amounted in this context to what Bossy termed a 'matriarchy' has rightly been questioned.[20] Nevertheless, the dependence of both English and Dutch priests on women must have had significant effects on the authority, role, and gender identity of both women and priests. In southern England in particular, Catholicism retained, during the entire seventeenth century, a seigneurial character, protected – and perhaps constrained – by the elite households that nurtured it.[21] In the Netherlands, by contrast, priests may always have depended on elite families, often their own, for financial support, but over time, as *schuilkerken* were constructed and coteries of *kloppen* gathered, they tended to become increasingly independent. Boards of laymen – not women – were established for the governance of the stations that replaced the old, pre-Reformation parishes and for the administration of Catholic poor relief. At least, this was the case in Dutch cities; much less is known about the situation in the countryside, a historiographic state of affairs opposite to that for England, where we are much better informed about rural than about urban Catholicism.

For Catholics in both the Dutch Republic and England, the Southern Netherlands formed a crucial point of contact with the wider Catholic world. Soon after Queen Elizabeth's accession in 1558, Catholics from England started to settle in the Netherlands. Scholars went to Louvain and Douai, where Philip II had founded a university in 1562 and where the English set up their own college in 1568, while laypeople were scattered over the prosperous Flemish and Brabantine cities. Much affected by the violence and devastation of the Revolt of the Netherlands, English and Irish Catholics were to remain a fixture in the Southern Netherlandish landscape through the remainder of the early modern period. For Catholics in the rebel territories of the Netherlands, the south took on key importance after all the United Provinces banned Catholic worship. Whereas many of the earliest refugees from the North had gone to Cologne, from 1585 northern Catholics increasingly looked to the Southern Netherlands for support.

Especially during the reign of the Archdukes Albert and Isabella (1598–1633), when a measure of calm and prosperity returned to the Habsburg Netherlands, Catholics from the British Isles and the Dutch Republic came to rely on these territories in a number of ways.[22] First, from 1596 until 1622 both the British and Netherlandish mission territories were governed from Brussels by apostolic nuncios, starting with Ottavio Mirto Frangipani, who acted in close cooperation with the Archdukes and who shaped much of the new arrangements that were made to try to keep Catholic life in the missions going. The provincials of the regular priests who worked in the mission territories also resided in the Southern Netherlands. Second, the territories functioned as a training centre for Catholic youngsters and especially, also, for new priests. Finally, believers in mission territories relied for much of their reading on the presses of Douai, Louvain and Antwerp, which in any case were supplying much of Catholic Europe with Missals, breviaries and other ecclesiastical print.

While a propagandist like Richard Verstegan, an English refugee of Netherlandish descent, worked for both Dutch and British Catholic audiences, the exile communities did not have as much to do with each other as one might expect.[23] This was partly because the English remained oriented towards Douai, while for the Dutch and Irish it was Louvain that supplied them with educational opportunities and new priests for the mission. More so than the English and Irish, who founded a range of religious houses of their own, Dutch believers with a monastic vocation simply joined existing religious communities of Flemish speakers. And while plots and plans to re-Catholicise both mission territories were being hatched in Brussels corridors, British soldiers played a much more prominent part in Habsburg armies than Dutch ones seem to have done. Too little is known as yet about lay migration to the Habsburg Netherlands. While a major project in Ghent is trying to survey the English presence in the Habsburg Netherlands – and finding many more people than first expected – information about Irish and Dutch migration is as yet mostly anecdotal.[24] While many Dutch Catholics were educated in the South, we know only of some prominent families who settled there permanently. The patrician Cornelis van Veen fled Leiden in 1572; when he returned to his native city, he left three of his sons behind in Brabant. The best known of these, the painter Otto van Veen, was never to settle in the North again, although he maintained contact with his hyper-Catholic kin in the Republic.[25] Although his father had been a prominent supporter of the Revolt, the Dordrecht patrician Jan Grijph Rochusz decided to move to Mechelen in the early seventeenth century and raise his young family there.[26] But even Dutch Catholics who did not migrate might nevertheless benefit from the proximity of the Catholic Habsburg lands. Catholics who lived nearby regularly crossed the borders in search of religious services that were no longer available at home. Marc Wingens has described frequent pilgrimages into Habsburg territories, while others might make the journey to go to school, be confirmed, or just hear Mass.[27]

Catholics who lived further away from the borders were, of course, not so lucky. One of the key problems for most Catholics in the Republic, as for those in England, was to retain regular access to the sacraments. In places without a resident priest, Mass was a special occasion, and there were only limited opportunities to receive baptism or make one's confession. Nevertheless, the spiritual difficulties this situation presented to believers may have been less dramatic than was assumed by earlier generations of historians. After all, Catholic teaching provided all sorts of special solutions for people who found themselves without a priest – in emergencies laypeople (or indeed Reformed ministers) could offer valid baptisms to newborn children, while it was also possible to take Communion 'spiritually', for instance. Recent historiography, moreover, has emphasised that laypeople without clerical support found alternative ways to worship. Walsham has explored the importance in England of new forms of domestic piety, which were sustained by books, songs, and private or family prayer, as well as the appropriation of elements in the natural landscape to create forms of sacred space to replace the parish church.[28] In the Netherlands we also find the use of such alternative sacred places; just as in England, holy wells, ruined chapels, and holy sites that were stripped of sacred imagery or object continued to appeal strongly to Catholic believers. For those who could not physically travel, some clerical authors promoted spiritual pilgrimages on which meditative exercises, prayers, and hymns marked the steps to a sacred destination. More simply, there were the prayer cards and cheap devotional books imported from the Southern Netherlands.

As Walsham has noted, the need to practise one's faith individually may actually have encouraged a type of interiorisation of religion that scholars have often associated with typical Counter-Reformation piety. Yet, whereas scholars like Bossy have emphasised that the Counter-Reformation turned against the family and the household as religious units, it is quite evident that in both England and the Netherlands the household also remained central to Catholic worship. While this may have to do with the special circumstances in the mission territories, it may also point to a general need to revisit Bossy's ideas on the relationship between communal and individual faith.[29] That is not to say, of course, that all of this spiritual activity met with clerical approval. Priests were understandably keen to assert their own sacerdotal indispensability. Yet most accepted that special conditions applied in the mission territories. Thus, the introduction of a Netherlandish songbook explained that the author had collected vernacular songs about saints and for feast days

> not so that people may sing them in the Lutheran manner during the service instead of the general Latin liturgy, no not at all. But in places in Holland or elsewhere where people are gathered without a priest or outside the normal service, where no Gregorian chant is sung or heard, the laypeople who don't know Latin may sing them for edification.[30]

Both in England and in the Netherlands Catholics strongly resented the takeover by Protestants of the parish churches. The English believers who were forced to attend those churches after the Reformation often considered the space to be contaminated, and felt themselves to be soiled when they had to attend services there. Dutch Catholics had a more ambiguous relationship to their former churches. Not only did they continue to bury their dead there, but because the Reformed churches did to some extent also function as a service centre for the whole community, the local minister was expected to perform the baptism of Catholic children and to marry people of all faiths. Netherlandish Catholics therefore continued to have a stake in church space, a sentiment which manifested itself in surprisingly long-lived hopes and fantasies about the repossession of 'their' churches, and which continued even when Catholics had already acquired new buildings.[31]

Some community life could, of course, be sustained in private homes and, when Catholics were fortunate, they had purpose-built places in which to gather for worship. Only some people had access to the foreign embassy chapels in London and The Hague, yet the family chapels in English and Dutch country houses were often also opened to trusted Catholic neighbours. In many Dutch cities, moreover, private houses and warehouses were refurbished and transformed into *schuilkerken*, the largest of which might seat several hundred people. Although it is evident that Catholics in both England and the Republic joined the confraternities and sodalities that were a central feature of Counter-Reformation community life, their functioning is yet to be researched, as are other aspects of Catholic community formation. A study by Michael Questier of the role of the Sussex Viscounts of Montague and their networks, offers an important example of how the study of Catholic community life can be attempted.[32]

Available evidence suggests that, even if Catholic piety was perforce often practised alone or in family settings, there nevertheless developed a common minority culture, or perhaps we should say minority cultures. There was considerable diversity among Catholics, not only between devotees of the Jansenist secular clergy, on the one hand, and of the Jesuits and other regular clergy, on the other. Although they require further study, cultural differences seem to have arisen also between Catholics in different regions of the Republic, based partly on the general cultural orientation of the different regions, and partly on the strength of the Catholic community relative to other local religious groups. Controversially, some historians have posited similar cultural differences in England between northern and southern, urban and rural Catholics.[33] In any case, Dutch and English Catholics were both also clearly united by common traits. Unsurprisingly, much attention among Catholics was focused on the past and emphasised the antiquity of their church. Catholic antiquarians worked tirelessly to document past splendours and old claims to ecclesiastical authority.[34] The apostolic vicars in the Netherlands strongly supported the cults of saints Boniface and Willebrord, who had first brought Christianity to the Low Countries, turning these 'national' saints into an instrument for competing with the Jesuits and their Marian predilections. Among English and Welsh Catholics too, there was a reviving interest in native saints like St Patrick and St Winifred, as well as in key figures like St Augustine, and his conversion of England.[35] More important for Catholic identity even than the history of the church were its martyrs. A number of Catholic priests in the Netherlands, usually regular priests, had met their deaths at the hands of 'beggar' (*Geuzen*) armies during the Revolt.[36] Many of these victims were commemorated in the martyrologies of Willem Estius and Petrus Opmeer, while the spot where the martyrs of Gorinchem had died became a focus for Catholic commemorative devotions that were said, in 1615, to have continued uninterruptedly since 1572; a miraculous plant that grew on the site also was taken on a tour through Holland and Utrecht. Yet it was really only after their bodies were disinterred in 1618 and taken to the Habsburg Netherlands that a series of spectacular miracles associated with the martyrs was reported.[37] Generally, the importance of Dutch martyrs pales into insignificance when compared with the veneration surrounding the English and Irish martyrs who lost their lives during the reigns of Elizabeth and James. Any priest working in England during this period knew that he risked dying a traitor's painful death, and potential martyrdom formed an essential part of clerical identity and preparation for the mission. When the worst happened, believers hastened to reap the salvific benefits, immediately collecting the blood, bones, and other relics of those who died so infamously at Tyburn and other places of execution.[38] For Catholics in England, more than for those in the Netherlands, martyrdom became a core element of minority identity.

As far as material culture was concerned, Dutch Catholics enjoyed the freedom to possess devotional objects at home, while they also felt secure enough to invest substantial sums in paintings, sculptures, and liturgical silver for their *schuilkerken*. Although the interiors and decoration of such churches have been studied extensively by Xander van Eck, little scholarly attention has as yet been paid to the wider spectrum of Catholic objects and images that Dutch Catholics used in their devotions, which formed a tangible link to the culture of international Catholicism.[39] In England, by contrast, where the possession of rosaries, crucifixes, and images of the Agnus Dei was much more problematic, Richard Williams, Walsham and others have started to consider a much wider range of material objects in their thinking about Catholic culture.[40]

That such objects were not always put to orthodox use has been known for a long time. Both in the Netherlands and in England, there was simply not enough systematic clerical supervision to be able to root out the use of devotional objects and sacramentals for purposes that the post-Tridentine church deemed 'superstitious'. Many priests in the missions, moreover, argued that to root out popular religious customs would alienate believers who were vulnerable to being lured away by the Protestants.[41] In the Netherlands, some of the deep-rooted disagreements between secular and regular priests revolved around the extent to which one could demand of such believers compliance with all the new norms. Yet historiography since the 1990s concerning the rest of Catholic Europe suggests it would be a mistake to see the survival of such practices as a sign of 'backwardness' that was typical for these mission territories alone. A new understanding of the difficulties encountered by Catholic reformers in Catholic states has done much to obliterate the alleged differences with the situation in England and the Republic.[42] Indeed, some would argue that the minority status of English and Dutch Catholics actually assisted the inculcation and acceptance of some Tridentine norms, in part because it encouraged a very conscious reflection on the faith by Catholic laypeople.

If some hybridity between old and new Catholicism was thus not unusual, the situation that prevailed in the mission territories was undoubtedly extreme. This seems particularly evident in the areas within these composite states where Catholics actually formed a majority of the population: Ireland and the so-called Generality Lands of the Republic. In both areas, the rejection of Protestantisation was strongly linked to political motives. In Ireland, both the Old English elite and the Gaelic Irish rejected interference from the crown. While the latter wished to impose a Protestant Reformation on Ireland, it never offered enough material and logistical support to make the conversion of all Irish subjects a real possibility. Coupled with the crown's encouragement of Protestant immigration and the Plantations, this led to a confessionalisation of political divisions, with consequences that have reached into the twenty-first century.[43] In most of the Generality Lands too, Protestantisation remained a dead letter. Although both Brabant and Limburg had seen plenty of support for Protestant heresies in the sixteenth century, the Counter-Reformation that got under way after 1585, when these areas were under Habsburg control, had been extremely effective; moreover, much of the Archdukes' political strategy hinged on presenting themselves as the guarantors of Catholicity.[44] When the Republic finally seized these territories from the Habsburgs around 1630, it decided not to give them the same political rights as the other provinces, but proclaimed that the States General were to rule them directly. Since the Habsburg Archdukes had made many concessions to provincial political elites and privileges, the Brabanters and Limburgers saw few benefits in the new arrangements and, just as in Ireland, the political divisions became confessionalised. When much of the local elite refused to convert, Protestant officials were imposed from above. It proved impossible, though, to effect a real Protestantisation of public life. Catholic priests worked almost openly, while a few independent lordships, like the County of Megen and Land of Ravenstein, offered safe havens for monastic refugees, schools, and pilgrims.[45] While the Catholic minorities in England and the seven United Provinces were mostly busy affirming their loyalty, or at least their harmlessness, in Ireland and the Generality Lands hostility to the state became a fact of life, with the populations occasionally, and at times violently, showing their disdain for Protestant outsiders. Some Protestant ministers charged with rural parishes found life in these quasi-colonised lands positively dangerous.

Even in England and the seven provinces, aggressive behaviour was not unknown, especially in locales where Catholics constituted a majority of the population, as they did in south-west Lancashire and the countryside of North Holland. Catholics in the Republic had a sense that the banishment of their faith from the public sphere was a product of purely political calculations on the part of regents, and they blamed the greed of local sheriffs for much of the sporadic harassment they suffered. They responded to raids on their services accordingly, with indignation. Both in England and the Republic, Catholic elites resented their exclusion from government office, but this exclusion simply could not be enforced consistently throughout the Netherlands, as it left too few 'qualified' persons to perform critical functions in certain locales. According to W.J. Sheils, Catholic elites retained positions of responsibility in English communities such as Egton and Madeley for similar reasons. Still, the legal exclusions Catholics suffered in both lands did tilt the balance of their occupations. In the Netherlands, noble families lived off their estates, or turned to military careers; patricians sent their sons to study medicine, or theology. The picture is less clear further down the social scale, but it does seem that Dutch Catholics were over-represented in some occupations, like painting, and under-represented in others, like textile manufacture.

In daily life, relations between Protestants and Catholics seem on the whole to have been amicable. However much relations varied by locale, 'getting on' and 'getting along' seem to have been more the rule than the exception in both England and the Republic. There is much evidence from the Netherlands that people of different faiths commonly lived in the same neighbourhoods, belonged to the same guilds and associations, did business, celebrated, mourned, worked, and played together. This is undisputed for the early seventeenth century, when the boundaries between confessional groups were still somewhat blurred and many Dutch people had not made a firm and exclusive commitment to any one of the rival faiths.[46] To what extent this situation changed over the course of the seventeenth century is a current question among scholars. As discussed by Benjamin Kaplan, one possibility is that, at least in the sphere of marriage and family life, Protestants and Catholics tended by the end of the century to form endogamous, mutually exclusive groups.[47] Such a finding would accord with the indications we have for other European lands, where the late seventeenth and early eighteenth centuries saw the religious differences dividing Catholics and Protestants articulating themselves increasingly in the social and cultural spheres. Sheils finds a similar tendency among Catholics in Egton and York, who by some point in the eighteenth century had 'settled into a denominational lifestyle alongside but somewhat apart from the Protestant establishment'. This very partial segregation does not seem either to have caused or been caused by some worsening of relations. To the contrary, it may have reflected, if anything, a greater acceptance of difference.[48]

However amicable most day-to-day interactions were, Catholics in Britain and the Netherlands remained discriminated minorities living in officially Protestant lands. Throughout the period studied in this book, their experiences were very unlike those of Catholics elsewhere in Europe. In some respects Catholic life in the mission territories was indeed backward and backward looking, yet this book also demonstrates that it was possible to accomplish much of the spiritual agenda of Trent without the institutional reforms and centralisation that have so often been seen as the *sine qua non* of Catholic reform. If the mission territories have a lesson for students of the Counter-Reformation, therefore, it is not to underestimate the ability of laypeople and their priests at the grass roots to forge religious change.

Notes

1 We wish to thank Professor Walsham for her very helpful comments on an earlier draft of this chapter.
2 Christopher Haigh, 'Catholicism in early modern England. Bossy and beyond', *Historical Journal* 45 (2002), 481–94, 493.
3 L.J. Rogier, *Geschiedenis van het katholicisme in Noord-Nederland in de zestiende en zeventiende eeuw*, 2 vols (Amsterdam, 1946).
4 John Bossy, *The English Catholic community 1570–1850* (New York: Oxford University Press, 1976); Alexandra Walsham, *Church papists. Catholicism, conformity and confessional polemic in early modern England*, Royal Historical Society, Studies in History, 68 (Woodbridge: Boydell, 1993).
5 Christine Kooi, 'Sub Jugo Haereticorum. Minority Catholicism in Early Modern Europe', in Kathleen M. Comerford and Hilman Pabel (eds), *Early modern Catholicism. Essays in honour of John W. O'Malley, S.J.* (Toronto: University of Toronto Press, 2001), pp. 147–62.
6 Bossy, *English Catholic community 1570–1850*, pp. 182–94; Walsham, *Church papists*.
7 Willem Frijhoff and Marijke Spies, *1650. Hard-won unity* (Assen: Royal Van Gorcum, 2004), p. 352; Marit Monteiro, *Geestelijke maagden. Leven tussen klooster en wereld in Noord-Nederland gedurende de zeventiende eeuw* (Hilversum: Verloren, 1996), pp. 53–7. Exceptionally, Jonathan Israel argues that Catholics comprised fewer than 20 per cent of the total population of the Republic, which would put their number at no more than 400,000. Jonathan I. Israel, *The Dutch Republic. Its rise, greatness, and fall 1477–1806* (Oxford: Clarendon Press, 1995), p. 642.
8 Peter Lake, 'Antipopery. The structure of a prejudice', in Richard Cust and Ann Hughes (eds), *Conflict in early Stuart England. Studies in religion and politics, 1603–1642* (London: Longman, 1989), pp. 72–106.
9 Lake, 'Antipopery'; Robin Clifton, 'The popular fear of Catholics during the English Revolution', *Past and Present* 52 (1971), 23–55; Willem Frijhoff, 'Prophecies in society. The panic of 1734', in Frijhoff, *Embodied belief. Ten essays on religious culture in Dutch history* (Hilversum, 2002), pp. 181–214.
10 Geoffrey Nuttall, 'The English martyrs 1535–1680. A statistical review', *Journal of Ecclesiastical History* 22 (1971), 191–2.
11 A. Th. van Deursen, *Plain lives in a golden age. Popular culture, religion and society in seventeenth-century Holland* (Cambridge: Cambridge University Press, 1991), p. 291.
12 In the northern Netherlands the one institution of ecclesiastic governance to survive was the chapter of the Haarlem cathedral, with which the apostolic vicars worked closely, usually in a

spirit of cooperation.
13 Bossy, *English Catholic Community*; Chris Haigh,'The continuity of Catholicism in the English Reformation', *Past and Present* 93 (1981), 37–69; M.C. Questier,'What happened to English Catholicism after the English Reformation', *History* 85 (2000), 28–47.
14 Alexandra Walsham, 'Translating Trent. English Catholicism and the Counter Reformation', *Historical Research* 78 (2001), 288–310; Michael Questier, *Catholicism and community in early modern England. Politics, aristocratic patronage and religion, c. 1550–1640* (Cambridge: Cambridge University Press, 2006).
15 On this clash, see for example the recent study by Gian Ackermans, *Herders en huurlingen. Bisschoppen en priesters in de Republiek (1663–1705)* (Amsterdam: Prometheus/Bert Bakker, 2003).
16 See Michael Mullet's chapter in this volume.
17 See the chapter by Charles Parker in this volume.
18 R. Po-chia Hsia, *The world of Catholic renewal, 1540–1770* (Cambridge: Cambridge University Press, 1998), chapter 5; see also Walsham, 'Translating Trent', as well as Charles H. Parker *Faith on the margins. Catholics and Catholicism in the Dutch Golden Age* (Cambridge MA: Harvard University Press, 2008), and the chapters by Alexandra Walsham and Judith Pollmann in this volume.
19 See Joke Spaans' chapter in this volume and Monteiro, *Geestelijke maagden*.
20 See the chapter by Marie Rowlands in this volume and Bossy, *English Catholic Community 1570–1850*, p. 153.
21 Haigh,'The continuity of Catholicism'; but see also Michael C. Questier, *Catholicism and community*.
22 See the chapters by Paul Arblaster and Claire Walker in this volume.
23 Paul Arblaster, *Antwerp and the world. Richard Verstegan and the international culture of Catholic Reformation* (Leuven: Leuven University Press, 2004).
24 The project is entitled 'Over het Kanaal. De Zuidelijke Nederlanden als toevluchtsoord voor Engelse bannelingen, 1603–1660' and is being run by Liesbeth De Frenne under supervision of René Vermeir.
25 L.J. Rogier, *Geschiedenis van het katholicisme in Noord Nederland in de zestiende en zeventiende eeuw*, 3 vols (Amsterdam, 1946), II, 716–17; *Nieuw Nederlandch Biografisch Woordenboek*, ed. P.C. Molhuysen and P.J. Blok, 10 vols (Leiden, 1911–1937), VI, 1297ff.
26 Jan Griep (ed.),'Een Hollandse familie Grijp', http://home.planet.nl/~artrako/Nederlanden/Holland-NL.html.
27 Marc Wingens, *Over de grens. De bedevaart van katholieke Nederlanders in de zeventiende en achttiende eeuw* (Nijmegen, 1994).
28 See Alexandra Walsham's chapter in this volume and Walsham, 'Holywell. Contesting sacred space in post-Reformation Wales', in Will Coster and Andrew Spicer (eds), *Sacred space in early modern Europe* (Cambridge: Cambridge University Press, 2005), pp. 211–36; Alexandra Walsham "Domme preachers"? Post-reformation English Catholicism and the culture of print', *Past & Present*, 168 (2000), 72–123.
29 Walsham,'Translating Trent' and Walsham "Domme preachers"?'; John Bossy, *Christianity in the West, 1400–1700* (Oxford: Oxford University Press, 1985). For one such revision, see Marc R. Forster,'Domestic devotions and family piety in German Catholicism', in Benjamin J. Kaplan and Marc R. Forster (eds), *Family and piety in early modern Europe: essays in honour of Steven Ozment* (Aldershot, 2005), chapter 5.
30 Judith Pollmann 'Hey ho, let the cup go round! Singing for reformation in the sixteenth century', in Heinz Schilling and István György Tóth (eds), *Religion and cultural exchange in Europe, 1400–1700* (Cambridge: Cambridge University Press, 2007), pp. 294–316.
31 See Judith Pollmann's chapter in this volume.
32 Questier, *Catholicism and community*.
33 See for example Lisa McClain, *Lest we be damned. Practical innovation and lived experience among Catholics in Protestant England, 1559–1642* (New York, 2004).

34 See for example Margaret Aston, 'English ruins and English history. The dissolution and the sense of the past', *Journal of the Warburg and Courtauld Institutes* 36 (1973), 231–55; Richard Cust, 'Catholicism, antiquarianism and gentry honour. The writings of Sir Thomas Shirley', *Midland History* 23 (1998), 40–70. For a Netherlandish example see for example P.H.A.M Abels, 'Inleiding', in *Ignatius Walvis, Goudsche onkatolijke kerkzaken* (Delft: Eburon, 1999).
35 Willem Frijhoff, 'The function of the miracle in a Catholic minority. The United Provinces in the seventeenth century in his *Embodied belief*, pp. 111–36, at p. 130; Walsham, 'Holywell'.
36 Brad S. Gregory, *Salvation at stake. Christian martyrdom in early modern Europe* (Cambridge, MA: Harvard University Press, 1999), p. 274.
37 Frijhoff, 'The function of the miracle', pp. 131–2.
38 Anne Dillon, *The construction of martyrdom in the English Catholic community, 1535–1603* (Aldershot: Ashgate, 2002); Alan Ford, 'Martyrdom, history and memory in early modern Ireland', in Ian McBride (ed.), *History and memory in modern Ireland* (Cambridge: Cambridge University Press, 2001), pp. 43–68.
39 Xander van Eck, *Kunst, twist en devotie. Goudse katholieke schuilkerken, 1572–1795* (Delft: Eburon, 1994) and his chapter in this volume.
40 See the chapters by Richard Williams and Alexandra Walsham in this volume.
41 Raymond Gillespie. *Devoted people: belief and religion in early modern Ireland* (Manchester: Manchester University Press, 1997).
42 For example K.P. Luria, *Territories of grace. Cultural change in the seventeenth-century Diocese of Grenoble* (Berkeley, Oxford, 1991); M.R. Forster, *Catholic revival in the age of the baroque: religious identity in southwest Germany, 1550–1750* (Cambridge, 2001). For the Habsburg Netherlands, see C.E. Harline and E. Put, *A bishop's tale. Mathias Hovius among his flock in seventeenth-century Flanders* (New Haven, CT and London, 2000).
43 See the chapter by Ute Lotz-Heumann in this volume.
44 Luc Duerloo, 'Pietas Albertina. Dynastieke vroomheid en herbouw van het vorstelijk gezag', *Bijdragen en mededelingen betreffende de geschiedenis der Nederlanden* 112 (1997).
45 See the chapter by Charles de Mooij in this volume.
46 See for example H. van Nierop and R. Po-Chia Hsia (eds), *Calvinism and religious toleration in the Dutch Republic* (Cambridge: Cambridge University Press, 2002).
47 See Benjamin Kaplan's chapter in this volume.
48 See Bill Sheils' chapter in this volume, as well as Alexandra Walsham, *Charitable hatred. Tolerance and intolerance in England, 1500–1700* (Manchester: Manchester University Press, 2006), chapter 6.

Index

Aberdeen 124, 133
Affligem, abbey of 131
Allen, William 149, 237
Amersfoort 225
Amsterdam 48, 56–7, 59–62, 86, 91, 95, 97, 114, 124, 127, 190–3, 219, 223, 225, 227, 230
Anglican Church *see* Church of England
Antichrist 8, 109
Antwerp 11, 57, 126, 133–5, 141, 143, 145, 162, 164, 219, 225, 227, 238–9, 256
apostolic vicars 20, 22–5, 27, 90, 162, 186–8, 195–6, 202, 209, 258
    see also Rovenius (Philip), Vosmeer (Sasbout)
archbishops 71, 77, 129, 134, 144, 151, 177, 223, 254
archdioceses 22, 69, 123, 125
Archdukes (Albert of Austria and Isabella Clara Eugenia of Austria) 123–4, 132–134, 141–3, 158, 255, 260
Arentz, Cornelis 187–90, 192–3
Arleboutius, Paulus 84–5, 89, 93–4
armies 22, 56, 128, 131–4, 144–5, 157–8, 164, 169, 252, 256, 259
    see also Flanders, France, Spain, States General
Aspinwall, Mary 41–2
Augustinians 139, 144, 149
    canonesses/nuns 146–7, 150–1, 210
Austria 134–5

Babthorpe, family 144
Baker, Augustine 149, 205
Ban, Jan Albert 24, 221–2

banishment 126, 251
    of priests 19, 21, 91, 163, 194
baptism 55, 71, 73, 91, 93–4, 111–12, 134, 208, 212, 221, 251, 256–8
Battle, abbey of 104, 230
Bavaria 5, 113
Bedingfield, family 146
    Edmund 150
Beggars *see* Geuzen
beguinages see Beguines
Beguines 95, 162, 188, 221
Bell, James 44–5
Benedictines 5, 36, 40, 105, 113, 128, 131, 134, 142–51, 205, 207, 244
Bergen op Zoom 52, 54, 60–2, 158, 164
Berkhey, Johannes le Francq van 96–8
bishoprics *see* dioceses
bishops
    Catholic 10, 19–20, 22, 33, 35, 42, 80, 89, 106, 108, 111, 116, 125–6, 128, 131, 133–4, 157, 160, 162, 169, 192, 203, 205, 208–9, 211–12, 221
    Protestant 172–3, 176
Bloemaert
    Abraham 216, 219–21, 228
    Hendrik 221
Blundell
    family 146
    William 43–4, 112, 151
Bohemia 130, 164
books 7, 15, 25, 76, 88, 90, 104–18 *passim*, 126, 139–152 *passim*, 164, 191, 201–2, 205, 210–12, 235, 238–9, 257

Borromeo, Charles 201, 225
Bossy, John 18, 33, 35, 139–40, 250–1, 255, 257
Boxtel 156–7, 160
Brabant 85–6, 90, 123–4, 130–2, 156–7, 159–60, 162, 255–6, 260
　see also States Brabant
Bray, Jan de 223
Breda 128, 130–1, 163–4
bribes 21, 165
　see also fines, 'recognition money'
Bridgettines 127
Den Briel 125
Brock, Wouter 94
Brooke
　family 72, 74
　Sir Basil 72
Bruges 129, 133–5, 141, 145–7, 151, 162
Brussels 11, 128–30, 132–5, 141, 143–5, 147, 220, 255–6
Bucke, John 108–9, 238
Buckingham, Katherine Manners, dowager-duchess of 146
Buckinghamshire 148, 234
Burgundian 9, 123, 132
　cross 164
burial 62, 73, 84, 87, 93–9, 111–12, 145, 172, 176, 208, 249, 258
　see also cemeteries

Calvinism 1, 4, 9, 27, 48, 50–1, 56, 60, 73, 93–5, 114, 123, 127, 202
Calvinist Church *see* Reformed Church
Cambrai 125, 146, 149–50, 205
Campion, Edmund 7, 107
canon law 125, 134, 184, 188, 211
Capuchins 10
Carajaval, Luisa de 205
Carmelites 135, 146–7, 150, 227
Carthusians 40, 113, 131
catechising 24–5, 27, 126, 145, 148, 174, 184, 196, 201, 209–12, 254
Cathedral chapters 22, 132, 134, 222
　see also Haarlem (Cathedral chapter of)
Catholic Reformation 2, 5, 8–9, 18–20, 27–8, 34, 40, 43, 86, 89, 104, 106, 112–13, 115, 117, 139–42, 147, 149, 152, 158, 170, 178, 188, 194, 200–1, 207, 216, 219–22, 225, 228, 249, 257–8, 260, 262
　see also Trent (Council of)
Cats, Judocus 27, 222
Cecil, Robert 204
　Sir William, Lord Burghley 109, 112, 174, 231, 242
cemeteries 84–5, 94–7, 112, 176
censorship, 126–7, 249
Challoner, Richard, Bishop 43, 111
chapters *see* Cathedral chapters
charity 13, 23–4, 26–8, 40, 51–2, 62, 70, 103, 144, 159, 175, 189, 193–4, 211, 254–5
Charles I, King of England 142, 171, 203, 252
Charles II, King of England 252
Church
　of England, 3, 44, 70, 77, 94, 127, 151, 202, 250–1, 253, 255
　of Ireland 169–77
　of Rome *passim*
　see also Reformed Church
church buildings 2, 5, 12–13, 18, 84–99 *passim*, 103–118 *passim*, 144, 149, 156–9, 160–3, 176, 184–5, 190–1, 196, 202, 208, 215–228 *passim*, 249–50, 258
　see also hidden churches, house churches, parish churches
church papists 106, 110, 203, 252
church property
　loss of 2, 12–13, 19–20, 25, 27, 86, 94, 96, 98–9, 156, 158, 162, 172, 175, 258
　see also iconoclasm
churchwardens 24, 26, 69, 77, 85, 95, 172
churchyards 71, 73, 114, 118
Cistercians 112, 130, 162
Clement VIII, Pope 128
Clement X, Pope 115
Clement
　Caesar 134, 144–5
　Margaret 144
clergy, Catholic
　numbers 4, 20–1, 23, 27, 38, 142, 186–7, 207, 223, 254
　persecution of 163, 207, 253
　see also martyrs

quality of 10, 20, 23, 24, 33–46 *passim*, 125, 186
recruitment 183–97 *passim*
regular 23, 25, 33, 39, 129, 169–70, 187, 202, 212, 227, 253, 256, 258, 259
  see also under individual orders
relations with laity, 18–28 *passim*, 33–46 *passim*, 104, 106, 109, 116, 175, 183–4, 186, 206–7, 254
secular 9–10, 22–3, 25–6, 33, 39, 53, 79, 91, 104, 128–9, 142, 164, 169–70, 187, 202, 207, 209–10, 212, 253–4, 258–9
Cleves 161
Clitherow, Margaret 81, 109, 116, 203–4
colleges, Catholic 125, 127–30, 133–4, 140–5, 149, 151, 174, 178, 186–7, 193, 237, 255
  see also Rome (English College in), seminaries
Cologne 11, 20, 26, 128–9, 184, 187–90, 193, 255
communion, receiving of 104, 110, 190, 210, 212, 215, 251, 257
Compton census 72, 76
confessionalisation 7, 19, 28, 118, 169–73, 249, 254, 260
confirmation 89, 212
confraternities 42, 50, 91, 185, 195, 212, 258
  see also rosary (confraternities of the), sodalities
consistories, Reformed 53, 55, 95, 96, 98, 163, 165, 195, 255
Constable
  Barbara 205
  Thomas 79
convents 80, 116, 117, 130, 139, 162, 190, 201, 205, 210
conversion 6, 15, 22–3, 37, 39, 56, 60, 139, 164, 192, 195, 221, 259–60
Coughton Court 244–5
Counter-Reformation *see* Catholic Reformation
Cousebant, Nicolaas Wiggerts 187–90, 192–3
crosses 96–8, 110–12, 114, 206, 233, 237, 244

Delft 27, 131, 191, 253
Den Bosch 92–3, 96–7, 131–3, 160, 162, 164, 219–20
Derbyshire 110, 210, 236
Deventer 128
Devon 35–6
Dijck, Anthony van 134, 219, 227
diocesan structure 10, 22–3, 27, 104, 125
  see also archdioceses, dioceses, parishes
dioceses 20, 38, 76, 124–5, 162, 189, 221
  see also bishops
Dominicans 44, 46, 142, 145
Dordrecht 24, 53, 132, 256
Douai 11, 40, 125, 127–9, 135, 141–3, 145, 148–9, 151–2, 201–2, 206, 253, 255–6
Dover 152, 234
Drenthe 23, 52, 54, 132, 251
Dublin 168, 171, 174, 177
Dunkirk 147
Durham 37

East Riding 79
ecumenicity *see omgangsoecumene*
education 2, 5, 25, 50, 52, 80, 124, 139, 141–3, 144–6, 148, 151, 159, 162, 177, 174–5, 184, 189–92, 194–5, 197, 205, 211, 249, 256, 260
  see also colleges seminaries, universities
Eggius, Albert 20, 26, 192–3
Egton 69–71, 73–4, 261
Eikenduinen 87–8, 94, 98
elites 2–3, 14, 19, 57, 68, 103, 133, 171, 176, 193–4, 237, 245, 254, 260
  Catholic (lay) 20–5, 27–8, 35, 37, 77, 80, 131, 160, 175, 249, 255, 261
  Reformed/Protestant 81, 160
  women 25, 28
  see also gentry, nobles, noblewomen, regents
Elizabeth I, Queen of England 35, 72, 74–5, 103–4, 109, 113, 141–2, 150, 169, 171, 230–1, 233, 235–6, 239, 241, 244–5, 252, 255, 259
Ely 239, 244–5
English Mission 20, 24, 33–46 *passim*, 69, 78–9, 103–6, 109, 115–16, 118, 126–9, 134, 139–52 *passim*, 207, 209, 211–12, 254
Enkhuizen 56–9, 62, 125

268 INDEX

Essex 142, 232
   Robert Devereux, Earl of 204
Est (Estius), Willem van 7, 259
exile 44, 124–5, 127–134, 138–52 *passim*, 159, 174, 180, 235, 256–60

Fenn, John 144–5, 150
Fernyhalgh 114, 211
fines 21, 69, 77, 91, 94, 96, 103, 126, 160–1, 163, 171–2, 190, 194, 203–5, 251–3
   see also 'recognition money'
Flanders 123–35 *passim*, 142, 144–5, 157, 162, 219–20, 228, 255–6
   see also Southern Netherlands, States Flanders
France 5, 16, 68, 77, 94, 96, 125, 129, 132, 144, 171, 203, 205–6, 210, 216, 227
   invasion of Dutch Republic by 11, 22, 91, 98, 163–4, 252
   refuge in/support from 124, 127, 129–30, 135, 170, 178, 201
   see also Louis XIII, Louis XIV
Franciscans 10, 35, 142–5, 162, 164, 177, 190, 207, 212, 225, 227
   Third Order of 143, 195, 212
Franeker 94
fraternities *see* confraternities
freedom
   religious 4, 77–8, 105, 163, 183, 259
   of conscience 4, 20–1, 49, 89
   of worship 11, 21, 89, 91, 98
   see also tolerance
Friesland 4, 52, 90, 124, 133, 189
funeral *see* burial

Garnet, Henry 106–7, 149–51
Gelderland, Gelre 21, 25, 56, 123–4, 131, 159
Generality Lands 3, 15, 54, 56, 90–1, 96, 130, 156–66 *passim*, 177–8, 252, 260
   see also Overmaas (Lands of), States Brabant, States Flanders, States Limburg
gentry 23, 35–8, 69, 72–6, 78–80, 105, 141, 152, 168, 170, 189, 204, 206–9, 211, 231, 244, 253–4
   see also elites, nobles
Gerard, John 35, 37, 106, 117, 142, 150

Germany 4, 9, 19, 103, 123–5, 128, 130, 132, 135, 225
Geuzen 9, 20–1, 116, 259
Ghent 90, 131, 134, 141, 145–7, 150, 162, 222, 256
Gillow, George and Richard 39–40, 42
Girls' Home *see maagdenhuis*
Godwin, Elizabeth 139, 149
Goes 133
Gorinchem 259
Gother, John 43, 211
Gouda 91, 93, 225
Grave 163
Gravelines 40, 150
Grebber, Pieter de 216, 219, 221–3, 228
Greek
   cross 241, 244
   language 117, 239
Groenveld, Simon 50–3, 62
Groningen 23, 52, 128
   Ommelanden of 54, 251
Guilday, Peter 140–1
guilds 48–50, 55, 62, 77, 85, 97, 162, 164–5, 261

Haarlem 26, 51–2, 62, 89, 93, 124, 127–8, 131, 187–94, 219, 221–3, 225
   Cathedral chapter of 23–5, 128, 186, 190–3, 221–2, 225
   see also Ban (J.A.), Cats (Judocus), Eggius (Albert)
Habsburg Netherlands *see* Southern Netherlands
Habsburg, House of, rulers of the Low Countries 3, 113, 123–4, 126, 129, 132, 134–5, 157, 177, 256, 260
   see also Archdukes, Philip II
Haigh, Christopher 36, 140, 250
Haks, Donald 57–9
Hammersmith 210
Hampden, Mrs 201, 234–5
Hardwick 236, 244
Harlingen 24
Harvington 206, 232
Hebrew 117, 239
Heigham, John 143–4, 201–2
   Roger 148

INDEX

Heiloo 86, 88–9, 94, 113–14, 116
Helmond 90
Henrietta Maria, Queen of England 10, 76, 116
Henry VII, King of England 40
Henry VIII, King of England 114, 168–9, 234–6
Henry, Earl of Huntingdon 77–8
Hereford 110
Herefordshire 111
's-Hertogenbosch *see* Den Bosch
hidden churches *see* house chapels/churches
Holborn 75, 235
Holland 4, 21, 23–5, 27, 52, 56–8, 60, 62, 86, 89, 91, 96–7, 126–7, 133, 159, 189, 201–2, 206–7, 209, 257, 259, 261
    States of 56–7, 128
Holland Mission 7, 9–10, 20, 22–8, 90, 128–30, 134, 183–97 *passim*, 253–6
    see also Eggius (Albert), Rovenius (Philip), Vosmeer (Sasbout)
Holywell 115, 206–7
Honthorst, Gerard van 220–1
Hooft, Pieter Cornelisz 132
Hoogstraten 146
house chapels/churches 18, 48, 89–91, 105, 117, 160, 163, 174, 176, 184–5, 189–91, 196, 204, 207–8, 211, 217, 225, 230–3, 245–6, 250, 253–5, 258–9
    see also hidden churches
Howell, James 49–50
Hoxton 235, 246
Huguenots 16, 171
huiskerken see house chapels/churches
Hungary 130, 132, 135

iconoclasm 88, 94, 103, 114–15, 125, 232
indulgences 2, 27, 106, 109, 115, 150, 202, 241
Inquisition 3, 19, 249
intermarriage *see* mixed marriage
Ireland 3, 6, 10, 61, 76, 112–13, 115–16, 123–35 *passim*, 140, 142–4, 147–8, 151, 168–78 *passim*, 183, 255–6, 259–60
Italy 103, 132, 135, 206, 219–20, 228, 237, 246

Jacobites 10
James I, King of England 132, 230, 234, 251–2, 259

James II, King of England 79, 209, 252
Jansenism 5–6, 10, 98, 129, 135, 254, 258
Jansenius, Cornelius 131
Jesuits 5–6, 8–10, 15, 25, 27, 35–7, 43, 90, 105–6, 117, 130, 139, 142–5, 148–51, 164, 174–6, 202, 205, 207, 210, 212, 218, 220, 225, 234, 251, 254
    female institution *see* Ward (Mary)
    relations with secular clergy 23, 26, 162, 191–2, 253, 258
Jews 184–5

Kempis, Thomas à 109, 201
kerkmeesters see churchwardens
Kilkenny 174, 176
klopjes, kloppen 1, 18, 25–7, 89, 90, 131, 184–5, 188–97, 206, 254–5
Knaresborough 206
Kooi, Christine 183, 250

Lancashire 34–5, 38–44, 105, 110, 112, 114, 142, 151, 202, 206, 211, 232, 261
Latin 109, 117, 194, 201, 210, 233, 239, 257
Lawson, Dorothy 104, 117
Leeuwarden 252
legislation, anti-Catholic 20, 53, 55, 70, 78, 81, 86, 89–90, 96, 112, 116, 160–1, 164–5, 183, 186, 195, 203–4, 209, 233, 249, 251, 252
    see also martyrs, persecution, prosecution, recusants
Leiden 16, 24, 57–8, 62, 97–8, 130, 134, 256
Leyburne, John, Bishop 80, 209
liberty *see* freedom
Liège 157, 161–2
Lier 131, 150
Lille 128, 134
Limburg 123–4, 131, 260
    see also States Limburg
Lingen 132
Lisbon 40
liturgy 13, 90, 93, 97, 104, 106, 109–10, 184, 197, 201, 209, 212, 225, 235, 257
London 10, 35, 69, 74–8, 80, 104, 107, 202, 204–6, 234, 242–3, 258
    Tower of 72, 106, 117, 150

Longford 210, 242, 244
Louis XIII, King of France 129
Louis XIV, King of France 11, 129
Louise, princess of the Palatinate 164
Louvain 11, 20, 26, 108, 125–6, 128–9, 131, 134–5, 139, 141, 143–4, 146, 149–50, 184, 187, 238, 255–6
Luria, Keith 177–8
Lutheranism 4, 42, 54, 60–1, 257
Lyveden New Bield 241–2, 244

maagdenhuis 190, 192–5
Maasland 60
Maassluis 57–9, 62
Maastricht 128, 157, 159, 163–4
McClain, Lisa 149, 151
Macclesfield, Thomas *see* Maxfield
Madeley 69, 71–4, 261
Mainz 128
marriage 13, 73, 78, 94, 111–12, 134, 146, 159–60, 168, 194, 203, 205, 212, 221, 249, 251–2, 258, 261
  clandestine 112, 208
  see also mixed marriage
martyrdom, martyrs 7, 9, 44–6, 107, 115–16, 129, 178, 183, 185, 203–4, 208, 211, 245, 250, 254, 259
martyrology 7, 45, 126, 140, 259
Mary, Queen of Scots 231, 234
Mary, Virgin 86, 88, 106–7, 113, 115–17, 130, 149–51, 185, 201–2, 206, 218, 234, 238–9, 245, 258
Mass 21, 37, 39–44, 79–80, 84, 89–91, 93–4, 103–5, 109, 117–18, 124, 144, 150, 160–2, 174–6, 186, 189–91, 193, 201, 204, 206–7, 210–12, 217, 219, 222, 230–4, 238, 241, 246, 249, 254, 256
Maurice of Nassau, stadholder, prince of Orange 128
Maxfield, Thomas 45–6
Mechelen 123, 125, 127, 256
medals 235
Megen, County of 260
Mennonites 15, 48, 51, 53, 60–2
Micklegate Bar 80
Middelburg 123

Midlands 38, 71–2, 202
Minster Yard 80
miracles 18, 88, 109, 115–16, 139, 147, 149–50, 259
mission, Catholic 3, 6, 33, 37, 112, 125, 135, 149, 169, 174, 200–1, 203, 205, 250, 253–7, 259–60, 262
  see also English Mission, Holland Mission, mission stations
missionaries *see* mission (Catholic)
mission stations 10, 184, 187, 189, 191, 195, 197, 217, 255
  see also parishes
mixed marriage 13, 48–63 *passim*, 71, 73, 162, 175–6
Monmouthshire 202
Montague Court 75, Viscounts of 258
Montague, Lady Magdalen, Viscountess 104, 106, 151, 203, 230
More
  Agnes 205
  Gertrude 149, 205
Münster 128 Peace/Treaty of 132, 157, 159
music 13, 25, 89–90, 95, 132, 150, 156, 189, 191, 194, 203, 206, 210, 221, 257

Nantes, Edict of 171, 252
Neercassel, Johannes (Joan) van 11, 24–7
Newcastle-upon-Tyne 104, 207
Nicodemism 15
Nieuwpoort 40
Nijmegen 9, 128, 133
nobility, nobles 6, 10–11, 21–2, 36–7, 90, 141, 168, 174, 189, 194, 254, 261
  see also elites, gentry
noblewomen 1, 230–1, 236
Noordam, D.J. 60
Noorderkwartier 60–1, 189
Norbertines 162
Norfolk 110
Northamptonshire 232–3, 240–2
Northumberland 44, 146
nuncios, apostolic/papal 128–9, 184, 255
nuns 1, 73, 112, 130–1, 134–5, 139, 142–7, 150–2, 194, 205–6, 210

INDEX 271

Oath of Allegiance 69, 75, 171, 173
oaths 72, 164, 173, 204
Oegstgeest 99
Old Catholics 10, 14
   see also Utrecht (Schism)
omgangsoecumene 7, 50, 63, 68, 98
Ommelanden *see* Groningen (Ommelanden of)
Orange, princes of 130, 159, 163
   see also Maurice of Nassau, William I, William III
Oratory, Oratorians 10
orphanages, orphans 13, 133, 162, 185, 192
Oudenaarde 125
Oude Tonge 24
Overijssel 21, 23, 132
Overmaas, Lands of 157, 159, 162, 165
Oxford 116, 141, 144, 207
Oxfordshire 111, 206

paintings 48, 91, 93, 98, 107, 134, 150, 216–46 *passim*, 256, 259, 261
Paris 149, 206
parish churches 86, 91, 94, 111–14, 159–60, 162, 202, 208, 249, 257
parishes 10, 22–4, 26, 28, 67–81 *passim*, 104, 106 172, 184, 197, 203, 208–11, 217, 227, 255, 261
   see also diocesan structure, mission stations
Parliament 76, 168–9, 170–1, 174, 204, 251
pastoral care/ministry 9, 22, 27–8, 73, 130–1, 145, 162, 190, 196, 201, 212
   quality of 23–4
patronage 13, 22, 24–6, 35, 37, 74–5, 113, 117, 123–35 *passim*, 143, 147, 201, 209, 227–8, 230, 233, 236, 246, 253–4
persecution, religious 3, 7, 12, 15, 19–23, 36, 56, 75–8, 91, 106, 113, 123, 126, 141, 163, 174–5, 177–8, 193, 204, 225, 232, 242, 250, 252–3
   see also Inquisition, martyrdom, prosecution
Persons, Robert 109, 237
Perth, Earl of 146–7
Philip II, King of Spain 51, 125, 141, 255
Pietism 6
pilgrimage 2, 18, 86, 90, 96–7, 113–17, 126, 162, 196, 206, 208, 256–7, 260

pillarisation *see* verzuiling
Pius V, Pope 171
plots 2, 12, 70, 72, 76–7, 79, 164, 204, 231, 252, 256
Poland 132
Poor Clares 40, 150, 188, 190, 219
poor relief *see* charity
pope 8, 77, 107, 125, 129, 168, 173, 187, 191–2, 212, 231, 233–5, 237–8, 251, 253–4
   see also Clement VIII, Clement X, Pius V
popery, popish 37, 70, 110, 142, 174, 176, 192, 195, 202, 231, 245, 252
Postgate, Nicholas 70, 211
Premonstratensians 130
priests *see* clergy
printing 2, 105, 126, 140, 143, 147–8, 150, 185, 238–9, 242, 256
   see also books
prosecution of Catholics 45–6, 56, 72–79, 85, 91, 103–4, 106, 109–10, 113, 116, 123, 126, 143, 149, 150–1, 160, 163–4, 194, 203–8, 210, 230–4, 244, 249, 251–3, 259
   see also banishment, bribes, church property (loss of), fines, martyrdom, persecution, 'recognition money'
processions 77, 90, 96, 112, 117, 125, 162, 249
public church *see* Church of England, Reformed Church
Puritans 75, 110

Quakers 79
Questier, Michael 140, 203, 258

Ravenstein, Land of 260
re-Catholisation 3, 256
   see also conversion, mission (Catholic)
'recognition money' 21–2, 91, 253
reconversion *see* conversion
recusancy, recusants 7, 34, 36–7, 43–4, 69, 71–2, 75–6, 78–9, 94, 106, 109–13, 115–17, 144, 146, 171–2, 176, 183, 203–4, 207, 232–3, 244–5, 250–3
Reformed (Calvinist) Church 4, 20, 53–4, 60, 89, 93–7, 109, 126, 159–60, 163, 165,

187, 190, 192, 196, 202, 251, 258
regents 21–2, 54, 158, 261
relics 86, 88, 90, 107, 109, 147, 149, 151, 208, 211, 218, 235, 259
Rembrandt van Rijn 4, 48–9, 216, 225
Remonstrant 48, 60–1
Reresby, Sir John 79–80
Rheims 109, 127, 134, 202
Rhenen 218
Richelieu, Cardinal 203
Roermond 125, 162
Rogier, Louis L. 1, 18, 250
Rome 11, 45, 128–9, 149, 219–21
    English College in 128–9, 134, 142, 144–5, 147, 235
    Church of *passim*
    see also pope
Rommes, Ronald 52, 60
Roosendael, Nicolaes 224–5
rosary 43, 88–90, 98, 106, 109–10, 139, 141, 148–52, 206, 210, 212, 234–5, 237–9, 259
    confraternities of the 105–6, 149–51
Rotterdam 27, 56–8, 62, 217
Rouen 127, 238
Rovenius, Philip 11, 20, 22–3, 26–7, 196
Rubens, Peter Paul 216, 219–21, 225, 227, 234
Rushton 232–3, 240–2

Saenredam, Pieter 92–3
St Anthony 104, 117, 245
St Augustine 115, 259
St Bavo 93, 221–2
St Boniface 115, 258
St Catherine of Siena 45, 117, 245
St Crispin 85, 156
St Francis Xaverius 220, 225
St Ignatius of Loyola 106, 109, 148, 208, 220, 225
St Michael the Archangel 115–17
St Nicholas 123, 234
St Omer 133, 143–5, 147–8, 150–1, 202, 206, 253
St Patrick 115, 259
St Teresa of Avila 135, 201
St Veronica 235, 241

St Willibrord 99, 115, 258
St Winifred 115–16, 206, 208, 259
saints 85, 113, 115, 117, 126, 147, 178, 185, 191, 201, 218–9, 232, 234, 245, 257–9
Sales, Francis de 126, 201, 205, 212
Scandinavia 123, 127
Scherpenheuvel 113, 115–16
schools *see* education
schuilkerken see hidden churches
Scotland 113–15, 123–5, 127–9, 132–5, 140, 142–3, 146–8, 151
sculpture 5, 225, 227, 233, 259
seminaries 20, 22–3, 25–6, 28, 40, 105–6, 125, 128, 130, 135, 140–5, 149, 151, 186–7, 194, 207, 237, 253
    see also colleges
Shrewsbury, Countess of 236, 244
Shropshire 69, 71
Singleton, John 41–2
Skippon, Sir Philip 145–7
Smith
    family 69
    Richard 35, 104, 203–4
    Sir Thomas 231
sodalities 40, 43, 90, 106, 150–1, 211–12, 258
    see also confraternities
Solihull 208
Southern Netherlands 5, 15, 85, 113, 123–52 *passim*, 160–2, 191–2, 201, 216, 219, 251, 255–7, 259
Southwark 75
Southwell, Robert 105, 117
Spain 11, 19, 22, 46, 103, 132, 144–5, 164, 187, 191, 206, 252
    relations with Britain 36, 75–6, 124, 128, 134–5, 140–2, 143, 170–1, 178, 204, 231
    Revolt against 20–1, 51, 157–8, 253
    see also Philip II
Spanish Netherlands *see* Southern Netherlands
spiritual virgins *see klopjes, kloppen*
Stafford 207
Staffordshire 73, 210–11
Stanley
    Sir Thomas 231
    Sir William 134, 144

INDEX

States Brabant 54, 131, 157–60, 162, 164–5
States Flanders 131, 157–60, 162
States General 11, 20, 56, 84–5, 125, 157–61, 163–4, 260
   see also Generality Lands
States Limburg 131, 160
States, provincial 11, 20, 52, 56, 125, 131
   see also Holland (States of)
Stoke Bucks 201, 234
Stolwijk 95
Struyck, Nicolaas 60
Stuart, house of 44, 103, 109, 246, 252
Suffolk 110
'superstition' 2, 97–8, 105, 110, 113, 115, 174, 176, 192, 209, 233, 235, 259
Sussex 104, 230, 258
Sutton 202
synods, Reformed 53, 97, 158, 196

Temple Bar 77
Temple, William 48–9, 62
The Hague, 86, 88, 98, 216, 258
theology 1–2, 5, 7, 9–11, 14, 42, 95, 103, 116, 125, 131, 176, 186–7, 203, 212, 238, 261
Tilburg 85–6, 93
tolerance/toleration, religious 6, 9, 15, 48–9, 52–3, 62, 68, 74, 81, 96, 112, 117–18, 143, 163, 171, 177, 194, 202, 209, 230, 246, 250
Trent, Council of 9, 20, 22, 27, 33–46 *passim*, 51, 104–6, 111, 118, 124–7, 131, 139, 141–2, 151, 169–70, 175, 183, 186–7, 189, 192, 201, 251, 254, 259–60, 262
Tresham
   family 104
   Sir Thomas 233, 235, 239, 241–2, 244–6
Trier 128
Tudor 168, 237
Twelve Year Truce 90, 158
Twente 132
Tyburn 116, 259

universities 2, 16, 104, 116, 126, 129, 132, 141, 144, 146, 174, 186–8, 193, 255
Ursulines 188

Utrecht
   city 52, 55–6, 60, 62, 86, 93–4, 98, 131–2, 163, 191, 218–19, 221, 223, 225
   diocese 124–5
   province 21, 23–5, 27, 89, 91, 133, 159, 259
   Schism (1723) 10, 254

Vavasour
   family 78
   Peter 79
Vaux
   catechism 201
   family 117
   Lord 238
Velsen 89
Verbeeck, Herman(nus) 86, 97
Verstegan, Richard 238, 256
verzuiling 7, 50–2, 62–3
Veryard, Ellis 49–50, 52
Vilvoorde 130
virgins, spiritual *see* klopjes, kloppen
Vlissingen 134
Vosmeer, Sasbout 4, 7, 20, 24, 115, 127–8, 186–7, 189–91, 193, 195–6, 253

Wake
   Lionel 134
   Margaret 134–5
Wales 89, 105, 112–13, 115, 140, 148, 206–7, 258
Ward
   Francis 134
   Margaret 204
   Mary (Institute) 143–4, 192, 205, 210
   William 134
Warmond 98
Warwickshire 206, 212, 244
Wassenaar 57–8, 60, 62
Waterland 53
Weston, William 116, 234
Westphalia 5 Peace of 15
Whitby 69, 71
widows 79, 184, 191, 206, 210, 212
Wiel(e), (Joannes) Stalpert van der 24, 89
Wigan 40
William I, prince of Orange 7, 128

William III, prince of Orange and king of England, 80, 130, 209
William I (the Conqueror), king of England 244–5
wills 26, 39–40, 42, 70, 73–4, 187
Wiltshire 242
Windesheim 210
Wingens, Marc 90, 96–7, 256
Wiseman
    Jane 116–17, 204
    William 142
Wit, Jacob de 219, 226–8
Worcestershire 232

Worthington, Thomas 144–5, 239

Yate, Appolonia 149
    family 146
yeomen 72, 111, 206
York 69–70, 74, 77–81, 109, 116, 144, 210, 261
Yorkshire 36–7, 69, 79, 113–14, 144, 202, 207
Ypres 134

Zaltbommel 131
Zeeland 21, 23, 25, 54, 86, 133, 159
Zutphen 128

EU authorised representative for GPSR:
Easy Access System Europe, Mustamäe tee 50,
10621 Tallinn, Estonia
gpsr.requests@easproject.com

www.ingramcontent.com/pod-product-compliance
Lightning Source LLC
Chambersburg PA
CBHW051050230426
43666CB00012B/2630